s\

Praise for
Death at the Little Bighorn

"Custer's last movements and decisions have been argued about since 1876, but, in my mind, no one has made a stronger case for what really happened than Phillip Thomas Tucker in this compelling and convincing narration."
—Bob Boze Bell, executive editor *True West* magazine

"Philip Thomas Tucker presents a fascinating, lively, and important reassessment of the famous Battle of the Little Bighorn that recognizes the role of Cheyenne as well as Lakota warriors in the decisive turning point that defeated Lieutenant Colonel George Armstrong Custer's flank attack, and explains vividly the military tactics that resulted in defeat instead of victory for Custer and his command. Where the 'Last Stand' happened and what it means will change dramatically for readers of this book."
—Clyde A. Milner II, co-editor of *The Oxford History of the American West* and co-author of *As Big as the West: The Pioneer Life of Granville Stuart*

DEATH AT THE LITTLE BIGHORN

DEATH AT THE LITTLE BIGHORN

A NEW LOOK AT CUSTER, HIS TACTICS, AND THE TRAGIC DECISIONS MADE AT THE LAST STAND

Phillip Thomas Tucker, PhD

Skyhorse Publishing

Copyright © 2016 by Phillip Thomas Tucker

Skyhorse Publishing books may be purchased in bulk at special discounts for sales promotion, corporate gifts, fund–raising, or educational purposes. Special editions can also be created to specifications. For details, contact the Special Sales Department, Skyhorse Publishing, 307 West 36th Street, 11th Floor, New York, NY 10018 or info@skyhorsepublishing.com.

Skyhorse® and Skyhorse Publishing® are registered trademarks of Skyhorse Publishing, Inc.®, a Delaware corporation.

Visit our website at www.skyhorsepublishing.com.

10 9 8 7 6 5 4 3 2 1

Library of Congress Cataloging–in–Publication Data is available on file.

Cover design by Rain Saukas
Cover art courtesy of Mark Churms, detail from *His Brother's Keeper—George & Tom Custer 1876* © Mark Churms 2003.

Print ISBN: 978–1–63450–800–1
Ebook ISBN: 978-1-63450-806-3

Printed in the United States of America

Dedication

To the small band of Cheyenne and Sioux warriors who bravely defended Medicine Tail Coulee Ford on the afternoon of June 25, 1876. These relatively few men and boys were the forgotten ones who repulsed George Armstrong Custer's last charge.

Acknowledgments

Many people across the United States provided gracious assistance and advice that resulted in the writing of this book. I am especially grateful to the expert staff at Custer Battlefield National Monument, Montana.

Contents

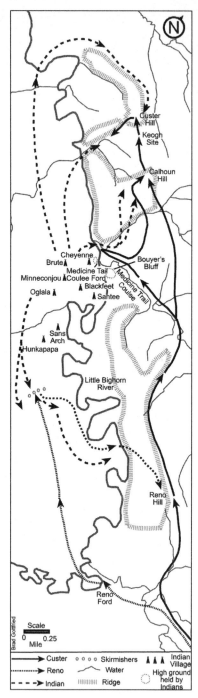

Map of the Little Bighorn battlefield, June 25, 1876. *(Courtesy Bradley M. Gottfried, PhD)*

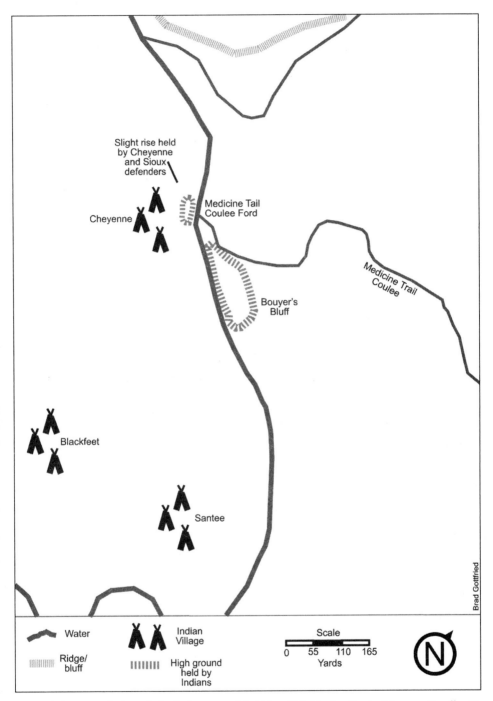

Map of the area of Custer's final charge on Medicine Tail Coulee Ford. *(Courtesy Bradley M. Gottfried, PhD)*

Introduction

No survivors of nearly half of an entire United States Army cavalry regiment (five companies) were left to tell the tale about what happened on June 25, 1876. As a result, no battle in the annals of American history has been more misinterpreted by layers of romance and fiction than the bloody showdown at the Little Bighorn. To this day, the hidden truths of no single battle in America's story have been more persistently elusive than "Custer's Last Stand." Therefore, the battle of the Little Bighorn in the remote Montana Territory has remained one of American history's most enduring mysteries and enigmas on multiple levels. The general assumption has been that nothing new can be said today about this iconic confrontation that represented the apex of a longtime culture clash and a defining moment in the American saga. However, nothing could be further from the truth.

To this day, this famous battle fought deep in the heart of buffalo country has been shrouded by sentimentality and romanticism, bestowing more myths than actual history. Few, if any, battles have been more distorted by so many contradictions and controversies as the fight at the Little Bighorn. Therefore, it is now time to more closely look at this iconic battle beyond the outdated traditional interpretations upon which the romantic myths have been based. More abundant Indian oral testimonies have now offered the inclusion of forgotten voices that reveal hidden truths about the battle at the "Greasy Grass River," as the Sioux called it.

To additionally obscure what really happened on June 25, a good many uncomfortable truths regarding one of the greatest fiascos in American military history had to be covered up to protect the reputations of America's top military leaders and the 7th Cavalry's officer corps. Therefore, Lieutenant Colonel George Armstrong Custer immediately became the most convenient scapegoat for the unprecedented disaster to preserve the American military's image and the reputations of his fellow officers and senior leaders, who were actually far more responsible for the fiasco than their regimental commander.

After dividing his 7th Cavalry to increase tactical flexibility for striking the largest Indian village yet seen on the Northern Great Plains, the exact final movements of Custer's five companies on the far north continue to be hotly debated to this day, because there were no survivors. Even the alleged final positions where the dead bodies of 7th Cavalry troopers were found have laid a shaky foundation for the exact course of actual events, fostering additional misconceptions and erroneous conclusions.

As part of the enduring romance, the immortal visual portrayals of Custer defending the open hilltop ("Custer Hill") and then falling heroically before masses of charging attackers have long been some of America's most iconic images. The heroic imagery of Custer's Last Stand became an early and enduring symbol of the vanguard of civilization pushing aside the barbarian horde of a different culture and color: America's rustic Thermopylae on the Northern Great Plains. This romantic portrayal of the disaster has been created by more than a thousand paintings, illustrations, and drawings. Custer's Last Stand has been marketed by an unprecedented outpouring of books, films (including D. W. Griffith's 1912 film, *The Massacre*), and documentaries over generations, ensuring that such myths replaced mundane and uncomfortable realities. What had been manufactured for public consumption was the enduring image of a glorious demise (like the ancient Greek warriors' so-called beautiful death in 480 BC at Thermopylae) and an apotheosis for one of the North's greatest Civil War heroes. A brigadier general at only age twenty-three and the winner of a long list of Civil War victories, Custer's horrific death on a once-obscure, lonely hilltop in Montana at the hands of "savages" seemed the most improbable of possible ends for a dynamic man of ability and destiny.

For young America on the verge of becoming a major world industrial and military power, Custer's annihilation shook the heady confidence of a vigorous republic when celebrating its Centennial soon after. Custer's defeat was truly a Greek Tragedy, but in a western frontier setting that mocked America's amazing success story, Centennial celebration, and national pride. Meeting an inglorious end, Custer's death at age thirty-six in leading more than 200 men to their doom has been one of the most controversial military actions in American military history. Hence, millions of Americans have been fascinated with this relatively brief and small clash of arms that has long captured the national imagination.

Paradoxically, despite the seemingly endless number of books devoted to Custer's Last Stand, the truth about what really happened has been obscured by the glorified myth that has faithfully endured to this day. America needed a heroic demise to mask the ugly realities, including a fabricated war based on self-interest as well as the most humiliating of defeats, so the much-celebrated Last Stand early on became an iconic national symbol of necessary heroic sacrifice (paradoxically a moral victory in defeat) that was required for America's "Winning of the West." Custer's sacrifice in the name of national progress has long been enshrined in the popular American memory and a traditionally myth-oriented American culture that usually only celebrates a winner (one of the many striking paradoxes of the Little Bighorn story). Ironically, the real losers on June 25 were the native people, whose Pyrrhic victory at the Little Bighorn ultimately signaled the end of their distinct culture and nomadic way of life.

Forgotten Turning Point

Since the time it had first become a place of tourist interest, the most visited location on the Little Bighorn Battlefield National Monument has been Custer Hill. Here, high above the clear waters of the Little Bighorn River nestled in the deep valley below, the final last stand was made by the ever-dwindling band of survivors of Custer's shattered and decimated command. Commanding a wide area, this dominant elevation stood around three-quarters of a mile above the river. "Last Stand Hill" overlooks the battlefield's openness and killing ground, offering a sweeping panoramic view of the picturesque river valley below. Of course, this remote Montana hilltop marks the spot where Custer's body was found with the last of his 7th Cavalry troopers, who found themselves short on luck, manpower, and support on one of the hottest afternoons of the year.

However, in one of the great ironies of American history and contrary to popular perception, the fabled Last Stand atop Custer Hill was not the scene of this famous battle's true turning point. In relative and overall tactical terms, what was played out on Custer Hill (Last Stand Hill) was not only tactically insignificant, but also actually anti-climactic. After all, what happened at Custer Hill represented only the final moments of the destruction of a command, after the battle had already been decided in the river valley's depths at Medicine Tail Coulee Ford. Indeed, the wiping out of the final band of survivors on Custer Hill was nothing more than the obvious closing scene of the systematic destruction of Custer's five companies, after command cohesion had earlier broken down, because of what had happened at the ford.

Today, hundreds of thousands of tourists from around the world continue to flock to Custer Hill. However, these visitors are not aware of the battle's true turning point. What happened at this isolated old buffalo ford along the river has been long misunderstood as the true key to ordaining the battle's final outcome. Quite simply, Medicine Tail Coulee Ford, located at the mouth of Medicine Tail Coulee, was the dramatic scene of Custer's last, but most forgotten, charge in his illustrious career. It was here that the most forgotten story of the iconic battle was played out in dramatic fashion. Most importantly, Custer's bold flank attack on the ford was his last opportunity to still achieve a decisive success, after the offensive effort of the other arm of his pincer movement (three companies under Major Marcus Albert Reno) had been thwarted upriver at the Indian village's southern end. This relatively forgotten struggle at Medicine Tail Coulee Ford, opposite the village's northern end, determined the fate of Custer and his five companies like no other single factor. However, no previous book has been devoted to this remarkable story of the battle's true turning point until now. In fact, relatively few people today can imagine that anything of any tactical importance, especially in deciding Custer's and the battle's fate, occurred at the then-called Minneconjou Ford (named after one of the seven Lakota—or Sioux—tribes). Quite simply, the battle's traditional narrative has completely overshadowed the importance of the showdown at the ford, dooming this important story to dark obscurity.

The multitude of errors in body identifications of where bodies of dead troopers were allegedly found, compounded by the fact that no markers of fallen men were erected in the ford sector, has continued to confirm the erroneous popular belief that the clash of arms at this vital crossing point was entirely insignificant. However, in truth, the mouth of Medicine Tail Coulee in the flats (river bottoms) before the ford witnessed the decisive repulse of the attack of the largest concentration of the 7th Cavalry on June 25: the most overlooked and forgotten story of the battle of Little Bighorn. In one of the great ironies of America's most famous battle, none of the many films or artwork has ever focused on the decisive struggle at Medicine Tail Coulee Ford.

The Blame Game

In the official cover-up of the facts about the battle in the Reno 1879 Court of Inquiry, prejudiced personal testimonies and outright lies of the 7th Cavalry's officers and others grossly distorted the official historical record in order to make Custer the scapegoat for disaster: a blame game that was urgently needed for pressing political and personal reasons, including the prevention of tarnishing the reputations of President Ulysses S. Grant and his top military commanders, who were the primary architects of one of the most disastrous campaigns in American history. The self-serving testimonies of Custer's two top lieutenants, Captain Frederick William Benteen and Major Reno, showed that they were primarily to blame for early obscuring the historical record, including the importance of Custer's flank attack at the ford and why they had failed to support Custer in his hour of need.

To save themselves from blame for having allowed Custer and his men of five companies to die on their own, Benteen and Reno refused to tell the truth of Custer's tactics that were calculated to win victory: Custer's bold flank attack of hitting the village's northern end (the Cheyenne village) in a pincer movement. Custer's masterful tactical plan would have almost certainly worked if his two top lieutenants had performed aggressively and supported his flank attack as he rightly anticipated and had ordered.

Reno and Benteen falsely testified that they had no idea that Custer planned to unleash a flank attack to strike the village's northern end. Therefore, because dead men don't tell tales, the importance of Custer's attack on the ford was obscured by the highest-ranking 7th Cavalry officers with personal, political, and professional agendas. In the end, consequently, the battle's most important chapter has been lost in the haze of lies, post-war politics (Custer was an outspoken Democratic critic of the Republican Grant Administration), and the well-organized effort that succeeded in protecting reputations and regimental honor in a massive cover-up of the truth. By conveniently ignoring the timely flank attack at the ford, Custer was then portrayed as the reckless and irresponsible fool who was solely responsible for the disaster instead of the actual guilty parties: President Grant and his top military commanders, Generals William T. Sherman and Phil H. Sheridan, as well as other highly respected leaders who had all manufactured an aggressive war against the Sioux without legislative consent or legitimate cause.

Additional misconceptions about the battle were then perpetuated by generations of writers and historians who focused on Custer Hill, while viewing the struggle at the ford as unworthy of notice. This situation also developed in part because so many white historians have long discounted the importance of Indian oral accounts with disdain and outright contempt. However, these revealing voices of the victors, who saw what really happened, deserve to be heard and given far more credibility to correct the outdated, traditional narrative.

Ironically, greater credence has been placed by Anglo historians, including academics, even upon highly questionable, second-hand, and erroneous white accounts instead of the Indians who fought there: perhaps the most bizarre paradox of the battle. This longtime routine and extensive dismissal of Indian accounts has even included the words of Sitting Bull, the diehard Sioux (Hunkpapa) religious leader. Unlike generations of white historians, Sitting Bull (actually Sitting Buffalo Bull) emphasized how "our young men rained lead across the river and drove the white braves back" at Medicine Tail Coulee Ford. Unfortunately, outright speculation by romantic-minded historians has been more often widely accepted as authentic history than Indian oral testimony. Therefore, central mysteries and misconceptions about the battle have remained not only alive and well but also deeply entrenched, providing a historical conundrum to this day.

Most importantly, the Indian oral accounts, especially from Cheyenne warriors who played the leading role in the ford's defense, tell us a much different story from the traditional histories. Reliable and corroborating Cheyenne testimonies (and a lesser number of Sioux accounts) have emphasized that Custer unleashed a full-fledged attack with all five companies down Medicine Tail Coulee in a desperate bid to cross the ford and charge into the Cheyenne village: proof of the wisdom of Custer's tactical plan of delivering a hard-hitting flank attack that might have prevailed, if only Reno and Benteen had provided the required assistance Custer had ordered. This was Custer's last charge (and the most overlooked one of his career, in another striking paradox), upon which the battle's entire outcome hinged. Consequently, there was nothing tentative or hesitant about Custer's last offensive tactics at Medicine Tail Coulee Ford, as long assumed by historians, because he had no other realistic tactical choice but to launch his maximum offensive effort at the ford in a final bid to pull out a victory from the jaws of defeat, after Reno had been repulsed at the village's opposite end.

However, to this day, historians have continued to casually dismiss even the most dependable Indian oral testimony (especially Cheyenne) of the ford defenders in their own forgotten last stand. For generations, Anglo historians have minimized what really happened at the vital river crossing, where the tide of battle was turned decisively against Custer: the unfortunate cost of assuming that Indian oral accounts were unimportant to understanding the battle. Therefore, this book will focus on those long-ignored Cheyenne and Sioux accounts as much as possible, because they are one of the forgotten keys to knowing what actually happened on June 25.

The most reliable of these invaluable warrior oral testimonies have revealed a great deal of the truth about what really happened at the ford in contrast to the battle's romantic and mythical views. Sioux and Cheyenne accounts, especially the latter, have proven more reliable and accurate than generally assumed, when correctly deciphered and validated by corroborating evidence, after methodically sorting out the existing ambiguities and obvious errors in oral testimony.

Along with other primary evidence, what these accounts have revealed is that this remote ford just east of the Cheyenne village was

Custer's most crucial tactical objective, at a time when not only the battle but also the fate of his command hung in the balance. In overall tactical terms, Custer's failure to achieve his tactical objective spelled the difference between victory and defeat. Relying on experience, Custer's flank attack was to be part of a classic pincer movement (Custer was the hammer, while Reno was the anvil) that had long proved successful, especially during the Civil War. For an increasingly desperate Custer, who knew that he had to regain the initiative after Major Reno had been hurled back, the realization that crossing the ford and attacking into the Cheyenne village was not only his last chance, it might have indeed been the key to his success as well.

Going for Broke

Custer's attack with five companies (the day's maximum offensive effort) on the Cheyenne village was launched down Medicine Tail Coulee and across the wide, open mouth of the coulee. Here, at the crossing point of low water where buffalo herds had long moved west in search for fresh grass, Custer attempted to deliver a flank attack to not only save the day but also to save Reno's hard-pressed companies and the regiment's remainder under Captain Benteen. In a tactical sense, Custer in fact emerged victorious by accomplishing this overlooked goal. Indeed, the destruction of Custer's isolated command of five companies ensured that most 7th Cavalry members (ironically those men and top officers who hated him and hoped for his destruction) survived to fight another day.

A golden tactical opportunity—catching the Cheyenne village virtually undefended since almost every warrior had converged on Reno several miles to the south—existed for Custer to fulfill his fondest tactical dreams. However, just when he was on the verge of success, the tide of battle was suddenly turned by a band of ford defenders to not only determine the battle's entire course, but also to seal Custer's fate. Indeed, up to this crucial point, Custer's bold tactical ambition of delivering a flank attack as part of the pincer movement had worked: a compliment to Custer's tactical skill, even under the most unfavorable circumstances. Ironically, this spirited defiance erupted from a mere handful of defenders (about thirty Cheyenne and Sioux warriors), who offered far stiffer resistance and for a longer period than has been acknowledged by historians.

The number of warriors was not the most important factor in guaranteeing the ford's successful defense, however. Significantly, they possessed the advantages of a concealed defensive position and the element of surprise: essentially an ambush that Custer, who was delivering his own surprise attack, never expected. His troopers were near the river's east bank, when a sudden volley of fire was opened by these hidden warriors in their concealed defensive position amid the saplings, willows, and underbrush near the west bank. Seemingly at the last moment, Custer's last charge was stopped by the heavy volume of firepower unleashed from a number of rapid-firing repeating rifles (especially the 16-shot Winchester rifles and, most likely, Henry rifles as well) of the concealed defenders, turning the tide of battle. Against heavy odds, this band of Cheyenne and Sioux defenders held firm behind a slight rise to thwart not only Custer's personally led main offensive thrust of the day, but also to fulfill his most ambitious tactical vision.

To protect their women and children who now fled west—while almost every other warrior was now fighting to the south in Reno's sector upriver—these warriors made the forgotten, but more important, last stand at the Little Bighorn. Firing rapidly and hitting targets from behind the cover of the low rise that ran parallel to the river, the defensive stand of these Sioux and Cheyenne fighters has long been the most overlooked story of Custer's Last Stand.

With their repeating rifles unleashing a heavy volume of fire in contrast to the troopers' single-shot and slower-firing carbines, these

Cheyenne and Sioux inflicted sufficient damage to force the withdraw of Custer's command of five companies and eventually up the open high ground from which there was no escape. Custer's sharp setback suffered at the ford (the battlefield's most strategic point at the time) guaranteed that the initiative was lost forever by Custer and his men, who were at that point, consequently, doomed.

Decisive Turning Point

Beyond its decisiveness, this was no ordinary setback at the ford for another reason as well. A number of reliable and collaborating Indian accounts (Cheyenne and Sioux) have revealed that Custer was hit (wounded, mortally wounded, or killed depending on the account) while leading the charge across the ford. In such a key situation, Custer's wounding at the ford—the far more likely case than his receiving a death stroke—also led to the fatal withdrawal of his five companies from the embattled ford. As verified by collaborating accounts, Custer was almost certainly hit at the ford, which significantly affected command cohesion.

Likewise, a number of the headquarters staff, whose members rode just behind Custer, were either killed or wounded in the attack on the ford. This also dealt a severe blow to the attackers' command and control center in the saddle. Indeed, these early significant setbacks led to a loss of confidence and morale among the troopers.

Clearly, the dramatic showdown at Medicine Tail Coulee Ford should have long been the centerpiece of any comprehensive and analytical study of the battle of the Little Bighorn. Without considering the importance of the struggle at the ford, no book about Custer's Last Stand is truly complete and fails to present a truly accurate analysis of the battle in its entirety. After all, Medicine Tail Coulee Ford, and not Custer Hill, was actually the scene of the battle's decisive, but long-forgotten, turning point.

After nearly 150 years of routine neglect of the most overlooked tactical aspect of the iconic showdown at the Little Bighorn, the hidden story of the battle's true turning point will now be told in full in a book-length treatment for the first time. First and foremost, this fresh analysis of this iconic battle has required the systematic stripping away of multiple layers of romance, stereotypes, and myths that have dominated Custer's Last Stand.

Unlike previous works, this book will focus on the centrality of the Cheyenne role (and Sioux to a lesser degree) at Medicine Tail Coulee Ford, instead of the overly emphasized Sioux role elsewhere on the field. After all, the Sioux fought mostly at the southern end (upriver against Reno) and not the northern end (opposite the strategic ford) of the vast encampment at the time of Custer's last charge. As the largest numbers of warriors present on June 25, the notoriously inaccurate and conflicting Sioux oral accounts have largely promoted the traditional views of the battle, which have obscured what actually occurred.

Clearly, these long-dismissed Cheyenne oral accounts now deserve greater attention and credibility than in the past. Therefore, Cheyenne testimony will serve as a central foundation in this study, more so than Sioux accounts. While the Cheyenne warriors were the primary ford defenders, they also fought beside a lesser number of Sioux in a true crisis situation. Most importantly, in revealing what actually occurred at Medicine Tail Coulee Ford, Cheyenne oral accounts are more accurate in general than Sioux oral accounts: the paradox of the longtime dismissal of Cheyenne testimony by historians.

Ironically, Custer's almost-certain wounding at the Medicine Tail Coulee Ford was most symbolic. This was Cheyenne revenge for Custer's November 27, 1868, attack (as ordered by his superiors) on the peaceful Cheyenne along the Washita. Family members of some Last Stand warriors had died in that unprovoked surprise attack—making this, clearly, a case of karma coming full circle at Custer's expense.

In classic irony, the tragedy suffered by the Cheyenne people at the Washita indeed came back to haunt Custer at Medicine Tail Coulee Ford during what had evolved into very much of a private war between them and Custer. It seems Custer's legendary luck finally ran out at this obscure ford on the Little Bighorn, where the mostly Cheyenne fighters thwarted his last charge. In this sense, the forgotten seeds for the 7th Cavalry's disaster along the Little Bighorn actually had been early sowed at the Washita.

In the annals of military history, seldom have so few fighting men made a more decisive impact on a famous battle's outcome than a relative handful of hard-fighting Cheyenne and Sioux, who succeeded in turning the tide of battle at the ford. Here, Custer met his match in terms of superior warrior firepower—repeating rifles—and warrior determination that had nothing to do with superior numbers. Clearly, the Great Prophet (also known as the Great Spirit and the Everywhere Spirit) looked down favorably upon these relatively few warriors at the ford during their never-say-die defense of their village, women, and children.

In traditional battle of the Little Bighorn historiography, while the Sioux's story at the Little Bighorn has been long explored in great detail, the Cheyenne warriors have been the most overlooked participants, whose story has been lost for the most part. Therefore, it is time to bestow—for the first time, and in full—recognition to the forgotten story of these Cheyenne (and a handful of Sioux warriors) of the all-important defense of Medicine Tail Coulee Ford. The decisive repulse of Custer's first and last charge by these warriors was the true source of the fiasco, rather than the simplistic explanation of the 7th Cavalry having encountered too many Indians. Racial and culture factors required defeat by vast numbers as an explanation of how dark-skinned "inferiors" could vanquish white-skinned "superiors": the culturally comfortable excuse to explain one of the most humiliating military defeats in American history.

This book is dedicated to revealing the true story of the most over-looked, but paradoxically the most decisive, catalyst that led to the wiping out of five companies of America's elite cavalry regiment.

To present the full story of the struggle at the ford for the first time, an ample number of dependable and collaborating Indian accounts (Cheyenne and Sioux) have revealed what actually occurred at the ford (including Custer's wounding) to dovetail with long-obscured facts found in the official personnel records of the 7th Cavalry troopers in the National Archives, Washington, DC. In this way, it has been pos-sible to fill in the long-existing gaps in the historical record to solve one of the battle's most enduring central mysteries by explaining the most forgotten cause of Custer's defeat: the decisive repulse at Medicine Tail Coulee Ford.

This most overlooked, but paradoxically most important, chapter of the battle—the struggle at Medicine Tail Coulee Ford—has been illu-minated to restore not only a much-needed balance to the traditional narrative, but also to provide a greater understanding about what actu-ally happened. This book is dedicated to unraveling some of the most central mysteries and myths about one of America's most iconic battles by presenting a host of new insights and fresh views, while restoring a balanced perspective from both sides. What is most remarkable is how the important story of a relative handful of warriors—who orches-trated one of the great delaying actions in American military history and turned the tide and course of one of the most famous battles of American history—has been the most forgotten last stand of June 25.

At first glance, it almost would seem impossible that so few war-riors could have possibly made such a decisive impact in the battle's final outcome, but this rather remarkable tactical development can be better understood by factoring in Custer's almost certain wounding in leading the charge across the ford. In a rather bizarre development, one of the battle's most important aspects has been ignored for more than nearly a century and a half, when in fact it was in many ways the most significant story of all.

However, for comparative purposes with regard to the overall importance of the ford's spirited defense by so few warriors, it should be remembered that for the 2015 bicentennial anniversary of the decisive battle of Waterloo on June 18, 1815 (another bloody Sunday like the fight at the Little Bighorn), a book has been recently released entitled *The Longest Afternoon, The 400 Men Who Decided the Battle of Waterloo*. This, too, was no isolated example of a relatively few fighting men altering a battle's course in the annals of military history. Less than 300 Georgians played a key role in defending Burnside's Bridge at Antietam on September 17, 1862, holding the attacking Federals of the IX Corps, Army of the Potomac, at bay and saving the hard-pressed Army of Northern Virginia during the Civil War's bloodiest single day.

Along with others in the annals of military history, these revealing Waterloo and Antietam examples (two battles that had decisive impacts on history on both sides of the Atlantic) share a distinct parallel with the ford's defense, although the battle of the Little Bighorn was only a mere skirmish by comparison. The defenders who rose to the supreme challenge at Waterloo and Antietam were armed with single-shot weapons like the 7th Cavalry troopers, who only possessed Springfield carbines to their great disadvantage. Meanwhile, the most effective Medicine Tail defenders blasted away with the most cutting-edge weaponry of the day: fast-firing repeating rifles, especially the legendary Winchester.

These representative nineteenth-century examples of superior combat performances of relatively few conventional soldiers at Waterloo and Antietam were in fact duplicated by a far smaller number of warriors who defended Medicine Tail Coulee Ford to make a disproportionate contribution to a famous battle's final outcome. Thanks to the heavy volume of fire from repeating rifles, seldom have so few men had a larger impact on a famous battle's overall outcome than the band of warriors who defended the ancient buffalo ford.

Therefore, this book is largely devoted to setting the historical record straight and finally giving credit where it was due. Most of all, the primary purpose of this book is to bring the long-neglected story of the struggle at Medicine Tail Coulee to life to reveal the heroism of the fighting men on both sides. A fresh approach in analyzing this iconic battle anew is long overdue.

While accurate Indian oral accounts of the ford's defense, the desperate determination of Custer's last attack of the day at the ford, and even those troopers who were killed have been dismissed by historians who declared that the ford fight was unimportant, the official 7th Cavalry service records in the National Archives simply cannot be so easily discounted. Military service records have revealed the identities of some officers and men who were killed in the charge across the ford to confirm the validity of Indian accounts, including the much-disparaged White Cow Bull, an Oglala Sioux defender of the ford. Additionally, Indian oral accounts, such as from Horned Horse, have verified the truth of White Cow Bull's words, and even the account of young Crow scout Curley, who saw Custer's last attack, before escaping the field.

All in all, the ample amount of corroborating Indian accounts and official army records have verified what actually happened at Medicine Tail Coulee Ford, including the loss of leading 7th Cavalry officers and Custer's wounding. Numerous accounts of soldiers who later found the remains of Custer's men, including officers, in the Cheyenne village (additional evidence of a full-scale attack at the ford), have also provided additional physical proof that they were cut down at the ford and its immediate vicinity. Here, during Custer's last attack, these officers had been either wounded or de-horsed and then captured to be later ritualistically killed in the village opposite the ford. Hence, trooper remains, including officers, were later found in the Cheyenne village.

Unfortunately, as with other oral testimony, White Cow Bull's account of shooting the courageous leader (almost certainly Custer himself) of the attack at the ford has been casually ignored by historians, although nothing else can better or more thoroughly explain not only the decisive repulse, but also the rapid collapse of trooper resistance thereafter. Dovetailing with Indian accounts and, most importantly, the validity of defenders' words of what happened at Medicine Tail Coulee Ford, White Cow Bull's account has been fully confirmed by the military service records of members of Custer's staff and officer corps who had been killed or wounded in the charge at the ford.

Ironically, historians have conveniently overlooked the fact that the Indian accounts are in agreement with the initial views of Reno and Benteen (and others) immediately after the battle, when they looked over the battlefield, as opposed to the self-serving 1879 Reno Court of Inquiry testimony: a premeditated closing of the ranks. After viewing the battlefield, experienced military leaders emphasized that the turning point of the battle was indeed at the ford. Therefore, given the existing ample evidence, one of the greatest paradoxes of the battle is why the importance of Custer's determined attempt to charge across the ford, and the tenacity of Indian resistance that stopped him, has been disputed or doubted at all, even at this late date.

One of the most obvious explanations was largely because of the enduring romantic myths that resulted in the longtime, routine dismissal of Indian accounts, as well as army, regimental, and national politics. After all, even the White House benefitted by making Custer the scapegoat for disaster. However, the words of the two leading regimental officers (Reno and Benteen, respectively) and others who viewed the battlefield immediately after the battle about what they saw on the field told a much different story. Most importantly, an ample number of reliable Indian accounts of the ford's successful defense (Cheyenne and Sioux, and even Custer's young Crow scout Curley, to a lesser degree) matched the early observations by Reno and Benteen and the last messengers dispatched from Custer's column, as well as military service records, and even archeological evidence (to a lesser degree): a corroboration of a good deal of reliable multiple levels of evidence that simply can no longer be ignored or dismissed as they have been so often in the past.

To additionally obscure what happened at Medicine Tail Coulee Ford, a central core of the myth of Custer's Last Stand and a longtime popular theme was that Custer himself was the last man (or one of the last) to fall atop Custer Hill, this romantic image has been enshrined in seemingly endless books, films, poems, and documentaries for more than a century. Therefore, the more plausible possibility and almost certainty that Custer was hit at the ford and then assisted or carried to Custer Hill has been routinely dismissed out of hand by historians.

Instead, the central myth of Custer's Last Stand has long dictated that Custer was doomed by overwhelming numbers of Indians and never had any realistic chance of reaping success: the romantic tale of a heroic band of troopers fighting against a cruel fate is the more popular fatalistic theory. However, this scenario does not correspond with the most accurate and reliable Indian accounts about the struggle for the battlefield's most strategic point, Medicine Tail Coulee Ford, about a quarter after four in the afternoon. Before the ranks were swept by the hot fire from the ford defenders, Custer had victory in his grasp when he unleashed his flank attack in his final bid to win it all.

In perhaps the battle's greatest irony, Custer was thwarted by Indians who had been recently armed, housed, and nourished by a government agency—the Indian Bureau—that perpetuated a misguided national policy advocated by a large segment of the American populace, especially in the northeast. In this sense and more than his own mistakes, Custer was actually killed as much by his own people as the Indians, a tragic fate that perhaps was appropriate because he had garnered his fame by winning so many victories against his own people: Southerners during the Civil War.

For the first time and in deviating from the long-accepted traditional versions of the battle, therefore, this book will focus entirely on the dramatic story of the struggle for the ford's possession and how Custer was repulsed at the battlefield's most strategic spot (not Custer Hill) to seal his fate. Here, in a lengthy (longer than generally assumed) contest that thwarted Custer's last charge during the forgotten "last stand" of Custer's Last Stand, the stirring showdown at Medicine Tail Coulee Ford was in fact not the insignificant feint as has been generally assumed by so many modern historians (unlike so many native Americans, who knew far better). More than the often-blamed culprits of Reno and Benteen playing leading roles in dooming Custer to defeat, it was actually the sharp reversal at the ford that had truly decided the tragic fate of Custer and his five companies.

Clearly, at long last, it is now time for the traditional story of Custer's Last Stand as we have been taught and led to believe to be entirely reconsidered and looked at anew from a fresh perspective, without the excessive layers of myths and romance—the necessary requirements for the unraveling of one of the final remaining mysteries and enigmas of this iconic battle. The central mythology and romance of the Last Stand has required that Custer should fall atop "Custer Hill," and certainly not at the remote buffalo ford, thus ensuring the permanent obscurity of what really happened at Medicine Tail Coulee Ford so long ago.

Indeed, the true heroism of Custer and the 7th Cavalry was perhaps more vividly revealed in Custer's last charge rather than the fabled final stand that was a hopeless, last-ditch defense of high ground of Custer Hill. Ironically, this maneuver, which was usually a distinct tactical advantage, proved to be a death trap that had no tactical importance and offered no hope for survival, especially after command cohesion had broken down.

Significantly, this forgotten contest at the ford revealed that Custer was a sound tactician, who attempted to deliver a bold flank that was part of a winning formula of a pincer movement: a brilliant tactical plan that would have certainly brought victory had he been properly supported by his top lieutenants as he expected. If Custer had Benteen and his three companies with him during his last attack on the ford as he desired, then victory very likely would have resulted; the vast majority of Indian warriors would have been focused on saving family members instead of killing bluecoats if eight 7th Cavalry companies instead of five had charged the village's northern end.

Agreeing with Indian accounts, recent historians and archaeologists have emphasized that the famous "last stand" never actually took place as long portrayed by romantic tradition. It was, in fact, little more than a systematic rout, followed by the wild flight of panicked troopers with relatively little organized resistance on the high ground above the ford. This situation certainly now places what had just previously occurred at Medicine Tail Coulee Ford in an even more important overall perspective. The most decisive confrontation in America's most iconic battle in fact actually took place at Medicine Tail Coulee Ford, the overlooked and forgotten turning point of the famous battle of the Little Bighorn. After nearly 150 years, it is now time for a new and close look at the most forgotten story of "Custer's Last Stand."

Phillip Thomas Tucker, PhD
Washington, DC
April 15, 2016

DEATH AT THE LITTLE BIGHORN

Chapter I

Custer's Surprise Attack Along the Washita

As unkind fate would have it, the desperate attempts of the Northern Great Plains tribes—the Lakota (or Sioux) and their allies (the Cheyenne)—to preserve their distinctive nomadic culture and way of life by the mid-1870s could not have been more ill timed. Quite simply, the Indians of the Northern Great Plains had never faced an opposition more powerful, or as deadly efficient in securing victory at any cost, as the American army. America's military leadership consisted of experienced former northern leaders of the Civil War.

With relentless single-mindedness, these highly placed commanders had led the Union to decisive victory during four years of brutal blood shedding. The American military machine's experience in the art of invading an enemy homeland dated back to the Mexican–American War in 1846–1848. They were also the architects of vanquishing the South by the merciless art of total war, sending the Confederacy into the trash bin of history. President Ulysses S. Grant and his top lieutenants, Ireland-born Philip Henry Sheridan and William T. Sherman, were now the primary orchestrators of another war against a free people far west of the Mississippi. During the Civil War, they crushed the Southern people's will to resist by waging war on civilian centers and their logistical support systems. Tough and ruthless, these hard men in high places had learned lessons that were now directed at the so-called hostile tribes of the Northern Great Plains, who resisted white encroachment and white civilization's relentless march.

America's leaders were now focused on the task of subjugating the latest threat to their nation's inevitable push west in the name of Manifest Destiny and national progress: the Sioux people. The Sioux were the most defiant of the indigenous people of the Northern Great Plains, but had never before faced a more relentless or successful opponent. During the 1864 Campaign in Virginia, then–Lieutenant General Grant had ordered his top lieutenant, Sheridan, to transform Virginia's fertile Shenandoah Valley into "a desert." This task had been accomplished with a destructive zeal by Sheridan and his boys in blue, including his cavalry. Among Sheridan's men was Brigadier General George Armstrong Custer, who skillfully commanded his hard-hitting "Wolverine" (Michigan) cavalry brigade of his division. The nation's top military leaders now brought the core concepts of total war to the Northern Great Plains.

Since the surrender of the battered Army of Northern Virginia at Appomattox Court House, Virginia, on Palm Sunday 1865, the chances of open conflict increased between the Indians and the white migrants who pushed ever further west toward the setting sun. As during the Civil War, America's military leaders knew that the key to decisive victory lay in targeting the civilian populace (the foundation of the Indian support system) to eliminate war-waging capabilities and the will to resist among Native Americans. Therefore, as early as 1868, the United States Army's top leadership adopted the highly effective tactical formula of reaping success: attacking Indian villages in winter during the harsh weather conditions of the Great Plains, when the tribes were stationary and vulnerable.[1]

For an expansionist nation with an insatiable appetite for gaining additional territory, stretching even beyond significant differences in race and culture, the real source of conflict between the two people boiled down to one basic issue: the Indians possessed what the American people wanted for their own, a seemingly endless expanse of rich and fertile land. After the Civil War, the United States government had established one treaty after another with the Indians, but these flimsy Machiavellian agreements—every one of them—had been systematically broken by the whites. Representing the young nation's pulse, the relentless push west of the American people never ended, ensuring the inevitable armed clashes with the Indians and shattering of treaties in their wake.

A Different Type of War

While America possessed a good many Civil War heroes, few of them successfully adjusted to a new type of warfare they were to now face. As a strange as it seems, the destiny of no United States officer was more eerily intertwined with the proud Cheyenne tribe (far more than the Sioux) than one of the North's greatest Civil War heroes, George Armstrong Custer. Ever since being assigned to service on the Great Plains not long after the Civil War's end, Custer had met the elusive art of Indian fighting with considerable frustration. Quite simply, much like other officers, he had trouble even finding Indians to fight. Therefore, Custer still had to prove himself in the Campaign of 1876. Since his Civil War glory days, Custer found the task of achieving success against the Northern Great Plains warriors to be far greater than he had imagined.

A West Pointer schooled in conventional warfare who graduated last in his class, Custer experienced frustration for the first time in his life when attempting to make the extremely difficult adjustment from conventional warfare to asymmetrical warfare on the seemingly endless prairies. The series of sparkling victories that had seemingly come so easily for Custer during the Civil War were only a distant memory. None of Custer's successes had been more important than on the third day at Gettysburg, Pennsylvania. There, in July 1863, he and his hard-charging Michigan cavalrymen had thwarted General Robert E. Lee's finest cavalryman, James Ewell Brown (Jeb) Stuart, from striking into the Army of the Potomac's rear in conjunction with "Pickett's Charge." By relying on his time-proven favorite tactic of leading the headlong attack, Custer played a key role in saving the day for the Union several miles east of Cemetery Ridge.

Then, near the war's end, the seemingly charmed "boy general" and his hard-riding cavalrymen had aggressively pursued what little remained of Lee's exhausted army after it had been forced to evacuate the fortifications of Petersburg, Virginia, and fled west in early April 1865. Custer had personally led the vigorous pursuit, including one of the war's last cavalry attacks. With his hard-hitting style, he had helped to force Lee's surrender at Appomattox Court House, Virginia, on Palm Sunday 1865, after cutting off his opponents' avenue of retreat farther west. It had been most appropriate that Custer had received the white surrender flag of the fabled Army of Northern Virginia.

Custer basked in the glow of a widely celebrated national hero of a victorious nation. After having earned a major general's rank, Custer never forgot his shining moment in the sun on May 23, 1865. At that time, he led his famed cavalry division during the victory parade of the Army of the Potomac down the broad Pennsylvania Avenue in Washington, DC. With long blonde hair flowing, he had impressed the new president and the nation's highest-ranking military leaders before a cheering populace. While serving on the western frontier, these resounding cheers still rang in Custer's memory, something that he still cherished while chasing Indians on the dreary Great Plains, now devoid of glory and far from national recognition. Any chance of reliving that golden time—the zenith of a distinguished military career that had reached unprecedented heights for the young American hero—had seemingly passed him by.

Instead of winning glory, the thankless job of hard service and fast-moving warriors slipping through his fingers deflated Custer's self-esteem. Victory proved elusive for Custer for the first time in his life. Most of all, by winter 1868 (more than half a decade removed from Gettysburg), a frustrated Custer needed a victory in this strange, primeval land so different from his native Midwest as never before.[2]

Surprise Attack on a Cold November Dawn

Since Lee's surrender more than three years before, as a professional military man, Custer had naturally dreamed of reaping still another smashing victory to once again electrify the American nation. The mundane service on the Great Plains seldom provided true opportunities for an ambitious officer long accustomed to victory, however. Therefore, Custer had been not only frustrated but also humiliated in attempting to achieve victory over the most elusive opponent he had ever faced.

Suddenly, like a gift presented by Mars, the Roman God of War, orders from headquarters and bitter winter weather suddenly became Custer's best allies to greatly enhance his chances for achieving a rare victory against a most confounding adversary. The harsh winter weather of 1868 ensured that the Southern Cheyenne, including Chief Black Kettle's village, remained stationary in winter's depths and vulnerable to a surprise cavalry attack. However, Black Kettle was friendly, presenting a moral dilemma. Unlike so many young warlike chiefs, the mature Black Kettle possessed the wisdom to have early realized that the Cheyenne's best chance for survival was peaceful accommodation with white people. He knew that attempting to defeat these powerful interlopers and their seemingly endless numbers was an unwise policy that would forever doom the Cheyenne.[3]

Doing the dirty work of General Sherman (who emphasized to "use all the powers [to vanquish] the enemies of our race") and General Sheridan, Custer had the odds in his favor by targeting Black Kettle's vulnerable village on the Washita in winter. Under orders from his superiors, Custer now possessed his best opportunity to reap a success. Not only were these peaceful Indians now encamped in Black Kettle's village, but also many warriors—particularly the ever-defiant Cheyenne Dog Soldiers, who wanted to fight white encroachment to the bitter end instead of trying accommodation like other Indians—were absent.

With Sheridan's personal blessings and under his orders, Custer and his 7th Cavalry departed their encampment amid a raging snowstorm that greatly increased the odds for a successful surprise attack on an immobile and unwary adversary, whose elusiveness in spring and summer was legendary. When the 7th Cavalry arrived in Washita's snow-covered valley, a personal reconnaissance by Custer and his trusty Osage scouts revealed that Black Kettle's sleeping village lay completely vulnerable in the tree-lined bottoms along the frozen river. After dividing his command to hit the village from multiple points, Custer prepared to unleash a sudden dawn surprise attack of four detachments. Typically confident, Custer believed at this time that there "[were] not Indians enough in the country to whip the Seventh Cavalry."[4]

When Custer struck the Cheyenne village at the cold dawn of November 27, 1868, he hit hard. Black Kettle was killed during the 7th Cavalry's relatively easy victory. Custer's losses were light in catching his opponent by surprise. His younger brother, Captain Thomas "Tom" Ward Custer, was slightly wounded while charging by his brother's side. Winning national recognition for his Washita "victory," Custer had succeeded in overwhelming a peaceful village, thanks to heavy snow and a totally unprepared opponent. In fact, this success was so thorough and easy that Custer thereafter viewed the overwhelming of Indian villages as a relatively easy undertaking: a dangerous delusion that was destined to have fatal consequences for him and nearly half of the 7th Cavalry in less than eight years.[5]

Indeed, in part because of Custer's one-sided Washita success, the stage had been early and partly set for the upcoming disaster at the Little Bighorn, especially after top military leadership lavishly praised Custer's tactics, including dividing the regiment, at the Washita. For such reasons, Custer's one–sided success renewed his old sense of confidence from the Civil War years. In Sherman's ruthless words from a letter that emphasized no mercy to any Indians who stood in the way of America's relentless march to the Pacific: "I am well satisfied with Custer's attack" on the Washita "and would not have wept if he had served [the other Indian bands] in the same style. I want you all to go ahead; kill and punish the . . . Cheyennes, Arapahoes, and Kiowas."[6]

Despite the glowing words for Custer's performance on that cold November morning, the truth was actually far different. Indeed, what was "most remarkable about the Battle of the Washita, as it came to be known, is how largely unremarkable it is" on every level.[7] Like military leadership saddled with the nasty business of trying to halt the brutal warfare that was impossible (offering no quarter by both sides) between the two entirely incompatible people, most Americans of the day conveniently overlooked the Washita's ugly realities. Nevertheless, this one snowy morning in late November along the Washita made Custer "one of the best-known Indian fighters of his age."[8]

Although he was only following orders, Custer's unprovoked attack on the peaceful Southern Cheyenne village followed the same relentless pattern initiated by his predecessors in the West. Under orders to "kill Cheyennes whenever and wherever found," Colorado soldiers had won another "victory" in attacking the friendly Southern Cheyenne village of the same ill-fated Black Kettle (who too willingly trusted the guarantees of whites) at Sand Creek, Colorado Territory, in late November 1864.

Personal ambitions and politics also explained the killing of mostly Cheyenne women and children at Sand Creek, whose male family members were away in pursuit of buffalo. Due to politics, the Colorado Territory's governor desired no peace with the Cheyenne, who actually wanted peace for self-preservation. Most of all, this consummate politician knew that his political success was based upon the slaughter of the Cheyenne to garner popular appeal and votes that guaranteed higher office. Equally ambitious military leaders also fell in step with political leaders in order to advance their careers. General Samuel R. Curtis, a former Civil War general, emphasized to Colorado's top military man that "I want no peace till the Indians suffer more."[9] Therefore, the Colorado soldiers had been ordered to "[k]ill all the Indians you come across," setting the stage for the massacre at Sand Creek.[10] However, to be entirely fair, whites and Indians equally demonstrated the evil capacity to display extreme levels of depravity in this bloody clash of divergent cultures on the Great Plains.[11]

Setting the Stage for Another Indian War

The settlers' relentless push west, and the resulting conflict with indigenous people, caused the United States government to attempt a more drastic solution. Since most native people were generally peaceful if left alone, only a relatively few warriors, usually young men, conducted raids against isolated settlers (to win individual recognition to elevate warrior status). The government took action to permanently separate the two people to halt the bloody clashes. Therefore, to confine the Great Plains Indians (a tragic fate for a wide-ranging nomadic peoples who followed the buffalo herds) to a stationary and unfamiliar way of life, the government established the reservation system. As the army's commander before he became president in March 1869 and before his personal positions hardened, Grant realized that "a good part of our difficulties arise from treating all Indians as hostile when any portion of them commit acts that makes a campaign against them necessary."[12]

Therefore, as a solution for dealing with the largest and most warlike tribe, the Lakota (Sioux of seven tribes), of the Northern Great Plains, the Great Sioux Reservation was established by the 1868 Fort Laramie Treaty. The overall strategic plan formulated at the White House seemed to be a workable solution at first, but only to a limited degree. By 1870, and according to the treaty's provisions, more than half of the Sioux were living on the reservations and drawing government rations—instead of leading a traditional nomadic life searching for buffalo over their traditional hunting grounds of the Powder River basin, including rivers like the Little Bighorn, south of the Yellowstone River.[13]

The Sacred Black Hills

The Black Hills was one of the last bountiful natural preserves, filled with game and distinguished by a pristine beauty, not yet overrun by white settlers. It was a very special place to the freedom-loving nomadic people who roamed it. Indeed, situated in the middle of the vast expanse of the Northern Great Plains and part of the Great Sioux Reservation, the Black Hills of the Dakota Territory were the most sacred ground of Northern Great Plains tribes. The Sioux believed that the Great Spirit dwelled among these rocky, forested mountains that rose up from the sprawling grassy plains like a giant beacon. The Lakota people called these magnificent hills—the home of the tribe's most revered ancient traditions and core religious beliefs—by the revered name of *Paha Sapa*. This Lakota name translated into the "Hills that are Black," and they were covered in dark carpets of luxurious Ponderosa pines and virgin Black Hills spruce of immense size. Consisting of the most sacred of grounds that lay at the very center of the moral, spiritual, and cultural world of the Lakota and

Cheyenne, the Black Hills were strictly off limits to white interlopers as guaranteed by the 1868 Fort Laramie Treaty. Placing the struggle of people, regardless of race, in its proper historical context—that of a larger struggle for possession of the best lands—the aggressive Lakota had forced the Kiowa out of the Black Hills to take possession and claim the lands as their own.

Open warfare between the Sioux and the whites was now inevitable, thanks to long-existing rumors that gold lay along the rocky bottoms of its clear streams and just below the thin topsoil. White trespassers on this holy ground were guaranteed to engender a violent response. Nevertheless, under orders from Division of the Missouri commander General Sheridan, Custer led his controversial summer 1874 expedition southwest from Fort Abraham Lincoln, located on the Missouri River in today's North Dakota, into the Black Hills situated in southwest South Dakota.

With President Grant's permission, Sheridan—the grizzled warrior who had so thoroughly ravished the Shenandoah Valley to play his part in destroying the Confederate Army's support system—planned to pry this central foundation of Lakota spiritual faith away from the Sioux people, weakening them internally. He planned for the building of forts in the area to all but guarantee complete subjugation. One of Custer's men, New York–born Private William Othneil Taylor, who had enlisted at age seventeen in the 7th Cavalry in mid–January 1872, wrote how the expedition was launched, "against the protest of the Indians, and in plain, direct violation of the treaty [of 1868 and] Gold was discovered, white men flocked to the El Dorado notwithstanding the gross violation of the treaty."[14] This transgression was deeply felt by native people. Like so many others of his tribe (the Sioux's closest ally) who also considered the Black Hills sacred, ancestral homeland, a Cheyenne warrior named Wooden Leg had been born in the Black Hills.[15] We'll hear more from Wooden Leg later, as his memoir brings the battle to vivid life.

Concern for another people's spiritual ground no longer mattered by the early 1870s, because the Black Hills became a national obsession of a growing nation on the move. After all, this was "the Gilded Age, and fortune–making was the national sport" [16] across America. An aggressive people on the march desired what was most revered by a highly spiritual people whose concept of the world was based upon the Black Hills. This situation guaranteed an inevitable bloody showdown along the Little Bighorn River, as if ordained by destiny and the Gods.

In 1875, after the gold rush to the Black Hills, the United States government launched the Senator William B. Allen Commission in an attempt to purchase the Black Hills. However, the so-called hostile Sioux, best represented by leaders Sitting Bull and Crazy Horse, intimidated any chiefs who dared to sign away the land. The leaders of the free-roaming (non-reservation or non-treaty) Lakota in the Yellowstone and Powder River country where the last of the great buffalo herds were found to support the nomadic ways, Sitting Bull (spiritual and political leader of the Hunkpapa Sioux) and Crazy Horse (war leader of the Oglala Sioux) were determined not to lose the Black Hills or their traditional way of life at any cost. Therefore, no treaty to hand over the sacred Black Hills was signed.

Given this frustrating situation that kept the Black Hills out of white hands, drastic action was needed by Washington, DC, to secure them. This required more devious means. At the White House on November 3, 1875, a cynical President Grant, Richmond's conqueror and head of a corrupt administration, along with other top officials and military leaders, agreed "that war was the best solution." [17] Here, along the Potomac's banks and under the Washington Monument's shadow, a new war against the Sioux was artificially "contrived" in the White House. However, no one in Washington, DC imagined the ultimate high cost of these calculated decisions: the destruction of the revered Civil War hero once known as the "boy general," [18] along with his elite cavalry regiment.

Clearly, because the Sioux refused to sell the Black Hills, a dark Machiavellianism dominated the White House proceedings to determine the area's fate and, ultimately, that of the Sioux. Almost everyone, including the commission, had been convinced early on that a good deal of coercive leverage (*i.e.,* military might) was now needed to forcefully convince the Sioux to sell the Black Hills. America's leaders, therefore, had fully realized that no purchase of the Black Hills was possible, until "the army had taught the Lakota a lesson"[19] that they would never forget.

After the sacred Black Hills had been violated, and knowing that these relentless whites now sought to gain the land by unethical means, the Lakota and Cheyenne chiefs (especially Crazy Horse, whose father and grandfather had been holy men) discussed the possibility of having to go to war only because they no longer had a choice. They knew that they would have to fight to the bitter end to save their ancestral ways and people.[20]

Victims of the insatiable greed for the yellow metal that made sane white men absolutely crazy, the Cheyenne's sad plight can be seen in the words of a Southern Cheyenne woman, Howling Woman (Kate Bighead was her reservation, or "white," name). She explained the setting of the stage for the eventual showdown at Little Bighorn:

> "I came to the Northern Cheyennes when their reservation was in the Black Hills country (1868–1874). White people found gold there, so the Indians had to move out. The Cheyennes were told that they must go to another reservation, but not many of them made the change. They said it was no use, as the white people might want their reservation too [so therefore] Many Cheyenne and many Sioux also, went to live in the hunting ground between the Powder and Bighorn rivers."[21]

The Bighorn, Little Bighorn, and Powder rivers (from west to east with the Tongue River and Rosebud running in the same direction between the Little Bighorn, the eastern tributary of the Bighorn, and the Powder River) flowed north into the Yellowstone River. Running northeast, the Yellowstone eventually entered the Missouri River. Free of white people and all traces of their corrupt, strange civilization, this magnificent land of unspoiled beauty and natural plenty was an unspoiled buffalo country. Here, some of the last remaining vast herds of buffalo still roamed free over an untamed landscape. Most of all, these pristine lands and best remaining hunting grounds provided an ideal haven for the most uncompromising Sioux bands under Sitting Bull and Crazy Horse. Sitting Bull was a "deep thinker," who bestowed insights and wisdom on his people, helping them to prosper.

As reported to the War Department in November 1875, increasing numbers of Sioux, including the bands of Sitting Bull and Crazy Horse, were now off the reservation in the unceded territory, which was overflowing with game, and breathtaking beauty.[22] Throughout the past, the Southern Cheyenne had often ridden north to join their Northern Cheyenne cousins to hunt the seemingly endless buffalo herds in the Powder River country.[23] Buffalo country also included the pristine region around the picturesque river that the Sioux called the "Greasy Grass": a name bestowed from morning dew simmering off the tall grass that lined the Little Bighorn River (the river's "white" name) that flowed west of the Powder.[24]

The Lakota people and their Cheyenne allies were not about to allow the desecration of the Black Hills and the loss of their best hunting grounds without a fight. As early as summer 1874, Lakota chiefs had warned the United States Army that war would erupt if the Black Hills were desecrated by whites. Nevertheless, the United States Government had dispatched a second (Custer led the first) expedition to the Black Hills during spring 1875, which had led to the congressional purchase attempt. Now the revered spirits of ancestors and the Great Spirit of this virgin land had been violated as never before. By the end of 1875, at least 15,000 miners had invaded the Black Hills, scaring off the game, polluting the land, and ensuring that the outbreak of war was only a matter of time.[25]

Feeling violated, angry Sioux looked upon the route of Custer's initial 1874 expedition into the Black Hills as the opening of "the Thieves' Road," which led to the holy ground's desecration. Clearly, by spring 1876, the Sioux and Cheyenne had plenty of old scores to settle with Custer, who was simply following orders from headquarters, thus becoming a symbolic representative of all that was immoral to the native peoples.[26] A final showdown had been brewing for many years. Deep-seated grievances of the Cheyenne went all back to 1864 with the attack on Black Kettle's peaceful village of Southern Cheyenne. A victim of a corrupt system of an aggressive alien people, a foreign nation, and their army, Black Kettle lamented how he once had been "the friend of the white man, but since they have come and cleaned out our lodges, horses, and everything else, it is hard for me to believe white men any more."[27]

Understanding why Custer and his men were about to pay the ultimate price for their society's and government's longtime—and seemingly endless—transgressions, Sergeant John Ryan, Company M, 7th Cavalry, correctly emphasized how the "Black Hills expedition did more to start the Indians than anything else and it soon became known that a general war with the northern Sioux was about to break forth."[28]

Ordered to Return to the Reservation

Literally pushed into a corner, the increasingly desperate Great Plains warriors would finally get their long-awaited opportunity to unleash their pent-up desperation and wrath along the pristine waters of the Greasy Grass River, because of serious bungling in high places of the army and government from the 1876 Campaign's beginning. Secret plans for waging an aggressive war against the Lakota had been in place early on, including a manufactured excuse for the launching offensive operations. During spring 1876, reservation agents reported increasing numbers of Sioux warriors departing because the buffalo herds were once again on the move in search of fresh grass, crossing the Yellowstone and heading south toward the Tongue River during their annual migration. Corruption led to famine on the Great Reservation, forcing an exodus to the rich hunting grounds of the unceded lands. Ignoring the fact that most warriors were only riding off to pursue the buffalo for their survival, like generations of warriors before them as part of a traditional way of life, Generals Sherman and Sheridan saw the building up of strength among the bands of Crazy Horse and Sitting Bull for only ill intent, as if they still waging war against the Confederacy.

As mentioned, an ideal excuse for initiating a new war against the Sioux had been established by the government with an artful skill calculated to achieve strategic and national goals, especially securing the Black Hills. Knowing that not enough sufficient time had been allowed for any compliance with the impracticable deadline, Commissioner of Indian Affairs Edward Smith had arbitrarily ordered that all wayward Sioux, Cheyenne, and Arapaho were to report to their respective agencies by January 31, 1876. As could be expected for such a late summons, only mere handful of warriors reported, but not the bands of Sitting Bull's and Crazy Horse's warriors who roamed deep in buffalo country and refused to recognize the white man's reservation system.

Nothing was more important to these fast-moving nomads of the plains than the buffalo, the most sacred animal of the Great Plains people. Indeed, the buffalo served as the very foundation of tribal life, both physical and spiritual. Noncompliance to this laughable government dictate to return to the reservations proved the flimsy excuse for the United States Army to launch a powerful punitive campaign against a free-roaming people who were now focusing on hunting the buffalo for subsistence at the traditional time and place.[29] Roaming at will in the Powder River country south of the Yellowstone, these surviving buffalo now fed on what was commonly called the "Buffalo curly grass."[30]

Of course, this calculated scenario that guaranteed widespread non-compliance to an arbitrary mandate manufactured by Washington, DC, was expertly contrived by hardened cynics. In Private Taylor's words, "many Indians from the different Agencies went out with the consent of their agents to hunt Buffalo in the unceded country [because] they had the right to do this under the treaty [and] []there was more reason for them to go at this time because there was an insufficient supply of provisions at the Agencies."[31]

Boding ill for future developments, especially with regard to the 7th Cavalry's eventual fate, an overconfident General Sheridan, the Division of Missouri commander, delegated the conducting of the 1876 Campaign to his two department commanders of relatively little ability, Generals George Crook and Alfred Terry. Crook was ordered to lead a column north from the Wyoming Territory, while Terry led a column from the north with the plan of catching the Indians in between them in a broad pincer movement. Confidence was high at headquarters for success against nothing more than "savages." Crook had already garnered a bold headline in the *New York Times* in May 1873 for his efforts in "Civilizing the Arizona Savages." He was now expected to do the same with the Sioux along with Custer.

Symbolically, Crook had been a player at the November 3, 1875, White House conference that orchestrated still another new war against the Sioux because they had refused to sell the Black Hills. Of course, entirely unknown to the Sioux and their Cheyenne allies at this time, a new war had been artificially created in Washington, DC, to bring the most serious threat to the Lakota's native homeland and way of life on a scale not previously seen. It did not matter that General Terry, a politician type rather than a man of action, possessed no Indian fighting experience, while Crook had relatively little experience, except in fighting the Apache in Arizona.

Quite simply, neither general was truly qualified for the stiff challenges that lay ahead in taking the war to the Sioux and Cheyenne deep in buffalo country, the unceded territory to whites and as designated in the 1868 Fort Laramie Treaty. Compounding these inherent weaknesses in the command structure for offensive operations in unfamiliar territory, an overconfident Sheridan initially dismissed reports of the growing strength of Indians in the Powder River area out of contempt for his opponent.

All of these diverse factors began to set the stage for a disaster along the Little Bighorn. Custer was about to pay a frightfully high price for the failures of top leadership, including his old Civil War commander, Sheridan. Nevertheless, with high hopes on May 17, 1876, the troops of the Terry–Custer column departed the newly established Fort Abraham Lincoln. Located in a remote region at the western edge of white settlement and the Union Pacific Railroad, this fort had been the 7th Cavalry's home in the Dakota Territory on the Missouri River's west bank since the early 1870s. It had been built as part of Sheridan's ambitious plan for creating an advanced position to strike at the Indians in their secluded sanctuaries. Leaving carefree days and the grassy baseball field behind (where they had played enthusiastic games as members of teams called the Athletes and the Actives), the 7th Cavalry troopers rode out of the fort with lofty expectations of an easy victory in Sioux country. They headed west for the south central section of the Montana Territory, riding toward a rendezvous with a cruel destiny.[32]

A Compromised, Yet Confident, Fighting Force

Unfortunately, at this time, the 7th Cavalry was not in the best of shape, after the long Northern Great Plains winter of inactivity. Even the regiment's elite reputation was somewhat of a deterrent to future success, engendering a dangerous sense of overconfidence, if not hubris. In an understatement, one modern historian diplomatically concluded with careful words how "the Seventh was perhaps not as good as its reputation."[33]

In addition, the expedition's launching from Fort Abraham Lincoln on misty May 17 was belated because of the late arrival of Custer and the lingering winter. A diehard Democrat, Custer had been caught amid the brewing sea of political intrigue and the scandals of Grant's Republican Administration, testifying before Congress about improper dealings at high levels. The precious time wasted before riding forth on a new campaign allowed even larger numbers of Indians to depart the agencies and join with Sitting Bull and Crazy Horse.[34]

Sergeant John Ryan, who had fought (as a Massachusetts infantryman) in the Army of the Potomac like Custer, described the departure from Fort Abraham Lincoln:

> The troops marched in columns of platoons with their guidons flying and their horses prancing [and] all the companies wore broad rimmed slouch hats, some black, others gray. The regiment never looked better, as all the men were in good spirits. Then came General Custer and his staff; next came the 7th Cavalry Band, all mounted on their magnificent gray horses, playing one of Custer's favorite tunes, 'Garryowen'.[35]

Reporter Marcus "Mark" Henry Kellogg described the extent of the overconfidence and even the commonplace delusion that distinguished the thinking of so many cavalrymen riding forth: General Terry "hopes the Indians will gain sufficient courage to make a stand at or before we reach the Yellowstone River."[36]

But some enlisted men in Custer's ranks of the dozen 7th Cavalry companies did not share the cocky optimism of their smug superiors, while riding away from the Missouri River country and toward where the sun set. One 7th Cavalry trooper, Ireland-born Private Thomas P. Eagan of Company E, was less sure of an easy success against the Sioux and their allies. As he had penned in a March 1876 letter to his sister: "We are to start for the Big Horn country [because] [t]he Indians are getting bad again [and] I think that we will have some hard times this summer. The old chief Sitting Bull says that he will not make peace with the whites as long as he has a man to fight. . . ."[37] Maintaining his distinct Irish sense of humor, Private Eagan then informed his sister in jest in the same letter, "As soon as I got back of the campaign I will rite you. That is if I do not get my hair lifted by some Indian."[38] Unfortunately for Eagan, who was in late twenties, this was precisely the future tragic fate that awaited him along the Little Bighorn.

Born in Bedford County, in the Piedmont of southwest Virginia in 1851, an apprehensive Private Thomas E. Meador of Company H, 7th Virginia, hoped for the best like so many other troopers, who rode out of Fort Abraham Lincoln to clanging of accouterments and the blare of martial music. He penned in a March 1876 letter to his sister: "We are to start on an expedition [which] [w]ill by my last one [and] I will come home next fall if nothin hapins."[39] Of course something indeed would happen, ordaining that Private Meador met his Maker on June 25, 1876.

Almost prophetically before they were killed along the Little Bighorn, Privates Eagan and Meador had ample reason for concern about the prospects for a successful summer campaign. Unlike in winter, success seldom came in summertime for United States soldiers, including Custer. Indian bands had begun coming together during April and May, concentrating as if correctly anticipating that a campaign would be directed against them.

Indian Forces Were Missing

Searching for the great buffalo herds with the warm weather of spring, after crossing to the Yellowstone's south side, the united bands moved west over the lush prairies, bright green from spring rains, and across the Powder River. They then continued west to cross the Tongue River, before settling down around the headwaters of the Rosebud River, west of the Tongue and just east of the Little Bighorn. They then steadily moved south up the lush valley of the Rosebud. Along the way in traversing the pristine, open plains region of southeastern Montana, they were joined by a steady, ever-increasing flow of agency Indians eager to hunt buffalo in the beautiful spring weather, when the green grass was high to provide ample nourishment to their ponies and the buffalo. Most of all, the Indian people were determined to defend "our beautiful country," in one warrior's words, against all interlopers.[40]

Remaining supremely confident for success, Custer shared little concern about what was happening with regard to his opponents' steadily gathering strength, because it was not fully realized. Like other experienced officers, he was most worried about the possibility of the Sioux escaping before his 7th Cavalry had an opportunity to strike a blow at an estimated 800 warriors.[41] However, by June 22, when he was destined to hold his officer's call when deep in Indian country, Custer and his officers believed that they would have to face from 1,000 to 1,500 warriors. This was still a significant underestimation of Indian strength that increased to outpace intelligence reports.[42] However, even this recent increase in warrior numbers from their earlier estimation still caused no great concern among these confident cavalrymen. Few men, especially officers, expected the Sioux to make a stand and fight, which was not their way of waging war, as Custer's men realized based upon Great Plains experience.[43]

For such reasons, ironically, "never had a more eager command started for hostile Indians," wrote New Hampshire-born Lieutenant Winfield Scott Edgerly, a West Pointer of Company D, 7th Cavalry. Clearly, a dark day of reckoning was in store for Custer and his men in a far-flung expedition that most troopers viewed much like an exciting adventure and little more than a lark.[44] Despite Custer having ignored General Sherman's May 8, 1876, warning to Terry: "Advise Custer to be prudent [and] not to take along any newspaper men, who always make mischief," Mark Kellogg, the *Bismarck Tribune* reporter, rode forward with the same confidence that dominated the column. He wrote how "Custer, dressed in a dashing suit of buckskin, is prominent everywhere [and is] full of perfect readiness for a fray with the hostile red devils, and woe to the body of scalplifters that comes within reach of himself and [his] brave companions in arms."[45] To be fair, Kellogg's words only reflected the day's common views among expedition members. Crook's recent success in hastening the surrender of Apache bands in Arizona was still seen as resulting from their "absolute fear of [Crook's] troops," which was now reflected in the common attitude among Custer's troopers.[46]

In truth, nothing was going to be easy during this campaign; it was going to be as lengthy as it was arduous. An emboldened Sioux warrior named Two Moons understood a reality still not fully appreciated by Custer and his troopers at this time: "Word came to us that the pony soldiers were coming after the Sioux [but] they are never good when they come on marches for that purpose."[47]

Symbolically, Custer and his men now rode on this expedition with newly cut hair, because this was an ambitious summer campaign that might well prove lengthy.[48] In the words of Trumpeter John Martin (Italian immigrant Giovanni Martini), Custer's "yellow hair was cut short—not very short; but it was not long and curly on his shoulders like it used to be."[49] Knowing that the newspaper's readership enjoyed such personal information about one of America's authentic war heroes, Kellogg wrote how Custer was called "the LONG HAIRED CHIEF" by his Indian scouts, "though he long since abandoned those golden ringlets, and now wears a FIGHTING CUT."[50]

Perhaps superstitious, men in the 7th Cavalry's column had heard, as expressed by a Sioux warrior, that the "Indians would not scalp soldiers with short hair [because there was] [n]o glory to scalp anyone with short hair . . . ."[51] Back in his glory days when the future never seemed brighter, Custer had his wartime locks first cut short by his wife in July 1865, which prompted him to inform his father-in-law, who disapproved of long hair, of the loss.[52]

Ironically, Custer's admiration for his superior, who was now sending him to his death deep in the Montana Territory, knew few bounds. As he had penned in a letter to wife, Libbie (Elizabeth Bacon-Custer), in the past, but the exact situation now applied to his ambitious expedition: "Some [7th Cavalry] officers think this may be a campaign on paper—but I know Genl. Sheridan better. We are going to the heart of the Indian country where white troops have never been before."[53]

However, because this campaign had begun too late in the year, precious time had been lost. Equally ominous was the fact that a good many veterans (about 100) of the 7th Cavalry, now together on a campaign for the first time since its formation in 1866, remained behind at Fort Abraham Lincoln because of the lack of horses.[54] Also staying behind at the fort along the Missouri were thirty-nine women who were about to learn of the high cost of choosing to become military wives. These unfortunate women at Fort Abraham Lincoln were all about to become widows.[55]

Ironically, Custer was riding forth on still another campaign because of fate and twists and turns in his own life. As early as March 1866, he had written to his wife, "I think it probable that I shall leave the army . . . I can obtain the position of Foreign Minister, with a salary in gold . . . I would like it for many reasons."[56] Meanwhile, Custer was now confidently leading the way in his most challenging and demanding campaign to date.

Chapter II

Forgotten Moral Foundations
of Custer's Opponent

For the inevitable climactic showdown of the 1876 Campaign, the upcoming confrontation was much more than a stereotypical clash of civilizations, cultures, races, and societies. It was an encounter between not only two worlds based on antithetical values and belief systems, but also on widely divergent religious views. While the Great Plains Indians wanted only to be left alone to roam free and hunt the buffalo, the whites still embraced a deep-seated cultural belief (which went hand-in-hand with westward expansion) of conquering nature. Even more, New Englander Herman Melville, the author of *Moby Dick* who based his view on a broad historical perspective, described one of these cultural views as "the metaphysics of Indian-hating."[1]

Indeed, even in June 1876 and for the last two centuries in America, the conquest of native people in the course of western expansion was viewed as a moral "achievement made in the name of humanity—the triumph of light over darkness, of good over evil, and of civilization over brutish nature."[2]

In this sense, Custer was widely viewed as the nation's cutting edge of the sword that was to cut its way through the obstacles like Great Plains warriors, who stood in America's path of expansion toward the setting sun. As Sheridan and Sherman fully appreciated, Custer and his mobile strike force (7th Cavalry) was the army's sharpest tool in its relatively small post–Civil War arsenal. A Cheyenne woman described Custer in detail, revealing how his charismatic appeal cut across racial and cultural boundaries, especially with regard to women: "Our people gave him the name of *Hi-es-tzie*, meaning Long Hair [and he] had a large nose, deep-set eyes, and light-red hair that was long and wavy [and] [a]ll of the Indian women talked of him as being a fine-looking man."[3] Certainly, wife Libbie thought so with regard to her bold cavalier. In a Civil War letter to Custer, she had implored with a sense of humor: "Old fellow with the golden curls, save them from the barber's. When I'm old I'll have a wig made from them."[4]

Ancient enemies of the Sioux in the struggle for diminishing natural resources on the Northern Great Plains were Custer's Crow scouts, who referred to white soldiers as "Light Eyes" and called Custer "Son of the Morning Star."[5] This name had been bestowed because Custer had struck Black Kettle's Cheyenne village along the Washita at sunrise when the Morning Star Voohehe was still high in the sky at daybreak.[6] Meanwhile, the Lakota people, or the Western Sioux Nation, knew Custer by the name of *Pehin Hanska*.[7]

Although he had been named after a Methodist preacher in the hope that he would one day enter the ministry, Custer was not entirely adhering to the belief that God and Manifest Destiny had ordained this land for whites only like most Americans. Instead, he looked toward the past. So many past successes during America's defining moment (the American *Illiad* of 1861–1865) still exerted a strong pull over him. Because it had been the key to so many past victories, Custer was obsessed with one tactical thought and winning formula: the headlong cavalry attack. Quite simply, the cavalry charge was something that Custer had always relied upon because it had brought him so much success. This faith had never failed him in the past.

Demonstrated repeatedly against the South's finest cavalrymen, including gifted Confederate commanders educated at West Point and military academies across the South, Custer's undying faith in the tactical wisdom of the frontal and flank attack had early transformed him into an authentic American hero. Custer described his well-publicized attack on the sleeping Cheyenne village at the Washita: "The moment the charge was ordered the band struck up 'Garry Owen' and with cheers that strongly reminded me of scenes during the war, every trooper . . . rushed toward the Village."[8]

Custer's obsession with this time-tested tactical formula for success against either whites or Indians was carried faithfully with him all the way to the Little Bighorn. However, what Custer failed to fully realize was that a new day had dawned. It was no longer 1865, when impressive victories had been relatively easy against an outgunned army and manpower-short nation devastated by nearly four years of war. Confident that he and his 7th Cavalry could beat any number of Indians, Custer's tactic of headlong and flank attack was his reliable ace in the hole, or so he believed. Consequently, this reliable tactical formula for success was something that he held close, especially if a crisis situation developed.

Prophetic Visions

Meanwhile, a lesser-known popular leader possessed another vision that he viewed as a special message straight from the Great Spirit. Sitting Bull was the most respected Sioux leader to emerge, not only because of his longtime defiance that mocked the accommodating agency— or reservation—chiefs, but also because he was the most revered holy man. He now served as a defiant symbol of resistance that united the tribes around him. Sitting Bull advocated a strict adherence of ancient cultural and religious ways as the best means to save a people under tremendous pressure.[9]

In pursuit of the buffalo herds that moved relentlessly in search of fresh bluestem grasses the covered the open prairie below the Yellowstone, Sitting Bull's band moved farther south and up the picturesque valley of the Rosebud from late May to early June. During the June Sun Dance at a medicine lodge on the Rosebud River (south of the Yellowstone and just east of the Little Bighorn River) and symbolically in the heart of buffalo country, a most significant event took place. A Cheyenne named White Bull, the nephew of Sitting Bull born in the Black Hills, recalled his uncle's inspirational vision that was greeted with deep reverence. The forty-five-year-old Sitting Bull, the most revered Hunkpapa Sioux holy man (*wicasa wakan*) who spoke excellent French, which he had learned from Catholic missionaries in Canada, sought to gain a revealing vision that might offer salvation to his beleaguered people. He hoped that this vision would come during what the Cheyenne called the "Great Medicine or Great Spirit Dance" (the "Sun Dance" to whites). He prayed for a great vision because he knew that the pony soldiers were on the move north of the Yellowstone and heading his way.

After hallucinating from intense pain caused by the tortuous Sun Dance, and then praying for a heaven-sent vision while atop a butte that overlooked the Rosebud, Sitting Bull gained his powerful vision: a good many enemies falling from the sky and into an Indian village full of well-armed warriors, who then destroyed them. In White Bull's words that described Sitting Bull's haunting vision that foretold of a great victory, "the Great Power had told him that his enemies would be delivered into his hands. He did not profess to know who these enemies were, but [he] explained that perhaps they might be [white] soldiers."[10] Ironically, in an eerily prophetic fashion, Libbie had gained a comparable vision of her husband rising into the midst of bellowing white clouds as if his soul was ascending to heaven. This pampered socialite and outgoing daughter of a respected Michigan judge was haunted by dreams like Sitting Bull's, and her dashing husband was caught in the middle.[11]

The Lakota's "Great Power" was named *Wakan Tanka*, and Sitting Bull had asked for assistance from this most revered spirit to save the Lakota people from destruction. Sitting Bull believed that his vision of soldiers attacking from the east (although the Terry–Custer Expedition was now located to the north above the Yellowstone) was bestowed to him, as he believed, from that most sacred source.[12] The Lakota people and their Cheyenne allies were told of Sitting Bull's vision guaranteed by Wakan Tanka that if the white soldiers had the audacity to attack the sizeable village (now larger than ever before), then they would be vanquished.[13]

Sitting Bull's spiritual vision gave the people new hope, especially with regard to the permanent return to ancestral and nomadic ways. The real name of this middle-aged holy man, who refused (like Crazy Horse) to be drawn into the seductive trap of the agency system or sign any treaties, was "A Buffalo Bull Lives Permanently among Us." Sitting Bull had long possessed his own sensible solution to avoid warfare: "to remain entirely out of touch with the whites" in every way. Therefore, he had led his people deeper in buffalo hunting grounds, the Powder River country, where they could roam free far from white government agencies, rules, or regulations.[14]

However, Sitting Bull was not the only voice that eventually proved prophetic. The Sioux believed in that the howls of the wolves were timely warnings. As late as "on June 24 [the day before Custer's attack], Box Elder, a Cheyenne prophet [who was also known as] Dog Stands on Ridge, sent a crier [through the village along the Little Bighorn] to warn the people to hold their horses [in preparation for an attack because] [h]e saw soldiers coming," in the words of Young Two

Moons.[15] Lamenting that these words fell on deaf ears of a complacent people who felt secure in the safety of numbers, Young Two Moons sent a crier to warn the people . . . "but people did not listen because they did not believe him."[16]

Indeed, as in the past when large numbers of Indian people were gathered in one place, these timely warnings were seen as unnecessary, and ignored. Low Dog, a tall Oglala Sioux warrior who had old scores to settle with Custer's men because one brother had been killed by the 7th Cavalry in a previous fight, said it best with regard to the representative view at the villagers along the Little Bighorn: "I did not think it possible that any white men would attack us, so strong as we were. We had in camp the Cheyennes, Arapahos, and several different tribes of the Teton Sioux—a countless number."[17]

By this time, the Northern and Southern Cheyenne were now united as one with their Sioux cousins, adhering to the wise adage of strength in numbers. Most importantly, these veteran hunters and warriors were well armed. Destined to fight Custer at the Little Bighorn like Low Dog, Brave Bear, a Southern Cheyenne Dog Soldier, was a typical warrior. He was proud of his painted war shield and colorfully decorated lodge that displayed designs of his past visions. Brave Bear was destined to lose his son to a trooper's bullet later that year during the attack on Dull Knife's village, located on the Red Fork of the Powder River, on November 26, 1876.[18]

The Oft–Overlooked Cheyenne

In relative terms, the Cheyenne, especially the Southern Cheyenne, were the most overlooked warriors at the Little Bighorn compared to the better-known Sioux, whose numbers were far higher. Since the Sioux were the principal opponents of the 7th Cavalry in this campaign, the far fewer number of Cheyenne oral histories have been long neglected by historians. Most importantly with regard to the final showdown, the Cheyenne were no ordinary warriors. In fact, they possessed a well-deserved warlike reputation and ferocity in battle that was equal to the Sioux.

An early pervasive attitude that evolved into one of the most cherished value systems of Cheyenne warrior society had been "let us fight all people we meet [then] we shall become great men," or warriors. The superiority of the Cheyennes' warlike ways was revealed by the fact that they were arguably the most mixed-race tribe (more than other tribes, including the Sioux), because so many past successes had garnered large numbers of captives over centuries. These war prisoners were then adopted into the tribe and married, with many different people becoming one. Consequently, and quite unlike the Sioux, almost every Cheyenne warrior had the blood from another tribe in his veins.[19]

The powerful meaning of Sitting Bull's and Box Elder's visions can only be fully understood within the context that they stemmed from perhaps the most spiritually focused and obsessed people in America. The Cheyennes' all-consuming spiritual nature combined with Spartan-like warrior ways to serve as the central foundation of their highly respected warrior societies that had long been the very heart and soul of the tribe: the Elk Soldiers (also called the Elk Horn Scrapers); the Fox Soldiers (also known as the Kit Fox men and the Coyote Soldiers); the Red Shield Soldiers; the Bowstring Soldiers (also called the Wolf Soldiers); and the Northern Crazy Dogs (Dog Men). Members of this last warrior society were called "Cheyenne Dog Soldiers" by whites, who had grown to fear them like no other Great Plains warriors. *Hotamitaneo* was the Cheyenne name for these fierce Dog Soldiers. Quite simply, the Dog Soldiers were the most warlike of the Cheyenne warrior societies. These warrior societies functioned as separate military units that operated and fought independently of each other to foster intense rivalries.

Serving as the traditional camp police and guardians of the village, these were crack fighting men of the warrior societies. Therefore, they possessed the greatest influence and commanded the most respect. These warrior societies were also the keepers of the tribe's rich heritage and ancient traditions, which were considered sacred. Consequently, besides protectors, these warriors were culturally important in the tribe like no other fighting men. Society members ensured the maintaining of order as much on the buffalo hunt (each family unit was entitled to an equal part in the hunt for their equal share of the meat) as in camp. All in all, each warrior society represented an *esprit de corps* of fighters to protect the people in wartime and preserve their nation's life. From an early age, members of these highly disciplined societies had been well–prepared well prepared for battlefield challenges, especially emergency situations when the tribe's very existence was in peril.

Representing the best fighting men of their respective warrior societies, the Cheyenne warriors wore clothing and possessed war regalia that distinguished them from other societies: a situation that fostered competition between warrior societies that heightened pride, morale, and war-waging capabilities to enhance the overall chances for the tribe's survival. Each warrior society possessed an easily recognizable tradition and legacy.

For instance, the warriors of the Red Shield Society were the only ones who carried a round battle shield, which was painted red. The Red Shield Society warriors believed that this distinctive shield have been a special gift from the Great Prophet. The shield's leather covering was made of the hide from a buffalo's hindquarters, including the long black tail that hung down from the shield's bottom to bestow a distinctive look. Most of all, this special shield spiritually linked these fighting men to the revered animal upon which the tribe's culture and survival was based. For these reasons, the Red Shield Society's warriors garnered the popular name of "buffalo warriors" among the people. They wore buffalo horn headdresses with horns attached during sacred ceremonies and dances, while bestowing God with thanks for the plenty provided by the buffalo herds and natural world.

The warriors of the Coyote (Fox) Society performed sacred ceremonies in the hope of gaining the legendary endurance and cunning of the coyote, which was one of the Plains' most stealthy, clever hunters. Meanwhile, the Dog Men Society was the Cheyenne tribe's largest warrior organization, its popularity stemming from its lengthy record of wartime successes. The waging of war was very nearly a full-time occupation among members of this highly respected society. Most of all, these men were the elite of the elite of these respective warrior societies. The society's symbol or emblem was the dog, which was a sacred animal. The reputation and prestige of the Cheyenne Dog Soldier Society exceeded all other tribal warriors.

Meanwhile, maintaining an exceptionally high moral code, the warriors of the Bowstring Soldier Society remained caste and morally focused. These men never married for the express purpose of remaining totally "pure" (more so than other society members) so that they stayed strong and were focused solely on nature's beauty to more clearly view God's masterful handiwork and the purity around them. The Cheyenne Dog Soldiers were not only stoic warriors, but also the sage philosophers among their people. Symbolically, they wore stuffed screech owls to signify the depth of their wisdom, which reminded them that their personal conduct in all matters should always be wise like the owl. In much the same way, the warriors of the Bowstring (Wolf) Society believed that they drew their power from the wolf's strength, cunning, and hunting skills.

Each warrior society of the Cheyenne nation had been created by a different holy man. He instilled moral qualities and strict codes of behavior. Acting independently of each other as separate entities, each warrior society performed actions that were focused on ensuring that the Great Prophet would bestow victory upon them. Warrior society members were truly the most Spartan of the Great Plains warriors. They were required to lead extremely strict, upright moral and virtuous lives (putting even some European monks to shame) in order to please the Great Prophet and guarantee his bountiful blessings, especially in wartime.[20]

Performing heroics in this crucial mission—their people's survival—brought greater respect and higher status for the individual warrior. Serving as the very "war force" of the Cheyenne tribe, these warriors bolstered military spirit among not only the society but also among the tribe in general.

Sacrificing their lives in order to save the people, especially defenseless women and children, was the greatest honor for these dedicated warriors of courage and faith. Against enemies regardless of their race and color, they fought with their hearts. Especially against white soldiers, these experienced warriors and veteran hunters expected no quarter and gave none in a Darwinian-like life-and-death struggle to the bitter end. Consequently, the war of the Sioux and Cheyenne warrior was a total one, against either whites or their ancient Indian enemies like the Crows.[21]

This situation of the Cheyenne was now especially desperate after the sacred Black Hills had been desecrated by the white miners. To these religiously obsessed warriors, too many whites had repeatedly proven that they "had no honor; they were lied to as Sitting Bull said [and therefore in] Lakota councils, the leaders talked of war."[22] Even white religious leaders demonstrated un-Christian qualities as the Cheyenne had discovered. A ruthless former minister, Colonel John M. Chivington, was the primary architect of the Sand Creek massacre, during one of the bloodiest days in the Colorado Territory's history where so many Cheyenne innocents had been killed on November 29, 1864. He had sworn to exterminate every Cheyenne that he and his Colorado men encountered, including even youths, if not infants (future warriors), because of the frontier philosophy that "Nits make lice."[23] Reflecting the day's common thinking, especially on the western frontier where racial hatred (on both sides) reached its savage peak, Chivington was convinced that "it is right and honorable to use any means under God's heaven to kill Indians."[24]

In contrast to the merciless Coloradoans, the Cheyenne warriors served and fought for the Great Prophet (God) to secure his blessings that were necessary for their people's survival. Everything that these warriors did was to honor this highest spirit and divine force as much as possible. Clearly, to a fanatical degree, these were true holy warriors who possessed a religious zeal. After all, these warriors knew that everything depended on God's favor for the people's salvation, especially at this time when their culture, society, and way of life were under threat from mounting white pressures as never before. By 1875, the majority of the buffalo herds had been decimated, and the white man was responsible for this systematic decimation of the most sacred animal for sport and profit. Quite simply, the situation was increasing desperate for the Northern Great Plains people by spring 1876.

Therefore, practically every thought and heroic deed of these society warriors was ordained by a powerful spiritual faith to save what was little was left of what they considered most precious and necessary to the people's survival. Quite simply, to these premier fighting men, the very life of the entire tribe depended upon the blessings of Divine Providence, which was believed to always direct the immense buffalo herds on their seasonal migrations straight to the people exclusively for their benefit. The people's mutual reliance and existence on this animal could not have been greater.

To their horror, the Southern Cheyenne had already witnessed the wiping out of the vast buffalo herds on the Southern Great Plains. Now, that same fate awaited the northern herds. Therefore, it was most of all necessary for these true holy warriors to stay in God's good graces to combat the evil that now threatened everything, especially the buffalo's mass destruction. The Great Spirit had always faithfully answered the ceremonial buffalo "calls" of the shamans by faithfully sending the herds on their annual migrations to the Sioux and Cheyenne to give them life, health, and vitality. However, now those herds were rapidly vanishing.[25]

While these warriors worshipped the buffalo, Custer was a battle-hardened military professional and war lover. In part because he had won so many victories during the Civil War, Custer worshiped at the altar of "the God of battles," as he had emphasized to his hard-riding troopers during the Civil War.[26] Reflecting their society's and leaders' prevalent views, the men of the 7th Cavalry already envisioned the final sunset of the Plains Indians as inevitable. Like everyone else, reporter Mark Kellogg embraced this widely shared view of a triumphant Anglo-Saxon race on the march west. While serving as a progress-minded member of the expedition to the Little Bighorn, he wrote philosophically about the fast-approaching end of an era with the inevitable extinction of a free people without remorse or a hint of sympathy: "the bee, the buffalo and the Indian are ever crowded ahead as civilization advances . . . the buffalo have gone [and] [t]he Indian must soon follow. The chiefs want the country and the Great Spirit has decreed that the red man must pass on."[27]

Even the number of warrior societies had diminished over the years. By the time of the battle of Little Bighorn, Wooden Leg, the Cheyenne warrior of the Elk Warrior Society and whose father defiantly refused to take his family to the reservation, concluded how there were "three warrior societies [which were] the Elk warriors, the Crazy Dog warriors and the Fox warriors."[28] He also emphasized how the "warrior societies were the foundation of tribal government among the Cheyennes [because] the members of the warrior societies elected the chiefs who governed the people. . . . The Elk warriors, the Crazy Dog warriors and the Fox warriors were the ruling societies of the Northern Cheyennes [and] those three were the only actives one in our northern branch of the double tribe," Northern and Southern Cheyenne.[29]

Custer understood the reputation of the enemy he was about to face along the Little Bighorn. With a hint of respect for their warrior ways that were not unlike those of the bright and the brightest from West Point, he wrote that the Cheyenne "Dog Soldiers [was] a band composed of the most warlike and troublesome Indians on the Plains . . . ."[30] He had early seen the warriors' formidable qualities. As an impressed Custer had confided to his wife in a November 1868 letter: "They are painted and dressed for the war-path, and well-armed with Springfield breech-loading guns. All are superb horsemen." Ironically, Custer, an excellent horseman himself, had been described by an eastern newspaperman after he lost control of his horse during the 1865 Union victory parade in Washington, DC, as having galloped ahead of the troops "like the charge of a Sioux chieftain."[31]

A Lengthy, Arduous Campaign

What had been now unleashed against the unwary Sioux and Cheyenne was a spring and summer 1876 campaign that was "an unprovoked military invasion of an independent nation that already happened to exist within" territory that later became part of the United States.[32] With a gift for understatement, the cynical Captain Marcus William Benteen, Custer's senior company commander, described this campaign as one not "initiated by the army for glory going purposes . . . but rather, was a little gentle disciplining which the Department of the Interior (the Department of the U.S. Government having charge of the Indian Bureau), had promised would be given the Indians if they, the nomads of the plains, declined to come in to agencies in the Spring; be good, and draw their pay."[33]

While the troops of the Terry–Custer Expedition continued to move relentlessly westward under adverse conditions and over rough terrain, the seeds of disaster at the Little Bighorn had already been deeply sown because of dysfunctional internal regimental dynamics and serious missteps of top leadership, both within the 7th Cavalry and higher up. As he desired, Custer continued to possess complete control of the 7th Cavalry, after Sheridan had made sure that the regimental commander, Colonel Samuel Sturgis, remained on detached service at the Cavalry Depot in St. Louis (more than 1,000 miles away) since 1873. One of the most confident military ventures ever launched in United States military history, the Terry–Custer Expedition consisted of two parts: the Dakota Column of the 7th Cavalry under Custer, and the Montana Column under Colonel John Gibbon—another hero of Gettysburg like Custer—at the northern edge of the unceded territory above the Yellowstone.

Before departing Fort Abraham Lincoln, Custer had divided the 7th Cavalry into two separate wings for greater tactical flexibility to meet the summer campaign's challenges. One wing was led by Major Marcus Albert Reno, a decorated Civil War veteran without Indian fighting experience, and the other wing was commanded by one of the regiment's best officers with ample experience in Indian warfare, Benteen. As if still fighting in the Civil War, Custer was taking some inherent risks in the overall name of regimental harmony and proper military protocol in this arrangement. Custer also made himself vulnerable because of his "forgiving nature," and tendency to overlook the depths of hatred among his personal enemies in his own ranks.

An extremely proud and haughty officer not revealed by the placid face of a schoolboy, the calculating Benteen was Custer's arch-enemy, second to none. Therefore, Custer should have known that Benteen could not be completely relied upon in a crisis situation. However, as during the Civil War years, when unity of purpose was paramount, he was hoping for the best in the overall name of the regiment, honor, and duty. For a variety of reasons, personal and professional, Benteen had been Custer's principal foe for years. The roots of this deep-seated animosity lay partly in jealousy stemming from Custer's glowing Civil War exploits and in what happened during Custer's attack at the Washita. On that late November day in 1868, a small mounted detachment under Major Joel Elliott, Benteen's friend, had been annihilated at the Washita. After Elliott and his men strayed and became heavily engaged in a hot fight after having chased fleeing warriors, Benteen believed that they had been abandoned by the regiment's commander to a cruel fate.

Captain Benteen also denounced Custer for having attacked recklessly without knowing the layout of the villages that spanned a long distance along the Washita, endangering the entire regiment. Custer's charge at the Washita was indeed a very close call. Custer's attack was unleashed without proper reconnaissance and knowledge of the enemy's strength and positions: a recipe for disaster. Still seething that Custer had ordered no search for the missing Elliott and his men from whom "nothing had been heard," in Custer's words, Benteen's open hostility toward Custer ensured that Benteen thereafter received the most remote assignments: a situation that led to the disease deaths of four of his children until only one lucky child, Fred, remained alive. This family tragedy was something that Benteen never forgot, or forgave.

For these reasons, Benteen's hatred of Custer was intense. He literally basked in his role as the leader of the 7th Cavalry's anti-Custer faction. Benteen fairly delighted in opposing what this native Virginian (born in Petersburg on the Appomattox River) derided as the "Custer Gang."[34] As late as October 1891, the depth of Benteen's bitterness toward Custer can be seen in his sad words that revealed the high personal price he paid for opposing Custer with such relish: "I lost four children in following that brazen trumpet around."[35]

The Summer Campaign

Custer and his men now expected a swift final victory this early summer on the high plains south of the Yellowstone. One of the most overlooked factors not taken into consideration to explain Custer's disaster was the grueling nature of this lengthy and demanding campaign. Indeed, this campaign seemed destined to leave the 7th Cavalry's exhausted men and horses (both out of prime battle shape in the aftermath of the long Northern Plains winter) at the very ends of their physical capabilities before the final showdown on June 25, when every ounce of energy and strength was needed.

Since departing Fort Abraham Lincoln on May 17, after riding west for nearly 300 miles east over wide stretches of rugged terrain in twenty-two days, the troopers now realized that this exhausting campaign was anything but "another pleasant summer outing." Custer and the 7th Cavalry reached the Powder River on June 7, after the long journey, having crossed from the Dakota Territory to the Montana Territory in late May.[36] In a letter to his wife on June 9, Custer wrote without a hint of danger: "We are now in a country hitherto unvisited by white men."[37]

Custer then turned north for a relatively short ride toward the Yellowstone—whose heavy silt bestowed upon the river its yellowish color and its name—and to where it meets the Powder. To support the expedition deep into Indian country, the Powder River Depot and encampment were established near the mouth of the Powder River.[38] Confident reporter Mark Kellogg wrote on June 10 that this concentration of troops "are so thoroughly organized that if the Indians can be found they will be taught a lesson that will be a lasting one to them [and] It is believed they INTEND TO FIGHT but they are no match for the force sent against them."[39]

On this same day, Kellogg described the newly formed strategy to subdue the wayward tribes in the unceded territory of the Powder River country:

> Taking the supposition that if the Indians have moved southward, that Gen. Crook [commanding the southern column from the Wyoming Territory] will meet and look after them. Gen. [Colonel John B.] Gibbon's four companies of cavalry were ordered to, and will arrive at the mouth of the Rosebud tonight to prevent the crossing of Indians at that point if any should attempt it. Major Reno,

with a battalion of cavalry . . . is ordered to march up the Powder river to its forks, then to push across the country [on a scout to locate the Indian's trail and then] Custer will outfit nine companies and with pack mules for transportation, will rampage all over the country, taking in the Rosebud and the Big Horn rivers, valleys and ranges. Gen. Custer declined to take command of the scout on which Maj. Reno is now at the head of, not believing that any Indians would be met with in that direction. His opinion is that they are in bulk in the vicinity of the Rosebud range.[40]

Consisting of half a dozen companies, Reno's scout began on June 12. He headed south up the Powder and to its headwaters and then farther west to the Tongue River, searching for signs of Indian movements to ascertain their location.[41] On Thursday morning, June 15, Custer led the 7th Cavalry's left wing (six companies) west along the south bank of the Yellowstone, after crossing the Powder River. Custer was directed to ride west to the Tongue River. The plan was for Custer to rendezvous with Reno's right wing about thirty miles to the west, where the Tongue River entered the Yellowstone. Custer reached the mouth of the Tongue River without incident.[42]

General Terry then joined Custer's encampment on June 16. Here, they waited three days for information from Reno's scout deep into buffalo country.[43] At this time, the Indians were continuing to move generally west because the buffalo migrated west across the arid high plains in search of fresh water and new prairie grasses that now stood high in the bright sunshine.[44] So far, most things had gone relatively well in this expedition. However, Boston Custer, the youngest of the Custer clan, who had never been a soldier, had gained more sober reflections that were right on target. Custer and brother Tom enjoyed nothing more than playing practical jokes on younger brother "Bos," continuing the teasing that was a Custer family tradition. On Thursday, June 8, the young man had written to his mother, Maria: "I do hope this campaign will be a success, and if Armstrong [George Armstrong Custer] could have his way I think it would be, but unfortunately there are men along whose campaign experience is very limited, but, having an exalted opinion of themselves, feel that their advice would be valuable in the field . . . I don't think we will get back to [Fort] Lincoln before September . . . ."[45]

On June 17, a delighted Custer wrote to Libbie how "I don't know what we would do without 'Bos' to tease." Ironically, on this very day when Crook was defeated along the Rosebud by Crazy Horse and his warriors, the overall situation was becoming far more serious and deadly than imaged by the fun-loving Custer. Back at Fort Abraham Lincoln, consequently, Libbie's fears had grown with each passing day. In one of her last letters to her husband, Libbie had prophetically written, in the third week of June: "I cannot but feel the greatest apprehension for you on this dangerous scout."[46] Perhaps she feared the worst also because Custer was not as religious as she thought he should be. Libbie admitted how her husband "though not a professional Christian yet [he] respects religion."[47]

Acting on the latest intelligence gained from Reno's lengthy scout—which discovered an extensive Indian trail that proceeded west all the way to the Tongue River and farther away from the Powder River than ordered—Terry formulated a plan for Custer to cross the Tongue River with six companies and link with Reno's six companies (the 7th Cavalry consisted of a dozen companies). He was then to pick up the Indian trail that had been discovered, after pushing south and up the Rosebud, west of the Tongue River.

Aboard the steamboat *Far West* at the Rosebud's mouth on the Yellowstone, Terry held a conference with his commander on the evening of June 21 to issue official instructions. By this time, it was clear that the Indians were located neither on the Powder or the Tongue. They were even farther west in the Rosebud, Little Bighorn, or Bighorn River (from east to west) country, where the buffalo roamed in greater numbers in the heart of the Indians' prime hunting grounds. Consequently, General Terry envisioned the three columns (General George Crook the Wyoming Column from the south [Terry did not know of his defeat and withdrawal], Custer the Dakota Column from the north, and Colonel John Gibbon with the Montana Column from the north) converging on their prey. Hopefully, the Indians then could be snared before they slipped away as so often in the past.

Therefore, on June 22, Custer and the 7th Cavalry rode south up the unspoiled landscape of the Rosebud Valley and away from Terry's command, after a formal review that impressed one and all. However, Custer's column was laden with its extensive pack train of heavily bur-dened mules, which was guaranteed to slow down movements and required too many guardians (one officer and six men) from each com-pany's ranks. Therefore, at total of 130, including all of Company B, were either part of the train or its guardians, representing twenty per-cent of the 7th Cavalry: vital manpower that was not part of Custer's two upcoming offensive strikes at the Little Bighorn.

The 7th Cavalry's march would be conducted about twenty to thirty miles per day, based on calculations formulated during Terry's confer-ence aboard the *Far West*. Most importantly as if worried that he would be able to gain full support from his top lieutenants in a crisis situation, Custer specifically emphasized at a commanders' conference that he would need the loyalty and cooperation of every officer for their mis-sion to succeed.

Following the trail of obviously a large number of Indians, Custer steadily led his troopers up the beautiful valley of the Rosebud, which was "clear running." Along the river's twisting course, the valley was radiant with new life, including an abundance of colorful spring flowers. As he desired, Custer had been allowed a free reign by Terry to locate the Indians, who were now expected to be either at the head of the Rosebud or on the Little Bighorn farther west. The morning (June 18) after the battle of the Rosebud, the immense village had

moved west to the Little Bighorn River. These two parallel river valleys were separated by a fifteen to twenty-mile divide of high ridges on
the open, rolling high plains. Now at the head of only the fast-moving
cavalrymen, Custer had been given discretion to attack immediately or
wait for the arrival of Gibbon's column, which was about half infantry
and of less strength (like Terry's column), depending on the tactical
situation that he found. Of course, since infantry moved more slowly
and Custer always struck as soon as possible, there actually existed
little possibility that he would wait, especially if he discovered a good
opportunity to strike as seemingly everyone at headquarters fully
realized.

Indeed, General Terry had emphasized to Custer that he was not
imposing "precise orders which might hamper your action when nearly
in contact with the enemy": a very clever way to delegate considerable
authority to Custer, while avoiding direct responsibility. Of course, this
situation now ensured that if disaster occurred, then the crafty Terry,
like an experienced lawyer skillfully orchestrating a favorable outcome
for himself regardless of Custer's fate, would not be held responsible if
Custer disobeyed his orders or acted rashly as in the past.

Hoping "of accomplishing great results," as he penned in a June 22
letter, Custer was so confident of victory that he might not have fully
grasped the somewhat sinister implications of Terry's carefully worded
order. If Custer succeeded, then Terry, after having cunningly created a situation that reflected the well-honed survival skills of a career
officer in a cut-throat military hierarchy long dominated by political
maneuvering, would be looked upon as brilliant by allowing his aggressive subordinate to reap victory with an independent command. If
America's popular hero failed, then only Custer would become the solo
scapegoat for defeat.[48]

Newspaperman Kellogg described the orders that directed Custer's
movements that began on June 22:

Custer, with twelve cavalry companies, will scout from its mouth up the valley of the Rosebud until he reaches the fresh trail discovered by Major Reno, and move on that trail with all rapidity possible in order to overhaul the Indians, whom it has been ascertained are hunting buffalo and making leisurely and short marches [and Gibbon's column] will march up the Big Horn Valley in order to intercept the Indians if they should attempt to escape from General Custer down that avenue [and] the hope is now strong [now] [th]at this band of ugly customers, known as SITTING BULL'S BAND will be 'gobbled' up and dealt with as they deserve.[49]

Kellogg's excessive optimism was not simply the result of his civilian status, because this underestimation of the Indian was universal among whites. Even General Sheridan saw these lethal warriors of the Northern Great Plains as little more than troublemaking "rascals" who only needed a good spanking from the 7th Cavalry.[50] Ironically, Custer was actually less optimistic than Kellogg at this time, because he feared that Reno's extensive scout too far west had alerted the Indians. As he penned in his letter to Libbie that revealed his fears at this time: "[Reno's] scouting party has returned [but] I fear their failure to follow up the trails has imperilled our plans by giving the village an intimation of our presence [and] [t]hink of the valuable time lost."[51]

With his men well-equipped for a fifteen-day expedition, Custer believed that he had the enemy on the run while following the trail. A feeling that an easy success was all but inevitable allowed some 7th Cavalry troopers to more fully appreciate the beauty around them. For protection against the searing sun, a number of cavalrymen, including officers, now wore new straw hats recently purchased from an opportunistic sutler aboard the *Far West*. They proved light and comfortable in the scorching weather, compared to the standard-issue heavy slouch hats.

On a hot day on which a vast network of converging Indian trails were all leading in the same direction—revealing that far more hostiles were on the move from the reservations than originally thought—Private William O. Taylor described with some awe on June 24 how "the whole valley [of the Rosebud] was scratched up by trailing lodgepoles [and therefore] [o]ur interest grew in proportion as the trail freshened and there was much speculation in the ranks as to how soon we should overtake the apparently fleeing enemy."[52] What the Indians and Custer's men were following was the ancient buffalo trail, always traversing the most favorable terrain for easy passage, that ascended up the picturesque valley of the Rosebud and ever farther from the Yellowstone to the north.[53]

In a recent letter to his mother, Boston "Bos" Custer looked upon the 7th Cavalry's confident advance deeper into the heart of Indian terrain as little more than a frolicking adventure. He expected little trouble with the region's migratory inhabitants (like the buffalo), who knew this land like the back of their hands, unlike the bluecoats. He wrote,

> Armstrong takes the whole command . . . on a Indian trail with the full hope and belief of overhauling them—which I think he probably will, with a little hard riding [and then] [t]hey will be much entertained [as] I hope to catch one or two Indian ponies with a buffalo robe for Nev [and] [j]udging by the number of lodges counted by scouts who saw the trail there are something like eight hundred Indians and probably more. But, be the number great or small, I hope I can truthfully say when I get back, that one or more were sent to the happy hunting-grounds.[54]

Custer's lofty expectations for achieving "great results" were highly–inflated, in part because he almost seemed to think that the 7th Cavalrymen were now comparable to the highly motivated troopers who he had led with distinction during the Civil War years: a dangerous assumption because these 7th Cavalry troopers were inferior in overall motivation, experience, and training, to those who fought to save the Union. During this exhaustive campaign and especially as the weather grew warmer with summer's arrival, conditions became harsher, diminishing the overall combat capabilities of the 7th Cavalry troopers. Under the broiling sun, officers and enlisted men rode onward mile after weary mile, moving south up the valley. With stoic resolve, the troopers steadily followed their officers on a grueling campaign, while half-choking on the yellow haze of sediments of finely grained dust. Some meager protection from the rising dust was provided by cotton scarves and bandanas that covered the noses and mouths of the hard-riding troopers.[55]

Now that his most aggressive cavalry officer had been unleashed to win laurels for him if he succeeded, General Terry had placed a smart high-stakes bet on the hardest-hitting cavalry commander in the United States Army. One officer marveled how Custer "was so full of nervous energy" that he had no patience whatsoever—the same kind of energy that had played a role in reaping so many Civil War victories.

What was largely overlooked was the fact that the 7th Cavalry was now not only in overall bad shape, but also far too few in number—less than 600 troopers—for the daunting task ahead. Custer was about to meet the largest concentration of Indians in the history of the Great Plains. In a most revealing letter to General Sheridan and unknown to Custer, a concerned Terry had recently warned prophetically how with regard to the 7th Cavalry's diminished strength that drastically reduced combat capabilities: "This number is not sufficient for the end [victory] in view. For if the Indians who pass the winter in the Yellowstone and Powder River country should be found in one camp (and they usually are so gathered) they could not be attacked by that number without great risk of defeat."[56]

Meanwhile, unknown to Custer in contrast to his growing confidence in following the Indian trial through the Rosebud Valley (the result of a movement that had been based on the annual pursuit of the buffalo and certainly not from fear of pony soldiers as assumed by the 7th Cavalry)—made especially vivid by colorful wild rose bushes in full bloom, which added to the almost festive mood—the strength of the Indians grew more imposing with each passing day. All the while, agency Indians continued to steadily arrive in the collective camp of Sitting Bull and Crazy Horse. They headed out of the reservations to not only hunt the buffalo in the Powder River country (the richest hunting grounds) but also to join Sitting Bull in partaking in the ways of their forefathers, including the Sun Dance, one last time, before everything seemed destined to be destroyed or consumed by the whites. Many departing warriors feared that this might be the last summer to enjoy the old life that was now on the road to extinction.

These gathered young warriors were of prime fighting age. Most importantly, for the first time they had come together in a united front against the whites. Sitting Bull's Hunkpapa Sioux, and Crazy Horse's Oglala Sioux, formed the heart of the resistance effort. This irresistible call to unite to fight against the common enemy especially appealed to the Cheyenne, who had old scores to settle. They were totally committed to defending the ancestral homeland that they loved. As never before, these warriors were prepared to fight to the death—to the last man, as Sitting Bull had declared. Therefore, Sitting Bull had wisely cautioned the ever-restless young warriors to remain patient and inactive while the pony soldiers steadily advanced toward them: sage advice that caused Custer to incorrectly conclude that the Indians were in flight from the 7th Cavalry. Instead of going forth to engage in the tantalizing prospect of harassing the Terry–Custer column, Sitting Bull, who headed the most militant Sioux tribe and bragged how he would never go to a reservation or sign a treaty as long as the buffalo roamed free, stood his ground, defiant in the unceded territory. He had wisely declared with regard to the advancing white soldiers, "Let them come" forth if they dare to receive the righteous wrath of a people, who had been pushed to the breaking point. Clearly, as the result of the sacred Sun Dance on the Rosebud, Sitting Bull's life-affirming vision of soldiers tumbling into the village (an attack from which they would never return) remained vibrant, inspiring an entire people with the faith of winning the ultimate victory. Therefore, it was now time for patience for even the youngest warriors. Sitting Bull's Sun Dance visions were derived from the Great Spirit, who had bestowed a vision of the enticing possibility of the "Long Knives" falling into their village "like grasshoppers" and then being destroyed like locusts who had invaded a ripe cornfield.[57]

Chapter III

To the Clear Waters of the Little Bighorn

The Indians Settle In

The upcoming showdown between the professional fighters from their respective societies was destined to be fought in the heart of buffalo county—including along the Little Bighorn, which was now covered in a luxurious carpet of buffalo grass that stood as high as four feet. The winter had lasted longer than usual, so the grass first began to turn green in April with spring's warmer weather and rains, providing the primary subsistence for the buffalo herds.[1]

In their relentless search for the buffalo herds, and because of their small numbers (unlike Sitting Bull's Hunkpapa, whose large numbers brought up the march's rear in case of a surprise attack), the Cheyenne had led the movement of mostly Sioux down the pristine timbered valley of the Little Bighorn River since it had first been reached by the Indians on June 15. As deemed by the chiefs, the Cheyenne people were led to their new camp site by the Kit Fox Society warriors. The primary responsibility of the Fox warriors was to maintain order and discipline among the people like true police during the movement south, up the picturesque valley, until the chiefs in front designated exactly where to set up the village along the Little Bighorn: a favorite camping place used for decades by numerous tribes because of good water, timber, and high grass for horses. If any argument arose among the people about the exact placement of lodges, especially proximity to the water, then the Fox warriors settled personal disputes in the fast-forming village.

Since times were now good for the people, there was a minimum of bickering and in-fighting (not even among in-laws) among a grateful people in the Little Bighorn's Valley. Giving their blessings to the Great Spirit for the bounty provided to them by the area's buffalo and ante-lope herds, they basked in their absolute freedom, fresh water, grasses for ponies, and plenty of game to feed the tribes.

As usual, the women of extended families and clans set up their lodges near each other in true familial settings. Here, across from the expansive mouth of the dry, eroded gully on the river's east side, known as Medicine Tail Coulee, the Cheyenne village on the far north quickly took shape on the west side of "the beautifully blue Little Big Horn" River. The entrances of the Cheyenne lodges faced east toward the line of bluffs rising up and lining the river's east side.[2] At this point, a wide opening in the terrain existed amid the wall of sage brush- and cactus-covered bluffs above the Little Bighorn to provide access to the river on the east side. The buffalo grass was new, green, and fresh, covering the hillsides below the top of the bluffs. Wooden Leg described how across "the river east of us and a little upstream from us was a broad coulee, or little valley, having now the name of Medicine Tail coulee."[3]

Extending several miles along the river, the lodges (each with its assigned place to maintain order in each tribal circle) of the vast Indian camp was quickly established with the Cheyenne (the smallest tribe) on the north and Sitting Bull's Hunkpapas (the largest tribe and most fanatical warriors) on the south or upriver: a formidable strength if an overconfident white commander made the mistake of attacking the strongest end of the village first. In fact, and in preparation for meeting the pony soldiers they knew would come during this summer of decision, this was the largest Indian village, consisting of a half dozen tribes, ever to take shape on the Great Plains in what could not have been more serene in its natural setting. Eight separate tribal circular villages (seven Sioux and one Cheyenne) were lined along the bottoms of mostly tall cottonwoods in full summer foliage. Older Cheyenne and Sioux knew this place well, because this valley had been a comfortable camping area extending back to their childhood days.[4] American Horse, a highly respected Cheyenne warrior born in 1847, described how "we moved on and camped in a big bottom where there is a bunch of timber": mostly giant cottonwoods, towering in stately fashion above the river's clear waters.[5]

Clearly, this favored camp location along the Little Bighorn was a beautiful place that had long drawn these nomadic people like a magnet. The sprawling village along the river exuded an air of supreme confidence stemming from the united strength of the tribes, and the growing sense of invincibility was palpable. After the remarkable victory over the over-confident Crook at the Rosebud on June 17, among the grassy hills, topped by Ponderosa Pines of dark green, the mood was one of absolute confidence, if not invincibility. After all, the Sioux and Cheyenne warriors, fighting more aggressively than usual, had caught Crook, who was guilty of underestimating his opponent, by surprise. Crazy Horse and his warriors had forced Crook to retire all the way back to the Wyoming Territory, eliminating him from this ambitious campaign for two months, precisely when Custer needed him the most. The entire village was dominated by a joyous mood; the recent Rosebud victory, and so many people concentrated in one place, bolstered faith and confidence to new highs. Quite simply, the Little Bighorn was a special place, and never more so than during this glorious June. Wooden Leg, a Cheyenne who knew the Little Bighorn River well from having encamped here during his youth, explained the representative mood at this time: "I had no thought then of any fighting to be done in the near future [because] [w]e had driven away [Crook's] soldiers, on the upper Rosebud, seven days ago [on June 17 and] [i]t seemed likely it would be a long time before they would trouble us again."[6]

As confident as Custer, but for entirely different reasons, Two Moons, a minor chief of the Kit Fox Society who had been born in the virgin lands of western Wyoming in 1842, described how when we "camped in the valley of the Little [Big] Horn [and] [e]verybody thought, 'Now we are out of the white man's country [and we] can live there, we will live here'," in peace—an illusion that disguised a sense of reality as thoroughly as Custer's was deluded by overconfidence.[7]

In some ways, the lush valley of the Little Bighorn was much like the pristine Black Hills, a lovely and quiet place considered sacred by the people for generations. Best of all, this favorite place for encamping was located deep in buffalo country and far from the white interlopers, serving as a safe and secure sanctuary, or so it seemed. Here, long ago, before the existence of the Northern Great Plains tribes had been seriously threatened, on "the Little Bighorn river, we had one day of Great Medicine thanksgiving" for the Great Spirit's and the land's seemingly endless bounty and natural beauty. Now, this religious and grateful people, who had faithfully adhered to a strict moral code, gave thanks for the recent victory of Crazy Horse over Crook and his Wyoming Column at the Rosebud.[8]

Like so many others, Wooden Leg, one of the tallest Cheyenne warriors, had old scores to settle with the white soldiers. He had lost his oldest brother, Strong Wind Blowing, in an 1866 clash with the hated pony soldiers, whose fast-firing revolvers and slashing sabers were lethal.[9] For such reasons as Wooden Leg explained, [h]is father "chose to stay away from all white people [and the reservation, while] his family all agreed with him."[10]

The warm night of June 24 was a special one that was cherished by the united tribes along the Little Bighorn. It was a time of celebration for not only the new sense of freedom, but also for the recent Rosebud victory. Thanks to this hard-fought success over Crook and the largest column in this campaign, the wives, mothers, fathers, and children were now safe from the "Long Knives," and "Long Swords," or so it seemed. Eighteen-year-old Wooden Leg never forgot how "That night we had a dance [but] [i]t was entirely a social affair for young people, not a ceremonial or war dance [around] a big bonfire [while] [t]he drums and Cheyenne dance songs enlivened the assemblage. It seemed that peace and happiness was prevailing all over the world, that nowhere was any man planning to life his hand against his fellow man."[11]

The picturesque setting and joyous mood were so seductive that everyone seemingly forgot that earlier in the day a crier had brought news that was based upon the recent reports of sharp-eyed scouts. Shouting a warning, the crier had ridden slowly through the camp yelling to inform the people: "The soldiers will be here tomorrow. Be ready."[12] However, no one heeded his warning, because this was the best of times.

The Serene Indian Village

With this massive concentration of Indians, it was a time for the beginning of new relationships between young people among the different tribes. To initiate courtship, the young women, dancing in customary groups, found the most eligible warriors who promised to be great hunters and win renown in battle to bring great honor to the family. Sioux men sought the prettiest and healthiest Cheyenne women, ensuring a healthy bloodline outside the tribe and a brighter future. It now seemed as if these days of plenty and prosperity would last forever. Consequently, the courtship and "virgin" dances were highlights of the celebrations that went far into the night of June 24.[13]

Fueled by an intoxicating mixture of mating instincts and lust heightened by meeting new women from other tribes, the ritualistic dancing of the sexes went deep into the night of June 25. In Wooden Leg's words: "At the first sign of dawn the dance ended [and] I walked wearily across to the Cheyenne camp. I did not go into our family lodge. Instead, I dropped down upon the ground behind it [and] [w]hen I awoke I went into the family lodge. My mother prepared me breakfast [and] [t]hen she said: 'You must go for a bath in the river.' My brother Yellow Hair and I went together. Other Indians, of all ages and both sexes, were splashing in the waters of the river. The sun was high, the weather was hot. The cool water felt good to my skin."[14]

Employing thin fishing line made of horsehair with metal hooks bartered from white traders like iron arrowheads, a Cheyenne warrior named White Shield spent the morning hours fishing for brown trout and rainbow trout in the cold waters, while so high up (south) the river with his nephew and another Cheyenne named Black Stone. Water from the melting snow of the Big Horn Mountains now filled the river, because summer had come later than usual following the winter's severity. Catfish and bass flourished in the warmer waters farther downstream to the north before shortly entering the Yellowstone. Now, along the Little Bighorn, good-sized trout supplemented the traditional meals of fresh, lean buffalo meat.[15] However, White Shield might well have thrown away his fishing gear and walked away from this pristine river had he known that the "favorite pastime" of Major Benteen was also fishing.[16]

After rising in northern Wyoming and then flowing north into the Montana Territory, the 138-mile-long Little Bighorn was a tributary of the Bighorn River that entered the Yellowstone. As the summer sun of this scorching hot Sunday, June 25 (in the Moon of the Ripe Juneberries to the Sioux) rose ever higher in a cloudless luminous sky, larger numbers of villagers headed for the river to wash and cool off.

Clearly, the Little Bighorn's soothing, clear waters on such a hot day were simply too tempting for the villagers to ignore. First children and women, and then late-rising warriors, flocked to the river's cold waters that meandered lazily through "the Indian camp [which] looked beautiful in the green valley" about a half-mile wide in an east-west direction. The village stretched nearly three miles along the bottom, covered in ancient cottonwoods and stands of young willows along the river's banks. Unlike the Sioux, the Northern Cheyenne called the Little Bighorn the "Goat River" and the "Little Sheep Creek." This fast-moving watercourse had been named after the magnificent monarch of the area's mountains, Bighorn sheep (the largest wild sheep in North America) that roamed free like Sitting Bull's Hunkpapa.[17]

Wooden Leg described the expansive village lying along the river's west bank as far as the eye could see: "Every one of the six [tribal] separate circles had its open and unoccupied side toward the east [and] [e]very lodge in each of these camps was set up so that the entrance opening was at its east side," to benefit from the sun's early morning warmth.[18]

Rejoicing in the purity of this special place along the peaceful river, one Cheyenne warrior also stated with racial pride, that revealed another appeal of this massive concentration, how: "One big lodge of Southern Cheyenne [under Chief Lame White Man] was in our circle" of Northern Cheyenne, and there "was not any white person nor any mixed-breed person with us."[19] Racial purity (not just a traditional white obsession) was still another consideration with regard to staying away from the white man and his inscrutable ways. Wooden Leg emphasized how, in the Cheyenne village circle, "[o]ur tribal medicine tepee, containing our sacred Buffalo Head [of the Northern Cheyenne] and other revered objects, was in its place at the western part of the open space enclosed by our camp circle [of around 300 lodges and] [o]urs was the only tribal medicine lodge in the whole camp [because the] Sioux tribes did not maintain this kind of institution. . . ."[20] Unfortunately for Custer and his 7th Cavalry troopers, who had no idea of what awaited them, "almost all of our Northern Cheyenne tribe were with us on the Little Bighorn."[21] In such tumultuous times, and having been warned from recently arrived agency Indians that the pony soldiers were coming, these native people understood the wisdom of the concept of united we stand, divided we fall. It was now the only and last hope for survival.

With so much to be thankful for this June, the people of this sprawling village along the Little Bighorn felt a perfect sense of contentment. It seemed like the days of old, before the arrival of the white man, who now threatened to destroy everything that these nomadic people cherished like their ancestors before them. The beauty of the natural setting and strength of the united tribes masked the harsh reality and ugly truth that the nomadic way of life was already now doomed.

Meanwhile, scattered reports from scouts had filtered into camp that the pony solders were headed their way, but this news continued to be routinely discounted by almost everyone. In fact, such timely reports were even openly mocked. As Wooden Leg explained the situation:

> We did not believe Last Bull's report [of soldiers heading toward the Little Bighorn because] [w]e thought somebody had told him what was not true. The treaty allowed us to hunt here as we might wish, so long as we did not make war upon the whites. We were not making war upon them. I had not seen any white man for many months. We were not looking for them. We were trying to stay away from all white people, and we wanted them to stay away from us.[22]

This was the sage philosophy of Sitting Bull. He was "the most consistent advocate of the idea of living out of all touch with white people," because he knew that this strategy was the key not only to his people's well-being, but also their survival.[23]

Accompanying a Sioux female friend on this warm morning of June 25 to the river's tempting cool waters, a Cheyenne woman departed her encampment at the village's lower end in the best of moods. Chatting along the way, the two native women walked upstream to visit their female friends in the Sioux camp on the far south. Howling Woman discovered that the river was swarming with people, who sought relief from the blazing heat. In Howling Woman's own words: "We found our women friends bathing in the river, and we joined them. Other groups, men, women, and children, were playing in the water at many places along the stream. Some boys were fishing [and] [a]ll of us were having a good time."[24]

In this relaxed mood that dominated the valley of unspoiled beauty, even some esteemed leaders also now enjoyed the Little Bighorn's refreshing waters, which continued to draw even more people this morning. One Cheyenne warrior mentioned that with the sun high "about noon, Crazy Horse, Yellow Nose, and other Indians were in the river bathing" seemingly without a care in the world.[25] Still fishing in the river for succulent trout to roast over an open fire, White Shield caught so many fish that he directed his nephew to search for grass-hoppers that were in the hills for additional bait (known as the Rocky Mountain Locust, the early hot weather had brought them out in larger numbers than usual).[26]

A Sioux warrior named Eagle Bear explained the village's lack of vigilance and concern about the approach of enemies, who were believed to be still far away: "Our people wanted peace. We did not want to fight the white men anymore [and] [n]one of the Indians expected a fight. The children were swimming in the river and playing on the bank. The women were cooking and packing their stores as we planned to break camp."[27]

However, this serenity and joy along the Little Bighorn was only the calm before the storm. One warrior in the Cheyenne village at the encampment's northern end realized as much. As mentioned, Box Elder's prophetic June 24 warning had been ignored, however. Box Elder, the blind prophet who had been born around 1790, "saw soldiers coming; but people did not listen because they did not believe it," in the words of Young Two Moons. Therefore, the usual daily pace of life in the Cheyenne village continued unabated, as if June 25 was just another ordinary day and that there were no white soldiers within 1,000 miles of them, partly because of Crook's defeat only twenty-five miles away. All in all, Custer and the 7ᵗʰ Cavalry was now presented with a golden opportunity to catch their unwary and overconfident opponent by surprise.[28]

Box Elder was also known as Old Brave Wolf, and this name had a direct connection to his most recent warning about the approaching pony soldiers. According to him, the wolves from the top of the hills had earlier seen Custer's men and howled their warnings that echoed through the night. These spine-tingling cries had alerted Box Elder, who understood their mysterious meaning. Nevertheless, even in an ancient culture that revered elders for their wisdom, he continued to be ridiculed as an old fool. His timely warnings rang hollow through a Cheyenne village dominated by playing kids, barking dogs, and women cooking.[29]

However, the arrival of additional numbers of agency Indians verified the early, sage warnings by prophets and holy men: serious trouble was on the way. In the words of Hump, a Sioux warrior also known as Big Chest and High Back Bone: "There was a good many agency Indians in our camp and all made the report to us that Long Hair was coming to fight us. So the Indians got all together that he might not strike small parties [because] they were getting ready to be strong to defend themselves."[30]

Despite the warnings, a good many warriors continued to sleep late in the buffalo hide lodges on the humid morning of June 25, because they had been "up all night dancing," in Brave Bear's words. These festivities were primarily military dances and social dances, with young warriors pursing the most alluring single women of their dreams to ensure that their minds stayed on lovemaking instead of approaching pony soldiers. In this sense, "Custer's Luck" was alive and well. Custer could not have asked for a more unwary or more overconfident opponent.[31]

At the same time, this was an emboldened opponent to a degree not seen before, thanks to the stunning June 17 victory over Crook. Two days after Custer and his command were wiped out, the increasingly worried editor of the *New York Herald* expressed the greatest concern for the fate of the Terry–Custer column: "When Crook, with thirteen hundred men, was unable to [win a battle over] Sitting Bull we may well be anxious over the fate of either of Terry's detachments, numbering less than seven hundred men, if they should meet them single handed."[32]

Custer's Tactical Flexibility

Relishing independent command, relying upon tactical flexibility, and following the ever-widening Indian trail, Custer no longer proceeded upriver farther south toward the Rosebud's headwaters. He swung west and headed toward the next valley, where the Little Bighorn River flowed, and toward where the buffalo herds and the Indians had gone. Custer pushed his men hard, resulting in two nights without sleep.

Just east of the high ground divide between the Rosebud and the Little Bighorn, after leaving the picturesque Rosebud Valley behind, Custer finally called for his men and horses to halt. He wisely hid his weary cavalrymen in a deep, wooded ravine to avoid detection during the sweltering midmorning of June 25. He planned to rest his exhausted command for June 25's remainder in preparation for an attack on the Indian village nested in the Little Bighorn Valley to the west, as revealed by his trusty Indian scouts. Custer was in an ideal high ground location just before the Little Bighorn Valley, and from which he could easily advance on the village to strike at dawn on June 26, once again in an Washita-like attack. Here, less than a dozen miles from the treeless divide located between the two river valleys, the tired bluecoats were ordered "to keep concealed, and to preserve quiet," wrote Private Taylor.[33] A former New York cutler who had enlisted in January 1872, Taylor felt increasingly nervous because they were now deep "in a section of 'the Indian's Paradise land,' where we had never been before."[34]

The much-needed rest break of Custer's weary men was not to last. Looking west from the dominant high point known as the Crow's Nest on the divide, at the northern end of the Wolf Mountains—the vast village nestled deep in the Little Bighorn valley, hidden behind (or west) of the high bluffs that lined the river's east bank—had been reconfirmed with certainty by the Indian scouts, including by the ever-reliable Bloody Knife. An experienced warrior whose words were respected in the 7th Cavalry, he was officially a "guide" and Custer's favorite Arikara scout. Then, fresh Indian pony tracks were ascertained near the 7th Cavalry's hidden position in the timbered ravine. Consequently, to Custer's shock, he now realized that "the Sioux discovered us in the ravine," wrote Trumpeter John Martin, who had served as a drummer boy in the Italian Army at age fourteen.[35]

With the startling news of having been discovered, Custer flew into action, and his well-laid plans of striking the village at the next sunrise were now sabotaged. Custer's plan for a much-needed day of rest for his exhausted command instantly vanished. An Italian immigrant whose strange fate had brought him all the way to the Little Bighorn, Martin described how: "At once [Custer] ordered me to sound officers' call, and I did so. This showed that he realized now that we could not surprise the Sioux [it was incorrectly feared], and so there was no use to keep quiet any longer [because] [f]or two days before this there had been no trumpet calls, and every precaution had been taken to conceal our march."[36]

With the midday sun scorching the high plains landscape, Custer called a hasty officers' conference. He laid out his new set of tactical plans and "gave his instructions about battalion formation"

TO THE CLEAR WATERS OF THE LITTLE BIGHORN • 61

into three battalions. Feeling that he had no choice in an emergency situation, Custer then explained his decision to ride west and strike the village immediately. After all, the village was located on disadvantageous low ground of the river valley and was "poorly situated for defense," as Custer realized.[37] Since Custer believed that the 7th Cavalry had been seen by Indians, which caused him to fear the worst possible scenario, the tactically astute commander emphasized the basis of his bold decision to attack, because "he would rather attack than be attacked."[38]

Private Taylor described the fast-paced chain of developments that so suddenly changed the entire tactical situation, which was destined to draw the 7th Cavalry toward the Little Bighorn: "our presence having been discovered," so the [Crow] scouts and the others reported, "it was necessary to act at once," and "we started off again crossing the divide a little before noon" on one of the year's hottest days.[39]

In the riskiest move of his career, Custer had decided to descend into the Little Bighorn Valley and attack the village in the middle of the day rather than wait for dawn, which was always the best time to strike an Indian encampment. Worried that the village was about to be warned and that the Indians would escape or rally to launch their own preemptive strike, Custer was in a high state of anxiety for fear of losing all that he thought he had gained: not a good mental state for an aggressive commander immediately before a major engagement. His mental state was bound to present a host of unprecedented challenges, as Custer knew so little about his opponent's numbers and exact locations. This situation was more motivation-inducing for Custer, because he'd recently made an enemy of President Grant and the Republican Administration. Therefore, obsessed with winning a victory to vindicate his stained name and honor, Custer was now determined to deliver an attack from the east before his command could be hit by a preemptive strike from the west. Custer's decision was tactically correct because, ironically, the large concentration of Indians had long engendered a dangerous complacency, making "them stupid—sure that no enemy would dare attack them," in one warrior's words.[40]

Therefore, Custer and his 7th Cavalry troopers, who had "cold water" in canteens, rapidly rode up the ascending ground leading to the divide's crest that separated the Rosebud and Little Bighorn River Valleys. Company I's Private Patrick Kelly, born in County Mayo, Ireland, in 1841 and married to an Irish woman named Ellen Flynn since March 1873, was one veteran in the fast-moving column. Crossing over the treeless divide at a good pace, the bluecoats continued to gallop over an unfamiliar landscape. With Custer leading the way, they rode through patches of sagebrush and tall grass, while trampling down spring flowers—white, purple and yellow—sprinkled on the hillsides alive with springtime color.[41]

Not long after noon, when there was no cloud in the sky, the 7th Cavalry reached the divide's east side on the eastern edge of the Little Bighorn Valley, around fifteen miles southeast of the village. However, Custer still did not know either the size or length of the village nestled in the wooded river bottoms lined with ancient cottonwoods; their full summer foliage disguised exact locations and numbers. Prudently, he had ordered his troopers to spread out to minimize the size of rising dust clouds and ensure a stealthy advance. Custer was convinced that it was now crucial to strike a blow before the Indians slipped away, guaranteeing that he still had the ability to make command decisions on the fly in a crisis situation, as during the Civil War. First and foremost, this called for overwhelming the small satellite village of the Sans Arc (Sioux), southeast of the main village, by surprise in broad daylight: something that Custer had never done before.

To enhance tactical flexibility against a guerrilla warfare–fighting foe whom he believed was now in flight, Custer divided his regiment into three battalions after crossing the divide. Based on seniority, the men of these two separate wings made final preparations for the attack on the small San Arc village. Just northwest of the Crow's Nest, Custer had divided a group that was already too small, inexperienced, and worn. Illinois-born Major Marcus Albert Reno now commanded the right wing. He wore one of the straw hats purchased from the enterprising sutler on the *Far West*. Reno, a West Pointer and Civil War veteran, now commanded Companies A, G, and M, composed of about 140 troopers.

Leading the left wing, Senior Captain Frederick William Benteen, a hardheaded Virginian, took charge of Companies D, H, and K—about 125 men in all. At the expedition's beginning, Custer had already divided the regiment into two separate wings under Reno and Benteen. Custer, meanwhile, took charge of two battalions (Companies C, E, F, I, and L) under Captains Myles Walter Keogh and George Wilhelmus Manicus Yates, consisting of about 200 troopers and civilians.

Usually uncooperative by instinct and general inclination, Benteen was a true contrarian. In his own words, Benteen's life was defined by a propensity for "rubbing a bit against the angles—or hair—of folks, instead of going with their whims." Benteen was disowned by his family because of his unorthodox decision to wear a blue uniform and serve in the Western theater during the Civil War. His own father had wished that he "should be killed by an avenging bullet [fired] perhaps by one of his own kin." Meanwhile, Captain Thomas Mower McDougall, another Civil War veteran of the western theater and a general's son, served as an escort for the extensive pack train that contained extra ammunition supplies—which was critically important in a long–term fight, if large numbers of Indians were encountered.[42]

However, a host of weaknesses lay in these divisions of the 7th Cavalry, including Custer's reliance on the seniority system that bestowed the ambitious second-in-command to Reno, and not in the pro-Custer clique. To be sure, Custer's choice of his five companies was rather curious under the circumstances. The 220 men and horses of Custer's five companies were in relatively poor shape. They had been part of Reno's scout in the Tongue River country that had been launched on June 10 and ended on June 18, a grueling and exhausting ordeal of nearly 250 miles.

Unfortunately for Custer and like the regiment in general, a good many of the most experienced officers were now absent on detached assignments, such as recruiting. Each company was officially authorized three officers, but none of Custer's five companies possessed more than two officers in the ranks. Company C, a relatively weak company, was Custer's younger brother's command. Equally of concern, Company E was "the most discombobulated component of the regiment," while Company F was only "of passable quality." Company L was also limited in overall combat capabilities. Company L was hampered by relatively junior officers in charge, and missing three of five of its sergeants, who would be much needed in the hours ahead. Then, some forty-five troopers of Companies C, E, F, I, and L had been detached to serve with the pack train to additionally reduce overall combat capabilities. Compounding this, larger companies led by more senior and veteran leaders were not part of Custer's immediate command. Company M, under Captain Thomas Henry French, born in Baltimore, Maryland, and the proud owner of the regiment's "best buffalo horse," was the 7th Cavalry's "strongest" company, and now assigned to Reno.

However, compensating in part for the lack of so many veteran officers, the bluecoat troopers of these companies had been molded by an Ireland-born sergeant who served as the unit's backbone and guiding force. Ireland-born Jeremiah Finley, of Company C and a Civil War veteran, possessed considerable experience. Finley provided a good representative example of these model sergeants who served as the sturdy backbone of each company. Ironically, in past centuries, the Irish Catholics of the Emerald Isle had been viewed by the English invaders (Protestants) as obstacles that had to be swept from their own native homeland during the conquest of their first colony, Ireland, and now the Sioux were seen as an obstacle that also had to be cleansed from the land.

Not all of these tough Irish sergeants were fully appreciated. In a towering rage, Company I's Private Adam Hetesimer, Ohio-born and of German descent, had hurled an axe at the head of Sergeant Milton J. DeLacy of Company I, a "red-haired Irishman." Unfortunately for Custer and Company I, the Irish sergeant was now assigned to the pack train escort. The Irish versus Germans tension was still another hidden fissure in the 7th Cavalry ranks, sapping the overall sense of regimental unity and cohesion and reducing overall command effectiveness.

Custer's dividing of his force into three different contingents enhanced his tactical flexibility. These separate commands conformed with his overall plan of spreading out his force to decrease the chances for the Indians' escape from the 7th Cavalry's clutches during its descent on the village.[43]

The 7th Cavalry troopers continued to gallop northwest, after having reached the outer reaches of the Little Bighorn Valley at around 12:15 p.m. While he hoped to surprise and capture the satellite village of the Sans Arc lying before the wooded valley of the Little Bighorn, Custer dispatched Benteen's contingent of three companies to the southwest, or left, to ascertain if another village lay upriver or if bands of warriors were fleeing in that direction. Clearly, Custer had learned his lesson at the Washita, where he recklessly attacked an immediate target (Black Kettle's Cheyenne village) without knowing that the string of villages stretched more than a dozen miles along the Washita River for reasons of sanitation and scarce natural resources in winter. Therefore, it was now prudent for Custer to dispatch Benteen on his mission to the left, because Custer had no idea if any villages lay hidden amid this rough, unfamiliar terrain that might conceal hundreds of warriors. Benteen might even strike the upper, or southern, end of the Indian encampment, if it extended for miles. In essence, the cantankerous but capable Captain Benteen would be guarding the rear of Custer's advance farther down the Little Bighorn Valley, as well as the all-important pack train that contained extra ammunition.

Moving steadily in a northwest direction, Custer's and Reno's battalions then advanced down a dusty defile side by side (Custer on the north and Reno on the south), while separated by today's Middle Fork of Reno Creek, before they entered Reno Creek proper to the northeast near the small Sans Arc village. This dry creek (Middle Fork) was also known as Great Medicine Dance Creek and "Green Grass Creek."[44] Trumpeter John Martin felt a sense of loneliness, after "Benteen, with three troops [companies], left the column and rode off in the direction that [Custer] had been pointing [while the] rest of the regiment rode on, in two columns," with Reno on the left, and Custer on the right.[45]

Captain Thomas "Tom" Ward Custer, his older brother's former Civil War staff officer, now rode in the forefront as a respected member of Custer's staff. The two brothers were inseparable and the bond was tight, although "Tom" had long resented having to live in his brother's giant shadow, leading to a complex love-hate relationship. He was more restless and perhaps even braver (both in the bedroom and on the battlefield) than the happily married lieutenant colonel. Custer had long looked after the welfare of "Brother Tom," a reckless bachelor, like a concerned father. At the expedition's beginning, the Custer brothers had often ridden far from the column to scout and hunt large game, as if this campaign was merely a leisurely excursion into a beautiful, pristine land. Despite his younger brother's achievements, Custer had earlier implored him to more diligently study tactics. Now, the two Custer brothers advanced at the column's head.

But while Tom and his impressive wartime contributions— including his winning two Medals of Honor—had been forgotten, his older brother was still America's hero. This widely celebrated "beau ideal of the Chevalier Bayard" of the Civil War, as Custer had been regaled in 1871, had recently written in a letter, "I think the 7th Cavalry may have its greatest campaign ahead."[46] However, Custer now conveniently overlooked an all-important observation that he had back in November 1868, when he had marveled in a letter to his wife how the

Great Plains warriors were "well-armed with Springfield breech-loading guns," because they had now significantly upgraded their weaponry in the intervening more than seven years.[47]

Indeed, overconfidence and optimism continued to blind many 7th Cavalry troopers to a host of harsh realities, especially their opponents' ever–increasing amount of modern firepower, including the Winchester and Henry repeating rifles. New Hampshire–born and curly-haired, Company D's Lieutenant Winfield Scott Edgerly, a West Point graduate (Class of 1870) and the over-achieving son of a humble farmer, caught the 7th Cavalry's mood when about to encounter its greatest challenge: "We all felt that the worst that could happen would be the getting away of the Indians."[48]

However, other 7th Cavalry officers felt differently. In his late twenties, Surgeon Henry Porter, 7th Cavalry, was embittered because of the enhanced combat capabilities of the "red devils, whom the government and Indian department have so splendidly armed with improved rifles to kill United States troops." At a recent night's encampment in the beautiful Rosebud Valley, a group of younger officers had sung the usual campaign songs by the bivouac fire. In an unfamiliar country not seen by the 7th Cavalry on previous campaigns, Private William O. Taylor explained how the officers began singing a solemn religious tune, realizing it was "rather strange song for Cavalrymen to sing on an Indian trail."[49]

Ironically, in an 1874 letter to his father, Philadelphia-born Private George Eiseman, a former brushmaker of German descent, was about to pay a high price for his love of nature. Little realizing that he was writing fondly about a picturesque region where he was about to be killed, Eiseman had written how "the yet unexplored Montana [Territory] has been of great interest to me. . . . Fortunately I have not yet lost my scalp," which ironically was about to be lifted in the hours ahead.[50]

These suddenly reflective 7th Cavalry officers had not forgotten what they had recently discovered in an abandoned Indian camp. Private Taylor described the chilling incident when

Custer, who was riding at the head of the column, suddenly came upon a human skull lying under the remains of an extinct fire, and stopping to examine it he found lying near by a portion of a U.S. Cavalryman's uniform as evidenced by the buttons on the overcoat being stamped with the letter 'C' [for cavalry] and the remains of a dress coat having the yellow cord of the Cavalry running through it. The skull was weather beaten and . . . was that of some poor mortal who had been a prisoner in the hands of the savages and who doubtless had been tortured to death. . . .[51]

Here, Custer had "halted to examine [the skull] and lying near by I found the uniform of a soldier," as he penned in one of his last letters to Libbie.[52] Sensing the dark foreboding, one Indian scout had watched silently while Custer "stood still for some time" staring down at the grisly remains while deep in contemplation.[53]

However, everyone was now focused on finding success in a bold undertaking by attacking the Indian village in broad daylight. Relying on his usual aggressiveness, Custer hoped to deliver an overwhelming blow, first on the Sans Arc satellite village, and then on the main village farther northwest in the river valley: essentially not one, but two, preemptive strikes. Divided in three parts in preparation for striking the village as at the Washita, Custer's command overlooked its increased vulnerability. Based upon the Washita's lessons, when having no thorough reconnaissance had almost cost him dearly, Custer's decision to send Benteen and his battalion to the left to search for any hidden villages in the low ground located between the ridges, or to ascertain if any warrior parties had prepared an ambush, was not appreciated by his cantankerous senior captain. As could be expected, given his personality, the habitually prickly Benteen, mounted on his favorite horse named "Dick," was not happy with this assignment. Nevertheless, this was a crucial assignment, because if Benteen found the village's southern end farther upriver, Custer had ordered him to immediately "pitch into" the encampment to protect his rear.

Suspicious of any order from Custer, Captain Benteen believed that he had been given a mission that ensured that he would miss the main attack, and that Custer would reap all the glory for himself; a firm conviction that boded ill for chances of possible future collaboration in the upcoming offensive operation. If Benteen found no Indians in the valleys to the left, then he was to turn north and then left to ride northwest (parallel to Custer and Reno) up the Little Bighorn Valley to rejoin the regiment in its offensive effort from the south. Clearly this might be expecting too much for Benteen. The angry top lieutenant harbored a host of grudges against Custer, and had old scores to settle. A tough, seasoned officer who never forgot a slight (real or imagined) from Custer, Benteen had long enjoyed telling his young troopers that the "government pays you to get shot at."[54]

With dust clouds rising from an arid land, the troopers continued galloping down the sloping terrain from the higher ground to the upper reaches of Reno (Ash) Creek, which was a mostly dry tributary of the Little Bighorn River. Perhaps wondering what strange fate had brought him all the way from Italy to this remote part of buffalo country, Trumpeter Martin described: "We followed the course of the little stream [Middle Fork of Reno Creek] that led in the direction of the Little Big Horn River [with] Reno [continuing to advance] on the left bank and we on the right."[55]

All the while, Custer continued onward with his headquarters staff in the lead. He, most of all, wanted to strike as soon as possible, almost as if still in pursuit of Lee's Army in the Appomattox River country in springtime 1865, when nothing had been impossible for the relentless "boy general." Custer's most immediate tactical objective was to overwhelm the satellite village of Sans Arc (meaning "Without Bows" in French for this tribe of the Lakota nation) located southeast of the main village and about two-thirds of the way to the Little Bighorn River.

Situated along the Middle Fork of Reno Creek that flowed for several miles west into the Little Bighorn, this small village was Custer's first objective: it had to be overwhelmed as soon as possible. Custer assigned Reno and his battalion, on the creek's south side, to the key mission of overwhelming this small satellite village lying before the main village, which was nestled in the river bottoms to the northwest—and to do so before these Sans Arc people could warn the main village in the river valley of the pony soldiers' approach. Like at the Washita, Custer evidently hoped to secure captives to deter an attack from a good many warriors of the larger village, especially since he believed that the 7th Cavalry had been spotted. If the Sans Arc fled as fully expected, then Reno was ordered to pursue with his three companies.[56]

However, as Custer feared, the Sans Arc had already fled the small village. Therefore, upon their arrival, in their dash to the village with revolvers drawn, Custer's detachment on the creek's north side discovered only a single lodge in place. Trumpeter Martin described how "we came to an old tepee that had a dead warrior in it [and] It was burning [because] The Indian scouts had set it afire."[57]

This somewhat humiliating setback of the first part of his offensive plan only brought increased frustration to Custer. Angered in realizing that his Sans Arc quarry was about to warn the main village along the river, Custer ordered the lodge burned down in its entirety, finishing the job the Crows had started. This job was completed by the time Reno's command arrived from the south side to the creek's north side, after Reno had spied the smoke of the burning lodge and Custer had signaled for him to join him. The two battalions were now united once again north of the creek.[58]

From nearby high ground above the Creek, scouts George Herendeen and Bouyer, and their Crow and Arikara followers, reported to Custer that about 40 Indians from the Sans Arc village were fleeing northwest down Reno Creek proper and heading toward the main village. Custer then directed Reno to pursue with his three companies and Arikara scouts. There was actual little, if any, chance of success, however, because of the fleetness of the smaller Indian ponies, who were now in prime shape. Reno's battalion now continued northwest, heading toward the Little Bighorn and the village's southern end that stood farther to the northwest. At this point, the Little Bighorn was "some fifty to seventy feet wide, and from two to four feet deep of clear, icy cold water," that flowed north into the Bighorn River. An ominous sign for future developments, the Arikara scouts, unnerved by what they knew lay before them, had refused to go onward because of the village's immense size.[59]

Now even more fearful that the main village had been warned by the Sans Arc, Custer believed that the Indians were in full flight as so often in the past, as indicated by his scout's reports. Meanwhile, no firing was heard coming from Benteen's direction upriver to his rear, increasing Custer's confidence that the Indians were not waiting in ambush or fleeing upriver from the 7th Cavalry's approach. Custer now knew that his rear was safe because the village did not extend upriver. Therefore, he could safely launch his attack down the valley without fear of being attacked in the rear.

With time of the essence, Custer could not wait for Benteen's command to return from its reconnaissance and catch up with the regiment's remainder to unite his divided command. Custer remained impatient; he knew that his command had been spotted and precious time was slipping away. In a Washita repeat to violate traditional axioms, Custer was forced out of necessity to unleash his offensive objectives despite having only limited knowledge about his opponent, the village's size, and the terrain before him.[60]

Ironically, with Custer drawing near, the sage Box Elder in the Cheyenne village was even more prophetic compared to the previous day's warning. He had received another detailed vision. Cheyenne warriors long remembered how "an old man harangued that the [white] soldiers were about to charge from the upper end and also from the lower end. When this was called out, men began to prepare for the fight and to mount their horses, but many of the horses had been sent out on herd [to the village's west] and most of the men were on foot."[61]

Meanwhile, Custer was now doing what would now be considered unthinkable, even under normal circumstances: launching an attack on a large Indian village in the middle of the day, rather than waiting for dawn to ensure surprise. Worried that the village's occupants would escape before his arrival, Custer's pace only increased when another group of warriors (evidently hunters in search of game) were seen galloping rapidly northwest toward the Little Bighorn. Rising dust clouds kicked up by horses in flight, combined with past reports from scouts, additionally confirmed to Custer that the Indians were in full escape mode. Indeed, Indian interpreter for the Arikara Frederic Francis Girard—a dark haired, full-bearded St. Louis Catholic, born of a French Canadian father and an Indian mother and educated at St. Xavier Academy in St. Louis—had just yelled to Custer from his high ground perch, "Here are your Indians, running like devils!"[62] Unlike most everyone else in Custer's column, Girard was lucky this afternoon, because he was about to be assigned to Reno's column.[63]

Despite the high bluffs along the river's east side blocking his view of the village situated deep in the river valley's timbered depths below, Custer was relying on aggressive tactics as he had so often during the Civil War. He feared that the entire village was shortly about to be devoid of Indians. Custer now envisioned a flank attack in a bold bid to not only strike an overwhelming blow, but also to encircle the village in a pincer movement by attacking at the village's opposite end. Having no time to conduct a reconnaissance, Custer was gambling in his eagerness to win a victory before his opponent fled.

Despite being unable to determine either the size of the main village or his opponents' strength because the high bluffs on the river's east side blocked his view, Custer now unleashed Reno to attack (the first arm of his pincer movement) straight ahead. Orders were relayed by Adjutant William Winer Cooke, one of Custer's most trustworthy and best officers, to Reno to advance northwest down the meandering Reno Creek to gain the Little Bighorn to hit the village's southern end. Custer, lingering in Reno's rear, planned to eventually move farther north to deliver a flank attack (the final pincer arm) to fulfill his tactical vision of a successful pincer movement: a very good tactical plan.[64]

Now serving on Custer's staff, Trumpeter Martin was well placed to see and hear the final formulation of Custer's tactical plan. He penned how Custer "told the adjutant to order [Reno] to go down and across the river and attack the Indian village . . . and that he would go down to the other end [of the village] and drive them, and that he would have Benteen hurry up and attack them in the center" to Reno's left.[65]

Custer was now relying on a time-proven tactic of the flank attack: Reno's attack of three companies was the anvil, while Custer's upcoming strike with five companies was the hammer. Indeed, his October 9, 1864, victory at the battle of Tom's Brook during Sheridan's Shenandoah Valley Campaign remained a vivid memory in Custer's mind, because of his employing a successful flanking movement. The Confederate general whom he vanquished that day was General Thomas "Tom" Lawrence Rosser, a former West Point classmate. In June 1873, Custer and Rosser, now wearing a blue uniform, talked at length about that battle. In a letter to Libbie, Custer described how Rosser admitted that this was the "worst whipping" that he ever received. The Confederate general had been confident for success until his shocked men in gray had started shouting, "We're flanked!"[66] Custer now sought to repeat this sparkling success along the Little Bighorn.

Reno's Failed Offensive Effort

At long last, the first offensive thrust of the 7th Cavalry was unleashed. Sergeant John Ryan, Company M, described how "Reno's battalion started down the valley, first on the trot and then on the gallop, marching in columns of twos."[67] Confidence was high and victory seemed inevitable because Reno's battalion contained the regiment's strongest and best companies. Capturing the mood, one of Reno's cocky officers yelled to his troopers, "Thirty days' furlough to the man who gets the first scalp."[68] After riding west down Reno Creek, the Massachusetts-born Sergeant Ryan described how: "We arrived at the bank of the Little Bighorn River and waded to the other side. Here the water was about three feet deep with quicksand and a very strong current [and] [w]e were then in the valley of the Little Bighorn and facing downstream."[69]

Major Reno launched his attack north across the river's open, level flood plain and toward the village's southern encampment lying in the timbered bottoms. However, Reno's charge never struck the village to deliver the hard blow, as Custer had envisioned. Instead, without making contact with the Indians and fearing an ambush in the large village, Reno halted his tentative attack while still far from the village, when the nearest warrior was not even within 500 yards of him.

Meanwhile, Custer expected Reno to deliver a hard-hitting blow (like he would have normally done in this situation) as part of the two-prong pincer attack. Besides sacrificing the element of surprise that Custer had won against all chances of probability, Reno almost immediately threw away the initiative instead of relying on his only hope for success: charging straight into the village to cause panic before the warriors could rally and take their own initiative. Worst of all, he handed this advantage back to his opponent who had been completely surprised by his attack. Reacting instinctively as if hunting an impaired animal to make a kill, the Sioux were emboldened by Reno's halting of his attack.

After having been given a reprieve, these warriors at the village's southern end immediately went on the offensive, knowing that the best defense was an offense. Reno's premature halt ensured that Custer's reasonable expectations of facing panicked warriors—who would have been more concerned about saving families than fighting, fleeing from an expected blow—ended forever. After his premature halt, Reno then compounded his folly by ordering his men to dismount and form a lengthy skirmish line: the worst possible tactic on the wide expanse of open ground against the best light cavalry in the world.

Having ended his dismal offensive effort even before losing a single trooper, Reno had not only lost his nerve and lost the initiative by forfeiting the crucial element of surprise, but also disobeyed Custer's orders to attack the village. Norway-born Private John Sivertsen, known as "Big Fritz," wrote how Reno's troopers "got pretty close to the Indian camp" that was larger than expected.

For disobeying orders, Reno later employed the lame excuse that he feared the Sioux less than the fear that Custer would fail to provide him support as promised (Custer was in fact supporting by way of a flank attack and not from the rear). Revealing his paranoia (perhaps made acute by alcohol consumption and a dysfunctional command situation) because he detested his commander, Reno had boldly confronted Custer on the night of June 21 to remind Custer that "if they were to get into a fight he hoped he would be better supported than he was at the Battle of the Washita."[70]

Going for Broke, Custer Rides North to Unleash a Flank Attack

As explained by Sergeant John Ryan, the son of Irish immigrants from County Tipperary and a tough soldier who still prized the Indian scalp that he had taken on the Washita, Custer was a commander who loved to maneuver "on his own hook, and did not care to be tied down" to limit his flexibility and initiative.[71] Indeed, Custer was now relying on all of his considerable experience and tactical ability to win a decisive victory, despite so many things having gone wrong this afternoon.

Custer was a gambler by nature and instinct, and these qualities were little tempered by past close calls in the Civil War and Indians Wars. The vexing tactical situation and fast-moving events beyond his control at the Little Bighorn were now forcing him to take greater risks, as if fate itself was dictating events. He was now relying on the boldest tactic of all—the pincer movement—in a desperate last bid to win the day. Coinciding with Trumpeter Martin's account, Custer revealed the core of his tactical plan with his telltale words related by Private John F. Donohue, Company K, 7th Cavalry, who had been born in Tipperary, Ireland, in 1852: "I will strike them on the opposite point and we will crush them between us."[72]

Trumpeter Martin wrote how Custer's five companies of two battalions continued onward "at a gallop," because "Custer seemed to be [in] a great hurry."[73] However, knowing that his already overheated and worn horses needed water on this blistering day, Custer had halted his men at Reno's rear, at the South Fork of Reno Creek (nearby the Middle and South Forks united to form Reno Creek proper) just past, or west of, the abandoned Sans Arc village. Here, on this scorching midday in a much-needed respite, Custer's thirsty horses drank from the clear waters in a position that Reno incorrectly believed was a strategic reserve to support his attack on the village's southern end. Trumpeter Martin described how the troops "just stopped once to water the horses." To gain intelligence, and demonstrating additional flexibility, Custer dispatched Adjutant Cooke and Captain Myles Walter Keogh—born in County Carlow, Ireland, and a Civil War veteran—to ride ahead and report back on the latest developments with regard to Reno's fight.

Lieutenant Colonel Custer was shocked when they reported that the Indians were not fleeing as anticipated. Instead, they were now swarming like locusts from the upper village in large numbers to confront the stationary Reno. Of course, this was the last development that Custer had expected, because Reno was to have charged into the village as part of his overall tactical plan to hit the village from two directions.

Conversely, Reno was equally surprised that Custer and his five companies were not immediately reinforcing him by advancing down Reno Creek and crossing the river to join him for a united front against an ever-increasing number of warriors. These sudden developments shocked both Custer and Reno, but for entirely different reasons. Meanwhile, to the rear, an increasingly sullen Benteen continued to believe that he had been deliberately left out of the fight so Custer could reap all the glory. This politically astute career soldier and acclaimed Virginia "lady-killer," distinguished by a full head of long, flowing white hair, was as ambitious and skilled as Custer.

As events demonstrated, Custer and his top lieutenants were as disconnected mentally in tactical terms as they were physically when unity of action was essential for the 7th Cavalry to achieve a success: the recipe for disaster. Custer now realized that his confident, tactical calculations about the assumed behavior of his opponent (flight instead of fight) and his subordinate (Reno, who adhered to flight rather than fight) were not only wrong but exactly the opposite of what was anticipated—although based on previous experience, long verified by ample evidence. Crow scout Hairy Moccasin, who had surveyed the village, had also presented intelligence of the unbelievable news that the camp was not breaking up in panic as expected (as had happened at the Washita). Clearly, something was now happening that was entirely different from what Custer had imagined possible from his previous Indian campaigns: a new reality that had been discovered by the chastised Crook at the Rosebud on June 17.[74]

Like General Crook had learned to the southeast, Custer belatedly began to understand that he faced experienced fighting men who could not have been more highly motivated this afternoon (another shock), because the lives of their women and children were in peril. These savvy fighting men at the village's southern end, who were previously considered nothing more than ignorant savages, were now on the offensive in Reno's sector to Custer's utter disbelief. Emphasizing a simple equation that was never really fully understood or appreciated by the upper class and career politicians in Washington, DC, or a self-satisfied army leadership resting comfortably on their Civil War laurels, one Lakota explained that the warriors' diehard determination was now fueled by the belief that these invading whites "had come to kill our fathers and mothers and us, and it was our country."[75] Consequently, a typical Cheyenne warrior now burned with the desire to reap vengeance upon the hated *wasichus* ("the [white] people you can't get rid of") because his mother and wife had been killed by 7th Cavalry troopers during that bloody morning on the Washita.[76]

Clearly, Custer now faced the greatest quandary and challenge of his military career. Much like his expectations of Reno's delivering a hard-hitting blow upriver, the foundation of Custer's plan, based on the anticipation of often-demonstrated Indian reactions (flight rather than fight) had completely fallen apart by this time. Hundreds of incensed warriors, including those from the Cheyenne village on the far north who had ridden rapidly south, continued to pour from the village to attack Reno's command. Now deployed in a lengthy skirmish line that offered no advantage for the defense, the fate of Reno's three companies was sealed. With the news that Reno was now heavily engaged with a resurgent foe whose counterattack was relentless, Custer ordered his sweat-stained men to once again mount up on their worn, but just watered, horses. This stunning tactical development now fueled his urgency: a bold flank attack was needed more than ever before.

The shocking news that Reno was in trouble guaranteed that the village's northern end was now more vulnerable, because a great mass of warriors had rushed south to confront Reno. Hoping to strike a blow, regain the initiative, and win the day despite so many initial setbacks, the tactically astute and flexible Custer ordered his five companies to turn north. He now planned to advance on the river's east side, parallel to Reno's advance on the river's west side, to deliver his attack from an entirely different direction. First and foremost, and as soon as possible, Custer had to gain the top of the bluffs to ascertain the exact village's location to strike the most effective blow with the pincer's other arm.

Custer now realized that his regiment faced a vexing crisis situation of a truly daunting magnitude. His tactical solution called for crossing the river downstream and striking the village's opposite end as soon as possible; a desperate last-ditch bid to snatch victory from the jaws of defeat. Consequently, Custer and his troopers departed the valley of Reno Creek, crossing its North Fork and riding north at full speed. They rode on the double up the dusty bluffs that ran east along the river and towered above the twisting contours of the Little Bighorn River. Knowing that Reno had his hands full at the village's upper and that warriors continued to surge upriver to meet the southernmost threat, their leaving the northernmost (Cheyenne) village on the far north empty of warriors now presented the most favorable of tactical situations to him to still win the day, Custer now relied on well-honed tactical savvy and years of experience that had served him so well during the Civil War.

Custer boldly envisioned a flank attack at the village's northern end to rescue the increasingly disadvantageous situation before it was too late; a double envelopment (tactics that almost always proved effective, including at the Washita where the 7th Cavalry had struck from multiple directions), if Reno managed to hold his own at the village's southern end. Perhaps Reno might even repulse the attackers and regain the initiative to resume his own offensive effort. In adjusting tactics as if still fighting Lee's Rebels back in Virginia, Custer's tactical plan corresponded to existing requirements of a fast-paced, fluid, tactical situation.

While Custer led the way north up the open slope bare of timber, he was now in hot pursuit of a solution to an increasingly vexing tactical situation with his regiment widely divided. Custer knew that the only solution now lay in delivering a flank attack. All that he now needed was to find favorable terrain (like a stream or ravine) leading west from the bluffs down to the river. Then, after reaching a fording point to cross to the river's west side, Custer would be in position to strike the village's northern end with another surprise attack: the second of the day. To reverse the hands of fate that had turned against him so suddenly, Custer's 200 troopers of the five companies continued to ride rapidly north and parallel to the river. All the while, exhausted horses and troopers struggled ever higher up the slope, with Custer leading the most audacious mission of his impressive career.[77]

Near the top of the open bluff that overlooked the river, and before reaching the commanding high ground above the swift-flowing river of blue, Custer met a returning Bouyer and four Crow scouts. They had ridden ahead to survey the Cheyenne village, whose lodges were distinguished by tribal markings, at the encampment's northern end and the ford at the mouth of Medicine Tail Coulee. The breathless scouts then turned around and led the column to the bluff's crest. Here, from this elevated perch and at long last, Custer knew that he would be fully illuminated about the great mystery concerning the village's exact size and location, especially with regard to how far it spanned north down the river. The bare, open crest of this "big hill [not "Weir Hill" or "Weir Point" as long assumed, but northwest of where Custer had turned north] that overlooked the valley," in Trumpeter Martin's words, dominated the timbered river valley to present a panoramic view for miles around, and Custer now obtained his closest and most commanding view of the village. Custer's eager surveying of his long-elusive target was enhanced by his binoculars. Lifting his spirits and expectations of reaping a success to yet reverse the day's sagging fortunes, Custer's fondest hopes were confirmed when he saw that there were no warriors were in sight in the Cheyenne village below!

Hardly believing his eyes, Custer was elated by the sight of a village absent of fighting men. Although he could not see Reno's sector far upriver, Custer also learned that Reno's men to the south had been driven back from their dismounted positions on the open bottoms and into the thick timber along the river, where a defensive stand was made by the three companies. This was a good position to make a defensive stand for Reno's men. To compensate for Reno's unexpected setback, Custer now saw even more merit in the enticing possibilities of unleashing a flank attack.

Trumpeter Martin heard Custer triumphantly proclaim that the 7th Cavalry had "got them this time," after having seen a serene village devoid of fighting men. With a well-trained topographical eye, Custer knew he had his opponent caught on disadvantageous low ground of the river bottoms. While waving his light-colored, broad-brimmed hat in elation, Custer turned to his troopers on the lower ground and shouted, "We've caught them napping." In response, the men of five companies cheered at the prospect of what seemed would be an easy victory over an ever-elusive opponent who now seemingly had been caught in a no-win situation.[78] Despite the high spirits exhibited by the horse-soldiers, this was not a good way to conduct a surprise attack, however. Alerted by the shouting, one warrior in the river bottoms recalled how, when "Custer and his men first saw the village, they gave three cheers."[79]

Nevertheless, Custer now possessed ample good reason to be elated, overcoming setbacks with tactical ingenuity. In the words of Trumpeter Martin, who had been beside Custer during his reconnaissance to a high ground perch that offered a good view of the sprawling river valley: "There were no bucks [males] to be seen; all we could see was some squaws and children playing and a few dogs and ponies. The General seemed both surprised and glad, and said the Indians must be in their tents, asleep."[80]

The incredible sight of the village's vulnerability was seemingly apparent because many women and children had already fled west to escape the pony soldiers, leaving behind what looked to be almost a ghost village.[81] Besides the warriors having streamed upriver to confront Reno, what other factors explained why the Cheyenne village was now so calm, as if Reno had never struck to the south? What has been overlooked has been the fact that, after Reno's threat had been successfully parried, Two Moons had already returned to the Cheyenne village and restored calm. Believing the danger over and the day won, he had ordered the panic-stricken Cheyenne women to cease removing lodges and to leave them in place, because there was no reason to now flee. Consequently, order and a sense of normalcy had been restored to the Cheyenne camp by the time Custer laid his eyes upon the unbelievable sight, while visions of victory danced in his head.[82]

Therefore, Custer had been electrified by the sight of a target that looked far softer than even he had imagined possible. In fact, Custer was so excited by the prospects for success that he yelled to his troopers, "Hurrah, boys, we've got them! We'll finish them up and then go home to our station."[83] In his own words in a 1873 letter to Libbie, he was now convinced that, "with 'Custer's luck'," a great victory was now possible, because this inexplicable potent force of nature was still by his side.[84]

Then, like an experienced hunter in pursuit of his prey, Custer ordered his command forward on the double to take advantage of the village's extreme vulnerability. In his eagerness, Custer led the way rapidly further north over the open ground, behind the river bluffs and parallel to the Little Bighorn, believing he had finally found the ideal tactical solution. All in all, this was a very good plan, and a credit to Custer's tactical flexibility in a crisis situation. Ironically, while Reno and Benteen held Custer in contempt, and even might have hoped that he would be defeated, Custer was gambling not only to save the day, but also the lives of his two senior leaders—who detested him— and their men: the majority of the 7th Cavalry.

In Trumpeter Martin's words: "We rode on, pretty fast" over the open high ground to fulfill Custer's bold tactical vision. The troopers' "fast trot" continued until around 3:45 p.m., when the command reached the vicinity of the head of the dry ravine, or coulee, which ran north behind the river bluffs to the east, known as Cedar Coulee. Just east of the treeless perch of Weir Point, this dry coulee had been cut by nature down the descending terrain and parallel to the river to the west. Cedar Coulee was named for the occasional clump of small cedars that lined this deep slash in the arid landscape.

Here, before entering the coulee's depths, Custer took advantage of this high ground point to again survey the relatively little that he could see of the village—shrouded in the heavy growth of full-leafed timber along the river—to the south before Reno. Even at this time, and as throughout the ride north, he was unable to see the village's northern end because of intervening high ground of the bluffs. Perhaps after reforming his men from column-of-four to column-of-two, Custer then ordered his command to enter the ravine-like depression and ride north up Cedar Coulee, which ran north for about a mile and a quarter to Medicine Tail Coulee. He now pushed toward lower ground that was cut deeply amid an open landscape. This indicated to him the greater tactical possibility of gaining an adjacent natural avenue of another coulee that led west to the river.

Even more, this wide coulee allowed Custer the advantage of concealing his command's advance from prying Indian eyes, in case advanced scouts or village guardians now occupied the high ground above Cedar Coulee: a secluded and deeply cut natural avenue by which to stealthy move five companies into a good position to catch the Indians by surprise, striking the village's northern end while keeping his movements hidden from view. Understanding the advantageous nuisances of descending terrain in this part of the high plains country when near a river, and having gained some knowledge about the immediate terrain's features from his Crow scouts who knew this area, Custer also sensed (or was informed by his Indian scouts) that this descending coulee eventually led to another descending coulee, an ideal avenue by which he could then lead his five companies west downhill and directly to a river crossing point. He hoped to gain this natural avenue that was deeply cut from centuries of massive erosion and silt washing down the coulee from endless rains and melting snow since time immemorial.[85]

As part of his extensive knowledge of Great Plains warriors, Custer had been convinced for days that the Indians had been fleeing because they had no desire to confront the 7th Cavalry. This was largely an ethnocentric and racial assumption (always dangerous to underestimate any opponent, especially one of a different race), which continued to serve as the central foundation of his aggressive tactics. Of course, Custer's assumptions seemed to be substantiated by the amazing sight of the all but vacant Cheyenne village that looked ripe for the taking. Contrary to the myth that they had set up a giant ambush of sorts along the Little Bighorn, the Indians had only been moving onward day after day in pursuit of the buffalo herds that had pushed primarily toward the setting sun, before settling down. White Bull, known to his fellow Sioux as *Pte San Hunka* (Lazy White Buffalo) and who had presented Sitting Bull with a .44 caliber Winchester rifle (Model 1866), explained what had actually taken the tribes farther west from the Rosebud River to the Little Bighorn: the tribes "did not move to fight but to find buffalo [but] did not find them on Little Big Horn creek."[86]

Lulled into complacency by the immense size of the combined tribal village and concentrated might of a massive gathering of so many tribes, these warriors were about to be jolted by the second part of Custer's calculated one–two punch: first Reno's attack, and now Custer's upcoming strike from an entirely different direction. Wooden Leg described the assumption that allowed Custer to achieve his initial tactical goal of catching his opponent by surprise against the odds: "We supposed that the combined camps would frighten off the soldiers."[87] As revealed by his aggressive tactics, Custer was not frightened by the prospect of facing superior numbers. In fact, the repeated warnings of his scouts, including Bloody Knife, about superior numbers only emboldened Custer with the desire to embrace an even greater challenge which, in his mind, equated to a greater victory if successfully overcome. As he had written Libbie back in September 1873, "With

'Custer's luck'," anything was possible, including this afternoon along the Little Bighorn, or so he believed.[88]

Descending into Medicine Tail Coulee's Depths

At the head of his five companies after moving down the deep and dusty ravine known as Cedar Coulee that angled down and away from the river in a northern direction after having crossed today's Sharpshooter Ridge, Custer soon found (about 3:20 p.m.) what he was looking for: an immediate means to descend all the way to the river. Amid a relatively low and sunken area surrounded by higher, open ground, covered in sagebrush and patches of prairie grasses on all sides, he finally encountered the dry bend where Cedar Coulee descended to join another deeply gouged coulee (Cedar Coulee was but a tributary of this larger coulee) that descended further down on even lower ground in a northwestern direction toward the river. With his topographer's eyes as trained at West Point and Great Plains service, the lay of the land now revealed to Custer that the Little Bighorn was close to the west, and this new coulee led straight down to the river: the golden avenue by which to descend to reap victory.

Here, under the blazing June sun, Custer ordered a much-needed brief halt for his worn men and panting horses at the intersection of the two descending wide, dry coulees. Both essentially dry ravines had been slashed deeply by erosion into the surrounding of a broad expanse of open terrain. Eager to reach the river and then cross the watercourse to strike the village's vulnerable northern end, Custer decided to lead his column into the unknown depths of Medicine Tail Coulee. Like Cedar Coulee, this larger and wider coulee offered an even better natural avenue to conceal his troopers during their descent straight toward the river and the village's northern end. Fortunately for Custer, who had been enlightened by his Crow scouts whose people had encamped along this Little Bighorn in the past, Medicine Tail Coulee led straight to the Little Bighorn and the old buffalo ford, for an easy crossing of the river.

As Custer now realized, this deeply cut coulee descended gradually toward the river in a northwest direction and toward the ford that lay at the foot of the river bluffs. Medicine Tail Coulee gradually widened until its mouth opened into a wide expanse of level ground (the bottoms or flats of the river's flood plain) for Custer's final approach to the ford. Seeing the combined buffalo or Indian trails leading straight west and down the coulee in a most inviting fashion, Custer now fully realized that the large–sized ravine led directly to the ford. Amid a sprawling open landscape covered in prairie grass (about a foot high and now green from recent spring rains), scattered cactus, occasional wild flowers, and patches of sagebrush, the coulee spanned nearly a mile from its head all the way down the gradually descending ground to the ford. Despite the unfamiliar terrain, Custer had chosen the correct natural avenue—broader and ever widening as it spanned farther west—by which to charge across the river and into the village's northern end barely one and a half miles away to the west.[89]

However, from his years of experience rising to the fore, Custer hesitated almost instinctively before ordering the lengthy column of more than 200 men down into the depths of this larger dry coulee that led to the river, which still could not be seen at this point. Was the lack of warriors in the village or surrounding hills an indication of an ambush? Not forgetting about the close call at the Washita, Custer could not be completely sure, but he had no time to investigate the surrounding terrain.

Here, demonstrating prudence at the head of Medicine Tail Coulee while his troopers rested and sucked hot water from tin canteens, Custer collected his thoughts on this day of surprises and took another measure of the tactical situation. With so much at stake, he wanted to make doubly sure that he was embarking upon the proper course of action. After all, Custer had never attacked a tactical objective by such an unorthodox natural route—and an unfamiliar one—during the Civil War. West Point textbooks said nothing about an advance of cavalry down a deep Montana coulee, especially one far from support and near an unconventional foe. Wary of his opponent because everything now looked almost too easy, Custer now must have wondered if he was about to lead his eager men into a clever ambush. What if warriors gained the high ground above the coulee, especially the adjacent high ground (today's Luce Ridge), and then the Nye–Cartwright Ridge that separated South Medicine Tail Coulee from North Medicine Tail Coulee? If so, then it would be a shooting gallery and slaughter of a good many troopers even before they struck a blow. With no time to launch a reconnaissance to ascertain the terrain's nuisances and hidden opponents, Custer boldly decided to take the command straight down into and through the heart of the deep "valley" of Medicine Tail Coulee.

This was a tactic never before undertaken by Custer during the Civil War years, but the tactical situation was now critical and urgent. As his mentor General Grant had long advised, and providing a clue to his own winning ways in both the western and eastern theaters during the Civil War, Custer continued to demonstrate considerable tactical flexibility and innovative thinking in a true emergency situation. He was not allowing himself to be restricted by the often obsolete dictates of tactical orthodoxy that so often resulted in the defeat of less flexible officers, who always went by the book and adhered to what they had learned at West Point regardless of a fast-changing tactical situation: a recipe often for not only defeat but also disaster.

Worried about a possible ambush while advancing along the deep coulee, especially since the Cheyenne village appeared too quiet, Custer must have felt a sudden uneasiness about entering this alien, eerie-looking environment of the deeper coulee. Therefore, Custer now saw the need to take a wise precaution before literally taking the plunge down this mysterious coulee with his entire command. Just before descending into the Coulee's depths, Custer possessed the wisdom to give a special mission of extreme importance to Trumpeter John Martin. Tom Custer, on his brother's order, had earlier dispatched Sergeant Daniel Alexander Kanipe on the same mission.

Now serving as Custer's "orderly trumpeter," the olive-skinned bugler had been born Giovanni Martini in Italy. He was an immigrant who had been imbued with a burning vision of making his American Dream come true like so many other hopeful immigrants. Custer sensed that heavy fighting lay ahead. After having seen the village's immense size, Custer also was wisely concerned that he lacked sufficient ammunition for a major confrontation. Unknown to Custer, Crook had lacked sufficient ammunition for a full-fledged battle at the Rosebud on June 17, and as now experienced by Reno to the south.[90]

Trumpeter Martin's words described Custer's decision: when at "a big ravine [Medicine Tail Coulee] that led in the direction of the river, and the General pointed down there and then called me [and] said to me, 'Orderly, I want you to take a message to Colonel Benteen. Ride as fast as you can and tell him to be quick, and to bring the ammunition packs."[91]

Despite feeling the natural thrill of the prospect of reaping a success, Custer was not taking any unnecessary chances at the point of descending down Medicine Tail Coulee, especially when he and his headquarters staff were leading the way. Neither was Adjutant William Winer Cooke taking any extra chances in this key situation of attacking a large village in broad daylight. He had been born in the tiny community of Mount Pleasant, Brant County, Ontario, Upper Canada, on May 29, 1846. Cooke was not a bookish bureaucratic type, but a dynamic man of action. In the past, he had commanded the regiment's company of sharpshooters with skill and good judgment.

Proving that he was a highly capable adjutant, Cooke wanted to make sure that the Italian immigrant, who spoke poor English, delivered the correct message when so much was at stake. Realizing the importance of Custer's message, and that Benteen should have no misunderstanding about the true meaning of its vital contents—to come to Custer's aid and to bring extra ammunition—Cooke acted with wisdom by making a timely initiative. He suddenly said to the twenty-three-year-old trumpeter, "Wait, orderly, I'll give you a message." The fast-thinking adjutant tore a page out of his small notebook. The capable Canadian then hastily scribbled down Custer's recent verbal order for Martin to personally deliver to Captain Benteen to ensure there would be no misunderstanding.[92] The dark-haired Martin, a devout Catholic who now must have especially longed to been safely back in his Mediterranean homeland, later sensed that riding away with Cooke's written message to secure assistance saved his life. The lucky Italian, who ironically believed that he was now about to miss out on a sparkling Custer success, wrote: "My horse was pretty tired, but I started back as fast as I could go."[93]

Clearly, with regard to extra ammunition, although each trooper carried 100 rounds for his Springfield carbine and another twenty-four rounds for his .45 caliber Colt single-action Army revolver (Model 1873, issued to the 7th Cavalry in early 1874), Custer had learned his tactical lesson well from his reckless attack on the Washita village. He was not going to make the same mistake twice. Clearly, Custer was attempting to place the odds in his favor as much as possible in striking still another Cheyenne village along a quiet river. Custer had emphasized the past close call at the Washita that he hoped would not now be repeated: "From being the surrounding party [of Black Kettle's village] we now found ourselves surrounded, Indians on all sides closing in on us [but] [h]elp arrived, a fresh supply of ammunition with which the Quartermaster, Major [James Montgomery] Bell, by heroic efforts had contrived to reach us."[94]

Indeed, the ammunition supply with the slow-moving pack train, drawn by around 150 unruly mules, was indeed the "Achilles' heel" of the 7th Cavalry on a far-flung campaign, especially after Custer had moved briskly over rugged, unfamiliar terrain and attempted to strike a blow as soon as possible. Custer wisely knew that he would need plenty of extra ammunition for the upcoming confrontation once he charged through the village, as revealed by its size.[95]

Although he had not heard of June 17's shocking defeat of the southern (Wyoming) column on the Rosebud, Custer's wisdom was verified by Crook's monumental folly: Crook allowed himself to be caught by surprise and attacked without a sufficient supply of ammunition. He had advanced deep into unfamiliar Indian country without his pack train (carrying extra ammunition), which had been left behind at his base camp. He faced annihilation after 25,000 rounds of ammunition had been expended by his men in a losing effort to inflict barely 100 casualties. Clearly, not taking any chances, Custer needed all of the ammunition that he could lay his hands on, and he fully realized as much.[96]

After smartly sending off his Italian messenger on a fast horse in his second attempt to gain the necessary assistance to ensure that he would prevail if he encountered large numbers of warriors, Custer then ordered his command to turn to the left and down into the gorge-like depths of Medicine Tail Coulee. Feeling a sense of uneasiness about where Custer was taking them in this plunge down a canyon-like coulee, Crow scout Hairy Moccasin, the son of Little Face who had enlisted as a scout in April 1876, described: "We went with the command down into a dry gulch where we could not see the village."[97]

In riding away from the column at full speed as ordered, Trumpeter Martin turned around for one last look from higher ground at the advance of five companies that had taken the plunge into Medicine Tail Coulee: "The last I saw of the command they were going down into the ravine. The gray horse troop [Company E] was in the center and they were galloping."[98] Custer fully realized that only a flank attack would now bring the sweet taste of victory. Confusing the narrower and small

Cedar Coulee with Medicine Tail Coulee, the dark-skinned Curley described how Custer's troopers moved down "a ravine [Medicine Tail Coulee] just wide enough to admit his column of fours."[99]

Besides the unbridled confidence that Custer had in more than 200 troopers of two battalions under Yates and Keogh, an intangible quality also now accompanied the command down Medicine Tail Coulee and toward the ford (called Minneconjou by the Sioux) opposite the Cheyenne village. This powerful "medicine" (as the Sioux would say) had reaped victory so often in the past: Custer's Luck. Custer and countless others (friends and foes) had long used this terminology to refer to the miraculous good fortune and amazing success of an overly aggressive, often reckless commander of cavalry.[100]

Major newspapers across America continued to believe in the sheer magic of Custer's fabled luck that was once again expected to bring a sparkling success, because "the net is gradually being thrown around the swarthy Sitting Bull" in one journalist's boastful words.[101] Most ominously, this bold promise from one of America's leading newspaper, the *New York Herald* of which Mark Kellogg now served as a correspondent, was made after Custer had been killed, however.[102]

Indeed, for the fate of five entire companies, a good deal now hinged upon a simple question: would the fabled Custer's Luck continue to hold true and bring the sparkling success so widely anticipated across America? Perhaps even more than tactics and numbers, was Custer's Luck still with him at the critical moment when he decided to lead the way down Medicine Tail Coulee to attack the village's lower end? Even Custer's men believed that Custer's Luck would not only bring them victory, but also save them if they suddenly found themselves in trouble when charging into the large Cheyenne village that had looked so inviting.

No one seemed to have wondered what might result if Custer's Luck—that he himself often bragged about as if tempting the Gods, something a Roman would never do—came to a sudden end in the valley below. Careful students of history had learned that disaster often lay at the end of the most impressive string of successes by even the most gifted and successful military leader. One only had to recall the extreme blind faith of tens of thousands of young men and boys from across Europe (more non-French than French in the fateful 1812 invasion of Russia) who risked all on "Napoleon's luck" when marching deep into Mother Russia to set the stage for one of the greatest disasters in the annals of military history. Not unlike Napoleon when he had resided in the Kremlin before conducting his ill-fated retreat from Moscow, Custer certainly believed that his fabled luck was still with him while leading the way with his headquarters staff farther down Medicine Tail Coulee.[103]

However, the native people along the Little Bighorn before Custer had their own special luck and spiritual "medicine" of considerable power, as the thoroughly chastised Reno had just learned upriver, and much like Crook who was equally humbled at the Rosebud. As fate would have it, this inexplicable spiritual and moral force that Custer was now approaching with such confidence would in fact be much stronger than any previous medicine encountered by Custer: a forgotten spiritual ambush of sorts with regard to the inexplicable quality of this revered medicine. In continuing to descend into the valley-like depths of Medicine Tail Coulee in a northwest direction, however, Custer continued to believe that his legendary luck was still fully intact, especially after having just seen a village without warriors, much less any preparations for meeting his surprise flank attack.

Even more than Custer could now possibly imagine at this time, he needed his luck more than ever before. After all, Custer's lofty Indian-fighting reputation was solely based on his success in attacking the sleeping Washita village of peaceful Cheyenne, and the national popularity of his 1874 memoir, *My Life on the Plains*. However, even his much-touted Washita victory of November 1868 had been stained by ugly charges of Indian women and children having been killed by the

7th Cavalry, leaving Custer with an unfamiliar uneasiness not experienced during the Civil War. Even more, Custer had been accused by his enemies (both inside and outside the 7th Cavalry) of having abandoned a handful of his 7th Cavalry troopers, under Major Joel Elliott. These troopers were wiped out to the last man in a small-scale Custer's Last Stand at the Washita: still another reason why Captain Benteen hated his superior and was more than willing to see him defeated on June 25. His growing list of both military and civilian detractors believed that Custer should have done far more to save Elliott rather than leaving him and his seventeen men to a tragic fate, while realizing that the regimental commander's first responsibility was to save the regiment when facing destruction.

Therefore, Custer now hoped that victory at the Little Bighorn might wipe away the unsavory Washita stain and the disturbing, if not haunting, memory of Major Elliott. As recently as the evening of June 21 while encamped along the Yellowstone—when there should have been perfect harmony among the officer corps for the stiff challenges that lay ahead—Custer and Benteen had engaged in sharp, mutual recriminations. During this heated exchange, Benteen had emphasized that he would need adequate support from Custer in the next battle so that he would not suffer Elliott's tragic fate of a grisly death. Giving as good as he got in the bitter back-and-forth, Custer had then angrily denounced Benteen (who had no choice) for having killed an Indian youth who was attempting to defend himself, at the head on the attack on the Washita village. Clearly, this personal in-fighting among the highest level of the 7th Cavalry's officer corps was not a good sign at a time when close cooperation was necessary not only for victory, but also for survival.

Custer now sensed the accomplishment of what might well prove to be his greatest victory, and perhaps even the zenith of a remarkable military career, if his masterful flank attack succeeded as he anticipated. While Custer continued to lead the way down Medicine Tail Coulee with the confidence of a lifelong winner and the firm belief that his troopers could rise to any challenge, a great success now seemed almost inevitable because the Cheyenne camp continued to appear relatively quiet.[104]

Intoxicated by a tactical vision of a flank attack that had proved so successful in the history of warfare, Custer realized (like the Cheyenne) that if he led his command in a charge into the village's northern end, then the "great victory" would become well publicized, if not legendary, across the United States. To Custer, it must have almost seemed to him that he was once again riding to decisive victory in leading his hard-hitting Wolverines, who charged overwhelming numbers of Southerners with their distinctive "Michigan Yell," while the brass bands had played inspiring martial music.[105]

Gradually descending down the deeply eroded coulee that looked so unlike anything seen among the gently rolling hills of his native east central Ohio (New Rumley), Custer's view of this deserted Cheyenne village was an exhilarating one. Covered in sweat, these troopers, who now wore their cotton and silk bandanas over their noses and mouths to keep out the fine dust particles kicked up by churning horses' hooves from the coulee's bottom, now believed in their own martial legacy. The troopers' feisty fighting spirit was embodied in the 7th Cavalry's regimental rollicking fight song (an old Irish jig) called "Garry Owen," which had echoed over the Washita to lift the attackers' morale: "We are the pride of the Army [and] [i]t matters not where we're goin' [because] [w]e'll do or die in our country's cause."[106]

Some 7th Cavalry troopers had been so convinced of victory that they believed that they would be home shortly after easily capturing the ghost-like Sitting Bull. He was a legend among his people, both old and young, like Custer was among his fellow citizens. One cavalryman felt that once this relatively easy mission was accomplished, and after teaching Sitting Bull a stern lesson that he and his people would never forget, then "the campaign with be over, and Custer will take us with him to the Centennial" celebration in Philadelphia.[107] In response, an equally confident 7th Cavalryman had laughed, and then offered his own witty retort: "of course, we will take Sitting Bull with us."[108]

While riding his prized thoroughbred sorrel named "Vic" (short for "Victory"), which was distinguished by four white feet and legs and face blaze, Custer led his five companies down the dusty coulee under the late June sun. Custer continued to sense victory in the air, as long as everything continued to go well. No doubt, the dual intoxicating visions of victory on Gettysburg's third day, in equally sweltering July weather, and in the Washita's snows swept across Custer's mind during his descent that seemed to have no end along the unfamiliar terrain of Medicine Tail Coulee. Both of those successful charges had rolled effortlessly across wide, open fields, not down a coulee that led to an obscure river ford suddenly made all-important by developments beyond Custer's control.

Fortunately for Custer and his men, in terms of making fairly good time in moving toward the river, the coulee continued to widen as they neared the old buffalo ford. The ever-optimistic Custer had written to wife Libbie on June 9, 1876, that he was "hopeful of accomplishing great results" in this campaign so far from not only Fort Lincoln, but also Terry's and Gibbon's columns by this time.[109] In his last letter written on June 22 to his wife, who still (in his wife's words) "managed to preserve the romance," he had advised an increasingly worried Libbie of "how closely I obey your instructions about keeping with the column."[110] Of course, now staying close to the column no longer guaranteed safety for Custer, while leading the way down the sweltering coulee in which a densely–packed column of troopers who were now vulnerable, if bands of warriors gained advanced firing positions on the high ground surrounding the coulee.

Back at Fort Abraham Lincoln on the turbid Missouri on this hot Sunday, and with her womanly instincts rising to the fore, Libbie was much less optimistic than her over-achieving husband about a forthcoming success for the 7th Cavalry so deep in Indian country. In fact, she was now haunted by a dark premonition that nagged at her conscience and increasingly fragile sense of well-being with regard to what was happening far away. Libbie spent sleepless nights, fretting and fearing the worst. She feared for her husband's life as never before, especially after having learned of Crook's recent defeat by warriors who had never before displayed so much confidence and aggression in confronting a large command of more than 1,000 men. Libbie's wifely intuition told her that things were about to go horribly wrong for "Autie" and his men.

Along with scores of wives of other 7th Cavalry officers now fearing the worst for their husbands on this risky expedition deep within an uncharted primeval land swarming with angry Indians, Libbie and her female friends began to sing old hymns from the innocent days of their youth. Almost certainly, these wives would have knelt in solemn prayer had they realized that their loved ones were now moving relentlessly down this obscure ravine called Medicine Tail Coulee straight toward the largest Indian village ever seen on the Great Plains.[111]

Perhaps as he neared the Cheyenne village now draped in an eerie silence, Custer might have entertained some doubts himself that went unsaid, especially after Reno had been repulsed. Custer still felt the disappointment that Libbie had not been aboard the *Far West* (that was destined to shortly bring her the news of her husband's death at Fort Abraham Lincoln) as he had anticipated: not a good sign or omen. Indeed, the strong-minded Libbie had long been Custer's talisman (like the regimental band recently dehorsed by Terry), whom he addressed as "my Sunbeam" in letters. Libbie had been a permanent part of the inscrutable formula of his good fortune going back to the Civil War years.[112] In Custer's grateful words from a May 1, 1867, letter: "You are indeed my guardian angel. . . ."[113]

However, now this time-proven formula for success—his wife and the regimental band—was absent when needed most by Custer. As if ordained by the Great Spirit, therefore, this obscure place which was called Muskrat or Water Rat Creek (Medicine Tail Coulee) by the Lakota people was steadily leading Custer ever–closer ever closer to a cruel fate. Where this broad natural avenue entered the Little Bighorn at the remote Minneconjou Ford was shortly about to become the most strategic and important sector of the entire battlefield, because Custer's fate and that of his five companies depended upon a successful crossing.[114] The coulee's deep expanse gradually widened even farther on the north and south as this natural ravine neared the river: a deep gouge cut by nature through the high bluffs that lined the river's east bank. Nestled between the ends of the commanding bluffs to the north and south, the terrain at the coulee's mouth was a wide flat extension of the river bottom.

Fortunately for Custer, this favorable geography seemed an ideal avenue for a mounted attack with all five companies across the ford. Clearly, the fabled Custer's Luck was continuing to hold true despite Reno's repulse, because good progress northwestward down the coulee continued to be made, and no Indians had yet fired on his column. He had finally found the perfect level ground that seemed tailor-made for a cavalry attack across the old buffalo ford. Ironically, the vast herds of buffalo that had long given the Great Plains people life now played a role (at least their trail and crossing point) in allowing Custer an easier means to strike them with his flank attack. As Custer had first learned from his Crow scouts, this was the closest natural opening, situated at this gap that opened so wide amid the wall of high bluffs. The mouth of Medicine Tail Coulee (sometimes known as South Medicine Tail Coulee) stretched for approximately 710 yards from one bluff end on the north to the other on the south, to present terrain that was ideal for a cavalry charge.

Custer felt thankful for having been presented with this broad natural avenue (an ever-widening coulee all the way to the Little Bighorn) leading straight to the river, because the high bluffs, towering above and dominating the ford, stood on either side of the coulee's expansive mouth. Butler Ridge, as the whites called it, rose north of the coulee. Looming some 170 feet above the ford like a rounded tower that was a butte, Bouyer's Bluff was the highest ground located immediately south of Medicine Tail Coulee's mouth. Providing a panoramic view from its windswept top to overlook a wide area west of the river, this bluff was open and without a tree or dense underbrush. Only the ubiquitous patches of bluish-green sagebrush and patches of the brighter green prairie grass, nourished by the recent deluges of spring rains, struggled for life in the thin soil atop the bluff. The commanding height of Bouyer's Bluff, a silent sentinel of the mouth of Medicine Tail Coulee, overlooked the old buffalo ford on this twisting, crystal clear mountain stream that flowed gently below in the tree-lined valley.[115]

For the troopers having to gingerly guide their horses down the coulee because of loose rocks and shale that were exposed when the top soil had been washed away, the invigorating sight of the river just ahead to the west presented a scene of natural beauty. The bluecoats now saw a ribbon of bright blue meandering its way lazily through the wooded bottoms, while the buffalo skin lodges were clumped together in a prescribed order with tribal circles on the grassy bottoms beyond the tall timber. Impressed by the river's beauty amid an unspoiled landscape, Private William O. Taylor, described how "the Little Bighorn [was] a stream some fifty to seventy feet wide, and from two to four feet deep of clear, icy cold water."[116] Unlike the rivers in his native northwest Ohio, Lieutenant Edward Settle Godfrey, Company K, 7th Cavalry, wrote how the "Little Big Horn River, or the 'Greasy Grass' as it is known to the [Sioux], is a rapid, tortuous mountain stream from twenty to forty yards wide, with pebbled bottom, but abrupt, soft banks [and the] water at the ordinary stage is from two or five feet in depth, depending upon the width of the channel."[117]

The level of the clear water at Medicine Tail Coulee Ford was on the lower side of these estimates with regard to depth and width at this narrow point, where the river was shallow to create a natural crossing point for man and animals, especially buffalo herds. Ironically, Custer could have attempted to cross the river at other points, but without the considerable advantages of the natural avenue of the ever-widening coulee leading directly to the water's edge. Therefore, besides Custer's own instincts and the words of Crow scouts, geography had pointed the way for Custer to advance. As if ordained by fate itself, this ford had become Custer's initial target out of urgent necessity, although according to one warrior, "At that season of the year, the river could have been forded almost anywhere with little or no difficulty, the water being very low."[118]

Attacking across a river, even at the ford's relatively low waters, was always a risky undertaking—especially when so close to a hostile village, in a place situated amid familiar terrain. With time absolutely crucial, there had been no possibility for Custer to conduct a thorough reconnaissance of either the surrounding ground or village, because his primary goal was to surprise the village, and as soon as possible. Custer's famed luck had not failed him at the Washita, which must have provided him with some comfort during his long advance down Medicine Tail Coulee, making it seem that his upcoming attack at the ford was less risky than was actually the case.

Nevertheless, Custer knew that unleashing a blind attack in an unfamiliar setting was always dangerous, especially against a crafty opponent who was a master in the art of setting up clever ambushes. After all, Custer had just narrowly escaped disaster at the Washita, perhaps even the annihilation of the entire 7th Cavalry, by only the narrowest of margins. At that time in late November 1868, he had no idea that the Cheyenne village at the Washita was located at the isolated end of a vast network of other tribal villages that extended much farther along the Washita.

After having easily overwhelmed the lightly defended immediate village of Black Kettle, only Custer's capture of women and children (who were essentially hostages) prevented a newly formed, heavy concentration of warriors from attacking and perhaps destroying his entire command. Consequently, as demonstrated at the Washita, attacking the remote end of an expansive stretch of villages was a most dangerous enterprise, even for a fast-moving cavalry. Relying on his usual blend of audacity and luck, Custer had been the sole author of that close call on that harsh winter day, and now he was in the process of seemingly repeating it out of urgent necessity. Revealing the depth of his recklessness and tactical folly on that late November morning in the Oklahoma Territory, Custer had initially desired to attack all the villages (containing thousands of warriors) along the Washita, which spanned for a length of ten miles, before he came to his tactical senses: a classic case of aggressiveness run amuck.[119]

Meanwhile, on this June day, the Cheyenne camp opposite the wide coulee was still largely vacant and relatively quiet while Custer and his command continued to move steadily down Medicine Tail Coulee, with Reno having drawn hundreds of warriors like a magnet to him. Two Moons—the highest ranking Northern Cheyenne leader who had initially organized resistance and a minor, or "little," chief of the Kit Fox Society—and his fully armed followers had ridden south to push Reno's three companies aside. Clearly, this highly-advantageous tactical situation provided Custer with his long-awaited golden opportunity to reverse the day's fortunes with a bold flank attack.[120]

In consequence, Two Moons, armed with his favorite repeating rifle, and most other Kit Fox Society members (the Cheyenne camp's policemen who also had initially served as "the special camp defenders") were now fighting several miles to the south. Confirming that Custer's Luck still held true while the five companies continued to advance down the coulee that seemingly now led straight to another Custer victory, the Cheyenne village appeared to be far more vulnerable than usual. Because of Reno's attack, the northernmost village was still almost entirely devoid of fighting men. Unfortunately for Custer and his men, the few remaining "Fox warriors" were so revered throughout the tribe, and represented some of the best warriors of the Cheyenne nation.[121]

The encampment's northern end had been earlier filled with large numbers of women and children who had fled north from Reno's attack. The chaotic scene that had consumed the Cheyenne village had entirely evaporated by the time of Custer's descent. Cheyenne warrior Soldier Wolf, born in the 1850s and who wore a special protective charm that hung over his chest (much like Captain Keogh's Catholic medal, *Pro Petri Sede*), described, "All the women and children gathered down at the lower village, and becoming more and more frightened as they listened to the firing [in the Reno sector], they decided to cross the river to the east side and so to get farther away from the fight. When these women were crossing the river and some were going up the hills, they discovered more troops coming. This was Custer's party."[122]

As mentioned, White Shield had been fishing downstream just north of the Cheyenne camp with his friend Blackstone, when his young nephew Dives Backward, who had been hunting for grasshoppers for bait in the hills east of the river, returned with startling news. He had seen a warrior in a full war bonnet riding toward the village's southern end. White Shield had only then belatedly realized that the pony soldiers had attacked upriver. Grabbing his weapon, White Shield mounted his favorite horse. He crossed the river at Medicine Tail Coulee Ford and rode up the high ground to investigate for himself. From the bluff (unlike in the low ground along the river bottoms below, because of acoustics) he first heard firing from Reno's attack. White Shield then galloped back to the Cheyenne village, knowing that a major attack on the Sioux village on the encampment's southern end was well underway.[123]

After riding back to the Cheyenne village, he was shocked because, "[w]hen I reached camp, all the men were gone [to fight Reno], but my mother [who risked her life instead of fleeing] was leading my war horse around, down in front of the lodge, waiting for me. I bridled my horse and said to my mother, 'Where is my war shirt?' She said that a man [Mad Wolf] had just been here who took it to wear in the fight

[and] [w]hile I was dressing myself [in full warrior regalia] and telling my mother which way she should go, I looked back and saw soldiers" in blue moving relentlessly down Medicine Tail Coulee with colorful flags waving under a blazing June sun.[124]

Catching sight of another large group of white soldiers on the high ground, "the hill of peace" and a "sacred place," above their village that extended a short distance north beyond the ford, a Cheyenne woman sounded the first alarm to warn of Custer's descent down the coulee. Terrified by the sight of seemingly too many bluecoats to count, she shouted in hysteria, "More horse soldiers are coming! They are on the sacred hill of the wild peas!"[125] Clearly, Custer's audacious decision to go for broke and mount an attack in broad daylight allowed this discovery, unlike during his dawn charge at the Washita. Having the flexibility to make tactical adjustments on the fly could overcome a disadvantageous situation.[126]

As Custer hoped to realize his tactical vision, the surprise was complete at the village's northern end. Incredibly, Custer had succeeded in surprising the Indians not once, but twice—first Reno, and now with his stealthy advance down Medicine Tail Coulee's length: an unprecedented tactical achievement in the annals of Great Plains warfare that spoke highly of Custer's tactical vision and skill, especially in an urgent crisis situation. Because it was located more than two miles from where Reno had struck, and due to the terrain's nuisances of a village lying deep in a river bottom while commanding bluffs lined the east bank, the firing upriver had not been heard by the occupants of the Cheyenne village located to the far north.[127]

Meanwhile, the terrifying sight of additional soldiers in blue coming and the chorus of frantic warnings alerted the Cheyenne village, unleashing a new round of panic among the remaining women and children. The Cheyenne raced west, away from the river and toward the pony herd now grazing in "other feeding areas on the valley and on the bench hills just [to the] west," to escape Custer's five companies.[128] A swift rider galloped south from the Cheyenne village to rally the warriors battling Reno's three companies to return to defend the village's northern end against this new and even more ominous threat that appeared seemingly out of thin air. Clearly, out of a mixture of urgency and sheer desperation, the old Custer of the Civil War had returned, galvanized by his most formidable challenge. Custer fully realized that the day's fortunes and even his regiment's ultimate fate, including that of Reno and Benteen, depended on what he did next.[129]

Most importantly during the confusion that resulted from the sighting of Custer's five companies, a mere handful of the sole and relatively few remaining guardians of the northernmost village somehow managed to keep their heads. Instead of bringing a crippling fear, the sight of the advance of Custer's troopers down the coulee only emboldened them to rise to the challenge. By this time, even Custer's thoroughbred that "was a sorrel with stocking [white] legs," in one Indian's words, could be seen, but no one knew that the leader before his pony soldiers was Custer.[130]

Despite having been caught by surprise as so often in the past, these warriors of the northernmost village were not running to escape this new threat, as Libbie had seemingly warned in her letter (about Crook's June 17 defeat on the Rosebud) to Custer that he was destined to never read. Ironically, while Custer relied upon tactical flexibility and boldness to yet win the day, he had not envisioned that this same boldness and tactical flexibility of only a few remaining defenders of the vulnerable Cheyenne village was about to thwart his glowing vision of repeating his Washita success.[131]

Likewise, the non-superstitious 7th Cavalry troopers, who had made "trinkets" from Indian bones found on the plains, would soon have their opponents "retaliate on them . . . and make trinkets out of their bones."[132] Eerily, during the Civil War years, Custer had lovingly referred to his wife as "My Rosebud" and "My dear little Army Crow." Now, Rosebud and Crow had entirely different meanings from when last spoken in their bedroom, while he eyed the blue waters of the Little Bighorn and the old buffalo ford.[133]

Chapter IV

Custer's Last Charge

In a March 1866 letter to his wife, Custer best summarized the quality of his dynamic personality that now guaranteed that he was now going for broke in his boldest bid to reap still another victory to add to a long list of successes, while attempting to reverse the hands of fate that had turned so suddenly against him: "I'm not partial to speechmaking [because] I believe in acts, not words."[1]

Lieutenant Colonel Custer was now determined to strike an overpowering blow with Yates's and Keogh's battalions, front to rear (west to east), by charging straight into the village. Hitting the village from the opposite side with a stealthy flank attack promised a great deal, because all of the warriors were now battling Reno well beyond the village's southern boundaries and even farther away because of his withdrawal from the timbered bottoms to the bluffs overlooking the river. As demonstrated so often during the Civil War, Custer now possessed a surefire tactical formula that was guaranteed, or so it seemed, to bring decisive victory to the 7th Cavalry, despite all of the setbacks this frustrating afternoon.

However, Custer now had only 220 troopers, which was a mere fraction (about one-third) of the regiment. Custer's Civil War charges were the stuff of legend. Unlike these Union troopers, the men of Custer's five companies no longer carried sabers, weighing three pounds and seven ounces. They had been left behind because the swords were generally considered useless in fighting Indians. This premature conclusion was about to come back to haunt Custer's men.

Even when Custer had been recently warned by the seemingly all-knowing scout Mitch Bouyer, of mixed French (a French Canadian blacksmith who had been killed in 1863 by Indians while trapping) and Sioux descent, that what lay before the 7th Cavalry was "the biggest village he had ever seen," Custer was only more determined to succeed at any cost. However, to be fair to Custer, this confidence and sheer bravado were understandable in purely tactical terms, because he was relying on tactics that had always proved so successful in the past, especially in the Civil War. He had earlier informed scout Charles "Charley" Alexander Reynolds, who likewise gave his own warning about large numbers of Indians along the Little Bighorn, that "he could whip them."[2]

Throughout the Civil War, "Custer's rule" for achieving victory had always included ignoring all obstacles, conventional wisdom, and such dire warnings like the ones recently gained from his scouts, including Bloody Knife, Custer's faithful "Ree" (Arikara). Custer had long relied on the shock value of a hard-hitting surprise attack to overwhelm his opponents, even if badly outnumbered, because that is exactly what his opponent least expected. If Custer found himself in trouble in the past, then he just fought his way out of the jam: a highly flexible and adaptive tactical formula that had worked even against the South's finest cavalrymen, when he had been a younger man.[3] Feeling that he could duplicate his Civil War feats that still resonated in his heart and mind, Custer now led, in his own words, "the proudest command in the world" down Medicine Tail Coulee and toward the ford that he knew he had to cross at any cost to reverse the hands of fate.[4]

Such unbridled aggressiveness had been precisely what everyone, especially in Washington, DC, and army headquarters, anticipated from Custer. After all, this aggressiveness was why Custer had been first chosen to serve as the heavy hammer, which Crook, Gibbon, or Terry could not manage, to deliver a devastating blow. If Custer was still very much of a captive of his romantic image of the hard-hitting "young American hero" as during the 1860s, he was trapped by his tactical rationale of always relying on the bold offensive strike, regardless of the odds or tactical situation: a formula that could backfire with disastrous consequences if Custer's Luck suddenly disappeared like a phantom.

Not disobeying any orders now, Custer was chosen from the beginning to accomplish exactly what he now hoped to do: strike an overpowering blow to reverse the fortunes of war and win the day. After all, Custer's bold plan of unleashing a flank attack across the ford was exactly why Terry had first designated the 7th Cavalry as his expedition's principal strike force, allowing Custer an inordinate amount of tactical latitude and flexibility to achieve their mutual goal. What everyone at headquarters fully understood was that "always Custer would hit hard at the first opportunity [which] was the precise reason, more than simple friendship, which explained why Sheridan had interceded with the president on Custer's behalf to negate 'Grant's Revenge'." He had only trusted Terry and Crook to formulate a winning strategic plan, but expected Custer to secure victory. Therefore, Custer had been allowed to develop his own tactical plan depending on the situation as he found it when entirely on his own. This explained why he had descended down the coulee on a single-minded mission.[5]

As if drawn by fate and perhaps even the Great Spirit itself, these were the existing realities and unusual circumstances that now sent Custer and his five companies ever-farther down Medicine Tail Coulee and toward the ford. A thoughtful officer who wisely steered clear of the bitter regimental politics as much as possible, Lieutenant Godfrey, Company K, 7th Cavalry, emphasized Custer's well-conceived tactical formula for success: "had Reno made his charge as ordered, or made a bold front even, the Hostiles would have been so engaged in the bottom that Custer's approach from the Northeast would have been such a surprise as to cause the stampede of the village and would have broken the morale of the warriors."[6]

Clearly, Custer's tactical plan was actually better than has been generally recognized by historians, offering the prospect of winning the day. If only Reno had accomplished what was expected of him by unleashing a hard-hitting attack, and if the divided elements of the 7th Cavalry had only acted together in harmony as a team as they'd done in the past, including at the Washita, then victory was obtainable. However, even Libbie astutely observed an inherent weakness—the shortage of officers and veterans after 1866 and 1871 enlistments had expired—of this non-elite (contrary to popular assumptions) regiment. In addition, the 7th Cavalry had not served as a single cohesive command for ten years. Libbie was unsettled by the fact that her husband's beloved regiment was "a medley of incongruous elements." This factor was already playing a leading role in sabotaging Custer's best efforts of reaping a dramatic victory this afternoon.[7]

While advancing farther westward down the coulee, now green with the fresh spring growth of buffalo grass, and ever closer to the river, Custer now must have felt the weight of the world on his shoulders, because it was up to him to turn the tide. Command responsibility never weighed heavier on him than now. He had twice sent messengers to request reinforcements (men and ammunition) after correctly sensing that every man and bullet would be needed this afternoon, because he knew of Reno's dismal fate. Unfortunately for Custer and his five companies, these desperate appeals for his reserves (Benteen) and extra rounds were destined to go unanswered. Quite simply, Benteen decided to disobey Custer's orders to rush forward partly because he wished to see him fail. Now, not only Major Reno, who equally detested his commander, and had "cut and ran" to gain safety on the bluffs above the river, but also Captain Benteen was letting Custer down as never before. Benteen's refusal to respond with alacrity to Custer's orders, leaving him and his command not only more vulnerable, but also on its own to do or die. Brought by the reliable Bouyer, the news that Reno had fled the field against all orders and expectations must have shocked Custer to the bone, guaranteeing no assistance from him and his three routed companies.

Custer would have been even more incredulous to know that Benteen now lingered far too distant from the action and far from recall. Three precious hours had passed since he had been dispatched to the left—and after having proceeded about five miles, Benteen was still taking his time. Now, when Custer (and Reno, for that matter) needed Benteen's command (his only reserves), the native Virginian was still too far away to provide assistance. As usual, regimental political, old hatreds, and egos rose to the fore. Disgruntled that he had been handed orders to deny him glory in reaping the widely anticipated victory, Benteen had turned not only sullen but also angry: a passive-aggressive attitude reflected in his "brooding pace" that guaranteed no support for Custer this afternoon. This deliberate foot-dragging eventually later included watering his command's horses at a spring surrounded by a swampy area on the Middle Fork of Reno Creek (before, or east of, the Sans Arc village on Custer's old trail) for perhaps as long as nearly half an hour, as if time and Custer's urgent orders for assistance were of no importance. The last thing that Benteen intended to do was to provide timely assistance to the one man whom he felt was most responsible for having made his life miserable, including the loss of his children due to remote assignments that he believed were handed out by Custer in vindictive spite.

Indeed, Captain Benteen's leisurely pace continued even after the arrival of Custer's message for assistance from Trumpeter Martin and

allegedly from Sergeant Daniel Alexander Kanipe. Benteen had continued riding too far west instead of immediately turning to assist both
Reno and Custer. When Benteen finally turned in the right direction
in a "right oblique" to regain the main trail (Custer's old route) and
then eventually picked up the pace when firing was heard from Reno's
command, it was already too late. Custer's plan to utilize Benteen
and the ammunition reserves with the pack train, now more than a
mile in Benteen's rear, was already impractical, because of the native
Virginian's stubborn intransigence. Benteen's dereliction of duty and
lack of responsibility to his commander guaranteed not only the lack of
timely support, but also disaster. On his own, Benteen had decided not
to go to Custer's assistance, despite repeated urgent messages for timely
reinforcements from his commander. Having made up his mind to
leave Custer and five companies alone to their tragic fates, he failed to
do "the right thing" to say the least, including after linking with Reno.[8]

If victory was to come for the 7th Cavalry, Custer would have to win
it himself, and this meant going for broke. With the awful realization that
Reno would provide no assistance and Benteen might well be too late,
Custer no doubt feared that he might be entirely on his own, because that
was indeed now the case. At this moment, he had nothing to rely upon but
himself, moral courage, and barely 200 men to attack the Cheyenne village.
In many ways, this was a symbolic (perhaps fitting) situation for his five
companies, because Custer could now count on a good many of his friends,
brothers, and relatives who were with him. These dedicated men, especially
the dependable officer corps of Custer's inner circle—the so-called "Custer
gang"—were literally the best and brightest of the 7th Cavalry, and their loyalty and resolve was guaranteed. Custer realized that he could count on these
men to the bitter end at the Little Bighorn, which was what was required
this afternoon of many surprises and new challenges on a scale previously
not experienced by Custer. Most of all, Custer gave no thought to accepting
the shame of ordering a humiliating retreat, even after the stunning news of
Reno's undisciplined flight from the field.

Consequently, sticking to his original tactical plan that was now the only hope of reversing the day's fortunes, Custer was even more determined to deliver a master stroke with his flank attack with all five companies. These were bold maneuvers that partly reflected the tactical lessons learned from Custer's diligent study of Napoleon's campaigns, which had been distinguished by their tactical brilliance. With everything at stake this afternoon, there would be no reserve force for Custer's flank attack with five companies. It was clear that Reno's three companies had been insufficient for their comparable task. Like at the Washita, the dense concentrations of cottonwoods along the river hid greater portions of this sprawling village along the Little Bighorn. Custer knew that so many tepees equated to a good many warriors that called for an overwhelming offensive effort with his entire command: an offensive thrust of both battalions that had to go for broke to reverse the day's fortunes.

Therefore, after now realizing the village's massive size that spanned about three miles down the river, Custer knew that he needed to employ his entire command for a maximum offensive effort at the ford. Given the increasing urgent tactical situation, and under desperate circumstances, Custer was now "desirous of massing the two squadrons [battalions] together, in order to make strong the line of attack," in the words of Private Theodore W. Goldin, a teenager, adopted son, and former brakeman of Company G, 7th Cavalry.

This meant that Yates's and Keogh's battalions were now employed by Custer in his last offensive effort: a maximum effort because the lieutenant colonel no longer had any realistic tactical choice, given the circumstances. After all, Custer realized that he must deliver an overpowering blow, instead of what too many historians have incorrectly viewed as nothing more than a weak feint at the ford that was launched to only assist Reno's command, instead of attempting to achieve a decisive success—the most implausible of scenarios given Custer's history, mind-set, abilities, and inclinations, especially when combined with the overall situation. Anything less than a full-fledged attack, including even a long-assumed piecemeal offensive, made no tactical sense under the circumstances. In keeping with the fighting style for which he was famous across America, Custer envisioned delivering a hard-hitting blow and not a mere feint. After all, a feint would have been defeatist; an admission of forfeiting the initiative and any possibility of achieving victory—the most un-Custer-like of tactical possibilities and outcomes under the circumstances.[9] Indeed, because the day's fortunes had turned so decidedly against him, Custer's last offensive down Medicine Tail Coulee was an all-out offensive effort that embodied "the chief ingredients of heroism and a dauntless courage."[10]

A concentrated assault of both of Custer's battalions across the ford was also verified by Captain Benteen, and others, not long after the battle in a letter to his wife. In addition, civilian John C. Lockwood also verified as much, agreeing with accounts of others who later saw the tracks of the horses of five companies going all the way to the ford. According to Lockwood's memoir (which is still controversial, but more reliable than previously thought by historians, who had mistakenly placed too much faith in Sergeant Daniel Alexander Kanipe account), he served—although not listed on the roster of Quartermaster employees but evidently used an alias like scores of other members in the 7th Cavalry—as a scout and packer under Chief Packer John C. Wagoner. Libbie later communicated with Lockwood, adding credibility. Even more, Lockwood enlisted in the 7th Cavalry on the last day of August 1876. He might have served in an unofficial capacity as a volunteer. This was very likely the case, since Lockwood was a longtime friend and companion (including trapping, exploring, mining, and hunting forays in the Black Hills) of guide Charles "Lonesome Charlie" Alexander Reynolds.

Reynolds served as Custer's top civilian scout. Ironically, Reynolds was known to the Indians as the "Lucky Man," (a badly misplaced nickname for the ill-fated native Kentuckian on the afternoon of June 25) but he was now haunted by a dark, but accurate, premonition that he would not survive the upcoming battle. Reynolds had twice appealed to Terry to be released from duty, but was refused. Clearly, fate had been unkind to "Lonesome Charlie."[11]

While on the high ground with a pack animal that had carried Custer's only extra ammunition (which was needed because the average trooper could use his 100 Springfield rounds in less than ten minutes in a hot fight), Lockwood verified the strength of Custer's attack. Again and as mentioned, this view also has been confirmed by Major Benteen's astute analysis gained not long after the battle. From high ground above the coulee, Lockwood saw "see [all] five companies moving together [and advancing south toward the ford] in line, all abreast with General Custer in the lead."[12] This analysis was in keeping with the fact, as verified by respected historian Larry Sklenar, that "all five companies" descended as one toward the ford during the advance.[13] In addition, and in agreement with what Lieutenant Charles Camilus DeRudio, Company H, after the battle, Curley's interviews also maintained that "Custer himself led all five companies down to the mouth of Medicine Tail Coulee."[14] Significantly, both white and red testimony coincided to verify as much in this regard.

Agreeing with Curley, Sklenar, and others with regard to Custer's maximum offensive effort to charge across the ford with all five companies, the Lockwood account has been long incorrectly lumped into those of a large number of men, who later falsely claimed to have been "last survivors" or "lone survivors" at Little Bighorn. One such long-dismissed "lone survivor," Sergeant Frank Frankel (George August Finckle), of Tom Custer's Company C, 7th Cavalry, has been only recently discovered to be grounded in more truth than had been assumed by historians for generations.

Despite numerous errors (to be expected of an older man with a faltering memory in dictating his story many years later), Lockwood's memoir has more merit than previously recognized. Of course, it only can be seen this way after weeding out what can be corroborated as valid from what has been clearly embellished: the same process in which the truth of Indian accounts can be deciphered by separating fact from fiction, and as recently achieved by author John Koster with regard to Sergeant Frank Frankel's story.

After separating fact from fiction, the Lockwood account rings true on a number of key scores, especially with regard to the confrontation at Medicine Tail Coulee Ford, and how Custer employed all five companies in the attack (as confirmed by some modern historians) and held none in reserve. These were perfectly in keeping with the desperate situation, and when Custer's only hope for success was in going for broke. Because of the importance of the struggle for the ford's possession, this often-ignored memoir has been now utilized to a limited degree in this work. First and foremost, Lockwood was almost certainly not a messenger, as claimed, like other alleged survivors, including Sergeant Kanipe. Most likely as a packer, he had been assigned to a pack horse of extra ammunition left behind on the high ground (the troopers carried too few rounds for an extended battle), after a final distribution of rounds before the five companies moved into the dusty depths of Medicine Tail Coulee.

Even if he never served as a messenger for Custer as claimed, which was almost certain, Lockwood's 7th Cavalry service almost immediately after the battle meant that he was in contact and close association with a large number of Reno's and Benteen's men, who saw the battlefield close up. This is a significant fact: Lockwood almost certainly learned of key details about the battle from them that were based upon personal experience and, most importantly, his own first-hand observations of events this afternoon.

Therefore, the Lockwood memoir should not be entirely ignored, because of its well-hidden revelations—despite its obvious errors, including having been written in a novelist style, which was typical of the day. As Lockwood's name does not appear on any rosters, he almost certainly used an alias, like more than 80 men (including former Confederate soldiers who concealed their past and identities) who served in the 7th Cavalry at this time. This long-dismissed Lockwood memoir might well have provided an example of historians having thrown the baby out with the bath water, especially with regard to the maximum strength of Custer's attack on Medicine Tail Coulee Ford, which has been verified by other accounts and makes the only tactical sense under the circumstances.

Lockwood enlisted in the 7th Cavalry at the end of August 1876: a situation quite unlike the many false storytellers, who had no comparable 7th Cavalry experience and, therefore, allowed their imaginations to soar. Unlike these false accounts of so many imposters, Lockwood's memoir was well rooted in, and deeply connected to, the overall 7th Cavalry experience, including his correspondence with Mrs. Custer, to a degree not evident with the false storytellers. Significantly, Lockwood's emphasis on Custer's maximum offensive effort in attempting to force his way across the ford and into the Cheyenne village was verified by Reno and Benteen from what they saw in analyzing the battlefield immediately after the fight.

In part because of their importance, the Lockwood Papers are housed in the Huntington Library, San Marino, California. Other key aspects of Lockwood's background have also provided greater validity to his memoir that has been entirely lacking in the accounts of so many false storytellers. He was from Bismark, near Fort Abraham Lincoln, like Kellogg. Lockwood also possessed a longer past personal association with Custer and the 7th Cavalry than either Kellogg or the mythmakers who claimed to have been with Custer: another foundation for his written communications to Libbie. In addition, Lockwood had long worked closely with the Kentucky-born "Charley" Reynolds before the battle as a scout and packer, including with the 7th Cavalry in previous active campaigning. Unlike the many imposters, Lockwood also possessed ample frontier experience, including as a hunter, trapper, packer, and explorer-miner in the Black Hills: a level of experience sought by

Custer for the 1876 expedition so deep in the dark heart of Indian country.

Lockwood described how he was with Custer's battalion, along with "four other packers" who had accompanied Custer's five companies with a small number of horses (almost certainly not slow-moving, balky mules with the main pack train—now a mile behind Benteen's battalion far to the rear—in order to keep up with their commander's rapid movements). Such an extra ammunition supply might have been one of Custer's wisest precautions as a veteran commander, just in case he became separated from the main pack train with the regiment's ammunition supply, or if the pack train was lost, captured, or just too slow, which was now the case. During the last halt before moving down Medicine Tail Coulee, Lockwood described that he and his fellow packers had "unpacked the [extra] ammunition and distributed it to the troops," before the attack on the ford.[15]

Hard-working civilian packers, like Lockwood, were the most forgotten participants of Custer's final campaign. All in all, especially with regard to Custer's attack on the ford, Lockwood's memoir rings true on key points, but only after the fiction is carefully separated from fact: as mentioned, in much the same way that author Koster achieved this feat in his 2010 book, *Custer Survivor: The End of the Myth, the Beginning of a Legend*, about Sergeant Frank Finkel. However, the Lockwood memoir's most glaring flaw was the story that "Charley" Reynolds was dispatched with a message at the same time as himself on a comparable mission. For all of these reasons, almost certainly Lockwood was simply a packer and not a messenger. In dictating his memoir in 1922, so long after the fact, Lockwood might have only desired to give recognition to his old friend, who lost his life in the river valley with Reno's command on June 25, by emphasizing that Reynolds served as a messenger. Of course, this is only speculation. Lockwood attributed his vital role to Reynolds rather than North Carolina–born Sergeant Daniel Alexander Kanipe, of Company C, and Trumpeter John Martin, respectively. Allegedly, Kanipe (although his account is disputed today) took Custer's first order (issued by Tom Custer) for assistance (first received by Benteen and then passed on) to Captain Thomas Mower McDougall, a battle-proven officer of Scotch–Irish descent. Born in Wisconsin and a Civil War veteran, McDougall now commanded Company B and the pack train—with the regiment's ammunition reserves—that lingered so far rearward.[16]

Ample Indian oral testimony also revealed that Custer descended on the ford in a staggered attack of two assault waves with all five companies—first one battalion, and then his final battalion: a prudent offensive tactic with the last battalion acting as a second assault wave for crossing a river. However, this full-fledged attack with everything that Custer had (five companies) was entirely in keeping with his hard-hitting tactical style and the overall situation after Reno's repulse. Consequently, with so much at stake, Custer utilized both battalions to deliver a maximum blow with his flank attack.

In a rarity of the battle of Little Bighorn historiography, white (Reno, Benteen, Goldin, Lockwood, and others) and red testimonies (including Crow scout Curley) coincided with regard to the day's final offensive effort, revealing that Custer in fact made his maximum offensive effort at the ford, where he went for broke because no other realistic tactical options were left open.[17] Curley, the youngest Crow scout, saw Custer's advance down the coulee and on the ford. Indeed, Curley "described the advance of several companies" in the attack on the ford.[18] However, Curley failed to see the second wave of attackers, Keogh's battalion, because he had departed the column with Custer's permission and was out of sight by this time.

Custer had actually accomplished what he had planned to do from the beginning: unleash an all-out offensive thrust with all five companies in a flank attack that seemingly could not be resisted, because almost every Cheyenne warrior was still far to the south confronting Reno. In purely tactical terms, he had managed to accomplish what was virtually impossible for the 7th Cavalry to achieve in either springtime or summer: catching an Indian village totally by surprise in broad daylight.

All in all, this was already an unprecedented feat in the annals of Great Plains warfare for the United States Army: a compliment to Custer's well-honed tactical sense and skills. Clearly, Custer defied the odds in having made this rather remarkable tactical achievement under the most disadvantageous circumstances, demonstrating flexibility by developing tactics on the fly. Custer and his five companies, including members of his inner circle, were seemingly about to reverse the day's fortunes and accomplish the most incredible victory in the 7th Cavalry's history.[19]

Of course, the key catalyst that guaranteed that Custer launched his assault with all five companies had been when Custer first learned of Reno's failure upriver, leaving him with no other tactical option if he desired success. As mentioned, this news came as a shock—the rout of a large percentage of his regiment (three companies) in retreat for the first time in the regiment's history. Therefore, it was now up to Custer to personally deliver the blow to reverse the day's fortunes and save the remainder of his regiment (along with its reputation and honor), before it was too late. Consequently, the overall tactical situation called for hurling his two battalions of all five companies across the ford as soon as possible as the only way to salvage a victory, after fortune had so unexpectedly turned against Reno, and Custer to a lesser degree.[20]

Custer was presented with a great opportunity because the Cheyenne warriors had ridden several miles south. Therefore, Custer's flank attack was launched to not only relieve the pressure on Reno, but also to rescue him. Custer's immediate target was still empty of Cheyenne warriors and left almost entirely undefended. Lodges stood vacant and silent. Relying on his best instincts, Custer continued to lead his assault of five companies down Medicine Tail Coulee to deliver his flank attack. He had long believed firmly that his 7th Cavalry could vanquish any number of Indians, and he was now backing up his words with action. However, many enlisted men were inexperienced (about one-fifth were recent recruits and young men from eastern cities), with little training and marksmanship practice.[21] Custer quite correctly believed in the high quality of his veteran officer corps, which was more reliable and experienced than the enlisted ranks. With pride, Custer wrote in a 1873 letter how "if ever a lot of hardy, athletic young fellows were assembled in one group it is found in the officers of the 7th Cav."[22]

With all five companies advancing down the dry coulee with colorful battle flags flying, Custer's attack looked as if it could not possibly fail, as so often in the past. After all, he was about to strike a village without warriors from what he could see with limited visibility because of the towering cottonwoods that lined the river bottoms: a correct assessment. As so often in the past, Custer now placed great reliance on his good friend and top lieutenant, Captain George Wilhelmus Mancius Yates. He was from Monroe, Michigan, like the Custer brothers who were closely bonded to him. Custer knew his man and fellow former Civil War officer well. With his usual skill, Yates now commanded the battalion that consisted of Companies C, E, and F.

Because its commander was so capable, Yates's battalion had been chosen by Custer to spearhead the attack of all five companies across the ford. Yates was the long-time commander of Company F, which he had transformed into an excellent unit. With Yates leading the battalion, this company was now commanded by Second Lieutenant William Van Reily. He had been too young to serve in the Civil War, having been born in Washington, DC, in December 1853.

Other than his brother Tom—who was basically Custer's alter ego throughout this arduous expedition—Custer trusted no one more in the 7th Cavalry than the native New Yorker. Captain Yates was the most literal example of a brother-in-arms with regard to his relationship with his regimental commander. Yates was blessed with dashing good looks, possessing "fine golden hair and long moustache." He was a polished and a somewhat rakish gentleman, and an occasionally reckless ladies' man. His romantic skills with other women in the true cavalier tradition had played a role in wrecking his first marriage with Lucretia Beaumont Irwin.

More importantly for this high-stakes offensive effort, Yates was the ideal officer to lead the way behind Custer and his headquarters staff, which advanced in the forefront as usual. As Custer fully appreciated, Yates's qualities were all-important for such a challenging situation that was in essence now the increasingly desperate lieutenant colonel's last gamble, where strength of character, experience, and leadership ability counted more than anything else. Captain Yates had led his men in the charge at the Washita on that snowy November day. Then, as always, he had proved cool and collected in emergency combat situations: qualities greatly admired by Custer because they were his own. Custer understood that Yates was exactly the kind of aggressive and talented officer who should lead the attack with his battalion.

Able to inspire troopers to follow him to hell and back if necessary, Custer knew that Yates could be depended upon in a crisis situation, when sound tactical judgment was required to reverse the day's fortunes. Clearly, as the leader of the disciplined "Band Box Troop" (Company F, whose members rode light bays that flaunted their elite status) and a hero at Gettysburg like Custer, Yates was clearly one of the regiment's finest officers. He was a Custer favorite because the two men were kindred spirits.

These two dynamic officers, who were totally committed to duty and a warrior ethos, shared a typical cavalier's bravado and aggressive manner on and off the battlefield. They also were natural showmen with the ladies, playing their parts as romantic cavaliers to the hilt. With plenty of experience in the art of love, Yates knew the right ways to capture the hearts of the ladies, including picking prairie flowers in a romantic natural setting far from prying eyes: a calculated strategy that had helped to win the hand of wife Annie, who was close to Libbie and who had fallen for the dashing cavalry officer's abundant charms.

Despite his conquests on and off the battlefield, Yates was more modest than his regimental commander, whom he so highly admired. Despite being part of the Custer clique, Yates still maintained good relations, both professional and off-duty, with the anti-Custer officer corps faction led with such prideful contrarianism by Captain Benteen. Custer had chosen correctly, because Captain Yates was just the kind of hard-hitting officer to lead the advance down Medicine Tail Coulee with his battalion across the river and straight into the village.[23] To Custer, Yates was more than a model officer, but also a close friend. Thanks to his easy-going ways, Yates was also respected by the enlisted men, who so often detested officers. Sergeant John Ryan recalled how Yates stood out in the officer corps because he was "a good-natured officer and fond of a joke himself. . . ."[24] Ironically, Yates was now only leading the advance at this crucial moment because, as he penned in a March 18, 1866, letter to his wife, Custer boasted, "I procured Yates' appointment to the regular army" by applying his influence in high places, particularly the Secretary of War.[25]

In the battalion's lead just behind the headquarters staff, thirty-seven troopers of Company E steadily advanced down the coulee. Known as the crack Gray Horse Company, this "show company" of the 7th Cavalry surged closer to the ford at the head of Yates' battalion in leading the way. About to add his bugle calls to those trumpeters of the headquarters staff, Company E's George A. Moonie, a twenty-one-year-old Irishman from Boston and who had enlisted in March 1875, had his bugle ready to blow upon Custer's orders. Tom Custer's Company C, whose troopers rode sorrels (light reddish color), followed Company E, and then Company F, which included troopers like France-born Private Joseph Monroe, who never saw his Gallic homeland or home in Cincinnati, Ohio, again.

First Lieutenant Algernon Emory Smith, who was part of Custer's inner circle, commanded Company E's men on their gray horses. He had born in Newport, New York, in 1838. Smith was a Civil War veteran who possessed a fine education from Hamilton College in Clinton, New York. Now a married man who had taken the hand of the charming Nettie, Smith had ridden through the Cheyenne village along the Washita with his revolver blazing. Lieutenant Smith now expected to win another such victory along the Little Bighorn. A feisty fighter, Smith led the way in Company E's front, despite unable to lift his left arm because of an old Civil War wound. He should have garnered a permanent disability discharge because of the injury, or remained behind at Fort Abraham Lincoln, but this was not Smith's style. He was dedicated to his men and the regiment. All in all, it took considerable courage for the native New Yorker to continue to ride ever deeper down Medicine Tail Coulee and straight toward the Cheyenne village with such a physical limitation: a situation that should have been an unnerving prospect for him, considering that close-quarter combat was sure to erupt among the maze of lodges filling the river bottoms, after crossing the Little Bighorn.

Smith was assisted in now leading Company E's troopers during their greatest challenge to date by his second-in-command, Second Lieutenant James "Jack" Sturgis. While a member of a New York infantry regiment, Smith had served with distinction during the Civil War. He won a brevet rank of major for heroics during the attacks on Fort Wagner, which protected the harbor of Charleston, South Carolina, in July 1863, and Fort Fisher, North Carolina, in mid-January 1865. From Newport, New York, which was divided by the waters of West Canada Creek, Smith had led his troops with inspired leadership. At Fort Fisher on the Atlantic coast, he received the wound that almost cost him his life, leaving him unable to raise his left arm on sweltering June 25.

Meanwhile, Captain Yates's "Band Box Troop," Company F, continued to follow close behind Smith's Company E down the coulee, while riding horses (light bays) that were darker than Company E's gray horses. Custer no doubt hoped that the dust kicked up by so many horses, filling the coulee in a fine–grained cloud, might mask the diminutive number (barely 200) of the attackers. He hoped to make the Cheyenne believe that a far larger number of troopers now advanced down the coulee, and to sow the seeds of panic in the village.[26]

A Sioux warrior named Horned Horse described the shocking sight when suddenly "the head of Custer's column showed itself coming down a dry watercourse [Medicine Tail Coulee], which formed a narrow ravine, toward the river's edge."[27] Just after 4:00 p.m., the sharp notes slated down the coulee, echoing loudly down the coulee and over the Little Bighorn's placid waters. Custer had ordered the buglers to sound the charge, despite still being a good distance away from the ford. The blaring bugles mystified young Curley, who knew nothing about the white man's psychological warfare. As in the past, Custer now employed the sounding of the charge (although not actually charging) as a time-proven psychological weapon (like his regimental band playing "Garry Owen"—his favorite song—in the Washita attack as a psychological weapon that he had successfully utilized since the Civil War years) to spread fear in the Cheyenne village. A terrified Sioux woman married to Spotted Horn Bull described her fear: "From across the river I could hear the music of the bugle and could see the column of soldiers . . . march down to[ward] the river to where the attack was to be made."[28] Crow scout Curley never forgot how Custer "ordered the bugles to sound a charge, and moved on at the head of his column. . . ."[29] The Indians of the village remembered how "the blare of Custer's trumpets told the Sioux [and Cheyenne] of his approach."[30]

Since Medicine Tail Coulee had significantly widened during the dusty descent, it now offered an even more ideal avenue leading all the way to the river, and Custer knew that he could easily ford the river at this shallow crossing point. From tracks, Custer knew that this was an old buffalo crossing point, ensuring that the river banks were relatively low and posed no serious obstacles to charging horses. Best of all, at "that season of the year," in one Indian's words, "the water being very low" for an easy crossing at this point.[31]

Ironically, Custer's choice of advancing down the coulee's extensive length and then fording the river at the well-worn buffalo crossing paid other unexpected dividends. At first, the rising dust from the white mens' horses had initially caused some Indians, as during Custer's earlier approach toward the Little Bighorn Valley, to believe that another buffalo herd was approaching the river to cross in search of fresh grass and water to quench their thirst in this scorching weather.[32]

Custer's choice of Yates and his battalion (Keogh's battalion still advanced, second in line behind Yates) to lead the way down the coulee was a good one. Yates's companies (like Keogh's battalion) contained less-inexperienced men than several companies—G, H, and K—serving with Reno and Benteen, in one of the vexing paradoxes of Custer's last attack. As could be expected, Custer naturally wanted to share the glory with his good friend and top lieutenant (Yates), and of course brother Tom. Ironically, nearly a decade and a half before, these two close friends had first met when Custer was a lieutenant and Yates a sergeant. During the Civil War's early stages, they had faced not only a common opponent but also a stiff challenge in confronting the obstacle of a river before them: the sluggish Chickahominy, in the Virginia tidewater located more than 1,600 miles away from the Little Bighorn. In the Peninsula Campaign of 1862 during General George B. McClellan and his Army of the Potomac's ambitious, but doomed, bid to capture the Confederate capital of Richmond, Custer and Yates rose splendidly to the challenge on May 24. Shouting "give them hell," Custer had encouraged the bluecoat infantrymen (including Yates) across the brownish-hued river (unlike the pristine Little Bighorn) under a hot Rebel fire to reap another success on the Virginia Peninsula.[33]

The tactical requirement of charging across the Little Bighorn now must have seemed as easy as when the 7th Cavalry had ridden roughshod through the Washita River Valley to strike Black Kettle's Cheyenne village to win Custer's only success on the Great Plains. Revealing the pervasive, almost complacent, attitude of Custer and so many troopers (ironically a factor that helped lead to Reno's reversal), this five company offensive effort launched so confidently down Medicine Tail Coulee was now seemingly little more than an exciting game. To many 7th Cavalrymen, the waging of war against the Great Plains Indians was seen as a sporting event, especially because no serious resistance was now expected at the northern end of the nearly deserted village. The ever-elusive Indians seemingly could be now trapped in the level river bottoms at the village's northern end, because they seemed to be entirely at the mercy of Custer's steadily approaching five companies, which had never known defeat.

Precisely because relinquishing the initiative was not considered even a remote possibility and certainly not a tactical option at this point, Custer had seemingly won the game of bagging his opponent, whose mobile style of warfare had so long frustrated the 7th Cavalry. The Sioux had long demonstrated an unsurpassed skill in slipping away before the troopers could strike a knock out blow. Large villages, especially this one of such an unparalleled size, never remained intact for long, because of the pressing need of the Indians to move on in search of new grass for horses and more plentiful game for substinence. Nearly a decade of Great Plains experience, in the antithesis of the inflexible ways that the 7th Cavalry waged war, showed Custer that the Indians always fought as individuals without orders, discipline, or organization: the height of tactical flexibility according to the existing situation, unlike white soldiers, who had been trained to follow orders to the letter.

As Custer fully realized, to additionally bolster his confidence, his opponent's asymmetrical style of fighting minimized the chances for a stiff defense at the village's northern end, especially when hit by a surprise attack by all five companies. Even if a relatively few warriors somehow managed to rally and offered resistance at the village at the last minute, then Custer still felt confident that his opponent would quickly disperse and offer no significant resistance, especially when suddenly under attack from five companies, because the warriors who had faced Reno several miles away had not returned by this time: a factor that no doubt also partly caused him to dismiss the warnings from scouts of the immense size of the village that spanned several miles upriver.

Not only were almost all warriors now facing Reno far away, but also Custer and his two battalions were now headed straight toward the smallest tribal encampment, the Cheyenne. Custer correctly realized that he had "caught them napping" (ironically, this was literally the case, as some fighting men of the warrior societies had slept late after their big social dance that continued until dawn) at the village's northern end, which continued to be now vulnerable by the absence of warriors.

Consequently, Custer perhaps could now almost envision the inevitable dashing portraits of the celebrated victor of the Little Bighorn in newspapers across the land, if he secured a dramatic victory as anticipated. After all, Custer's heroic image of leading a bold cavalry attack had been emblazoned on the front cover of New York's *Harper's Weekly*, on May 19, 1864, to electrify the Northern people. Now, Custer was seemingly about to accomplish the same news-grabbing feat that would be broadcast widely across the United States. Indeed, he now seemed on the very threshold of once again being thrust into the national spotlight by a successful charge across the ford and straight into the Cheyenne village with all five companies.

Indeed, it now seemed as if the man and the moment had met. In the heady celebrations of a vibrant American people's progress during this glorious Centennial year, especially in the United States' first capital of Philadelphia, the confident American nation was waiting to celebrate a dramatic Custer victory to forever end the Indian Wars, which would be a gift just in time for the Fourth of July celebration. Not surprisingly in this pervasive national mood of exuberance, the American people also had complete faith in Custer and his crack 7th Cavalry to push aside so-called savages, who dared to challenge America's national destiny. After all, these Indians were commonly viewed as nothing more than irritating, gnat-like obstacles to national greatness. The confident people across America now fully expected Custer to win another smashing victory, as if he was still the famed boy general waging his hard-hitting style of war that had helped to pave the way to Appomattox.

Not unlike his regiment (which was widely considered to be more elite than was actually the case), and despite his well-honed tactical skills, Custer was still in truth a media creation, especially the New York newspapers, thanks to his so-called victory at the Washita. Even now, in the steady descent of his two battalions down Medicine Tail Coulee, he was still very much trapped inside his heroic image of the dashing cavalier that he could never escape—even in slightly balding middle age. In consequence, Custer now felt the pressure of having become the media darling that America had created at such a young age. Therefore, the native Ohioan now had to live up to the lofty image that an entire generation (from private citizens to top military leadership) had long expected from their golden boy of Civil War fame.

Now with a receding hairline, a light-complexioned face "somewhat worn" from so many military campaigns, and with hair newly cut short for this summer campaign, the thirty-six-year-old Custer had embarked upon his greatest challenge while past his prime. Worst of all, his military expertise was in the art of conventional warfare rather than Indian warfare, but he was now blending the two when they could not have been more different. Seemingly, Custer was now steadily pulled farther down the coulee not only by fate, but also by the media hype and his wide readership, especially in *Galaxy Magazine* (his last article had been recently completed while encamped on the Tongue River), as a popular writer across America. He was about to engage in the battle to determine the fate of not only the Sioux people but also the 7ᵗʰ Cavalry , which now hung in the balance. A mix of the past legacies, high expectations, soaring ambitions, and destiny itself now pointed the way down Medicine Tail Coulee for Custer.

As when he had so aggressively led the "Wolverines" of his crack Michigan Cavalry Brigade, one of the North's finest cavalry commands, to one victory after another, he was now relying on the "relentless power" of a typical Custer attack. In his adrenaline rush of engaging, in still another battle in which he felt that he was sure to win, and like brother Tom, who was also a gambler by nature (on the battlefield, in the bedroom, or at the poker table), Custer remained blissfully unmindful of his command's long list of liabilities. Most of the enlisted men lacked the necessary experience and firing skills to defeat Indians, especially a good many city boys. Recent immigrants, like Ireland-born Private John D. Barry of Company I, who hailed from major northeastern urban centers, now pushed down the coulee with far more misplaced confidence than combat prowess. Barry had enlisted in Boston in late September 1875. While leading the advance, Custer also seemingly overlooked the obvious that he now wore a wide "white sombrero," with the right side turned up in a jaunty manner: a dashing style that enhanced his visibility not only to his men but also to experienced warriors, including sharp-eyed hunters who could shot down a bounding black-tail deer or antelope at long-range with ease, unlike a good many troopers in blue.[34]

Custer always led the way, and the descent upon the Medicine Tail Coulee Ford was no different. He had taken the usual risks in leading the Washita attack, when he "would allow no one to get ahead of him," wrote an amazed scout.[35] Custer, therefore, had been fortunate not to have been killed at the Washita, like Captain Louis McLane Hamilton, the promising grandson of Alexander Hamilton, who had been hit in attempting to keep up (an impossibility) with Custer.[36]

Indeed, to his relatively few opponents in the valley below, Custer's low-crowned and broad-brimmed white hat, not to mention his large trademark red scarf around his neck, which was worn as when he had led his Michigan boys to glory, served as a white beacon at the column's head: an ideal target to sharp-eyed Indian marksmen. Even Custer's thoroughbred sorrel mare "Vic" (just remounted by Custer after the older brown horse "Dandy" had been left behind after his observation of the village from the Crow's Nest) was also distinctive in its markings and overall appearance, standing out from the other 7th Cavalry mounts. Custer should have realized that the relatively few fighting men in the valley below were veteran warriors who possessed a skill unmatched by the whites, including greedy buffalo hunters who killed with such a merciless impunity for profit.[37]

Custer and his men were about to discover other harsh realities. In the words of one lucky 7th Cavalry survivor of the Little Bighorn, the Sioux were "better armed, better prepared, and as well, if not better, led" on June 25.[38] As usual, when conditioned to so many past successes, Custer remained confident during his descent down Medicine Tail Coulee. A survivor of many close calls that seemed to defy the too-often vindictive Gods of War (especially to overly successful leaders who casually tempted fate from hubris), Custer had no fear of death as demonstrated on almost too many past fields of strife to count. Annie Yates, the foremost battalion commander's pretty, blue-eyed wife with a dual romantic and intellectual bent, had recently told Custer of a haunting nightmare. Hailing from a leading Philadelphia family, she had dreamed of Custer getting shot in the head by an Indian warrior. When Annie told Custer of her vivid nightmare, he was amused. His fatalistic response revealed his sense of optimism, daredevil qualities, and lively personality. Stoically, he merely said: "I cannot die before my time, and [then] if by a bullet in the head—Why not?"[39] Custer, who often teased Annie like a sister, should have listened to Yates's insightful wife. He failed to heed the ominous warning, believing that his own destiny and star were more powerful than this dark portent. An open-minded thinker who confounded many eager suitors before her marriage to Yates, this rather remarkable and smart army wife often relied on fortune tellers and believed in the words of prophesy, when combined with her own intuition.[40]

Even now, Custer still remembered the words of the psychic who he had visited in the bustle of New York City. This psychic had confirmed what he already knew to be true from the Civil War years: "I was always fortunate since the hour of my birth and always would be. My guardian angel has clung to my side since the day I left the cradle," as Custer emphasized with his trademark confidence.[41]

Now, this fabled good fortune seemed once again to be smiling on Custer by sending him and his troopers farther down the coulee and ever closer to the undefended Ford and village located on the flank an enemy encampment. Clouds of dust rose higher to reveal the movement of five companies to additional Cheyenne and Sioux. All the while, the sun beat down hot, and the fine grains of dust choked Custer's men on this blistering afternoon. They were about to meet the enemy on his own terms, and on his own territory, too far from Fort Abraham Lincoln. Weary troopers were drenched in sweat, which mixed with a fine layer of dust to cake uniforms that now looked almost more yellow than blue. After having ridden for so long today, the throats of the troopers were parched from the intense heat, creeping fear, and anxious nervousness about striking a blow on a large village.

As usual in going headlong into action, Custer was accompanied by his faithful personal headquarters staff, which consisted of some of the regiment's most qualified men. This was additional evidence that Custer now advanced with all five companies in the attempt to charge into the Cheyenne village with his entire command. Unlike at the beginning of the attack on the Washita village, Custer had no bandmaster to order "Give us 'Garry Owen,'" (his lucky talisman) or

"Yankee Doodle," as when attacking Rebels in the previous war. Custer now must have thought about the Washita, which had garnered headlines that appeared in the *New York Herald*: "DECISIVE BATTLE WITH THE INDIANS." All the while, trumpeters Vose (Chief Trumpeter), McElroy, and Dose, along with the bugles of Companies E and F, immediately behind them, continued to blow their notes to unnerve the opponent.

One of the great myths of the battle was that Custer remained safely behind the advance of Yates's battalion and that Keogh's battalion, after having taken a stationary on the high ground and far from the ford, almost as disinterested as if forcing a crossing was tactically insignificant. This popular misconception has fueled the additional myth that this advance (Custer's most important one this afternoon) down Medicine Tail Coulee Ford was nothing more than an insignificant feint: the absolute most un-Custer-like of his actions and entirely uncharacteristic of all realistic possibilities under the circumstances, when decisive offensive action was most of all needed to reverse the day's fortunes. After all, Custer remained to this moment one of the most aggressive cavalry commanders in the history of the American military.

Capable Headquarters Staff

In this crisis situation, Custer was wisely relying on a highly capable staff, forging a tight bond that was evident in the descent down the coulee. Even before he won his brigadier general's stars in the Civil War, he had relied upon capable staff officers. And now, he depended upon his staff more than ever before, because there was literally no tomorrow for the 7th Cavalry. Trusting in his abilities and those of his men, Custer continued to confidently lead the advance beside brother Tom, who essentially acted as his chief of staff, toward the shallow ford with his trusty headquarters staff at the head of his five advancing companies. These talented professional military men were some of the regiment's most useful soldiers, and Custer appreciated that fact to the fullest. Representing the regiment's command and control center, the staff was now protected by a trusty honor guard of crack troopers. This honor guard most likely consisted of a dependable lieutenant and hand-picked troopers of Yates's Company F, because Yates' battalion advanced just behind the headquarters staff. This honor guard excluded a recent "showman" from a New York City circus, an inexperienced Private William A. Lossee, who had enlisted in late September 1875 and was in his mid-twenties. All the officers' watches were synchronized to display the same time as the regimental commander for better coordination and unity of action on a fast-paced battleground once fighting erupted. Some of the 7th Cavalry's top officers were now part of Custer's staff, representing an elite cadre.

Like growing up in Ohio, the three Custer brothers were all together with the headquarters staff, their destinies now joined together as one. They now advanced in the forefront of the advance down the dusty coulee. Custer's staff naturally included brother Tom, who the lieutenant colonel trusted like no other officer, and most likely Boston "Bos" Custer, who was the butt of so many jokes by his older brothers. Born on Halloween 1848, sickly "Bos" had come west to improve his health! Six years younger than his more famous but less decorated brother, who once taunted an unlucky opponent during a game of chance and skill how "relationships don't count in poker," Tom served as Custer's aide-de-camp, advisor, and confidant while riding by his brother's side. Whenever an order needed to be completed without delay, Custer counted on Tom to accomplish the task efficiently: an invaluable right-hand man. In advancing down the coulee by his brother's side, Tom was now stylishly dressed in a buckskin shirt and wore a broad-brimmed white hat.

Tom continued faithful staff service to his brother from the Civil War years. He was shorter, a bachelor more popular with the ladies (white or red), coarser in behavior and with a wilder streak, a better shot, and smaller in build compared to his older, more lanky brother, whose natural rambunctiousness had been nipped in the bud by a happy marriage. Tom had served capably on Custer's staff during 1864–1865, gaining invaluable experience. The captain's hair was "not so golden" as the lieutenant colonel's, as if reminding everyone that Tom had been the black sheep of the family and lived under his brother's giant large shadow that he could never step out from, despite his own impressive military record. Nevertheless, these sibling dynamics had fueled a healthy rivalry, pushing each man to excel. Like his brother, Captain Thomas Ward Custer had been born in New Rumley, Ohio, near the Pennsylvania border. Tom possessed more of the Irish traits of his Scotch–Irish mother, Maria Ward Kilpatrick, than George, who was more like his father's German side. As during the later years of the Civil War, Tom remained close to his older brother's side in active campaigning, especially during offensive operations. Throughout the 1876 Campaign, he continued to offer sage advice and council to his older brother, because of his well-known good judgment. The left cheek of Tom's handsome face still carried the scars of a Confederate bullet. He was known to the Cheyenne as "Buffalo Calf," while his older brother was known as "Strong Arm," which accidently coincided with his middle name.

Besides hunting together (when one tried to outdo each other), the two brothers had often engaged in scouting and reconnaissance far ahead of the main column, revealing the close bond that made them inseparable. Quite simply, the Custer brothers were a team whose well-honed abilities matched their high-octane energy level. They had charged together side by side into the heart of the Cheyenne village along the Washita. For such reasons, Tom had made his will out in summer 1873, and his mother was about to inherit his worldly possessions.

Since the campaign's beginning, the more decorated Custer brother (two Medals of Honor) had been assigned from his Company C, whose troopers now advanced down the coulee behind Company E. A devoted reader like Libbie, who was extremely fond of him, Tom was a fan of the popular works of Mark Twain (Samuel Clemens). Captain Custer's old company was now commanded by Second Lieutenant Henry Moore Harrington, in his late twenties. By any measure, he was a fine officer and steady as a rock. Now leading Company C because Tom served on the brother's staff, Lieutenant Harrington, about to receive his baptismal fire, was especially nervous, believing that he was fated to be shortly captured and tortured to death.

The importance of the noncommissioned officers, especially sergeants, who filled the leadership gap, was to make Harrington's job easier and his inexperience less of a liability. Like other companies, Company C included quite a few Irish troopers, who still loved the Emerald Isle. Sergeant Jeremiah Finley had migrated from County Tipperary, Ireland, to the United States in 1860. He had been long one of the steady influences of Company C, including this sultry afternoon deep in the Montana Territory. The Custer brothers had complete trust in the dark-haired Harrington, despite the fact that he had yet to see combat as a company commander. Wearing a stylish buckskin coat, or perhaps even one of the popular firemen's shirts, like other officers, Harrington was part of Custer's charmed inner circle.

A physician's son from a wealthy family of Ontario, Adjutant William "Willie" Winer Cooke was a tall and trim Canadian with outsized and luxuriant mutton-chop dark whiskers known as Dundreary sideburns. He likewise rode down Medicine Tail Coulee near Custer as the regimental adjutant, who had been at the heart of Custer's inner circle since the regiment's formation. Second only to Tom, Custer depended upon Lieutenant Cooke, age thirty and the well-educated son of two wealthy Upper Canada families, to obey and relay orders of importance. With a superb build and standing more than six feet tall, the popular Cooke was a dependable and highly competent staff officer: another excellent right-hand man for Custer. One of the 7th Cavalry's best marksman and finest horsemen from having served in a New York Cavalry regiment in the eastern theater (like Custer) during the Civil War, he was known as the "Queen's Own," having been born a British citizen in Canada. Adjutant Cooke was also called "Cookie" by his friends, including of course the Custer brothers. Distinguished by lengthy, dark whiskers that hung down to his upper chest that gave him a distinctive look, Cooke was a seasoned veteran whose judgment was widely respected. In the past, Custer had presented him with the grim task of ending his wife's life with his legendary marksmanship, if she was ever about to be captured by Indians. He was appointed regimental adjutant in December 1866, when the 7th Cavalry was first organized. During the brother's war, Cooke had won promotion for valor while serving in the1864 campaign, when Grant's Army of the Potomac was focused on capturing Petersburg, Virginia, just south of Richmond. The Custer brothers and the well-spoken (near-perfect English) adjutant were close. However, despite his social skills and charm, this magnificent Canadian was less capable with regard to some manipulative American women, whose well-honed wiles made him more vulnerable than on a battlefield, where he excelled.

Blowing his bugle as part of Custer's own unique brand of psychological warfare to unnerve opponents in the valley below and mounted on a gray horse like all of the regiment's trumpeters, blue-eyed and fair-haired Chief Trumpeter Henry Voss also now served as a member of Custer's staff. Born in Germany, he had been appointed to this position from a lowly private's rank on May 8, 1876. Voss was every inch of a fighter, thanks partly to a hot temper. He had even assaulted one of the regiment's saddlers (a sergeant no less).

Also with Custer's staff in the advance down Medicine Tail Coulee was Trumpeter Henry C. Dose. He had been born in Holstein, Germany, in 1848, when liberal revolution was in the air. At only age twenty-five, he had enlisted in Company G on February 1, 1875. Dose was the father to two children, Charles and Hattie, who were being raised by his regimental laundress-wife, Elizabeth Fettis. A Company

G member, Dose had been assigned to the staff as Custer's trumpeter orderly.

Trumpeter Thomas Francis McElroy, born in 1844 in Neigh, Ireland, and who migrated to America in 1863, also now blew his bugle as ordered by Custer to create panic in the Cheyenne village. A Civil War veteran with blue eyes and a light complexion who still spoke with an Emerald Isle brogue, the Irishman was in the forefront in the advancing ranks that moved relentlessly onward down the broad coulee. Meanwhile, Color Sergeant Robert H. Hughes, born in Ireland in 1840, was also in the forefront close to Custer during the advance, when the afternoon heat and humidity were stifling. Hughes sweated under the blazing summer sun like everyone else now pushing down Medicine Tail Coulee, which now seemed as hot as an oven. Especially confident because he knew that Custer was still proud of never losing a battle flag, going all the way back to the Civil War, the brave Irishman now "carried Custer's battle flag" of his headquarters with a firm grip. This colorful banner was half red (on top) and half blue (on bottom), with the design of the two white crossed sabers of the traditional cavalry insignia.

Leading the way down the coulee before the headquarters staff and bouncing up and down not far from Custer's side, this swallow-tailed guidon was another most distinctive banner above the mounted column. This unique flag had served as Custer's personal standard from the Civil War years. As a general officer (brevet rank earned during the Civil War), Lieutenant Colonel Custer possessed the official right by regulations to fly his own personal flag, distinguished by two white stars of a major general's rank, at the column's head. Taller than the average troops that served him well as the flag-bearer, especially when mounted, Color Sergeant Hughes was a Dubliner with brown hair and blue eyes. He had enlisted in the 7th Cavalry during fall 1873. Hughes was a father of three and husband to wife Annie, who prayed in vain for his safe return. Some troopers had seen an ill omen when this "headquarters' flag" had been blown down twice within minutes at the site of an empty Sun Dance lodge on the Rosebud, just after Custer's command separated from Terry on June 22.

Reliable and efficient, Sergeant Major William H. Sharrow was one of four noncommissioned officers who now served on Custer's staff. Toughened early in life, he had been born at sea, having this only unique distinction in the 7th Cavalry. Born in 1843, Sharrow had grown up in York, northeast England, and still spoke with traces of his English accent. Sharrow had been detailed from Company F to serve as the regimental color bearer: a position of honor and respect.

Of German descent and noted for a Teutonic meticulousness, Sergeant John Vickory (his actual name was John H. Groesbeck who had been born in Toronto, Canada, in July 1847) was not carrying the regimental colors. This prized flag had been stored away back with the pack train that was now bringing up the rear behind Benteen's three companies (D, H, and K). Ironically, for the most famous battle fought in the 7th Cavalry's history, the regimental colors, with the design of a large American eagle in flight position in the flag's center, were not unfurled.

With a dark complication, brown hair, and blue eyes, this battle– hardened sergeant rode tall in the saddle at five feet, ten inches, while moving down the coulee. Like Custer's other most trustworthy men in the advance's forefront, Sergeant Vickory was also a Civil War veteran. Vickory's family had moved from Upper Canada to New York during the antebellum period. During fall 1862, Vickory had first served in a New York artillery regiment. He deserted his regiment, and then changed his name to John Vickory. This identity change allowed him to re-enlist in a Massachusetts cavalry regiment in May 1864 to collect the lucrative enlistment bounty. Instead of the silk regimental colors, Vickory now carried the cherished yellow battle flag that Custer had fought under, while commanding his cavalry division during the Civil War.

Faithful orderlies were also part of Custer's headquarters staff, including two other Custer boys who were both civilians: the naïve and religious-minded Boston "Bos" Custer, also born in New Rumley, like his two brothers, and nephew Harry "Autie" Armstrong Reed, who had been born in Monroe, Michigan. "Bos" had forsaken his duties to the rear to join the column just in time for its descent down Medicine Tail Coulee. The stepdaughter of Custer's father, Emmanuel, Lydia Ann Kirkpatrick, had married David Reed. Only age eighteen and officially assigned to quartermaster duties, "Autie" should have stayed safely on the *Far West* as Custer desired, because of his youth and inexperience. However, Reed, Custer's oldest sister's son, had forced his soft-hearted uncle, who admired his spunk, to relent. Like "Autie," Custer thought very highly of his youngest brother "Bos." In fact, Custer had instructed the *Far West's* captain, Grant Marsh, to keep the youngest Custer aboard, but the young man would have none of it. Custer had written glowingly to his wife, "I am proud of the way he is beginning life" by connecting himself to the regiment in a civilian capacity in 1871. As mentioned, an honor guard of crack troopers continued to ride down the coulee near the Custer brothers, a true fighting clan, to protect the regimental commander and his staff.[42]

Assistant Surgeon George Edwin Lord, the aspiring adopted son of a Congregational minister, was another respected member of Custer's headquarters staff. Born in Boston in mid-February 1846, he had graduated from Bowdoin College (BA in 1866), Brunswick, Maine. He then graduated from the Chicago Medical School (today's Northwestern University) in March 1871. Not long after graduation, he had promptly enlisted as assistant surgeon in the 7th Cavalry in late April 1871, casting his fate with Custer as now in advancing ever closer to the Cheyenne village.

However, for facing his greatest challenge, Lord was now in physically poor shape. In fact, he should have been left behind at Fort Abraham Lincoln as Custer, who always pushed his men hard in active campaigning, fully realized. On June 23, Dr. Lord had suffered from a serious "indisposition" (the so-called "trail colic") that had plagued him in the past. Custer, consequently, had kindly presented the assistant surgeon with the sensible option to remain behind. However, knowing that casualties were inevitable and with duty calling, Lord was determined to go not only with the command but also in the advance with Custer's personal headquarters staff in the attack on the Cheyenne village: still another display of moral courage in the 7th Cavalry's ranks on a day when it was abundant.[43]

Also near the column's head as part of the headquarters staff was the most unorthodox member of Custer's staff: newspaperman Mark Kellogg. Hailing from a leading La Crosse, Wisconsin, pioneer family, he was now writing for the *Bismarck Tribune*. Kellogg was an experienced newsman with literary talent and soaring ambitions. He seemed almost cursed by a long-lasting streak of bad luck, because plans never seemed to go quite right for him, despite his best efforts. The ever-optimistic Kellogg now hoped to break his hard luck once and for all at the Little Bighorn. Also a correspondent for America's premier newspaper, the *New York Herald*, he now hoped to get the "biggest scoop of the century." Hitting a home run with an unprecedented journalistic scoop, he now envisioned being the first to broadcast the exciting story of Custer's latest victory: a proper analogy because Kellogg was also a passionate baseball player at Fort Abraham Lincoln like other 7th Cavalry members.

The forty-three-year-old Kellogg, a father of two daughters and married since May 1861 to wife Mattie (or Martha), sensed that he was about to write the biggest story of his life. Kellogg had repeatedly missed his big breaks in life, business ventures, jobs, and politics: a fateful situation that explained why the hard-luck newspaperman now rode down the coulee and toward a grim fate: "I go with Custer and will be at the death." So many unexpected twists and turns in Kellogg's life had forced him to scratch for everything to make a living, while hoping that his hard luck would turn at the Little Bighorn. If Kellogg expected some of Custer's Luck to rub off on him, then he was badly mistaken.

With an eye for promotion, Custer had been the first to make the necessary arrangements to secure this *Bismarck Tribune* reporter to tell the story about his latest military success in the last great battle of the Indian Wars as he closed a chapter in America's saga. While riding down the coulee, Kellogg might have wondered about the strange destiny had brought him in a tragic sojourn of no return. What better story was there than the saga of America's former "boy hero" leading a successful charge to reap another victory as during the Civil War?[44]

Ironically, after moving to Bismarck, the territorial capital in the Dakota Territory, Kellogg had joked in a boasting letter that seemed to tempt fate, if not the ever-capricious Gods of War: "I have cruised in all directions excepting west; and as my acquaintance with the Sioux who occupy the country in that direction [because] I have no particular wish to seek game in the happy hunting grounds"[45]

Near the campaign's opening, a confident Kellogg also empha-sized in writing how the greatest challenge to the 7th Cavalry now came from "Sitting Bull's band of mountain Unkapapas [sic], num-bering about 1,500 warriors, well-armed, who are a mischievous, devilish set [and now] [t]he red devils will hunt their holes," before the powerful expeditionary force.[46] However, from his earlier scout to the Tongue River, Reno had estimated 800 warriors (the figure that Boston Custer quoted to his mother in his June 21 letter), but that number was revised upward to 1,500 warriors just to be on the safe side. As Custer and his troops were about to discover to their shock, the 1,500 figure was far too low.[47] These overall numbers of warriors had changed quickly, and faster than anyone realized, especially in part because of the steady flow from the reservations. Indian agents, who secured funds and resources based on high numbers under their con-trol, failed to report the volume of this flow to military authorities out of self-interest. Nearly 1,000 warriors had been concentrated around Sitting Bull and other revered leaders by early June, but thousands of Indians had poured in an exodus from the reservations to swell warrior numbers in the thousands since that time. In this sense, the giant encampment along the Little Bighorn had reached unprecedented proportions in stealthy fashion. A host of intelligence failures, far more than Custer's tactical decisions, paved the way to disaster.[48]

Kellogg became more realistic as the campaign lengthened and became more demanding on men and horses. In mid-June, after Custer's men had recently found a lone grave of an unlucky Company L, 7th Cavalry, sergeant who had been killed in summer 1873, a sober Kellogg suddenly became more reflective and philosophical, understanding how his life was in the hands of God and fate:

> This brave fellow died here surrounded only by his brave comrades, hundreds, perhaps thousands of miles [if from Europe] from mother or sister, or the home of his childhood. Life is beset with hidden footfalls. When we least expect it death approaches. . . Shall we leave beneath the sod of the almost limitless prairies the forms of any of those now with us, who are so full of life and hope?[49]

Clearly, in reflecting upon fate, Kellogg was also prophetic about his own fast-approaching demise along the Little Bighorn.

Kellogg's growing apprehension was an exception to the rule. The men who Custer now had around him on his headquarters staff and part of his inner circle were optimistic about winning a success, because their leader had won so many past battles. They now reflected their commander's optimism. In a close-knit group of mostly experienced officers advancing at the column's head, these trusty staff members of Custer's headquarters continued to lead the way down the coulee that they were convinced was not a natural avenue of no return.[50] All in all, the regiment's headquarters staff was an impressive collection of talented men. One Company C private concluded, "It would be difficult to find a finer set of officers in the service of any country."[51]

All the while, Yates's battalion of well-equipped troopers followed close behind the headquarters staff, with Company E leading the way down Medicine Tail Coulee. Then came the troopers of Company C (Tom Custer's old company), which was followed by Company F. In advancing ever closer to the seemingly all-but-abandoned Cheyenne village and the obscure ford that had suddenly become strategic in this remote corner of the Montana Territory, tension among the troopers steadily increased. Despite Reno's repulse, victory now seemed inevitable for Custer's contingent pouring with increased momentum down the coulee, because it gradually widened and was no longer less ravine-like. Perhaps some troopers already envisioned the ceremony at Fort Abraham Lincoln when the glorious name of "Little Bighorn" would be placed on the beautiful regimental banner, just as "Gettysburg" had once decorated the regimental flags of Custer's Michigan troopers.

Serving as Yates's orderly after having been assigned from Company F, Private Edward Henry Pickard was also in the forefront of the relentless advance under the searing sun. Born in Boston and having dreamed of becoming a soldier since he was a small boy in Boston (instead of going to sea, like so many young New Englanders consumed with wanderlust), the twenty-two-year-old Pickard was also optimistic about future success. He had been told by "old timers" of the Washita fight "that about all there was to it was to surprise an Indian village, charge through it, shooting the Indians as they ran, and then divide the tanned buffalo robes and beaded moccasins [spoils of war], before burning the lodges and destroying supplies. . . ."[52]

Clearly, a great surprise and a host of the ugliest of realities now awaited the more than 200 troopers of Custer's two battalions: a fact entirely unimaginable to them at this time. Nevertheless, the dust-covered cavalrymen continued to advance closer to the ford with confidence and with unity of purpose, while their colorful flags flew under the Montana sun that never seemed so hot. Although "few of his troopers or officers could claim any Indian-fighting experience, Custer still expected them to acquit themselves proudly when the time came," which was now coming very soon along the Little Bighorn.[53]

Most of all, when about to enter still another battle, Custer was delighted to have so many family members by his side, especially brother Tom. Custer had been proven prophetic in his November 1864 estimation in a letter that "Tom, with a little more experience will make a valuable and most efficient aide."[54] No 7th Cavalry officer was more faithful or trustworthy than Tom, who was indeed his brother's keeper on June 25—continuing a guardian role from their Civil War days. Back in March 1866, a triumphant Custer had been ecstatic when his younger brother had gained an officer's commission in the postwar army, concluding in his letter to Libbie: "So the 'Custer's luck' has again prevailed."[55] However, that fabled luck was about to change forever at an old buffalo ford called Medicine Tail Coulee, and when least expected.

The Initial Response

Confirming what Custer and Trumpeter Martin had seen from the higher ground, when the comatose village was first targeted with high expectations for success, White Shield revealed the complete vulnerability of the Cheyenne camp and the extent of Custer's golden tactical opportunity, after he had quickly returned to the northernmost village from fishing in the river. In his own words: "When I reached camp, all the men were gone," to fight Reno far to the south.[56] Fully prepared to sacrifice what she loved most in life for the preservation of her people, White Shield's proactive mother now assisted the young warrior beyond just words of advice. She played a timely forgotten support role that other women fulfilled in assisting young Great Plains fighters, which has been often overlooked by white historians, who had underemphasized the importance of family dynamics in fueling the warriors' fighting spirit during the supreme crisis situation on the afternoon of June 25: "my mother was leading my war horse around, down in front of the lodge, waiting for me. I bridled my horse and said to my mother, 'Where is my war shirt?' She said that a man [Mad Wolf] had just been here who took it to wear in the fight."[57]

White Shield was a battle-hardened veteran (the son of Spotted Wolf) who had helped to defeat Crook's bluecoats with the large number of his Indian allies at the Rosebud on June 17. Initially unknown to White Shield was the fact that Two Moons and his Cheyenne had ridden south to fight Reno at least a half an hour, and perhaps as long as forty minutes, beforehand. An Oglala warrior who spoke fluent Cheyenne and was visiting the Cheyenne village, White Cow Bull, age twenty-eight, had remained beside his good Cheyenne friends Roan Bear and Bobtail Horse to guard the sacred Buffalo Head at the Medicine Lodge: a sacred responsibility. They had deeply felt the extent of the northern village's vulnerability down to their bones even before the sighting of Custer's column. Here, at the sacred "buffalo hat lodge" at which Roan Bear served as the primary guardian, they had shared their thoughts about the crackling gunfire and the progress of the distant battle raging to the south and its implications.

All of a sudden, upon hearing the blasting of Custer's bugles that he had ordered blown for maximum psychological effect in the hope of causing the greatest possible consternation and fear in the village, Bobtail Horse was shocked by an unnerving sight upon peering east. With the bluecoats advancing across the higher ground to the east opposite Medicine Tail Coulee Ford, he first saw this new threat that had so suddenly emerged like the arrival of a summer thunderstorm: large numbers of confident pony soldiers advancing with flags flying. Jumping to his feet in shock and instinctively knowing what now had to be done, Bobtail Horse shouted, "They are coming this way! Across the ford! We must stop them!"[58]

In such a true crisis situation, these three experienced warriors knew most of all that the best defense was to take the offensive as they had been taught since children, which was the best way to defend their village and people. Not even the solemn responsibilities of guarding the sacred Buffalo Head and its revered medicine lodge were sufficient to deter an immediate effort to defend the ford. Quite simply, the warrior responsibility of defending the village and the people even superseded the mission of protecting the sacred Buffalo Head. Such a flexible response partly explained the survival of the Cheyenne as a people for centuries, despite so many enemies who had long wanted to exterminate the Cheyenne people like a surrounded band of buffalo.

Shaken, but not unnerved, by the sight of so many bluecoats advancing down the coulee and heading straight toward the ford in overwhelming numbers, these few warriors now at the Cheyenne village busily prepared for their greatest challenge to date. These bluecoat intruders had to be met head-on at the ford, before another Washita disaster became a harsh reality along the Little Bighorn. Therefore, undeterred by the shocking sight of Custer's seemingly unstoppable advance, they grabbed their weapons. They then attempted to find their horses for the dash east to somehow defend Medicine Tail Coulee Ford before it was too late, despite being so few in number, and against all odds for success.[59]

White Shield responded to the new threat with alacrity, like White Cow Bull who was about to mount his favorite horse, an iron-gray gelding. From the low ground of the Cheyenne village nestled in the timbered river bottoms, and not far from the sacred Buffalo Medicine Lodge, White Shield continued to be astounded by what he saw on the high ground opposite the ford. Looking east to the open terrain above the wide mouth of Medicine Tail Coulee, the stunned Cheyenne warriors obtained a better view of their opponent during their steady approach. As he explained: "While I was dressing myself and telling my mother which way to go, I looked up and saw soldiers" on their big horses coming down the Medicine Tail Coulee in overwhelming numbers.[60] Even Sergeant John Ryan, who possessed the Celtic–Gaelic love for horse racing long after his parents had migrated from County Tipperary, Ireland, lamented how the 7th Cavalry possessed "heavy cavalry horses" that had long made chasing Indians, who rode smaller and faster horses, a futile exercise.[61]

Moving relentlessly toward this village were seven distinct groups of attackers (both battalions but acting as one in tactically and in overall offensive terms), heading toward the ford with determined resolve and colorful banners waving in the sunshine.[62] A stunned White Shield marveled at the sight of the bluecoats' disciplined order (so un–Indian like), and the advance of many troopers on the backs of such large horses of multiple colors. Appearing more vivid, these colors now shined and glistened off the sweating horses of Custer's troopers in the intense summer heat. He watched the fast-approaching pony "soldiers in seven groups (companies)" moving relentlessly toward the ford in a confidant manner: "One company could be seen a long way off [since their] horses were pretty white," in the words of White Shield, who had sighted the grayish horses of Company E, Yates' Battalion.[63]

From White Shield's stated observations and other evidence, Custer had divided both Yates's and Keogh's battalions into thirds (the headquarters contingent was the seventh group) for six separate groups of troopers to allow for Custer to make a staggered attack in depth in seven successive waves. Custer's unconventional deployment in successive waves made good tactical sense because of the descent down the coulee early on was along a narrow front, before the coulee gradually widened into a broad expanse of open terrain. The advancing ranks of the troopers were now fully extended as the coulee widened to a great length of open ground in the flats at the coulee's mouth.

Partly because he had been initially more exposed on the open, high ground above the coulee's mouth, Custer's tactical plan also diffused the front's length to minimize losses that would have inevitably come with a more concentrated, or traditional, assault formation of a massed column, if and when fired upon just in case of an ambush in the timbered river bottoms that just lay ahead: a distinct tactical possibility that no doubt flashed through Custer's mind because of the seemingly complete serenity of the Cheyenne village. As verified by a good many Indian participants, what was most significant about Custer's last advance was the fact that all five companies of Yates's and Keogh's battalions advanced as one and descended toward the ford with the intent of charging into the Cheyenne village to redeem the day's fortunes.[64]

To the Mouth of Medicine Tail Coulee

The level of absolute shock experienced by the Cheyenne upon first observing the avalanche of bluecoat pony soldiers descending Medicine Tail Coulee revealed the success of Custer's bold plan of catching his opponent by surprise. Conversely, and as could be expected in approaching a large Indian village, Custer's men, even veterans, felt greater tension upon advancing ever near to their target. At this point, some troopers, especially the rookies, might have well lost their once lofty confidence.

Perhaps some of Custer's men now thought about how much had changed (especially after Reno's repulse) since they first heard the bravado of the ever-confident Tom Custer, when this ambitious expedition rode out of Fort Abraham Lincoln. At that time, he had shouted how a "single company of that [column] can lick the whole Sioux nation." Now, the troopers, including so many inexperienced men in their first battle, now eyed the sight before them in the wooded river valley below with more nervousness, because even more of the Cheyenne village gradually came into view and a larger number of lodges were revealed. Clearly, this village was much larger than anyone had expected. Anxiety increased and sweat continued to pour down the dust-covered troopers amid the heightened tension that continued to increase along with the day's intense heat. "Bos" Custer and Harry Armstrong Reed—the two novices of the Custer clan who had deserted their assigned duties and positions to the rear to join Custer, so as not to miss the fun and glory—no doubt now had some second thoughts about what they had thought would be nothing more than a "colorful adventure."[65]

From higher ground to the rear a good distance from Custer's column, after having been left behind as a packer when the last ammunition had been distributed (instead of being a messenger to Benton and Reno, as alleged), civilian scout John "Jack" C. Lockwood knew that Custer was nearing his target because of rising dust and blaring bugles. In his words, "I [now] could see the five companies moving together in line, all abreast with General Custer in the lead."[66]

As Custer realized at this point, this tactic of using all of his troops in a flank attack was the only possibility for fully exploiting the tactical situation, especially because no better tactical option remained to reverse the day's fortunes and win a decisive success. In this regard, Custer's experience and tactical instincts were right on target, and he sought to exploit the golden opportunity that lay before him.[67] After his recent humiliation by President Grant and his corrupt administration of self-serving cronies, Custer continued to prove that he "would not hesitate to take the greatest risks to redeem himself," in Trooper Taylor's words.[68]

Company C, part of Yates's battalion, and Tom Custer's company of troopers on sorrels (like Company K, now with Benteen's battalion) that he had long groomed with personal, if not loving, care, was one of the finest companies that now surged down the coulee. With an average age of twenty-seven, which was two years older than the regimental average, these were generally inexperienced men (including one private with only six month's service) because the average service experience was only two years. Company C's troopers (along with Companies E and F of Yates's battalion) continued to advance toward the ford and the village just beyond it with increasing trepidation. Interestingly, this company contained the highest percentage of immigrants, primarily from Ireland and Germany, with thirty men from foreign lands.[69]

Riding not far from Englishman Private Jeremiah Shea, born in London, with gray eyes and brown hair, and having enlisted in September 1875, a Russian trooper of Company C continued to advance toward the ford. It was the Russian who now seemed most out of place at the Little Bighorn, instead of serving in a Cossack regiment in his native homeland. A proud Slav from Mother Russia with penetrating blue eyes, Private Ygnatz Stungewitz, a former clerk in his late twenties from New York City's crime-ridden streets and ethnic ghettos, had enlisted on September 1873.[70] Company C also possessed members with ample experience, including Private Ludwick St. John from Columbia, Missouri. He had been caught in the horror of Missouri's guerrilla war (like Captain Benteen, who served with distinction in a Missouri Union cavalry regiment), after having enlisted in 1861 at age thirteen. St. John was now a tough, seasoned trooper, who had been disciplined for having spoken with disrespect to an officer.[71]

Meanwhile, Cheyenne warriors continued to notice that the horses of Lieutenant Smith's Company E in front were whitish in color (gray) and lighter in color than any other of Custer's five companies. And they could also see that Company C's troopers, who wore gray slouch hats and advanced behind Smith's men, were mounted on sorrel-colored mounts of a reddish or copper-red tone: a sight that these lifelong horse-lovers of the Northern Great Plains must have marveled with a sense of admiration.[72]

To Company C's rear, meanwhile, Company F (Yates's old company, and whose members wore black slouch hats) continued to be led ever closer to the ford by Second Lieutenant William Van Wyck Reily. Wth a dashing look, the handsome, dark-haired officer with a square jaw had taken command of the company after Yates recently took charge of the battalion. A bizarre fate now had young Van Wyck, age twenty-two, leading his Company F troopers ever closer to the ford of destiny. The young man's father was a distinguished graduate of the United States Naval Academy on the Chesapeake in Annapolis, Maryland. However, the father's fate was as tragic as his son's along the Little Bighorn. His father, William, Sr., had been lost at sea when his vessel, *USS Porpoise* (which was formerly of the West Indies Squadron), sank in the China Sea in September 1854, before William, Jr., was a year old. Ironically, like other 7th Cavalry members under the broiling sun, Lieutenant Reily now might have worn a straw hat, quite possibly naval surplus for service in the tropics, recently purchased from the *Far West* sutler.

However, for a while earlier in life, William's future had never seemed brighter. He had attended school not only in Dresden, Germany, but also at the Jesuit's Georgetown University near where he had been born. Clearly, Reily had gained a high-quality education that was superior to the vast majority of Americans. At only age sixteen, William had been then appointed to the Naval Academy in September 1870. He proved deficient in his studies, especially in math and science. This personal setback perhaps developed because of the usual distractions for the young man with his home, friends, and family, perhaps even a love interest, nearby. For such reasons, Reily had finally resigned from one of America's most prestigious military academies on October 17, 1873.

Then, swept by wanderlust that might have stemmed from a failed relationship with a pretty woman, William had charted another course for himself in life which was far more risky than attending classes. He had then journeyed to the disease-infested jungles of Nicaragua on a surveying expedition. Upon his return and still looking for adventure after his experiences in Central America, he had joined the 10th Cavalry, a Buffalo Soldier regiment, in Washington, DC, on mid-October 1875. His most fateful step had been in transferring to the 7th Cavalry in late January 1876. Clearly, a strange fate had ordained the destiny of this former Naval Academy student, who was now 900 miles from the nearest ocean (Pacific) while riding down Medicine Tail Coulee and toward the ford that Custer now needed to possess to win the day.[73] Like others in Custer's column, Lieutenant Reily should have been left behind at Fort Abraham Lincoln because of illness, but his eagerness to join the expedition got the better of him. He had eagerly galloped away from the fort on the Missouri with his company in the lengthy column on May 17: a fatal miscalculation that he was bound to lose along the Little Bighorn.[74]

With his five companies deployed to his satisfaction across the open ground of the wide flats at the mouth of Medicine Tail Coulee, Custer was ready to make an overpowering strike. Ordering his last charge at full gallop when well within full sight of the ford (now made strategic by a host of developments beyond his control) and the Cheyenne village that lay straight ahead, Custer shouted, "Charge! They are sleeping in their tepees." As earlier in descending the coulee to unnerve villagers, Chief Trumpeter Voss and trumpeters Dose and McElroy unleashed the notes of the charge with renewed vigor. Then, with the old buffalo ford and the river's blue waters in sight, and with the treeless butte later known as Bouyer's Bluff dominating the skyline up ahead to the left, or south, the troopers broke into "on the run" with cheers. At the head of the blue formations charging across the open flats, colorful flags flew in the bright summer sunshine, especially the swallow-tailed banners that flapped more in a slight breeze than traditional, rectangular flags.[75]

It now must have seemed to Custer that he was fighting Confederates of old back in Virginia on a warm Old Dominion day, when he had known his opponent far better than this more mysterious and elusive foe, who he only thought he knew intimately. Custer was going confidently into his most risky battle, and unleashing his last charge with all five companies, but without a large percentage of highly qualified 7th Cavalry officers. A good many of the most experienced officers were now absent (a full twenty percent of the regimental officer corps) and far away from the Little Bighorn. However, Custer had no choice but to ignore such unsettling realities that he could not change. As he had glowingly promised Libbie in the last letter that he ever wrote to her: "A success will start us all toward [Fort Abraham] Lincoln" and home.[76]

With the ancient buffalo ford lying before him and no opposition to be seen anywhere, Custer saw visions of an outstanding success that would send him and his victors on their way home. As he had recently told his scout White Man Runs Him (formerly White Buffalo That Turns Around), born in 1858 and who had enlisted on April 10, 1876: "I am going to teach them a lesson today. I am going to whip them."[77]

Custer possessed plenty of good reason to be optimistic, despite Reno's setback. After all, he was facing Great Plains warriors who were much less formidable, or so he believed, than Lee's Rebels, when Custer and his cavalry division that compiled an impressed string of military accomplishments seldom achieved in the annals of American military history. Even wife Libbie marveled how, in only a six-month period, Custer and his hard-hitting cavalry division "had taken 111 of the enemy's guns, sixty-five battle flags, and upward to 10,000 prisoners of war, while they had never lost a flag" in battle.[78]

Seemingly, while leading his troopers at a fast pace over the wide, open ground, Custer could not possibly fail to charge across Medicine Tail Coulee Ford and straight through the Cheyenne village to reverse the day's sagging fortunes. He might have even recalled a lesson from ancient history, when Alexander the Great all but ensured his conquest of the Persian Empire by leading a bold cavalry charge across the ford on the Granicus River to win his first great victory. To Custer (and much like Alexander the Great on another hot afternoon, but in 334 BC), destiny had seemingly called him all the way to the Little Bighorn for just such an opportunity now presented to him. Therefore, as so often in the past, he was leading the flank and surprise attack in typically bold fashion, going for broke. Embracing the dictum that fortune favors the bold, he was not remaining on the high ground above the ford, as commonly assumed by modern historians, forsaking the advantage and all the initiative. Historians of the traditional school, including James Donovan in his popular book *A Terrible Glory,* have continued to maintain that no serious offensive effort was launched

by Custer in attempting to cross the ford, almost as if nothing significant could be gained from striking the village's northern end in
a flank attack: the most implausible of possibilities for a commander
like Custer and one of the great myths about the battle of the Little
Bighorn.[79]

Chapter V

The Most Forgotten Last Stand of June 25

While charging relentlessly ever nearer to the ford, pounding horse hooves raised a larger cloud of choking dust, protected by iron horseshoes shod by 7th Cavalry blacksmiths like Rhode Island–born Henry Allen Bailey, who now rode in Company I's ranks and was eager to conquer "Sitting Bull and his cut throats,"[1] as he penned in a letter. Fine dusty particles stung troopers' eyes during the sweeping charge toward the ford. Custer felt a surge of excitement while moving ever closer to the Cheyenne village, seemingly all but vacant, where lay the victory—or so it seemed.

By this time, Custer almost certainly would have now recognized the distinctive markings of the lodges (like those of the Washita) were Cheyenne. Custer might have now wondered of the strange destiny that had seemed to have ensured a longtime private war between him and the Cheyenne, especially with regard to his attack on Black Kettle's Cheyenne village on the Washita. This was no unimportant consideration: Custer overlooked the possibilities of an angry people's revenge and a terrible retribution in charging still another Cheyenne village to tempt fate.

In his typically self-assured manner, Custer had also already overlooked the wise warning from his favorite scout, Bloody Knife. The son of a Sioux father and "Ree" (Arikara) mother, Bloody Knife met his Maker not far from Major Reno in the chaos of the valley fighting amid the timber (second position) along the river, before the wild flight to the bluffs. Custer dismissed Bloody Knife's startling conclusion that an incredibly large village lay hidden amid the timber, mostly cottonwoods, that filled the Little Bighorn's bottoms, and more warriors than ever seen before.

He was now going for broke in a final bid to gain the kind of victory that had been so elusive since the beginning of his rather mundane military service on the Great Plains. As he had so often in the past, Custer was relying on his famed luck, tactical savvy, and experience on thrashing a good many opponents, both red and white. The faithful husband of She Owl and the devoted father of a son, Bloody Knife had warned about a more formidable opponent than previously encountered. However, Custer was only amused by the mere thought of what he considered most improbable; the "Sioux won't run" in Bloody Knife's words.[2] Troopers like Blacksmith Henry Allen Bailey, Company I, expressed the representative mood in a letter to his sister just before the campaign was launched. He wrote that when "Custer gets after [Sitting Bull] he will give him fits for all the boys are spoiling for a fight."[3]

This same determined resolve of Custer and his troopers now equally applied to the village's few Cheyenne, members of three warrior societies of elite fighting men, including the Kit Fox Society, who served in a guardian role as the "camp police," the Cheyenne Dog Soldiers, and the Elk Scrapers Society. Respected for their combat skills and leadership abilities while serving as the tribe's principal protectors, the expert fighters of these warrior societies would defend their women and children to their last breath in this critical situation.

For generations, these were the most defiant warriors, especially the Dog Soldiers, who had always refused to recognize any peace treaties with the hated whites. Remembering the horrors of the 1864 Sand Creek Massacre when rampaging Colorado soldiers had killed a good many Cheyenne women and children, the late November 1868 horror of the 7th Cavalry's attack along the Washita, and other Indian villages that had suffered the wrath of the pony soldiers, these veteran warriors were determined to protect their village at all costs. Tactically flexible and experienced, and despite being few in number, the Cheyenne of the elite warrior societies needed no orders or commands about how best to fight, especially in this emergency situation. Most of all, these premier fighting men were motivated by the firm conviction that their moral duty called for now defending their people with their lives. Ironically, they were motivated by the same deep bonds of a warrior ethos that cemented the relationship among Custer, his younger brother, and their inner circle of close friends and relatives now charging toward Medicine Tail Coulee Ford.

The Cheyenne camp opposite the ford was still devoid of almost every warrior. They were still now far to the south, after having rushed upriver under Two Moons, the leading Cheyenne war leader, to confront Reno's threat. Custer's chance for success was never greater, because only a handful of members of the warrior societies had been left behind to protect the northern camp. After Two Moons and his warriors had already ridden south upriver, only a few Cheyenne warriors now remained in the village, to Custer's maximum tactical advantage: those with guardian duties, or those warriors who were now asleep in their lodges (without specific duties or responsibilities), after the night's dance until the red dawn rose over the Little Bighorn.

After catching sight of Custer's descent down the coulee and charge across the open ground opposite the ford, additional warriors hurriedly grabbed their weapons and made personal preparations for once again meeting the pony soldiers. Frantic warriors attempted to find their

horses, while others remained at their lodges to make final preparations for battle. Fulfilling a religious obligation by ensuring that their
sacred regalia for battle were exactly in the right place as prescribed in
fast-induced visions or advised by respected holy men before entering
into combat, these warriors had to look just right as prescribed by rigid
religious guidelines. Warriors also carefully painted faces and bodies
with sacred vision–related designs that they had seen in vivid religious
dreams that had dictated the specific course of their lives.

These remaining few warriors in the Cheyenne village were in the
right place at the right time, although quite by accident. Bobtail Horse,
a seasoned Cheyenne warrior, had slept late because he had been
dancing the entire night and seeking an attractive lover, as the odds
were high for success with the large number of young women now
at this massive encampment: the same reason why White Cow Bull,
the Oglala who was a ladies' man in his own right, had been visiting
the Cheyenne village since morning. Bobtail Horse had emerged half-
asleep from his lodge after Two Moons and his Cheyennes had ridden
south in a great hurry to save the village's southern end. Bobtail Horse
had attempted to retrieve his horse from the herd to join the fight
against Reno. This had taken more time than expected, because the
herder boys, too young to be warriors but fulfilling a necessary tribal
responsibility, had still not found and brought his favorite war horse to
the village. However, the delay allowed Bobtail Horse the opportunity
to now face Custer, paying an unexpected dividend to the village in this
crisis situation.

In such a desperate situation, where five full companies of
troopers were charging toward the village—without any obstacles
before them except the shallow river at the ford—these relatively few
warriors clearly now needed assistance from the Great Spirit for a
successful defense of Medicine Tail Coulee Ford. Again, the crisis was
also especially severe because the few remaining Cheyenne warriors
in camp were now without horses, which were still part of the vast

pony herds and beyond immediate reach. Since the early morning, the tribe's horses had been set out to graze in the lush bench grass- lands on the gently rolling hills to the west: a situation that made the village especially vulnerable and increased Custer's chances for success.

For an inordinate period of time, consequently, what continued to be presented to Custer was a golden tactical opportunity to reverse the day's fortunes to not only compensate for but also to negate Reno's defeat: the most favorable tactical situation that stacked even greater odds in Custer's favor. Unfortunately for Custer's ambitions, these pre- cious few warriors who still remained in the village—the only ones who were close enough to meet the attack down Medicine Tail Coulee— were some of the Cheyenne's tribe's best fighting men, especially the reliable Buffalo Head Lodge guardians, such as Roan Bear. These vet- eran warriors could be depended upon in this critical situation that was now presented in full.[4]

Mostly Buffalo Head Medicine Lodge guardians, these few war- riors in the Cheyenne village finally secured the nearest horses that belatedly became available, because Custer's troopers were now so near to the ford. Finally, after much time had passed, the herder boys finally brought additional horses into the Cheyenne camp, including Bobtail Horse's mount. But for other warriors, there was no time to retrieve their own animals from the vast herd now out grazing in the expansive grasslands that stretched west of the river far beyond the cluster of buffalo hide lodges, whose openings faced east to catch the warmth of the morning sun. In a hurry, and evidently at the village's west side, where he had not initially seen Custer's approach, Bobtail Horse hur- riedly mounted his war horse. At long last, he was now fully prepared to ride south to face Reno's interlopers, until he looked east to the high ground above the ford. The astonishing sight of Custer's troopers pouring down the coulee had shocked him to the core and no doubt took his breath away. In his own words: "It was not long . . . when I first saw Custer [and his] body of soldiers coming down a little dry creek; not in it, but following down by it."[5]

After having gained fresh horses (unlike Custer's men, who were now seriously disadvantaged by exhausted and thirsty horses) and after completing their final ritualistic preparations for battle, Bobtail Horse (Elk Scrapers Society) and a mere handful of Cheyenne warriors were now finally ready to meet the greatest threat at the village's northern end as best they could. These premier warriors, so respected by their tribe, now realized that not only hard fighting lay ahead, but also an unprecedented crisis situation and one upon which the tribe's very life now depended. They realized that so few fighting men had absolutely no chance of stopping Custer's attack, but that did not matter because a solemn duty called. Hysterical shouts of terrified women that the pony soldiers were "about to cross the river and get into the camp" still rang in their ears, fueling the warriors' determination to do their best against impossible odds: a desperate attempt to buy time for the warriors' arrival from Reno's sector. In White Cow Bull's words: "We saw the soldiers in the coulee were getting closer and closer to the ford, so we trotted out to meet them."[6]

As an "elk dreamer" who drew moral strength from his mystical vision of a majestic Bull Elk that had made him part of the Elk Scrappers Society, Bobtail Horse was now donned in full battle regalia. He had made his required ritualistic war preparations, including those that were time-consuming. Wearing a sacred elk tooth in his hair to protect him for the white soldiers' bullets, he now rode rapidly toward the ford. On the way, he met other warriors, including White Cow Bull, also galloping east in a mad dash to reach Medicine Tail Coulee Ford before the fast-moving troopers gained this vital crossing point: a forgotten race for this key ford when much was at stake, including the battle's outcome.

Fearing that his companions might lose strength of heart at the unnerving sight of so many bluecoats headed straight toward them with flags flying when almost every warrior was still far away in the Reno sector, Bobtail Horse felt the need to encourage the few fighters galloping forth to reach Medicine Tail Coulee Ford. Therefore, Bobtail Horse shouted to other warriors that they must rally with courage to meet the day's greatest threat that had appeared so suddenly to catch everyone by surprise. These few defenders, including White Cow Bull, Bobtail Horse, Dull Knife (Lame White Man), and Roan Bear dashed on bareback toward the ford at breakneck speed to reach this strategic point before the 7th Cavalry's arrival. As fate would have it, and as Custer had hoped, this handful of fighting men were the only warriors who were now in the way of five full companies under America's celebrated Indian fighter. Clearly, this was a most formidable challenge. Beside his older brother at the head of five charging companies, Captain Tom Custer believed that "a single company of can lick the whole Sioux nation!"[7]

Ironically, no warrior realized that the dark blue formations were led by Custer himself. At the same time that the defenders galloped toward the ford, a handful of Sioux were now fleeing before Custer's relentless push toward the river. Along with an Oglala Sioux warrior called Shave Elk, who was on his own, these five warriors had ascended the coulee in an attempt to gain Reno's rear—now located atop the bluff after the retreat from the river bottoms. With Custer's troopers getting ever closer to the low-lying river valley filled with virgin cottonwoods and the concentration of Cheyenne lodges, the six Sioux warriors (five in a group and Shave Elk on his own) now fled for their lives, riding down the coulee at a frantic pace. To escape Custer's last charge, they headed straight for the village's safety. These Lakota were literally showing Custer the way down the dry coulee and straight to the ford and village's northern end. In their desperate effort to escape the 7th Cavalry's most concentrated and largest onslaught of the day, they were now only concerned about slipping out of harm's way before it was too late.

These fast-moving revered cousins of the Cheyenne were not decoys for an ambush, as long assumed, because the village was still not defended at this time. At the right place at the right time, these five Lakota warriors from the same tribe now benefitted from ample wartime experience. They knew that the only possible defense of the village was by taking cover and making a defensive stand among the brush and trees that grew thick in the bottoms. However, these warriors realized that any offensive effort or attempt to slow the 7th Cavalry's advance was all but suicidal. Therefore, these five Sioux continued to ride their swift ponies, small and fleet compared to Custer's larger mounts, rapidly down the coulee to escape the bluecoat onslaught. The Lakota's lithe ponies (fed on native green grasses that also nourished the buffalo) more easily navigated rough terrain than by the larger 7th Cavalry horses (fed on oats).

Fortunately for the upcoming defense of the ford, the five Sioux warriors now headed straight toward the band of Cheyenne (and the Oglala White Cow Bull), who were also racing toward the ford from the opposite direction by accident rather than any planned design: a fortunate development when the village was never more vulnerable. What was about to result was a most-timely union of Cheyenne and Sioux warriors: a mere handful of veteran fighters who banded together at the right time and place in a desperate bid to meet the day's greatest threat.[8]

After having spent a relaxing morning catching trout for dinner, White Shield likewise rose to the challenge in splendid fashion, after detecting Custer's relentless advance. In a hurry like everyone else, he finally joined the small group of warriors now heading on their fast ponies toward the ford in the hope of reaching some good defensible point from which to defend their village. Clearly, this was now literally a deadly race between Custer's men and the foremost warriors to gain the ford first. White Shield explained how Custer's attacking formation "was coming fast, making for the Little Bighorn [and] [n]ear me I could see only Roan Bear, Bobtail Horse and one other man" named Mad Wolf.[9]

With Custer's troopers getting ever closer to the well-worn buffalo ford, and with time of the essence, these foremost Cheyenne now found themselves with an opportunity to make a disproportionate contribution far beyond their numbers in saving their people, including their relatives. These were the right warriors: veterans of strong religious faith who could be depended upon to make the supreme effort and sacrifice, if necessary. In the face of Custer's onslaught, they had mastered their own fears, refusing to flee and save themselves, which seemed entirely sensible under the circumstances. Among this small group were warriors and hunters who were determined to stand firm in the ford's defense at any cost: Bobtail Horse, Buffalo Calf, White Cow Bull, Dull Knife (Lame White Man), Mad Wolf, and Roan Bear.

Although short in stature, and excessively modest for a proud Great Plains warrior in a culture in which boasting of martial deeds was encouraged, Bobtail Horse was every inch of a fighter, whose veteran leadership could not be underestimated in such a key situation. He was a revered member of the Elk Society warriors that guaranteed that he possessed hard fighting qualities and astute tactical judgment. With traditional warrior society rivalries ever in mind, and that now merged with his deep hatred of the pony soldiers, Bobtail Horse was determined to represent this revered society to the best of his ability in the ford's defense. Having been left behind since morning to guard the sacred Buffalo Head at the Cheyenne Medicine Lodge (which was the most honorable of protective roles), Roan Bear was a Fox Society fighter who could be depended upon to defend the ford to his last breath. He, too, was a proud representative of this highly revered warrior society. Roan Bear had been named after the light-colored brown bear of the Big Horn Mountains that had long awed these warriors with its legendary strength. Roan Bear was destined to play an inspiring leadership role in the ford's defense when it was needed the most, along with Bobtail Horse and his Sioux friend White Cow Bull.

As fate would have it, they had engaged in story telling about "our brave deeds in the past" and assisted Roan Bear in guarding the most sacred lodge of the Cheyenne before the 7th Cavalry's sudden arrival, which now allowed them the opportunity to defend the ford.

Roan Bear and his friends now realized that the best way to protect the Cheyenne people's Buffalo Head "sacred hat," with horns, was to defend the ford. The Northern Cheyenne believed that this "buffalo cap" possessed powerful medicine in exemplifying the animal's abundance and promise of its annual return to provide for the people.

Buffalo Calf (ironically, the Cheyenne name for Captain Tom Custer) was another hard-fighting member of the elite band of warriors now heading rapidly toward the ford in the hope of quickly establishing an ad hoc defense. He was part of the Crazy Dog Society, whose members were the fiercest Cheyenne warriors in their untamed world dominated by the harsh laws of survival of the fittest. These warrior society members consisted of elite fighting men who knew that this emergency situation was now their special destiny. They possessed experience not only in hunting but also in battling not only pony soldiers and Custer's Indian allies like the hated Crow and Arikara or Arikaree (known as "Rees" by the whites), especially Custer's Crow scouts.

In this crisis situation, these warriors naturally put aside all of their clan societal and tribal differences, and often-heated rivalries, to unite together as one. All that now mattered now was riding together toward the Medicine Tail Coulee Ford with the common goal of creating a united defensive effort, before it was too late. Clearly, these defenders of the Cheyenne village, who had suddenly come together at the last minute by circumstance, when Custer's troopers had nearly reached the ford, were highly motivated.

Mad Wolf was another warrior now riding toward the ford with White Shield and the others. He was a veteran fighting man who offered no mercy to opponents. Mad Wolf had been hit by two bullets in an 1865 clash, which engendered a passionate hatred of white soldiers.

Gaining a lofty reputation among the people as a revered shaman, Mad Wolf was an inspirational force among this band of warriors. It had been early believed that he possessed the power to make warriors bulletproof to projectiles from the revolvers and rifles: a spiritual belief that had played a part in fueling the repeated mounted attacks on the band of white frontiersmen and scouts trapped on Beecher Island (known as the battle of Arikaree Fork), Colorado Territory, in mid-September 1868.

However, the death of warriors, especially the emboldened Chief Roman Nose, in leading the mounted attacks had convincingly proved the fallacy of his "medicine" at Beecher Island and elsewhere to diminish Mad Wolf's credibility. Of course, the defenders' combat prowess, thanks to repeating rifles, was the true source of the defeat. Nevertheless, an undaunted Mad Wolf displayed a stubborn streak by continuing to believe in his own supernatural abilities. He never doubted that he possessed special power, taking the loss of prestige because of the Beecher Island setback in stride. To enhance that power by now wearing a prized "war shirt," Mad Wolf was not only now properly but also specially attired for the ford's defense. He now wore White Shield's prized "war shirt" that he had taken from his friend's lodge to thoroughly prepare for battle, securing additional spiritual protection and power. Despite not being a holy or medicine man in the traditional sense, this respected older warrior was also called Mad Hearted Wolf (a name incorrectly interpreted by whites as Rabid Wolf—the English corruption of his true Indian name, Wolf That Has No Sense).[10]

Although a poor man (without large numbers of horses) as evident from the thin, bony horse that he now rode bareback, Mad Wolf was respected for his deep knowledge, especially as a mystical shaman. Mad Wolf was also a Cheyenne Dog Soldier. As mentioned, this was no ordinary warrior society. The Cheyenne Dog Soldiers were correctly considered by whites to be "the most mischievous, bloodthirsty and barbarous" warriors on the Great Plains. Born among the Southern

Cheyenne in 1825, Mad Wolf was now in his early fifties. The depth of Mad Wolf's knowledge and wisdom was respected even among the younger warriors, who would follow his lead into battle regardless of the odds. Therefore, when Mad Wolf first rode up to the fast-moving band of crack fighting men heading toward the ford, this sage elder warrior shouted words of wisdom that caught the younger warriors' attention. A rare alliance because of the emergency situation, the ford's defense was about to be undertaken by both young and older warriors, when traditionally only younger warriors fought.

Shouting the correct tactics most needed with an air of authority, Mad Wolf yelled: "No one should charge yet—the soldiers are too many." Knowing that this second major threat posed by Custer's men, who had dared to confidently descend into the Little Bighorn Valley, was the day's most serious, Mad Wolf offered sage tactical advice to hot-headed youngsters, who only wanted to charge the pony soldiers and count coup. For all to hear, he emphasized the best possible tactic for defending the Cheyenne village: it made no sense for a mere handful of Indians to madly charge headlong into the mass of pony soldiers (as the over-eager young warriors saw as the most courageous possible act), because the overall situation was so desperate. The young men wanted to engage the pony soldiers in hand-to-hand combat to gain the greatest individual honors as dictated by their warrior society. According to their warrior values, they saw no honor at all in shooting down an opponent from behind cover with long-range shots. Mad Wolf fully understood that it was now necessary to employ a more sensible tactic to confront the pony soldiers at the ford, because this was all about saving the tribe and not individual honors. Knowing exactly what he was talking about in tactical terms, and with no illusions about time-honored concepts of bravery that would have ensured the quick wiping out of the small band of warriors by Custer's men, Mad Wolf screamed that it would be a grave mistake to charge in the midst of the bluecoats who seemed too many to count.

Instead, he emphasized to his comrades that what was now most required to save the vulnerable Cheyenne village was a clever defensive stand amid underbrush and trees along the river bottoms to disguise their diminutive numbers. To convince the young warriors, who were determined to die in a glorious charge that would become an enduring legend to future generations, the ever-sensible Mad Wolf repeatedly shouted words of wisdom to the young warriors. While heading toward the ford at a brisk pace, he continued to scream that there were simply far too many enemies before them, and it was absolute folly to charge all of them.[11]

While his old nag, "a rack-of-bones horse," could barely keep up with the young men's more fleet horses, now fat and full of life from the new spring grass that stood high, Mad Wolf continued to emphasize the wisdom of taking a good ambush position. Shouting at the top of his voice, he implored the stubborn and proud young men to listen: that charging so many pony soldiers was absolute folly because "they had no chance against a whole army."[12] In response, a fatalistic, if not slightly irritated, Bobtail Horse shouted back at Mad Wolf and his repeated advice and warnings with the typical warrior psychology in this crisis situation: "Uncle, only the Earth and Heavens last long. If we four can stop the soldiers from capturing our camp, our lives will be well spent."[13]

Proud to have been named for the powerful animals that roamed through the Bighorn Mountains to the south at the Little Bighorn's headwaters, Roan Bear was the brother of Cheyenne warriors Little Fish and Hard Robe. Known for his wise ways, he was a sub chief of the Kit Fox Society, whose members guarded the village as "camp police." Besides having held the prestigious position of serving as the guardian of the tribe's "sacred Buffalo Head" at the Cheyenne Medicine Lodge, Roan Bear also possessed a never-say-die disposition and what whites called command presence: qualities that now transformed him into the highest-ranking leader (more moral, and in terms of respect, than military in the traditional white sense) of the upcoming defensive stand against the odds at the ford. Demonstrating his own good tactical sense in the day's greatest crisis, Roan Bear readily agreed with Mad Wolf's tactical wisdom. As members of a democratic society, a common consensus was now reached with regard to exactly what was now most of all needed to save the village: a defensive stand in a good ambush position, instead of a foolish headlong charge that was doomed even before it was launched. Like Custer, these warriors had formulated their tactics while literally on the move and based upon the fast-changing circumstances.

Roan Bear possessed the depth of character, and experience level, that were about to pay dividends in the ford's defense. By any measure, he was a capable natural leader. He was occasionally hot-headed as much as the overly aggressive young warriors, but he now kept this trait under control. When his wife eventually ran off with another man to shame him before the tribe and diminish his lofty standing, Roan Bear responded in the most appropriate manner that he could possibly imagine.

He only made a simple request for a dog meal as the equitable settlement to compensate for the loss of his wayward wife. In this novel way, he publicly showed absolute contempt for his unfaithful woman in order to maintain his personal dignity in the face of a public humiliation. As everyone realized, Roan Bear was basically revealing to one and all that his philandering wife was worth nothing more than a lowly dog meal that was a poor substitution for tasty roast buffalo meat: the ultimate insult to the loose woman he had once loved. In much the same way, Roan Bear was the kind of experienced and inspirational leader who was about to make still another strong personal statement in the ford's defense, when personal revenge, determination, and pride likewise played their roles, as in losing his wife.[14]

After having ridden toward the ford from a different direction (the north) than the other warriors because he had been fishing in the river, White Shield would belatedly join the mounted group of warriors heading toward the ford just in the nick of time. In many ways, he was one of the most remarkable warriors of this contingent of determined fighting men. White Shield's previous displays of heroism in the face of the enemy (red or white) were fueled by his courage and, as he believed, his protective charms that he believed had saved him numerous times.

White Shield had recently earned greater recognition for killing several of Crook's men at the Rosebud. He basked in the recognition of what he had achieved in that day-long clash that had sent Crook's forces reeling in defeat. A no-nonsense fighter regardless of the odds, White Shield was a ruthless killer without compassion for his people's enemies, especially if they were white. He was engaged in a true holy war on this afternoon when so much was at stake, guaranteed that he would fight with his heart and head this afternoon. White Shield was proud of his eldest and most handsome son, Porcupine, who also aspired to be a great warrior like his father.[15]

With Custer's two battalions advancing relentlessly as if nothing could possibly stop them in a full-fledged assault on the ford, White Shield viewed the onslaught of Custer's "soldiers in seven groups (companies) [and] [o]ne company could be seen a long way off [because] the horses were pretty white [or grey which signified Company E, which was leading Captain Yates' battalion, and] the company was coming fast, making for the Little Bighorn" to cross the ford with this powerful concentration.[16]

Fortunately, for the Cheyenne village's defense, a handful of stalwart warriors who rallied together in timely fashion were literally the only fighting men who were now even remotely close to the ford at this time. This upcoming resistance effort would be something told around campfires and in lodges for generations to come, if they could somehow stop the pony soldier onslaught. Despite the odds, confidence remained surprisingly high among so few warriors, thanks in part to their strong spiritual faith that fueled resolve and even the recent success over Crook. After all, this surprising victory on the Rosebud had eliminated one column (the largest) of the overall strategic plan of converging on the Indians to ensure no escape, or so it had been optimistically hoped in

Washington, DC, while causing an anxiety-ridden Libbie to worry even more about her husband's fate, when so deep in Indian country.

In addition, the fighting spirit among some of these warriors had been earlier lifted by the sight of an elated Cheyenne warrior, who had earlier returned to his village from the Reno fight with a war trophy, before riding back upriver. In triumph, he had frantically waved a blue blouse, with the brass crossed saber insignia with the number "7" on the collar, back and forth for the Cheyenne people to see. This was one of the first war trophies of the battle. Yelling that "this day my heart is made good" by killing some of Reno's men, this warrior's bloodlust was now satisfied, because "he had seen [this uniform] before, on the soldiers who had killed his mother and his wife on the Washita."[17] In the Cheyenne camp, a number of women had recognized the distinctive insignia and its awful implications, rekindling horrific memories of the killing of relatives, including noncombatants, by these same 7th Cavalry soldiers on the bloody winter day that they would never forget.[18]

Likewise, these few Cheyenne warriors who were about to defend the ford with their lives might have recalled the sage words of the ancient Cheyenne Great Spirit, Sweet Medicine, to inspire them to perform extraordinary martial efforts against the odds. This legendary story had been passed down as long as anyone now encamped along the Little Bighorn could remember. Consequently, the warriors about to defend the ford had heard about Sweet Medicine since their earliest childhood days when they had been consumed with grown warrior dreams, while sitting around campfires or inside warm lodges of buffalo skins. For these young men, such stories had long brought a sense of spiritual warmth even in the most severe winter. Sweet Medicine had long ago warned of the sudden arrival of a strange, light-skinned people, whom the Cheyenne had never seen before, from some faraway land of an unknown name. It was most ironic that these interlopers on big horses who were now attacking toward an obscure place buffalo crossing called Medicine Tail Coulee, which might prove to be a "Sweet Medicine" trap for Custer and his men, if the Great Spirit still look favorably upon his people in their greatest hour of need.

For the hard-pressed Cheyenne people, the longtime westward push of thousands of white settlers and the pony soldiers, who protected them, had been nothing less than the coming of the Apocalypse. Sweet Medicine had warned of this alien people with "light hair and fair skin," who had become a dark blight upon the land. This was still another horrifying prophetic vision that had come true, and this was now personified in these 7th Cavalry troopers now nearing the ford. Worst of all, the white interlopers had caused the disastrous turn of events that was spelling the doom of the Cheyenne people, bringing an unprecedented amount of death, disease, and destruction, especially with regard to the buffalo herds, with them. Therefore, the ugliest vision and most haunting prophesy of Sweet Medicine was now most tangibly represented by Custer to symbolize awful warnings of Sweet Medicine so long ago, but never forgotten by the people.[19]

Also fueling their fighting resolve to new heights, these Cheyenne warriors now galloped rapidly toward the ford in a desperate bid to reach it before Custer's troopers gained the river's west bank, was their own worst nightmares if their women and children were captured. They already knew of the possible horrors lay in store for some women (like the tragic fate of an eight-year-old Southern Cheyenne girl raped by troopers in an abandoned village just before Custer attacked Black Kettle's Washita village) if captured by lustful pony soldiers.

Some warriors now dashing toward the ford might have now recalled the fate of three Cheyenne children who had been captured by Chivington's Colorado boys at Sand Creek in 1864. One child was taken to Denver for public display. Another child, a five-year-old boy, when captured, became part of a sideshow of the popular Wilson and Graham traveling circus. In negotiations with the United States government, Cheyenne leaders obtained the return of the three Cheyenne children, including the Indian boy who was finally mercifully released from being a living circus exhibit. These were only a few reminders that explained why these warriors were about to fight with an abandon and almost maddened desperation to defend their village and people.[20]

Additionally, the haunting screams of panicked women and the crying children, who had fled the village before Custer's attack, still rang in the ears of these warriors. They now wanted revenge on the pony soldiers for having caused so much havoc in this once-peaceful village. By this time, the majority of the panicked throng of women and children "had run away to the hill benches to the westward," allowing the upcoming showdown at the ford to be fought without risking noncombatant lives.[21] However, these defenseless ones might still be threatened if these relatively few warriors allowed the troopers to ford the river and charge through the Cheyenne village.

These warriors were prepared to sacrifice themselves if necessary for the greater good of their people. As this was an emergency situation in which they were literally ready to die, they had taken their time to exchange their "ordinary" clothing for their "best clothing" and "fine garments." In preparation of getting killed at the ford's defense (which now looked inevitable), these experienced Cheyenne fighting men were not only dressed in their finest war regalia, they had also taken the time to create sacred designs, as instructed long ago by medicine men and as deemed by visions, on their faces and bodies for self-protection with colorful war paints made from plants. Such necessary ritualistic formalities were just part of the warrior ethos. All of these time-consuming preparations were necessary according to custom for not only protection against enemy bullets but also, as Wooden Leg explained, "for presenting his most splendid personal appearance [to the Supreme Being because] he got himself ready to die."[22]

Death, however, was only briefly contemplated by these fighting men, as they were focused on somehow stopping Custer's five companies from riding through the Cheyenne village. Wooden Leg emphasized the thinking of these warriors at this crucial moment when everything was at stake, because each one "wants to look his best when he goes to meet the Great Spirit," if killed in defending the ford.[23] In her last letter (written in June and never received) to her husband and with a wife's intuition, Libbie had warned Custer that something had changed from the past ways of fighting Indians, because these same warriors no longer fled before pony soldiers. As she penned prophetically after having learned of Crook's shocking Rosebud defeat while literally tortured by worry for her husband's welfare, as if knowing that he was about to meet a grisly end far from his Fort Abraham Lincoln home: "The Indians were very bold [and now] They don't seem afraid of anything."[24] As Custer was about to be discover at Medicine Tail Coulee Ford, the Indians' lack of fear was also about to be demonstrated against the other arm of Custer's pincer movement.

While riding onward to the east toward the buffalo ford, few warriors felt that they would see the sunrise of June 26, quite unlike Custer's confident men who only envisioned victory. Therefore, while galloping rapidly toward the ford, two or three of them began to sing their high-pitched Cheyenne death songs. Possessing a spiritual power all their own, the words of these hauntingly eerie songs now helped to steel their fighting resolve, once they made their final stand. Some inspiring words of these songs included "Nothing lives long only the earth and the mountains." Despite the fact that these battle-hardened warriors, now dressed for glory and death, felt that they could not possibly survive the attack of so many bluecoats, who continued to charge onward as if nothing in the world could stop them, they were determined to do their best "to stop the soldiers from capturing our camp," in Bobtail Horse's words, and winning the day.[25]

By this time, the first shots in the ford's defense had already been fired at Custer's advance, but these first shots came belatedly. As was customary at a tribal encampment, two lonely Cheyenne guards of the Kit Fox Society had been earlier assigned to guard positions on the river's east bank at either side of the coulee's mouth. This first precautionary measure was just part of routinely guarding the ford because of its proximity to the Cheyenne village. Even as Reno unleashed his attack on the village's opposite end, the fact that the two warriors had still remained in place in their guardian role displayed the high discipline of these fighting men, who whites (more civilians than soldiers) believed possessed no military discipline because they were nothing more than lowly savages, according to the pervasive stereotypes.

All the while, the troopers looked big on their large horses (including thoroughbreds, which Custer rode with his usual equestrian grace, purchased in Kentucky by regimental quartermasters) branded with "U.S." and "7C" for 7th Cavalry, to these two warriors in the river valley. They realized that these hated "Long Knives" had proved extremely audacious by having attacked from two different directions to hit opposite ends of the vast village complex. Perhaps these Cheyenne warriors even wondered if the long-haired white leader, who they called "Son of the Morning Star" (known as "Old Iron Ass" by disgruntled troopers for his martinet ways), was now leading the way toward the ford.

The solitary guardian on the north side of the coulee's mouth earned the distinction of firing the first shot at Custer's attackers. Relying on their best instincts instead of forfeiting their lives for nothing, these two Cheyenne ford guardians retired across the river to take cover in the brushy bottoms. Here, they were about to be reinforced by the handful of Sioux and Cheyenne warriors who were coming from the opposite direction. Displaying moral courage, these two ford guardians had not fled west through the village to save themselves, but remained defiant despite the impossible odds.[26]

Meanwhile, the Cheyenne warriors and White Cow Bull, the Oglala who loved these Cheyenne warriors like brothers, continued to ride east through the northernmost village in the hope of reaching a good advanced defensive position to defend a ford, before it was too late. It now appeared to White Shield that Custer's formations were about to "force their way across the river" with ease because there was no opposition to stop them.[27]

When near the river's sparkling blue waters and the old buffalo ford, the Cheyenne warriors and White Cow Bull were encouraged to literally stumble across several Lakota boys (old enough to fight) and a few old men (spry enough to fight, but beyond the traditional fighting age of about age fifteen to about thirty-seven). These Sioux youngsters were already situated in concealed positions amid the thick underbrush and willows along the river. Taking the initiative without having been told and working together as a team, they had prepared their own ambush out of urgent necessity, because they realized that they were the only available warriors to do their duty in protecting their village and people. Not far from the river's west bank, the mounted band of Cheyenne and Sioux (there were only subtle, tribal differences—unrealized by pony soldiers—in their appearances) were now united with this small band of Lakota, adding strength to the collective warriors who hoped to somehow stop Custer's attack.[28]

With Custer and his companies charging in full sight, these warriors might have wondered about Sitting Bull's Sun Dance vision of so many pony soldiers falling helplessly into the village "like grasshoppers" and then being systematically destroyed: a source of moral strength. With so few ford defenders available, there seemingly was no possibility that all five of Custer's companies could possibly be stopped by only a handful of warriors, however.[29]

Nevertheless, with their spiritual faith and Sitting Bull's prophesy bolstering fighting resolve, these warriors had reason to believe that the "Great Spirit" was now by their side in their darkest hour. Perhaps they now took heart from the fact that at the battle of the Rosebud, Crazy Horse "rode unarmed in the thickest of the fight invoking the blessing of the great spirit on him—that if he was right he might be victorious and if wrong that he might be killed."[30] The fighting men fated to defend the ford felt much the same, because they were most of all moral warriors now united with the holy mission of saving their village and people.

Ironically, in a strange coincidence, White Shield had been fishing in the river with grasshoppers as bait when he had first learned of the attack, which had a direct prophetic connection to Sitting Bull's vision of enemies falling into the village "like grasshoppers" had become a reality as the people had believed.[31] With satisfaction, a woman named Pretty White Buffalo heard Custer's blaring bugles and saw the column surging down Medicine Coulee, knowing that the "Great Spirit had delivered the white men into the hands of the Lakota."[32]

Indeed, in overall tactical terms, this was true because Custer's pincer movement had been reduced to a flank attack without adequate support: Reno had been repulsed, Benteen was still too far away to assist, and Crook's force had retired all the way back to the Wyoming Territory instead of applying pressure from the south as planned. A veteran Civil War cavalry general correctly understood as much after later surveying the Little Bighorn battlefield: instead of "an open field, in which you could handle your command . . . Custer was buried in a deep ravine or canyon [coulee], and, as he supposed, stealthily advancing upon an unsuspecting foe, but was, by the nature of the ground" now placed the five 7th Cavalry companies at a tactical disadvantage.[33]

With a sense of pride, White Cow Bull described the most audacious, but most forgotten, Indian effort of the day that set the stage for the dramatic showdown at Medicine Tail Coulee Ford, which was destined to determine the battle's outcome. He emphasized one of the most improbable sights at the Little Bighorn at about quarter after 4:00 p.m.: "We charged [toward the ford] and we rode straight to Custer."[34]

Natural Defensive Position of a Low Rise
To compensate for Reno's sharp reversal, Custer was now in an ideal position (facing almost no opposition) to charge straight through the

Cheyenne village to reap a sparkling success as at the Washita. Custer now posed the ultimate nightmare scenario for the relatively few warriors who voluntarily chose to defend their village on their own without guidance or advice from leadership (religious or military). Indeed, Custer was seemingly about to gain a key position between the warriors upriver facing Reno and the greatest mass of women and children who had fled west from the Cheyenne village.

Recovering from the shock of a most serious new threat suddenly coming from a new direction and one of the first fighter-hunters, to dash east to defend the ford, American Horse, a respected Cheyenne warrior who also took the initiative on his own, described how he "saw Custer coming down the hill and almost to the river. I was one of the first to meet the troops and the Indians and the soldiers reached the flat [opposite the ford] about the same time. When Custer saw them coming, he was down on the river bottom at the river's bank."[35]

Most importantly, the first ford defenders had won their race by the narrowest of margins. Incredibly, the visions of Sitting Bull and Box Elder had now proved prophetic, first at the village's upper end with Reno's repulsed attack, and now at the village's northern end with Custer's charge: the decisive one–two punch.[36]

The sight of Custer and a mass of bluecoat troopers surging down Medicine Tail Coulee and across the open ground at the coulee's mouth was literally a prophetic dream come true for these few warriors, who fully understood what was at stake. After quickly surveying the river bottoms for the best defensive position with the eyes of an experienced hunter upon nearing the riverbank, Bobtail Horse shouted, "Let us get in line behind this ridge" to make a defensive stand. Members of this band "slid off our ponies" and quickly took "whatever cover we could find" and the best firing positions on the river's west side along the slight rise or "low ridge," in White Cow Bull's words. Covered in underbrush and saplings, including the silt-loving willows, this slight elevation (or rise) of sand and sediments that had been washed up by the river at flood stage. The Cheyenne village was located on ground that was several feet higher than the river, while the land gradually rose to the west. This slight rise just west of the river bank was situated on a shelf of land that stood about several feet higher than the village and about six feet higher than the rocky, lower-lying bottom on the river's opposite side (east) that was the lowest-lying part of the flood plain. Therefore, despite positioned in the river bottoms, this united band of Sioux and Cheyenne possessed a slightly elevated advantage. They could now deliver a slightly plunging fire on the troopers once they reached the lower ground at Medicine Tail Coulee's mouth and attempted to cross the swift-moving Little Bighorn.

Here, amid the relatively light cover of underbrush, willows, and cottonwood saplings that grew along this sandy rise, or slight "low ridge," consisting of silt and sand that had been created from the once-flooded river, which had since shifted farther east closer to the bluffs, this slight rise (perhaps the edge of an ox-bow, a former river bank) ran parallel to the river and was located inside a wide bend of the mean-dering river. The bend swung to extend east and near the bluffs on the river's other side, and on either side of the coulee's mouth. Here, along the brushy rise of soft soil, the warriors had found an excellent defensive position to make their last stand. They were now situated in good cover that effectively hid them from the view of Custer and his troopers, who were about to fall into an ambush, when least expected. The density of the bright green vegetation of the stands of small wil-lows and cottonwoods was now in full summer foliage, these estimated initial ten to fifteen warriors were concealed in a natural ambush posi-tion, unrealized by the advancing troopers.

Symbolically, this united defensive consisted of the Sioux and their Cheyenne cousins, representing that vital alliance that had become the key to mutual survival for both people. The band of Sioux (the handful of Sioux boys and older men who had earlier been found in place in the bottoms just in front of the low rise by the mounted warriors before the two bands united) were also highly motivated to stand firm. These Sioux defenders were partly inspired this afternoon by the memory of the spiritual legacy of White Buffalo Calf Woman. She had long served as the foundation to the identity of the Lakota people, and brought good fortune year after year. Fueling determination to defy the odds, they feared that the bluecoats were about to capture the women and children as hostages like at the Washita. Custer evidently contemplated the duplication of his old Washita trick of capturing women and children to keep any future concentration of warriors at bay to leverage a victory, especially after Reno had been repulsed.

Meanwhile, Custer had no idea that he was leading his five companies straight into an ambush by an ad hoc band of recently gathered warriors, because of the Indians' naturally camouflaged defensive position and since he had only recently viewed a peaceful camp from the high ground. Knowing that they had to make every shot count, the concealed warriors, including good fighting men armed with the 15-shot repeating rifles, waited only briefly for the bluecoats to get closer to the ford, after having taken good firing positions under cover. Then, at about 4:18 p.m., when the first "few soldiers reached the river's edge and began to cross, the Cheyenne–Lakota contingent opened fire" at targets that they could not miss at such close range.[37] One Indian woman saw the terrible effect of the "withering fire which greeted [Custer's] approach from the willows on the Indian side of the stream."[38] The Sioux warrior named He Dog claimed that the number of defenders was from "fifteen to twenty" at this time, but there were certainly more warriors, including a Sioux named Big Nose, than this lowest estimate.[39]

Symbolically, and evidently by deliberate design or tradition (or both) to invoke Great Spirit's assistance when it was most needed, the defenders of the tribe's sacred Buffalo Head were the first to unleash their fire on Custer's men, looking big on their large horses, when they neared the ford. In the words of Long Forehead, "Roan Bear, a [Fox warrior] Cheyenne, was the first to fire at Custer's command."[40] Clearly, the mighty brown bear's magical power, as so often seen in the most remote locations in the Big Horn Mountains, now roared in defiance near the Little Bighorn's west bank at the troopers' determined bid to possess Medicine Tail Coulee Ford. Then, Dull Knife (Lame White Man) opened fire on the mounted targets of blue that were already at the river and attempting to cross, after having paused briefly to realign at the riverbank on Custer's orders.[41] Along with the other defenders who realized that they had to hold firm at all costs, White Cow Bull blasted away with his fast-firing repeating rifle at seemingly too many targets to count.[42] While rapidly firing, silent prayers were said by these fighting men "to the Great Spirit, or God . . . the Great Controlling Power of this Universe" which determined all outcomes.[43]

Wisely understanding psychological warfare (ironically, much like Custer in long relying upon the music of the 7th Cavalry's regimental band for unnerving opponents and the early blaring of bugles in the advance down Medicine Tail Coulee), the ford defenders had their own trick up their sleeves. To disguise their small numbers, the warriors now unleashed a chorus of war cries that coincided with the crescendo of barking guns that they now fired as rapidly as possible. These defiant shouts and war cries coincided with the roaring gunfire that had so suddenly exploded from the underbrush and willow saplings, catching Custer and his troopers by surprise. This cacophony of noise, this wild shouting from the thick underbrush echoed over the wooded river bottoms, helped to unnerve Custer's hard-hit men in the front ranks.[44]

These Cheyenne and Sioux warriors, including Bobtail Horse, who blasted away with a muzzleloader, were now resolved to do or die because, in the words of Low Dog: "The Indians held their ground to give the women and children time to get out of the way [to the west because] our men were fighting to save their women and children," which the Cheyenne warriors had been unable to accomplish at the Washita, where the 7th Cavalry had run roughshod over the village.[45]

So highly motivated were these warriors that Mad Wolf continued to admonish the young fighters not to do what they still wanted to unleash: to launch a headlong charge the pony soldiers at the ford. Exhibiting more of his trademark wisdom that was much-needed in this crisis situation, Mad Wolf shouted to these young fighting men how "the soldiers are too many [to charge therefore] [j]ust keep shooting at them."[46] From the high ground above the ford, Crow scout White Man Runs Him, the son of Bull Chief and Offers Her Red Cloth, saw that the "Sioux [and Cheyenne] were right across the river" from Custer's attackers.[47] White Cow Bull was mesmerized by the daring leader of these pony soldiers, who had decided to attack such an immense village in broad daylight: "One white man [who was clearly the leader] had little hairs on his face and was wearing a big hat and a buckskin jacket [and] riding a fine looking big horse,"—Lieutenant Colonel Custer. Firing from his well-concealed position behind the slight rise amid the underbrush, White Cow Bull also described this dynamic officer who was leading the way in the forefront: "The soldiers came down to the ford led by one with mustache and buckskin jacket on [a] sorrel."[48]

However, the daunting spectacle of so many enemy soldiers advancing ever closer was an unnerving sight that was too much for even one of these battle-hardened men. Dull Knife (Lame White Man), after firing at the bluecoats for some time, suddenly lost his nerve. He bolted rearward where his horse was tied, leaving his fast-firing comrades behind the brushy rise on their own. After having reached his psychological breaking point under the stress of an intense battle, especially with the 7th Cavalry troopers now so close it seemed they could not possibly be stopped, Dull Knife gained his horse. He leaped on the horse's back, and then shouted to his fellow fighters, "It's no use. We cannot stop them."[49]

Fortunately for Indians today, the other defenders along the slight rise in the river bottoms were far more steadfast than Dull Knife, whose name proved especially symbolic. Continuing to fire as fast as possible at an ample number of moving targets around the ford, the defenders believed that they had no choice but to stand firm and do their best in this critical situation, because so much was at stake. Bobtail Horse shouted encouragement for the warriors to hold out as long as possible, yelling that they had to "try to stop or turn them. If they get in camp they will kill many women."[50]

At this crucial moment, not long after Dull Knife rode away to the west at a brisk pace, the defenders' steely resolve had been additionally solidified by the unexpected arrival of the five Sioux warriors who had been recently chased down Medicine Tail Coulee. They had only narrowly escaped Custer's advance. After whipping their horses and splashing across the shallow ford, they had circled around and ridden in behind the defenders crouching below the low rise, covered in the clumps of underbrush and small willows. A most timely reinforcement that raised spirits in the face of Custer's onslaught, these five Sioux fighters took good firing positions behind their busy Cheyenne and Lakota comrades. These newcomers likewise began to fire with rapidity, utilizing the marksmanship skill of lifelong hunters. As part of a culture than emphasized selfless sacrifice for the tribe's general good, the warriors as individuals continued to demonstrate initiative, good judgment, and tactical flexibility. The lifelong experiences and abilities of these fighting men were ideally suited and tailor-made for such a key situation as the ford's defense. Perhaps an arrow or lance, more than six feet long and ritualistically decorated, was driven into the ground to signify this last stand along the slight rise. Ironically, Custer would have better served had he assigned a company of his best marksmen atop Bouyer's Bluff, just to the south and overlooking the ford, to rake the defenders along the rise with a plunging fire. Custer, however, had believed that the charge across the ford would not be opposed—until the ambush revealed otherwise. Consequently, no time had existed for such a sensible tactic, although three of Custer's Crow scouts had fired at the five fleeing mounted Sioux from this commanding height,

The "Boy General" George Armstrong Custer, during the Civil War years, in a non-regulation uniform he designed so his men could recognize him on the battlefield. By 1876, he was considered America's best Indian fighter. *(author's collection)*

Sitting Bull was the most revered Hunkpapa Lakota Holy Man of his day. He inspired his people to follow traditional Lakota ways and unite in defiance to white encroachment. His prophetic sun dance vision of enemies falling into a large Indian village would come true on June 25, 1876. *(author's collection)*

Crow scout Curley was nineteen at the time of the battle. He enlisted for scouting service in April 1876 and narrowly escaped Custer's last battle. *(author's collection)*

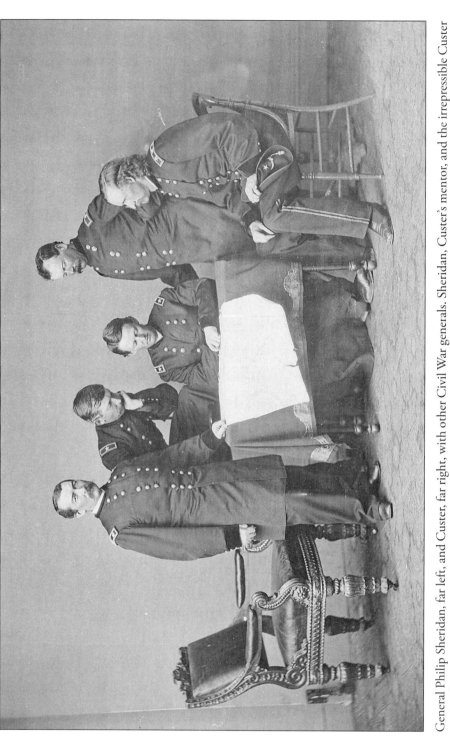

General Philip Sheridan, far left, and Custer, far right, with other Civil War generals. Sheridan, Custer's mentor, and the irrepressible Custer made a formidable leadership team during the Civil War, and beyond to the Indian Wars. *(National Archives)*

Custer married up when he took the hand of the pampered daughter of a Michigan judge, Elizabeth "Libbie" Bacon Custer. She was Custer's greatest supporter before and after his death. *(Library of Congress)*

CAPT. TOM CUSTER

Captain Thomas Custer, George's right-hand man, was one of many Michigan Staters in Custer's entourage. The winner of two Medals of Honor during the Civil War, Tom fell beside his older brother on "Last Stand Hill." *(Wikimedia Commons)*

Lieutenant James Calhoun was known as the Adonis of the 7th Cavalry. Married to Custer's younger sister Margaret, Calhoun was a respected member of Custer's inner circle, and he died fighting to the bitter end. *(Wikimedia Commons)*

Major Marcus Reno was Custer's second-in-command at the battle of the Little Bighorn, but his inexperience in Indian fighting helped to doom Custer's plan of striking the enemy village from two directions in a pincer movement. *(Library of Congress)*

Captain Frederick Benteen was a capable Indian fighter but lacked the will and desire to support Custer, partly because of personal animosity and jealousy. *(Library of Congress)*

Neither Reno nor Benteen provided timely assistance, leaving Custer and his five companies on their own.

Edward Sheriff Curtis's photo of the Indian village on the Little Bighorn River, July 6, 1908 (photo courtesy National Park Service, Little Bighorn Battlefield National Monument, Montana)

"Benteen—Come on. Big Village. Be quick. Bring Packs." Carried by Trumpeter John Martin, Custer's last message and desperate plea for ammunition and manpower was never answered. *(author's collection)*

In 1879, photographer Stanley J. Morrow took this photo of Medicine Tail Coulee Ford, where Custer unleashed the final charge of his life. *(Library of Congress)*

This rendering by Kicking Bear was one of many Native American drawings and accounts that have surfaced that shed new light on what was known by the Lakota as the Battle of the Greasy Grass. *(author's collection)*

These two renderings of Custer's heroics appeared shortly after the battle. Gross distortions of the facts began almost immediately when artists around the United States allowed their imaginations to soar. *(author's collection)*

THE BATTLE ON THE LITTLE BIG HORN RIVER—THE DEATH STRUGGLE OF GENERAL CUSTER.
[DRAWN BY MR. W. M. CARY FROM SKETCHES AND DESCRIPTIONS BY OUR SPECIAL CORRESPONDENT.]

This wood engraving of W. M. Cary's "The Death Struggle of General Custer" ran in *The Daily Graphic* on July 19, 1876, depicting Custer as the last white man standing. Cary played an early part in establishing the Custer myth. (*Library of Congress*)

In this scene from Pawnee Bill's *Wild West Show*, circa 1905, a fanciful battle plays out, with "Sitting Bull" himself slaying "Custer." The real Sitting Bull actually toured with Buffalo Bill's traveling show. (*Library of Congress*)

One of the world's most famous paintings, *Custer's Last Stand* by Edgar Paxson hangs in the Whitney Gallery of Western Art. No battle in American history has been more shrouded in romance and myth than the dramatic "Last Stand" at the Little Bighorn. *(Wikimedia Commons)*

No. 5. Custer's battlefield on Crow Agency, Montana, along the R.R.M.R.R. Battle fought June 25th, 1876. Custer and all his men were killed. Photographed and copyrighted by H. R. Locke in 1894, Deadwood, S. D.

A photo taken in 1894 shows the markers where Custer and his men fell. Future archaeology and forensics analysis would provide further clues about the 7th Cavalry's last moments. (*Library of Congress*)

GENERAL GEORGE A. CUSTER, U. S. A.

Custer lives on in our collective memories, frozen in time. We now know his real heroics took place as he attempted to cross the Little Bighorn River at the Medicine Tail Coulee Ford. *(author's collection)*

because it would have taken too long for already-weary troopers to climb to the bluff's top.

Meanwhile, the number of defenders increased, including another new addition—a veteran Cheyenne warrior named Rising Sun, who joined his fellow Cheyenne defenders. He also now fought beside two separate bands of Sioux defenders: the youngsters and older warriors who they had first encountered under natural cover just before reaching the slight rise, and the other band of timely reinforcements—the five Sioux mounted warriors who fled down the coulee before Custer's advance—who had recently united with them. Like a handful of others, Shave Elk, an Oglala Sioux who also had fled down Medicine Tail Coulee to escape the advance, also might well have joined the defenders at this time. Regardless, the last reinforcements brought the total number of defenders to about twenty-five to thirty warriors, and possibly even more.[51]

Never having seen or fought white men before, dark-skinned White Cow Bull, who rapidly fired his repeater, felt astonishment mixed with curiosity at the sight of so many strange-looking Caucasians in blue uniforms before him. These odd-looking, light-colored fighting men looked exceptionally big on their large horses. To White Cow Bull, who had seen only dark-skinned people for his entire life, Custer's men appeared not only white but also eerily pink and hairy.

Indeed, at this time, Custer's troopers had an extra shaggy growth of facial hair from the past thirty-one days since departing Fort Abraham Lincoln with high hopes. With the 7th Cavalry troopers now so close, White Cow Bull was surprised at the sight of so much facial hair, especially their beards, unlike the Indian people, whose insular culture viewed these white characteristics with disgust. Custer's men were now close enough that White Cow Bull plainly saw their pale reddish color (like a buffalo calf in spring) and blonde hair. These were strange-looking hues on humans never seen before by him. This veteran warrior might have been reminded of having seen a white buffalo, a spirit or "medicine animal," roaming free on the plains, or a white buffalo robe, a sacred object. No animal of the Great Plains was more eagerly sought with greater zeal by the warriors than the revered white buffalo.[52]

After unleashing the first shots that caught Custer and his men by surprise, and with the Sioux and Cheyenne warriors now firing rapidly at will, this was developing into a showdown that would have the greatest impact on the battle's overall outcome. Clearly, the highly flexible Indian style of fighting as individuals now paid immense dividends, because this divergent group of warriors of different ages, tribes, and warrior societies (although they looked the same to Custer's men) had suddenly come together to create a masterful ad hoc defense on the fly to face the day's crisis situation.

Of course, precise testimony about the effect of the Indians' fire is lacking from whites, because none of the attackers of Custer's five companies survived the battle. Pretty Shield learned from warriors, such as White Cow Bull, that Custer, Mitch Bouyer, and a color–bearer were the first to enter the ford's waters and were cut down. Do any white accounts substantiate the words of Pretty Shield? Before riding off to safety and agreeing with Curley's account, packer Lockwood saw what happened to the troopers, with Custer and his headquarters staff leading the way, including flag–bearers carrying their colorful banners in front.

To the warriors in the low-lying river bottoms, the words from the Old Testament's Song of Solomon 6:10 were now appropriate, because nothing is as "terrible as an army with banners." In Lockwood's words, which agreed with Indian oral testimonies, "the Indians were waiting for them [along the slight rise and when] those Indians opened fire on the general and his staff, and they all fell at the first volley."[53] Again, Lockwood's account is in agreement with ample Indian oral testimony that he never saw. For example, two warriors, the Cheyenne Bobtail Horse and Sioux White Cow Bull, and others described how the leader of the charge was hit and fell into the river.[54] Custer always led from the front, so this could have been Custer as alleged by the collaborating Indian oral testimony, including that of Pretty Shield. Indeed, Custer went all the way down to the river, leading the way as usual, with Bouyer and a color–bearer. With a commanding high ground view above the ford, Scout White Man Runs Him also verified as much, emphasizing how Custer "went right to the river bank [as] I saw him go that far," reaching the ford.[55]

Of course, watching this fight from a distance, Lockwood was incorrect about so many staff members falling, but a number of men went down as Indian accounts revealed. Dr. Lord, in front with the headquarters staff, might have fallen at this point because his surgical case was later found in the Cheyenne village. From his higher ground perch and even from a good distance, he could have seen Custer because of the prominence of his white hat and buckskin coat (verified by scout White Man Runs Him and ford defender White Cow Bull) while he led the charge as usual, especially in a crisis situation.[56]

In general terms, Lockwood's words were verified by White Cow Bull and Horned Horse, who described how "several men tumbled into the water" of the Little Bighorn, and Pretty Shield, who emphasized that Custer was one who fell.[57] This heavy volume of fire maintained by the ford defenders was also confirmed by this same warrior. Horned Horse told how Custer and his foremost troopers were swept a "tremendous fire from the repeating rifles" (rapidly firing 15-shot weapons, either the Winchester or Henry repeating rifles, or both) of the ford defenders.[58] Crow scout Curley "saw two of Custer's men killed who fell into the stream."[59] One woman described this "withering fire . . . from the willows [because] [o]ur people, boys and all, had plenty of guns and ammunition to kill the new soldiers."[60]

With regard to Custer's fall, Less Spotted Hawk, the grandson of Little Bighorn veteran Spotted Hawk, learned from the family's oral tradition that "Custer was riding at the head of his troops [when] [h]e was shot in the chest as they prepared to cross the river."[61] As mentioned, both Bobtail Horse and White Cow Bull also verified that the leading officer in the charge on the ford fell, after having been shot in the chest.[62]

This traditional story from the warriors who defended the ford matched the chest wound when Custer's body was found atop Custer Hill, where he might have been eventually carried or assisted by staff members for the famous Last Stand.[63] One of the great mysteries of the battle of the Little Bighorn has revolved around the question of which warrior hit Custer with a well-aimed shot at the ford: White Cow Bull or Bobtail Horse? Pretty Shield said that the Sioux warrior named Big Nose was the one who shot Custer, but this was a least likely possibility. Bobtail Horse cut down at least one trooper, who fell from his gray horse and then tumbled into the Little Bighorn's waters. White Cow Bull specifically targeted officers with his Winchester or Henry repeating rifle that blazed at a rapid rate. A veteran warrior, he instinctively knew that the key to repulsing the attack was to eliminate white leaders, who were obvious by their commanding appearance and behavior. Just before hitting his target with a fine shot, White Cow Bull "aimed his repeater at one [officer in front] in a buckskin jacket who appeared to be the leader." More important, he correctly identified not only the exact attire of the leader of the charge across the ford, but also the correct horse that Custer rode, to reveal that White Cow Bull [as he explained] shot Custer, who "was wearing a high hat and a buckskin jacket [riding] a fine looking big horse, a sorrel with a blazed face and four white stockings. On one side of him was a soldier carrying a flag and riding a gray horse, and on the other side was a small many on a dark horse [Mitch Bouyer] . . . so I gave the man in the buckskin jacket my attention" with the fast-firing reaping rifle.[64] Again and as mentioned, Crow scout White Man Runs Him emphasized that on this afternoon Custer "wore buckskin," providing additional proof that the lieutenant colonel was indeed hit at the ford.[65]

The heavy volume of firepower unleashed by the fast-firing band of ford defenders was also revealed by Crow scout Curley, who witnessed the attack down the coulee from the vantage point of higher ground. Emphasizing that Custer ran into an ambush in the river bottoms, Curley described how, when the troopers "neared the river, the Indians, concealed in the undergrowth on the opposite side of the river, opened fire on the troops. . . ."[66] Telling what he had learned from his warriors after their most successful day against the pony soldiers in Sioux history, Sitting Bull revealed the effects of superior firepower. He emphasized the tenacity of the defense of Medicine Tail Coulee Ford, stating how: "Our young men rained lead across the river. . . ."[67]

Based on first-hand information that he obtained from Custer's youngest Crow scout, Curley, Custer was not the first to be hit. Trooper William O. Taylor wrote: "After the head of the column reached the river, Curley saw a man on a gray horse with stripes on his arm, meaning a Sergeant, ride into the river, evidently to see if he could find a ford [by ascertaining the river's depths and] [a]t that moment the Indians opened fire on the column."[68]

Despite relatively few defenders blasting away from the brushy rise and clumps of willows, the rate of fire was not only heavy but also accurate because Custer's hard-hit troopers suffered losses from the beginning. What was the most-forgotten factor that explained the unleashing of such massive firepower from so few men from their good defensive positions? First and foremost, the forgotten answer lay in the superior weaponry of the 15-shot repeating rifle, which was vastly more lethal and faster-firing than the single-shot Springfield carbines of the 7th Cavalry troopers.[69] White Cow Bull fired a repeater, either a 15-shot Winchester or Henry rifle, during the ford's defense, including in blasting away at Custer. Almost certainly a number of defenders, perhaps even the majority although it cannot be verified with any accuracy, also possessed repeating rifles. Therefore, a relative handful of defenders unleashed a tremendous volume of fire—verified by Sitting Bull and others—that was all out of proportion to the low number of defenders.[70]

The erroneous impression has been that only White Cow Bull possessed a repeating rifle, while the other defenders were armed with only bows and arrows, which was certainly not the case.[71] The Sioux warrior named Horned Horse and others, including Sitting Bull, explained the secret that revealed exactly why their defense of the ford was so effective against the odds. Horned Horse emphasized how Custer's men "made a dash to get across, but was met by such a tremendous fire from the repeating rifles" from the Cheyenne and Sioux that a crossing was impossible.[72] Encountering such a heavy volume of fire from the finest repeating arms in America should have come as no surprise to the 7th Cavalry troopers. Ironically, a concerned Captain Yates had sagely warned in December 1874, "I observed the Indians [Sioux] were splendidly armed principally with Henry and Winchester Rifles."[73]

Ironically, the Winchester rifle has been commonly viewed as "The Gun That Won the West," especially the famed Winchester model '73. Ironically, and although unrecognized, this gun actually played a far larger and disproportionate role in winning the battle of the Little Bighorn. In fact, this June 25 reality was even more appropriate and on–target in terms of deciding the crucial contest at Medicine Tail Coulee Ford. Consisting of models 1866 (known as the "Yellow Boy" because of the yellow color of its brass receiver), 1873, and 1876, the massive volume of firepower unleashed from this classic lever action repeating rifle far outmatched and outclassed the 7th Cavalry's single-shot Springfield carbines: a forgotten explanation about how so few warriors could prevail at the ford. All in all, these fast-firing Winchester rifles played a key role in determining loser from victor on June 25.[74]

What was happening was very much a showdown of weapon technology. Manufactured in New Haven, Connecticut, and like the Winchester rifle, the Henry rifle was actually the first authentic Winchester rifle. The Henry rifle had first proved its lethality during combat by a relatively few Union soldiers, mostly in the western theater. These Yankees had been armed with the day's most innovative weapon, which decimated attacking Confederates, who were severely handicapped by using single-shot muzzle loaders. Firing .44 caliber bullets from metallic cartridge casings, the rate of fire (like the Winchester) from the 16-shot Henry was devastating, and unlike anything experienced by Southern soldiers.

Quite simply, the Henry repeating rifle was the best weapon in the Union arsenal, while the Winchester was the best weapon of the Indian Wars.[75] However, some defenders, more Sioux than Cheyenne, in the ford's defense only possessed bows and arrows. Even these ancient weapons proved effective in arching arrows high across the river to rain down on the lower ground on the east side. With long iron heads obtained from white traders, Cheyenne arrows were marked by three wavy lines on the wooden shaft (designating the sacred spirit that had long assisted in bringing and killing buffalo for subsistence) that distinguished them from Sioux arrows.

Amid the underbrush and willows that covered the slight rise, those warriors, like White Shield, without firearms continued to fire a hail of arrows, with lengthy points, at the attackers. These arching arrows repeatedly flew high and across the river to strike targets, now well within deadly range. While unleashing arrows in a high arc and in quick succession, the experienced archers remained behind protective cover that allowed them to be unseen by Custer's men. Consequently, they were able to let loose with arrows without exposing themselves to the troopers' return fire from the .45–70 caliber Springfield carbines.[76] With either rifles or bows and arrows, these veteran hunters, in the words of one officer, were "a most dangerous warrior within two hundred yards [because this is] the range which he is accustomed to kill game. . . ."[77]

Most symbolic like the timely (but entirely unplanned) unity of Cheyenne and Sioux warriors who now stood firm before the battlefield's most strategic point at this time, the ford's defense proved formidable, thanks to a strange combination of the most ancient weapons, the bow and arrow, combined with the most advanced weapons technology of the Winchester and Henry repeating rifles: a somewhat bizarre synergy of old and new weaponry that were ideally suited in the ford's defense when least expected by Custer. Unfortunately for the attackers, they encountered the fire of more advanced weaponry than imagined and at a closer range than from bows and arrows: a shock that shook confidence and sapped the charge's momentum.[78]

Leading the "Gray Horse Company" (E) in the attack at the head of Captain Yates's battalion on the ford was "Fresh Smith." He was known by this nickname to separate him from Captain "Salt Smith." As his sobriquet indicated, "Salt Smith" was a crusty officer and a 7th Cavalry wagoner of the Black Hills Expedition, possessing a seaman's background in the merchant marine. The modest, less-worldly "Fresh Smith," a quiet married man, was the antithesis of "Salt Smith." Smooth-faced and handsome, Lieutenant Algernon Emory Smith was a popular young officer of outstanding promise. He was called "Smithie" by his best friends, including Custer. They preferred this more familiar nickname to "Fresh Smith," a name that revealed a measure of disrespect from the older officers that indicated a strict regimental pecking order.[79]

As sad fate would have it, Lieutenant Smith was almost certainly fatally cut down at the ford, while leading the advance of Yates's battalion. Respected historians Sandy Barnard, Brian C. Pohanka, and James S. Brust concluded: "Lieutenant Algernon E. Smith of Company E—whose presence, a considerable distance from the other men of his company, may indicate that Smith was an early casualty."[80]

In overall tactical terms, and thanks to the fast-firing repeating rifles of White Cow Bull and other warriors, what was now happening in the ad hoc defense of the ford was quite remarkable by any measure. Against all odds, a mere handful of warriors were in the process of thwarting the lofty ambitions and boldest tactical plan (flank attack) of one of America's greatest Civil War heroes. All the while, a good many factors continued to ensure that these defenders could not have been more highly motivated or determined at this time.

As mentioned, these warriors knew that they must hold firm to protect the village's women and children, doing their duty to their people. To fuel the determination of the Cheyenne warriors at the ford, thoughts reverted back to the searing memories of Sand Creek. Here White Necklace, the wife of Wolf Chief, found her niece decapitated by Colorado's unrestrained soldiers. Likewise, the memory of the killing of an estimated seventy-five women and children (mostly accidental) by the 7th Cavalry at the Washita proved a grim reminder of what might happen along the Little Bighorn, if these warriors were now pushed aside. Therefore, the battle cry for the Cheyenne warriors on this hot afternoon was "Remember the Washita." This war cry was a powerful motivating factor for them to hold firm against the odds.

The tenacity of these Cheyenne and Sioux warriors can also partly be explained by the inspirational power of spiritual faith. All in all, a host of complex factors now combined to make these men some of the best fighters of their respective warrior societies. Quite simply, they were the elite fighters of the tribe, and they were now demonstrating as much in the ford's defense. These young men and boys (Cheyenne and Sioux) had been thoroughly indoctrinated in the cherished values of their respective warrior societies, which now fueled their motivations to new heights. Making them supreme fighters when everything was at stake, these warriors stoically believed that it was far better to die in battle in defending their people (especially helpless women and children) than to live to old age and then quietly fade away when well past their prime. Consequently, this crisis situation at the ford was exactly what the Cheyenne warrior most gloried in, providing the ultimate challenge.

Since childhood, these warriors had heard the fables that glorified the heroic actions of fighting men in protecting the tribe. Therefore, Cheyenne war heroes (in the past and the present day) were the most respected and popular members of the tribe, much like Hollywood and sports stars in America's popular culture of today. Such warrior heroes were long idolized by young males preconditioned in warrior values from infancy in a society in which battle courage was the most revered quality. They were moral fighting men and holy warriors whose lives were devoted to giving thanks to God for His blessings and the tribe's protection. These Cheyenne and Sioux defenders of the ford believed that the "Great Prophet" now gave them the strength to stand firm against the odds after having met Custer's column head-on.[81]

Among the thick underbrush of the sun-baked river bottoms, the defenders of the slight ridge needed all of the spiritual power to face the attack of five companies of a proud regiment that was considered elite across America. With only three companies, Reno should have delivered an offensive blow as Custer had ordered. Despite the heavy fire pouring from the repeating rifles, an increasingly alarmed Bobtail Horse still "believed they would cross the river and get into the camp" and win the day.[82] Clearly, Custer realized that crossing the river at this point was the key to victory. Lieutenant Winfield Scott Edgerly, Company D, 7th Cavalry, later realized the excellent tactical possibilities for Custer to reap a sparkling success in gaining the Cheyenne village, because the river at the ford was "only about fifteen or twenty yards wide. . . ."[83]

Fueling their determination to hold firm, these warriors were now also inspired by the moral legacy of the Cheyenne holy girl who had existed so long ago. Bestowed with the spiritual power of sacred animals and the Great Spirit, this female orphan had directed the basic shape of Cheyenne tribal council and leadership. Even more symbolic, the Cheyenne warriors now battling with their hearts from behind the brushy rise also fought in the honor of Sweet Medicine, the Cheyenne's mythical hero. Serving as the sacred tool of the Great Spirit atop the "Sacred Hill" in the Black Hills where she gained wisdom, Sweet Medicine had first presented the warrior societies with their sacred rituals and regalia centuries before. She had been granted four sacred arrows by this personified great spirit. Not unlike those now let loose in rapid succession toward Custer's men at the ford, these arrows were the supernatural means, or "grace," by which the Cheyenne people survived in the future.

In purely spiritual terms, the Cheyenne also hoped to repulse the threat from Medicine Tail Coulee Ford to gain favor from Sweet Medicine's sacred memory. These warriors now fought for the survival of everything that they knew and loved: a distinctive culture, a unique way of life, and freedom-loving people who were now under threat not only from the 7th Cavalry, but also the relentless push of modernity and progress. Providing inspiration, these crack fighting men of the Northern Great Plains were convinced that the all-knowing "Spirit who Rules the Universe" was now beside them in the ford's defense, bestowing moral strength and courage to them. The centrality of this all-consuming religious faith in the daily lives and traditional value systems of these Cheyenne and Sioux warriors led them to defend the ford with a tenacity and stubbornness unexpected by Custer's men.[84]

Protective Charms and Audacity in the Face of All Tactical Reason

Last but not least, and like Bobtail Horse, who wore his protective elk's tooth, the warriors defending the ford also believed in the spiritual power of their special charms, including eagle feathers and buffalo tails that were darker in color than the bison's tan-colored body hair. The most colorful protective charms in the ford's defense were the "helper birds," including stuffed hawks worn in long black hair, which had been long envisioned by these warriors in dreams to protect them and give them strength in the heat of battle. A typical medicine pouch (a counterpart to Dr. Lord's surgical case) might contain a buffalo tail and eagle feather, or these sacred charms might hang from the warrior's body. To these battle-hardened fighters, these revered charms offered guidance and protection from harm, especially the lead bullets of the white man, while fueling a tenacious defense along the Little Bighorn.[85]

To heighten resolve in the ford's defense along the slight rise, no stuffed bird now worn by these warriors atop their heads or tied to their hair was more symbolic than the kingfisher. Therefore, White Shield now wore a stuffed kingfisher atop his head, believing that it provided spiritual power that protected him from harm. This was all part of the complex Cheyenne spiritual belief system (like that of the Sioux) that explained why they were so carefully dressed in full battle regalia. If killed, then these fighting men wanted to look their best when they entered the next world of their ancestors, and the stuffed kingfishers were among the finest war regalia to impress the Great Spirit. Since children, these warriors had watched in amazement at the expert hunting prowess of the brightly colored kingfisher (whose magnificent colorful plumage consists of bright blue and yellow breast feathers) that patrolled swiftly above the waters, including along the Little Bighorn, in search of fish. Sighting an unwary target near the surface, the kingfisher then dove into the water to spear fish with its long, dagger-like beak. Imitating the kingfisher's cry in the heat of battle, these warriors took inspiration from its amazing hunting skills, because "If it dives into the water for a fish, he never misses in prey,": a fact that these warriors now sought to emulate against the tribe's enemies, and especially now in defending Medicine Tail Coulee Ford.[86]

Like his superiors who believed that the worst of all fates would be for the "savages to beat us" on the battlefield, in General Sherman's words, Custer had badly underestimated the overall martial qualities of these warriors, especially with regard to motivations. When his Crow scouts had recently informed him that there were a sufficient number of Sioux in the village to ensure a battle of two or three days, an amused Custer could hardly keep from laughing. He had responded, with a smile, "I guess we'll get through with them in one day."[87] Despite his bold words, Custer was still not able to break through only a mere handful of defenders at the ford, all the while knowing that everything was now at stake. In Bobtail Horse's words, the warriors now "were firing as hard as they could and killed a soldier," whose horse then bolted across the river at the shallow ford.[88]

At this time, ironically, the ford defenders had no idea who led these attackers, despite knowing of Custer because of his devastating Washita attack. Cheyenne and Sioux accounts have revealed that no one expected that these bluecoats were led by Custer. Custer's recently cut hair made their identification of him (including after the battle) impossible. Therefore, the Indians believed that they were now once again battling Crook's soldiers from the Rosebud fight, where they had emerged victorious after demonstrating that they were "the best cavalry in the world."[89]

However, the oral account of Sioux warrior Hollow Horn Bear revealed that a fellow warrior had told him "that he saw a man with a red and yellow handkerchief around his neck and a buckskin jacket on [and] the warrior who made this remark said it must be Long Yellow Hair."[90] After having become the Union's youngest general at age twenty-three during America's fratricidal conflict, Custer had created a special uniform for himself. As if to remind him of his glory days (and like other members of his inner circle, who wore these colorful "neckties,") Custer had worn, in the words of one of his men, "a conspicuous red tie."[91]

A number of Custer's officers of the inner circle, including Tom Custer, wore stylish buckskin shirts or coats. Now covered in alkali dust, these buckskin garments had been long popular among the officer corps of the 7th Cavalry. Custer wore a buckskin shirt and pants, and esteemed members (officers) of the Custer clique followed the lieutenant colonel's example. In fact, even officers outside the clique, like the dashing Irish wing commander Captain Myles Walter Keogh (who now carried a photo of Captain McDougall's sister) also wore buckskin shirts or coats. Custer clique members now wearing buckskin shirts or coats included Keogh's top lieutenant now commanding Company I, Lieutenant James Porter, Lieutenant Henry Martin Harrington, Tom Custer, who rode on his Kentucky thoroughbred near his brother in the charge down the coulee, Lieutenants James Calhoun and Algernon Smith, Adjutant Cooke, and the other wing commander, Yates. Marveling at the bravery of the 7th Cavalrymen, Red Horse described one especially courageous "officer [who] wore a large-brimmed hat and deerskin coat." This was most likely Tom Custer, who wore a buckskin coat and a white broad-brimmed slouch hat while serving as part of his brother's staff at the forefront during the attack on the ford.[92]

One of the misconceptions about the battle of the Little Bighorn was that Custer wore no buckskin shirt or coat during the combat. With a penchant for confusing details in later years, it was thought by Trumpeter Martin that Custer had taken off his own buckskin coat or shirt and then placed it behind his saddle. The Italian immigrant-turned-bugler stated that Custer wore a blue shirt with buckskin pants. Even if questions have continued to exist in this regard, Custer might well have put his buckskin back on (serving as a duster) in leading the charge on the ford, because a number of other officers wore buckskin shirts or coats as verified by numerous Indian accounts.[93]

As mentioned, ample evidence and testimony exists that Custer was hit early in the attack. Sioux warrior White Cow Bull presented oral testimony that he shot down the leader of the charge donned in a buckskin shirt or coat during the charge across the ford: a claim that packer Lockwood, who never knew about White Cow Bull's testimony, supported and verified in his forgotten memoir. Hairy Moccasin, Goes Ahead, and White Man Runs Him "saw [or heard of] Custer's fall at the river" that fateful afternoon.[94] In this regard, this was one of the few times that white and Indian testimonies were in agreement. Lockwood emphasized that he saw Custer "fall at the head of his advancing troops, and that he was 'the first to fall' *before* the real battle began."[95] After analyzing the often-confusing details of the battle (due to no white survivors) to a degree like few other historians, Jack L. Pennington concluded in no uncertain terms that "Custer must have been shot at the ford. . . ."[96]

From a good many Indian accounts that he carefully analyzed, historian David Humphreys Miller also emphasized how "Custer . . . fell, a hostile bullet through his left breast."[97] All of this testimony (white and red) by those who witnessed what actually happened at the ford was additionally verified by the words of a Northern Cheyenne, the grandmother of Sylvester Knows Gun. Having heard the personal views of the battle from surviving warriors, including those men who had defended the ford, she explained how the leading officer in a buckskin jacket was "the first one to get hit" by the ford defenders' fire. Pretty Shield, wife of Goes Ahead, learned from warriors, including her husband, that Custer fell at the ford.[98] Just when the officer appeared about to fall off his saddle and into the clear, cold waters at Medicine Tail Coulee Ford, three men (staff members, if this was Custer) rushed to his assistance. "They got one on each side of him," in the oral testimony of this Northern Cheyenne woman, "and the other got in front of him, and grabbed the horse's reins [and then] they quickly turned around and went back across the river."[99]

White Cow Bull, one of the Sioux who fired a repeating rifle (either a Winchester or Henry rifle), described the destructive fire from the last stand defenders that led to the fall of the leading officer whom he believed was Custer himself, because it had the effect of eroding the overall momentum of the attack (as verified by Curley and Lockwood) at the ford:

> The man in the buckskin jacket seemed to be the leader of these soldiers [and this] man who seemed to be the soldier chief was firing his heavy rifle [not the standard issue cavalry carbine] fast [and] I aimed my

repeater at him and fired. I saw him fall out of his saddle and hit the water. Shooting that man stopped the soldiers from charging on. . . . Some of them got off their horses in the ford and seemed to be dragging something out of the water, while other soldiers [Keogh's battalion on higher ground behind Yates' battalion in the low ground at the mouth of Medicine Tail Coulee and the ford] still on horseback kept shooting at us.[100]

White Cow Bull's revealing words seemed to indicate that if this was Custer who was hit (which is most likely the case), then he was only wounded. If so, then an injured Custer was eventually assisted up by his men (most likely staff officers and other inner circle members, especially Tom Custer) and eventually carried all the way up to Custer Hill, nearly three-quarters of a mile away, where his body was later found. Fully convinced that Custer had been killed at Medicine Tail Coulee Ford, Sioux warrior Horned Horse concluded that the "Little Big Horn [River flows and] cuts off the edges of the northern bluffs sharply near the point where Custer perished."[101]

Blazing Repeating Rifles

Like other warriors, White Cow Bull revealed why this blistering fire pouring from the slight rise amid the underbrush and willows was so devastating (something that even amazed Sitting Bull) for a lengthy period of time: some defenders, perhaps even a majority, possessed weaponry far superior to the men of the 7th Cavalry. Firing beside White Cow Bull, who blazed away with "my repeater," Bobtail Horse also shot a trooper (the first bluecoat to fall at the ford according to White Cow Bull) "out of the saddle" and off his gray horse while most likely firing a repeating rifle.[102] Sioux warrior Horned Horse revealed that the key to Custer's unexpectedly harsh reception and sharp setback at the ford was due to "such a tremendous fire from the repeating rifles" that roared.[103] The number of repeating rifles used in the ford's defense was not an unusual situation, because large numbers of warriors along the Little Bighorn were armed with repeating rifles on this day: the ultimate shock to Custer, who had hoped to surprise his opponent, but instead had been surprised in this regard. Two Young Moons, the Northern Cheyenne leader born in 1855, described: "We were pretty well armed [including] rimfire Winchesters [and the] Indians had many .45 and .50 caliber guns and Winchesters at [the] time of [the] Custer fight."[104]

Ironically, Custer already knew about his opponent's superior weaponry, but certainly not with regard to the ford's defenders until it was too late. In referring to Sitting Bull's Hunkpapa band, Indian agent John E. Smith had warned Custer in February 1874 that "two-thirds were well-armed [and] [a]bout half the warriors remaining at Agencies have repeating rifles, Winchesters & all others have breech–loaders [and] I have known Indians . . . to have 3,000 rounds of ammunition for a single gun."[105]

The undeniable reality of the vast superiority of Indian weaponry was also realized throughout the 7th Cavalry. Private Taylor emphasized how the warriors were splendidly armed. He mentioned how "many of the Indians carried . . . Winchesters."[106] An embittered Sergeant John Ryan, Company M, described the supreme disadvantage now faced by Custer at the ford: "Sitting Bull's trusty and most persistent allies were the Indian Department and the Indian traders who supplied him with Winchester rifles and patent ammunition" in large quantities.[107] Indeed, in the words of one modern historian (and unfortunately for Custer and his men), "The Interior Department and its Bureau of Indian affairs looked after their charges, providing arms and ammunition for the hunt, while the army suffered the consequences of superior weapons in the hands of already able warriors."[108]

Ample archaeological evidence from the Custer battlefield has revealed the truth of the Indians' large number of the day's cutting-edge firearms technology, the Winchester and Henry repeating rifles.

Archaeological studies have also coincided with the analysis of Reno and Benteen and their lucky survivors, who lived to fight another day thanks to Custer's flank attack.[109] Therefore, the words of Baltimore, Maryland–born Captain Thomas Henry French, who rode a Kentucky thoroughbred as the commander of Company M, the son of an Englishman, and a Civil War veteran, were not an exaggeration with regard to the Northern Great Plains warriors: "These Indians *all* had Winchesters 17 shooting breech loaders, which may be fired as rapidly as a slight turn of the hand can be made. They had, some of them whom I have seen at the agencies, four belts of cartridges—two about the loins, one each way from the shoulder over the chest."[110]

Custer's attack was so hard hit at the ford by the rapid fire from superior weaponry only because these guns had been sold to these warriors by white traders, including licensed Department of the Interior traders.[111] One Arapaho (who were allies of the Sioux and Cheyenne) warrior named Left Hand explained the central foundation of the longtime mass arming of the Northern Great Plains Indians with superior weaponry: "The white men used to trade us guns for buffalo robes. . . ."[112]

Sitting Bull correctly saw the ford contest as a mismatch because of a broad disparity in weaponry in the most fundamental terms that proved the decisive in the end: "They fired with needle [single-shot carbines] guns [and] [w]e replied with [16-shot] magazine guns—repeating rifles."[113]

If Custer was not hit, despite ample Indian and white testimony that has deemed otherwise, then two possibilities existed with regard to the identity of this officer who fell at the ford. Charging immediately behind Custer and his headquarters staff, Yates' battalion (Companies E, C and F, respectively) was also swept by same fire that hit the headquarters staff. When Smith's Company E was hit by the hot fire erupting from the brushy river bottoms, Company C reinforced

Company E out of urgent tactical necessity after the shock from the first volley and sustained fire. Exposed in the open and an easy target, Lieutenant Smith also wore a buckskin shirt or coat when he was cut down.[114] By this time, Company C's soldiers, including dark-haired and black-eyed Private Patrick Griffin, who had been born in Dingle, County Kerry, Munster Province, in southwest Ireland, were shocked by the rapid fire and "sharp crack of Winchesters and Henrys as the Indians killed" members of Yates's battalion, which was swept by the ford defenders without let up.[115]

Continuing to throw the odds in favor of the relatively few ford defenders as the firefight lengthened, Custer's men simply could not match this heavy volume of gunfire, especially when they were mounted during the charge, which guaranteed an inaccurate return fire. The single-shot Springfield carbines were simply no match to the Winchester and Henry repeating rifles. No doubt, these fast-firing weapons included those decorated brass tacks on wood stocks, a popular style among the Northern Great Plains warriors. The embattled ford was now impassible, in part because Custer's men no longer possessed the superior weapon that had once unleashed a greater volume of firepower than their Springfield carbines The troopers no longer carried the Spencer seven-shot carbine, a fast-firing repeater.

Even more symbolic, Custer's Wolverines of his Michigan Cavalry Brigade had been so effective in the Civil War years in no small part because they relied upon Spencer rifle's firepower. However, in its conventional wisdom that now doomed a good many its own members to cruel deaths along the Little Bighorn, the United States Army had decided to discontinue the superior Spencer carbine (capable of firing ten shots in a minute) in favor of the inferior model 1873 Springfield carbine that was so badly outmatched this afternoon at the ford, when the battle's outcome was being decided.[116]

Charging Across Medicine Tail Coulee Ford

In the absence of so many veteran officers, lower-ranking leaders rose to the fore as best they could under difficult circumstances. Commanding Company C in Tom Custer's absence and in his first battle, Second Lieutenant Henry Moore Harrington also wore a buckskin shirt or coat. In this regard, Harrington followed the habit of their esteemed commander and other leading officers, especially Custer's close-knit inner circle who wore this popular attire. As mentioned, the so-called buckskin scout jacket or shirt was a popular style among the leadership corps of the 7th Cavalry, including among Custer's staff.[117]

Captain Tom Custer (or "Brother Tom," in Libbie's words), Captain Myles Walter Keogh (who possessed an Irishman's sensitive heart hid under a rough-hewn hardened exterior), and the highly competent Adjutant Cooke, Boston "Bos" Custer (the youngest of the Custer brothers, who now served as a civilian guide officially assigned to the quartermaster), Ohio-born Lieutenant James "Jimmy" Calhoun (a Civil War veteran known as the handsome "Adonis of the regiment"), and other highly respected men all wore buckskin shirts or coats. Married to Custer's sister Margaret, or "Maggie," the mannerly, blond-haired (like his brothers-in-law) officer of Scotch-Irish descent, Lieutenant Calhoun possessed intellectual inclinations and now rode at the head of Company C. All of these respected officers, Custer's favorites, wore buckskin shirts or coats at the Little Bighorn.[118]

At the head of thirty-four enlisted men of Company C, now that Tom Custer continued to serve on the commander's staff and at his company's head, acting company commander Lieutenant Henry Moore Harrington looked the part of a dashing leader in his light buckskin shirt. He led Company C's troopers in his first combat as company commander. Meanwhile, the buglers continued to blow the charge for Company C. Trumpeter William Kramer was in his late twenties, married to wife Elnora, and proud of his infant son, Orren. No doubt having briefly admired the picturesque landscape of the high plains around him before the attack, Kramer had been an idealistic painter—before enlisting in the 7th Cavalry in October 1875 to learn about a cruel world from which he would never return. At age twenty-seven and a Michigan man like the Custer brothers, Harrington was a West Point graduate (number seventeen out of fifty-eight members of the Class of 1872) when he was age twenty-three. He had been married to the granddaughter of a respected West Point professor since November 1872, Grace Berard, after he graduated from the America's top military academy on the Hudson.

Despite leading the company for the first time, Harrington possessed solid leadership experience on the Yellowstone Campaign of 1873 and Custer's 1874 expedition to the Black Hills. He had been at home on leave with his wife and children (Grace and Harry) in the community of Coldwater, in south-central Michigan, when he learned that Custer had been reinstated to lead the regiment on the 1876 expedition. Despite a month remaining on his long-awaited furlough, the call was simply overwhelming for this duty-minded second lieutenant, and the conscientious Harrington had immediately telegraphed Custer. Despite being saddled with familial responsibilities, he requested to be allowed to rejoin the 7th Cavalry. Custer, of course, was delighted to have another capable Michigan officer by his side. Harrington, verifying Custer's trust in him, led Company C's charge on the ford to the sound of bugles blaring in the afternoon.

With the cherished Christian medal that he now wore providing no protection against the bullets from Indian rifles, Second Lieutenant Harrington was struck in the upper left side of his forehead just above his left eye. A large-caliber bullet smashed through his head. The massive bone structure damage revealed that the young lieutenant's death was almost instantaneous. The fall of Harrington, who had long idolized Custer as Michigan's greatest Civil War hero, also revealed that Company C advanced immediately behind Company E during the attack.

Yates's battalion (Companies E, C, and F in this order of advance) surged forward close behind Custer and his headquarters staff during the charge on the ford. An Indian revealed that Harrington was "among the first killed in Custer's [five companies in the] attack of the Indian village."[119] Reno believed that Harrington was only wounded and was then held captive in the valley, because he was hit so close to it. In fact, the lieutenant's massive wounds proved otherwise. His grieving wife, Grace, was later presented contrary information by the 7th Cavalry's regimental surgeon, Dr. John W. Williams, about her husband that convinced her that he remained a prisoner even long after the battle. However, all of this collaborating evidence is still another indication that the promising lieutenant was cut down in Custer's attack at the ford.[120] Like Company E, Company C was also swept by the fire from repeating rifles which roared from the brush-covered rise that could not be overcome by inferior single-shot firepower.[121]

Like other officers and enlisted men who were in the forefront of Custer's final offensive effort of the day at Medicine Tail Coulee Ford, additional evidence (besides Reno's account) that Harrington was killed at the ford and near the village was verified because of the fact that his body was never found after the battle. Evidence exists, including a dead trooper and his horse later found in the village, that some attackers crossed the ford and rode into the village. In addition, enraged Indian women later dragged wounded cavalrymen (tragic trophies of an angry people), who had fallen around the ford into the village that night during the victory celebration in which decapitation occurred. With field glasses from the bluffs above the river after his retreat from the river valley, and after the warriors had streamed north to face Custer's threat, some 7th Cavalry officers, including Reno, saw three captives tied up "to the stake." Here, their remains were eventually consumed by the flames. In looking northwest up the river valley, this horrifying sight provided additional evidence that Custer's last charge on the ford was a greater attack and succeeded in making a far greater westward penetration than has been generally recognized by historians.[122]

In Reno's words: "I [am] strongly of the opinion that [Harrington] was burned at the stake [because] while the great battle was going on I, and some officers looking through field glasses, saw the Indians miles away [in Cheyenne village] engaged in a war dance about three captives. They were tied to the stake and my impression was that Harrington was one of them."[123] What was significant about Reno's observations was that these captives were taken prisoner very early and tied to the stake while Custer's five companies were under attack on the high ground, after the repulse at the ford: additional proof that these men were captured in the attack on the ford.[124]

As could be expected among a thoroughly vanquished people, almost every Indian later denied (during careful oral testimony to white interviewers when they and their families were vulnerable after the tribes had been subjugated) the taking of 7th Cavalry captives (true MIAs, or Missing in Action, because their bodies were never found). They offered excuses to the point of explaining that quicksand was responsible for having "swallowed" up the bodies of troopers who fell into the river. Most revealing, Little Knife explained, "One prisoner was taken [who] had stripes on his arm. . . . He was bound hand and foot with a '*shag a nappe*' (stripped buffalo hide), and left in a lodge [and later] A wild dance followed in the night after the battle, and a few men . . . sought out the lodge in which the captive was held and killed him with a knife. . . ."[125] Little Knife's words corresponded with what Reno saw from the high ground perch above the river.[126]

The most accurate words of what happened to the dead and wounded at the ford was revealed by Two Moons, the minor chief of the Cheyenne Kit Fox Society. The son of an Arikara (or "Ree") captive named Carries the Otter who became a fully accepted member of the Northern Cheyenne tribe, Two Moons emphasized how at Medicine Tail Coulee Ford "some soldiers were killed and were afterward dragged into the village, dismembered and burned at [the] big dance that night."[127] During the attack on the ford, amid the hail of lead from the slight rise, some men were unhorsed by a shot or a fall—the ultimate "ignominy for a [cavalry] officer of being dismounted" from a favorite horse.[128]

From reliable Indian oral accounts that coincided with what Sergeant Daniel Alexander Kanipe saw (*i.e.,* the body) after the battle, it has been determined at least one 7th Cavalryman crossed the ford and charged straight into the Cheyenne village. Foolish Elk, a Sioux warrior at age twenty-one, related that "one soldier did ride his horse across [Medicine Tail Coulee Ford and then] into the village and was killed. . . ."[129] In fact, at least two recent recruits and "green troopers on scared horses broke loose from the company [C] and rode right through" the swift-moving waters of the ford and into the Cheyenne village. Coinciding with existing other evidence, Curley also saw a noncommissioned officer (Ireland-born Sergeant James Bustard of Company I who had experience, unlike the recruits), not only cross the river but also enter the village. However, Bustard's marble burial marker has been misplaced far from the river as part of the overall blundering and errors that resulted in the erection of 252 markers for the around 210 who were killed.[130]

Indeed, ample evidence exists that more 7th Cavalry attackers gained the west bank, contrary to what has been generally assumed by historians. In fact, from what they saw at and around the ford, both Reno and Benteen were convinced that part of Custer's command penetrated into the village. *According to The Custer Myth,* Benteen emphasized in a Fourth of July 1876 letter to his wife: "I am of the opinion that nearly—if not all of the five companies got into the village—but were driven out immediately." After studying the field immediately after the battle, Major Reno, the regiment's most senior officer next to

Custer and a Civil War veteran, concluded in his official report on July 5, 1876: "Company C and I, and perhaps part of Company E, crossed to the village, or attempted it at the charge . . . ."[131]

Another trooper of unknown name was shot and fell off his horse, but was saved by fast-thinking comrades. In a courageous act under heavy fire from the brushy rise in the bottoms, nearby troopers dragged their wounded comrade back to the relative safety of the east bank, before he drowned or was left to be later captured.[132]

Other 7th Cavalrymen were killed and wounded besides officers in a full-fledged attack, which fully confirmed Reno's evaluation (coinciding with Indian accounts) based upon surveying the battlefield not long after the combat. As mentioned because his surgical case was later found in the Cheyenne village, sickly Dr. Lord (of Custer's staff), who wore eyeglasses, also might have well fallen at or near this point. The surgeon's body, like Harrington's remains (either killed or captured at or near the ford), was never found. After all, Custer's staff had been the first contingent swept by the fire from the slight rise covered in underbrush.[133] Assistant Lord's fall near the river corresponds with the high casualties among Custer's staff and the foremost companies, and agrees with an ample amount of Indian collaborating oral testimony of how the column's front was hard hit by ford defenders' fire.[134]

Chief Trumpeter Henry Voss did not escape the hail of bullets, unlike other staff members, which seems to indicate that the Indians were selective in choosing targets. This coincides with White Cow Bull's testimony of deliberate targeting and firing at officers, including Custer, and flag-bearers in front. At five feet eight inches tall, the talented musician of German descent was conspicuous atop his horse while blowing his bugle, when his sharp notes slanted over the Little Bighorn's valley to mix with the sound of crackling gunfire.[135] Later, in looking over the field, it was discovered by white soldiers that "the body nearest the river was that of chief trumpeter Voss. . . ."[136]

Near the front of the attack column, the other trumpeter on Custer's staff was also unfortunate during the attack on the ford. Like Voss, he offered an easy target to the ford defenders. Born in Germany and riding a gray horse during the attack, Trumpeter Henry C. Dose was "[k]illed near Medicine Tail Coulee."[137] Clearly, in leading the way, Custer's headquarters staff was hit hard by the blistering fire that spat from the rise, as revealed by Indian testimony and official service records. White Cow Bull revealed as much after shooting the "soldier chief," and then targeting other bluecoats in the forefront of the attack.[138]

Also advancing at the head of Custer's headquarters staff and riding near Assistant Surgeon Lord (before hit) and Chief Trumpeter Voss, Sergeant Robert H. Hughes now carried "Custer's battle flag," or "personal guidon." Highly respected as the "Regimental Color Sergeant," he was likewise killed in the charge on the ford. According to Pretty Shield, Custer was hit beside a color-bearer, which was most likely Hughes, while in the ford's swift waters. With the colorful flag so prominent near the column's head and at five feet nine inches tall, Hughes presented a most inviting target to the concealed Cheyenne and Sioux along the slight rise covered in underbrush.[139]

Once again, the fast and accurate firing of White Cow Bull, who blazed away with "my repeater," proved devastating, especially to those troopers at the front. As if shooting at a flock of turkey gobblers roosting high in a tall cottonwood by aiming at the lead bird in the full plumage of spring mating season, White Cow Bull shot Sergeant Hughes, who was beside Custer in the ford's waters. Destined to never again see the serene Liffey River that ran gracefully through his native Dublin, the devoted Irishman was hit on horseback and nearly dropped his banner of silk. Like others, Sergeant Hughes also "tumbled into the river." As White Cow Bull described the hot fire streaming from his reaping rifle: "I fired again, aiming this time at the soldier with the flag [and] I saw him go down as another soldier grabbed the flag out of his hands."[140]

White Cow Bull's words coincided with other reliable Indian oral accounts that were collected by historian Miller. Therefore, this careful and dedicated researcher Miller, who obtained a large number of Indian interviews over a lengthy period, wrote how "the orderly [near Custer and part of his staff] with the flag crumpled from his saddle [but] a trooper grabbed at the flag and kept it from falling" in the river.[141] The fact that Sergeant Hughes (who left behind a widow, Annie) fell at the ford was additionally verified by the later discovery of the blood-stained waistband of the Irishman's light blue trousers in the Cheyenne village.[142]

With his fast-firing Winchester or Henry rifle, White Cow Bull toppled a number of troopers. By all accounts, he was the best marksmen among the ford defenders, tabulating a number of hits with his well-aimed fire. After shooting the buckskin-clad officer who fell off his horse and into the river with a splash, as mentioned, White Cow Bull then "shot another soldier [Sergeant Hughes] who was carrying a flag [and] [t]hey all fell from their saddles and hit the water."[143]

Despite the lack of artifacts recovered at the ford more than a century after the battle, Sandy Bernard and other top Little Bighorn historians concluded, but underestimated, that "at least a few individuals, possibly some Army privates or newspaper reporter Mark Kellogg [indeed] made it to the vicinity of the river."[144]

A sufficient amount of evidence caused one modern archeologist, Doug Scott, to conclude: "I can see Kellogg or someone else got popped down there" at the ford.[145] Scott's opinion corresponded with the Indian accounts, and even what Lockwood allegedly saw with regard to the decimation of the head of Custer's column (headquarters staff), after having been swept with the initial volley of a destructive fire. These accounts are additionally reinforced by data in individual 7th Cavalry service records in the National Archives, Washington, DC, to reveal what really happened at the ford.[146] Indeed, while riding with the headquarters staff near the column's head, Mark Kellogg was "killed on flat near the river below Custer Hill."[147] The fact that Kellogg fell close near the river and close to Medicine Tail Coulee Ford was later confirmed when it was discovered that "the body nearest the river was that of chief trumpeter Voss, and near to it was that of Kellogg [and] [b]oth of these bodies were within a stone's throw of the river."[148]

In the words of respected historian Sandy Barnard, who relied upon available existing evidence: "One must conclude that during the decisive phases of the battle Kellogg remained close to Custer, probably with the headquarters element of the regiment [and] [h]is clothed body [found afterward] strongly suggests he was an early casualty of the battle."[149] Barnard's expert analysis was also in keeping with an abundant amount of Indian testimony, and even what Lockwood and others (including Indian accounts and military service records) allegedly saw in the first Indian fire taking a high toll on the forefront headquarters contingent.[150]

These losses among Custer's headquarters staff that came so very near the Cheyenne village (at the ford) ensured that the bodies of a number of men were never found: additional convincing evidence that they fell either in the river or around the ford, and that their bodies were later then dragged into the village by young boys and women to be desecrated in a ritualistic manner so that these enemies would never be faced in the afterlife.[151]

North Carolina–born Sergeant Daniel Alexander Kanipe, allegedly the second-to-last messenger to secure assistance (before Martin) was a tall, twenty-three-year-old ex–farmer and noncommissioned officer of German descent from Company C, 7th Cavalry. He explained what happened to the most unfortunate 7th Cavalry soldiers: "There were 14 men and two officers, Lieutenants Harrington and Lieutenant Sturgis, that never were found. It was said that the Indians cut off their heads and dragged them around as they powwowed during the night."[152]

This ultimate horror for a number of 7th Cavalry troopers—more officers than enlisted men, which indicated that they were at the head of the charge when either wounded or dehorsed—was also the tragic fate of young Lieutenant James Garland Sturgis. He was at the forefront of the attack because he was second in command of Company E, the "Gray Horse Company." The popular "Jack" Sturgis evidently took charge of the company after Lieutenant Smith was either killed or wounded, if he himself had not fallen before that time. Born in Albuquerque, in the upper Rio Grande country of New Mexico, Sturgis was the twenty-two-year-old son of the 7th Cavalry's commander, Colonel Samuel Davis Sturgis, who was now on detached service. The seasoned colonel was a Mexican–American War and Civil War veteran and West Pointer (Class of 1846) of proven ability. Despite his commander father officially commanding the 7th Cavalry, the amiable "Jack" was modest and unpretentious.

As could be expected from a courageous officer leading his company into the teeth of the defenders' hot fire, the fate of the youngest 7th Cavalry officer was a tragic one. Of course, Lieutenant Sturgis would never have charged the ford with Company E if his father had been killed instead of captured by the Mexicans during a risky mounted reconnaissance just before the bloody showdown at Buena Vista between an outnumbered American Army and Antonio Lopez de Santa Anna's Army in northern Mexico on February 23, 1847. Only because the colonel now served on detached duty, Custer led the command in his final charge toward the old buffalo ford. Young Sturgis, distinguished by a thick mane of wavy, dark hair like his father, which graced his face that revealed youthful innocence, was hit before his charging Company E troopers. He was not only cut down, his body was also lost at the ford and never recovered, because he fell so close to the village. Lieutenant Sturgis was another promising young officer, a graduate (twenty-nine in a class of forty-three cadets) of the West Point Class of 1875. As listed officially on the muster roll and in the military service records, "he was missing [in action during the attack on the ford] and presumed killed."[153]

Like other officers who led their troopers in attacking the ford, Lieutenant Sturgis's body was never found. Additional evidence of the severity of the fighting at the ford and the fact that Sturgis fell in this struggle (quite possibly either in or near the water), was that his blood stained clothing was later found in the Cheyenne village. The young lieutenant's body had been dragged into the village by women and children for the purpose of what one historian has called "special attention": systematic dismemberment and ritualistic burning (as Reno saw) of an opponent rooted in spiritual beliefs and the hope that the victim would never attack the people in the afterlife.[154]

Like the gory remains of other unfortunate men cut down at the ford and its vicinity, Sturgis's head (distinguished by a shock of black hair and handsome face), bloodstained shirt, and undergarments were later found in the village.[155] Colonel Sturgis had advised his son in a pleading May 1875 letter, when about to graduate from West Point, to make a much wiser career choice by serving in the artillery instead of the cavalry. Prophetically, the father had warned his headstrong son that the cavalry was the worst possible choice. Attempting to convince his son to forsake all romantic notions about the grandeur of cavalry service, he mocked the "boyish notion . . . of being mounted and dashing about on their horses, I hope will find no place in your mind in making up your choice. An Indian, for that matter, is mounted also and does a great deal of dashing around, but for all that, he is an Indian still. You I hope will take a higher view of your future than all that."[156] Clearly, young Lieutenant Sturgis should have listened to his father's wise words. In this sense, a strange and tragic fate had brought "Jack" Sturgis to this obscure ford.

As mentioned, Major Reno and fellow officers from the high ground above the river later saw three 7th Cavalry prisoners tied to the stake in the village. Therefore, it is quite likely that what Reno and other 7th Cavalry officers saw were "Lieutenants Porter and Sturgis and possibly Assistant Surgeon Lord."[157] As previously mentioned, Major Reno fully believed one of these individuals might have been Lieutenant Harrington.[158] Revealing what was acted out in gory fashion on the night of June 25, Reno and his men later found the remains of 7th Cavalry comrades, who had been burned in bonfires until nothing more remained but ashes and pieces of bone.[159] Ironically, these unfortunately captives very likely had been cut to pieces by axes and hatchets marked "Dept. of the Interior."[160] Sergeant John Ryan was later horrified by the sight of the "bodies cut up in a most brutal and fiendish manner [which] was done by squaws. . . ."[161]

Revealing the penetrating depth (long minimized or entirely overlooked by historians) of Custer's last charge as ascertained by Reno and the 7th Cavalry's surgeon with regard to the tragic fate of captives (Lieutenant Harrington, in the case of Surgeon John W. Williams), these prisoners had been captured after having been wounded, had their mounts shot from under them, or had fallen off their horses during the attack on the ford. Lieutenant Harrington's skull was eventually "found near the Cheyenne camp" at the village's northern end and near the ford, providing additional evidence.[162] Scout George B. Herendeen also discovered to his horror that "some of our men were captured alive and tortured [and] [t]he heads of four white heads were found [in the village] that had been severed from their trunks. . . ."[163] One of these almost certainly belonged to the trooper, perhaps the red-haired corporal, who charged into the village. Grace, the wife of Lieutenant Harrington, was eventually not only informed of her husband's death, but also that he had been captured and tortured in the Cheyenne village on the night after the battle.[164]

Corresponding with individual service records housed in the National Archives and contrary to traditional views of historians, Indian accounts revealed that a larger number of Custer's men than generally recognized were in fact cut down at the ford, including those who fell in the water, or had been left behind, after having been unmercifully swept with a "tremendous fire" at the ford that even Sitting Bull later marveled at with regard to its intensity.[165]

In striking contrast and most significant, the words of the modern white historians do not correspond with the views presented in the dependable Indian oral accounts, especially those of the Cheyenne, whose testimonies have been long ignored and dismissed. Most importantly, these accounts have verified that Custer and other troopers were hit by a hail of bullets from a blistering fire, including repeating rifles, while riding through the river's waters and so far west in attempting to cross the ford in Custer's first and last attack on June 25.[166]

The ability to explain why a number of officers' gory remains were found in the village has given solid credence that Custer's last charge went farther than generally assumed by historians. Again, from his analysis of the battlefield not long after the fighting concluded, Major Reno even believed that the charging troopers of three companies "crossed to the village," including fording of the Little Bighorn in a deep westward penetration.[167]

The Crucial Time Factor

Besides having been nothing more than an insignificant showdown at the ford according to the traditional view of so many modern historians, another myth of the struggle at the ford was that it was of only brief duration, and hence its unimportance. Most of all, historians have failed to appreciate that Custer attempted a crossing with all five companies, and that this was a full-fledged flank attack and not a mere feint, because he knew that everything was at stake. Again, this dismissal of ample evidence by historians simply does not conform with the most reliable and best Cheyenne and Sioux accounts, white accounts (including Lieutenant Charles Camilus DeRudio) or the data found in military service records: a key collaboration of white and red accounts. According to Brave Wolf, the troopers "had got down toward the mouth of the little, dry creek and were near the level of the bottom [where] they began fighting, and for quite a long time fought near the river, with neither party giving back."[168] Cheyenne and Sioux oral testimony have revealed that this dramatic showdown along the river was a lengthy and hard-fought contest for possession of the battlefield's most strategic position (Medicine Tail Coulee Ford), in which all five companies played a leading role in attempting to force a passage across the river in consequence.[169]

However, in American Horse's words that described after Custer's attackers reached the river, the "troops fought in line of battle, and there they fought for some little time." American Horse arrived at the latter stage of the fight at the ford, but still emphasized a fight of lengthy duration.[170] A Cheyenne warrior, born about 1820 and formerly the husband of Corn Woman (Chief Crazy Head's sister, who had left him because of his infidelity), Brave Wolf was another Cheyenne late arrival to the ford fight. Proving that a lengthy struggle for possession of the strategic ford was played out in full, he described: "When I got to the Cheyenne camp, the fighting had been going on for some time. The soldiers [Custer's] were right down close to the stream."[171]

Entirely contrary to these collaborating Cheyenne and Sioux accounts, which have been long ignored, the overall consensus of historians and archeologists has been that the struggle at the ford was inconsequential and so brief as to have been nothing more than a light skirmish hardly worthy of a footnote.[172] This striking paradox has represented one of the great myths about the battle of Little Bighorn, obscuring of the significance of what happened at Medicine Tail Coulee Ford, which was the battle's forgotten turning point.[173]

Quite simply, these long-accepted views of modern historians simply fail to correspond with some of the most reliable Cheyenne oral testimony—which has been long erroneously considered less valid than Sioux accounts, when the opposite was actually the case. Presenting the collected testimony of the Cheyenne warriors, knowledgeable historian George Grinnell summarized: "according to Brave Wolf—a part of Custer's troops had got down toward the mouth of the little, dry creek and were near the level of the bottom [and] [t]here they began fighting and for quite a long time fought near the river, neither party giving back."[174] Again, what was most significant about Grinnell's summarization was the verification of a lengthy struggle for the possession of Medicine Tail Coulee Ford.

However, in part because of their single-shot carbines, the return fire of the 7th Cavalry's five companies proved largely ineffective, going too high and over the defenders' heads on the lower ground behind the low rise. The fact that the warriors were well hidden in the underbrush, willows, and saplings also kept them secure from return fire, because quite simply the troopers could not hit what they could not see. Relatively few 7th Cavalry troopers could see the ford defenders concealed in the thick underbrush and behind the slight rise.[175] Nevertheless, the fire of Keogh's cavalrymen of Companies I and L helped to cover the withdrawal of the foremost of Yates' troopers (Companies E, C and F), who had been so hard hit that they retired, playing a role in restoring much-needed stability under the hot fire, after the decisive repulse.[176] This was especially the case with regard to the fire's destructiveness because Indian accounts emphasized how: "One company [E] started to run when Custer was near and the rest fired . . . and made them come back." Of course, this was the Gray Horse Company.[177]

Soldier Wolf, a teenage Cheyenne warrior, provided some of the best testimony of the contest's length at the ford: "By this time, Custer had gotten down to the mouth of the dry creek and was on the level flat of the bottom. They began firing and for quite a time fought in the bottom, neither party giving back."[178] Likewise, White Shield described how the exchange of fire across the river continued for an extended period. He emphasized how the "shooting [lasted for] some time. . . ."[179]

Like Lieutenant DeRudio and others, Sergeant John Ryan saw ample evidence of a larger fight at the ford than has been not emphasized by modern historians. Investigating the ground in the Cheyenne village near the ford, this tough Ireland-born sergeant wrote with insight, "We found quite a number of dead horses and ponies lying around the camp [and] I heard there were some" Indians dead in camp.[180] Most significant, Ryan's words that described the large number of dead horses in the Cheyenne encampment coincided with Cheyenne warrior Soldier Wolf's words. Soldier Wolf described how during the attack on the ford, the troopers' heavy firing "killed quite a good many horses" in the bottoms and in the Cheyenne village, where "the ground was covered with the horses of the Cheyennes, the Sioux. . . ."[181] All of this evidence has revealed a significant clash of arms at the ford.

In addition, to verify Custer's determination to charge across the ford, other warriors emphasized how the pony soldiers attacking the ford were "shooting into the camp."[182] From what he had seen in surveying the battlefield, Major Reno also believed that Custer's last charge spilled over to the west bank and into the village.[183] Clearly, this was no contest of short duration or insignificance, as long assumed by generations of historians. The hard-hit 7th Cavalry troopers in the forefront evidently believed that the fire was coming from the village instead of the concealed rise. All in all, such dependable testimony and time considerations have provided additional evidence that Custer attacked with all five of his companies, which unleashed a sufficient amount of firepower, as revealed by Soldier Wolf, that thoroughly swept the bottoms and Cheyenne camp to kill larger numbers of horses, but not the hidden warriors.[184] In addition, some warriors, evidently coming to the assistance of the ford defenders in the village's eastern edge, were hit by the bullets pouring from the five companies. Consequently, one of the luckiest men in the 7th Cavalry (because his messenger mission saved his life), Trumpeter Martin later "saw the dead Indians in the brush on [the] river bank in [the Cheyenne] village. . . ."[185]

Most importantly in overall tactical terms, the precious time bought by the ford defenders in preventing a crossing not only succeeded in thwarting Custer, but also decided the battle's course, as Sitting Bull later appreciated after learning the truth from warriors. The precious time purchased by the well-aimed fire of the ford defenders ensured the arrival of the first few warrior reinforcements from Reno's sector. Down river, the cry had been early raised among the warriors: "Look! Yonder are other soldiers!" This alarm about the sudden appearance of Custer's threat had electrified hundreds of Sioux and Cheyenne warriors who were battling Reno. In Wooden Leg's words: "The news of them spread quickly among us [and] Indians began to ride in that direction."[186]

It was the rapid fire pouring from the repeating rifles that had bought precious time to ensure the arrival of the first additional warriors from Reno's sector. Thanks to the intensity of the fire from the Indians' repeating rifles and other weapons, not only Company E but also Company C (both of Yates's battalion), immediately to the rear, was thrown into some confusion. Indeed, because of the intense fire from the "Winchesters and Henrys" proved devastating, and "Company C balked."[187] Indeed, the "size of the village and the rapid gunfire from the Indians [had] left the men [of Company C and like those of Company E] dumbfounded."[188]

Second Wave Attack of Keogh's Two Companies after Yates's Repulse

It was now the turn of the second wave of the battalion's staggered attack, as first envisioned by Custer, who was going for broke. Yates's repulse now called for Keogh and his battalion of Companies I and L to strike a blow: a one-two offensive punch envisioned by Custer. As mentioned, Curley had already seen all five companies descend to the coulee's mouth (which was later verified by officers and troopers after the battle), and they were all part of Custer's last charge. After the front ranks of Yates's battalion—especially Companies E and C—also had been hard hit by fire, perhaps even after gaining the village itself (as Reno fully believed after studying the ground not long after the fight), and especially if Custer was hit, then senior battalion commander Captain Myles Walter Keogh now took charge of the five companies. Amid the heat of combat, the transition to a new commander was more difficult because of losses among the headquarters staff. Keogh called his senior commanders together in an ad hoc conference to discuss the vexing tactical situation and brainstorm about their next move, after the failure to cross the ford and Custer's wounding, which was almost certainly was the case.

Captain Keogh was experienced and cool in a crisis situation, ensuring that the command in good hands. The seasoned Ireland-born senior captain wore a Catholic medal on a gold chain around his neck as a protective charm, much like the warriors viewed the spiritual power of buffalo tails and eagle feathers. He was a capable replacement if Custer was indeed knocked out of action, which was most likely the case. The handsome Irishman, age thirty-six, was a dashing ladies' man who had never married. An adventurer in and outside of the bedroom to flaunt society's conventions, Keogh's charisma and good looks were sufficient to have caused concern among his fellow officers. The gallant Irishman's effortless ability to catch female hearts even made Benteen worry about the effect of Keogh's boundless charm on his own wife's heart. To be fair, Benteen had good reason for worry about Keogh's charm affecting his wife. Keogh's sexual transgressions were well known, including the taking of a captive Indian woman to bed, as he revealed in a boastful letter to his brother, Tom. Like so many other world-weary officers who were sick of war's horrors, Keogh was inclined toward heavy drinking when off duty. Nevertheless, this true Irish soldier of fortune was one of the regiment's finest officers.

In keeping with Custer's original tactical plan, Keogh launched an attack with his battalion (or, more properly, his wing) of Companies I and L in an attempt to force a passage of the ford, after the offensive effort of Yates's battalion faltered. The troopers of Keogh's companies rode light bays, which fueled an *esprit de corps*. One of Keogh's attackers was Company I's Private Charles Banks, born in Dublin, Ireland, in April 1845. He was former waiter from a New York City restaurant before casting his fate with the 7th Cavalry. However, Banks's Company I comrade, a native New York City boy named Private William J. Logue, was made of tougher and more volatile stuff. He had been charged with verbally abusing two laundresses and then threatened to end the life of a fellow private in early 1871.

After later analyzing the battlefield, Reno later found ample evidence that Company I (Keogh's old company, now led by acting commander First Lieutenant James Ezekiel Porter) charged as far as Yates's Companies C and E, perhaps even into the village itself. Contrary to the traditional assumption and generally accepted version of events that Keogh's battalion remained impotently on the high ground far above the ford and a good distance from the initial fighting, as if nothing of importance was at stake, the battalion's offensive effort at the ford was verified by the fact that a number of its members were killed at the ford, and what was later seen by troopers in analyzing the battlefield. Again, in a key tactical situation of the battle's turning point—at a time when he had known that Reno had been hurled back from the village's southern end—Custer had early realized that he had to make the maximum effort (as Keogh would have realized as well if now in charge after Custer's wounding or death in leading the attack, which was most likely the case) to cross the ford and charge into the village: the other arm of the pincer and the only tactical movement (flank attack) that could possibly bring success at this point in time and place.

After all, there was no other realistic tactical option for Custer and his five companies at this stage of a true crisis situation. Quite simply, the charge across the ford was the last bid to reap a success in accordance with Custer's original plan. The challenges were most formidable and entirely new (including their not having been part of his Civil War experience) to Custer in their entirety, presenting a daunting tactical quandary: crossing a river under fire, facing a strong natural defensive position manned by determined enemies armed with repeating rifles, attacking in the middle of the afternoon, unfamiliar terrain, charging across an old buffalo ford, etc. Most significantly, all of these diverse factors at Medicine Tail Coulee Ford were the antithesis of Custer's attack on the Washita village. The longtime common view that Keogh and his battalion were non-players and stood idly by (like allegedly Custer himself!) to passively watch Yates's offensive effort at this critical moment, when aggressive action was desperately needed to reverse the day's fortunes, makes no tactical sense. It would be illogical, especially when the ever-aggressive Custer was in command of an offensive movement that was calculated to save the day.[189]

In this desperate situation and as mentioned, Sergeant James Bustard was in the forefront of Keogh's attack on the ford to yet force a crossing at any cost. He was a seasoned member of Company I, Keogh's old company, and now part of his battalion. Born in County Donegal, Ulster Province, northern Ireland, in 1846, and having enlisted in July 1870, Sergeant Bustard was one of Company I's best noncommissioned officers. In leading the way for Company I during the attack's second wave (as Reno and DeRudio verified with their analyses of the battlefield after the fight), the light-haired, fair-skinned Bustard was still another trooper who was "killed near Miniconjou [Medicine Tail Coulee] Ford."[190]

With Captain Keogh, the confirmed bachelor from County Carlow, Ireland, now commanding the battalion, a reliable lieutenant had taken command in leading the charge of his thirty-six Company I troopers. Ahead of his men as usual, First Lieutenant James Ezekiel Porter led the way in Custer's staggered attack, wearing his trademark buckskin shirt. Born in Maine in 1847 and a West Point graduate (sixteenth of thirty-nine graduates in the Class of 1869), the dark-haired Porter was also almost certainly killed at an advanced point near the ford. As mentioned, he was reported "missing" (like Harrington, another young lieutenant who was in his first battle like Porter) because he fell so close to the Cheyenne village.

Young Porter enjoyed a fulfilling personal life before meeting his end in a cruel rendezvous with disaster at the Little Bighorn. Married to Rhode Island–born Eliza Frances Westcott since late July 1869 and the father of two sons, the ruggedly handsome and square-jawed Porter was a most promising young officer. Porter's wife had given birth to their second son (James Francis), named after him, on March 25, 1876, at Fort Abraham Lincoln. Clearly, young Porter had everything to live for, especially after James's birth had brought him additional personal joy. Therefore, Lieutenant Porter, who possessed the distinguished look of a wealthy English aristocrat, had officially requested less-hazardous duty (a general staff position that guaranteed faster advancement while enjoying a safe job far from the often-nightmarish frontier duty) and healthier environment to raise his new family

Cruel fate had deemed otherwise for the Porter family, including his infant son's death before the year's end. Porter's request for reassignment and his eagerly anticipated dream job had already been approved at the highest levels at headquarters. However, this process had taken too much time in a typical army bureaucracy. Indeed, the necessary paperwork at headquarters for the coveted transfer had slowed the official confirmation process down to a crawl. Lieutenant Porter led his troopers in this charge to meet a grim end, not only because of an Indian bullet, but also thanks to the red tape of a cumbersome bureaucracy. Porter was hit with a well-placed shot that revealed the nature of the close-range fighting for the ford's possession. He fell with a bullet through the chest, which entered his body near the heart. Like Lieutenant Harrington, whose body was never discovered, Porter's fall so near the ford ensured that his body was later taken to the village by Indian women and hence never found.[191]

Later, after investigating the battlefield, Lieutenant Edward Settle Godfrey described the horror of Porter's sad fate. He wrote, "I found Porter's buckskin blue in the village . . . and from the shot holes in it, he must have had it on" when "shot from the rear, left side, the bullet coming out on the left breast near the heart."[192] Again, and most significantly, Major Reno saw ample first-hand evidence that Company I's troopers had in fact made a deep penetration, charging across the ford and making it all the way to the west bank, and perhaps into the village itself. Providing additional evidence of the attack across the river, Company F's Private William A. Brown, a blue-eyed trooper with more than three years of service in the 7th Cavalry, was killed near the ford, and his body was likewise later found in the Cheyenne village. [193]

Albany, New York–born First Sergeant James Butler, of Keogh's battalion, was still another good fighting man who was cut down in the attack on the ford. At age thirty-three, the dark-haired Butler had been reenlisted at Fort Abraham Lincoln by Tom Custer on the last day of May 1875. He had married a woman of Irish descent and the same socio-economic status as himself, Mary Elizabeth C. Murray, on July 7, 1875. The fact that this capable Company L sergeant' fell near the ford was confirmed by Lieutenant Edward Settle Godfrey, a West Pointer of Company K, 7th Cavalry. In walking the field after the battle, Godfrey wrote: "One of the first bodies I recognized and one of the neatest to the ford was that of Sergeant Butler of Tom Custer's troop."[194]

Additional evidence has revealed that Keogh's battalion (Companies I and L) attacked the ford not long after Yates' battalion struck: all part of Custer's one-two punch of an all-out offensive effort to force their way across the old buffalo ford. A member of Keogh's Company I now commanded by Keogh's second-in-command First Lieutenant James Porter, Private Gustave Korn, born in Silesia in 1852 and perhaps of Jewish descent, had the wildest ride of his life. He nearly reached the river during the charge's deep penetration: again a fact verified by Major Reno. Here, at the Little Bighorn's east bank, Korn's "horse bolted near the river" and raced south or upriver. Frightened by the gunfire, Korn's mount was entirely out of control, taking its rider on a hair-raising dash.

However, in the end, Korn was fortunate. He eventually reached the safety of Reno's defensive position atop the bluffs. Korn's amazing good luck (which Custer had lost so suddenly in meeting the unexpected stubborn opposition at Medicine Tail Coulee Ford) was destined to finally run out at Wounded Knee, South Dakota, in late December 1890. Here, he was killed in the attack on another Sioux village to officially end the Indian Wars.[195]

Private Marion E. Horn, age twenty-five and Indiana-born, also served in Company I's ranks during the attack on the ford. Perhaps he was recalling his prophetic words recently written in his final letter back home to Richmond, Indiana, with some alarm that he and his comrades now realized was well–founded: "there is one of the greatest Indian war expected this year. . . ."[196]

Again, Yates' battalion of three companies and Keogh's battalion of two companies had attacked at the ford with "the five companies moving in line," which revealed that Custer had launched a full-fledged offensive effort.[197] This fact corresponded with numerous Indian accounts (and later trooper evaluations of the field) that emphasized the might of Custer's attack, which revealed that he was not holding back with regard to offensive capabilities as long assumed. Indeed, "many of the Indian participants . . . believed that both battalions fought as one group [at] Medicine Tail Ford" and later in retiring up the high ground.[198]

As mentioned, Custer's fall at the ford has been disputed in part because a number of officers, especially those of Custer's inner circle, wore buckskin coats, such as Lieutenant Harrington and Tom Custer.[199] Horned Horse explained how he "did not recognize Custer, but supposed he was the officer who led the column that attempted to cross that stream."[200] Like other warriors, especially White Cow Bull, Horned Horse was convinced that "Custer perished" near the river, however.[201] Two Eagles also told that "a few" troopers were killed in the attack on the ford and others were wounded.[202] And significantly, at least one Indian account coincided with that of Sergeant Kanipe. Thunder Hawk explained why more officers and men were lost at the river than has been generally recognized: because the foremost troopers charged across the ford and all the way into the Cheyenne village. In relating that the attack was not only harder hitting but also more successful than has been generally recognized by historians, he emphasized "that Custer did cross the river and moved down the west side [of the river] firing into the tepees."[203]

In one of the rare agreements in white and red testimonies, the words of Thunder Hawk coincided with those of Major Reno with regard to what he later saw around the ford, revealing that at least several companies "crossed to the village, or attempted it at the charge. . . ."[204]

Again, the fighting at the ford continued for an extended period and longer than believed by today's historians, who have mistakenly concluded that the struggle at the ford was insignificant and hardly worth mentioned. Making a later arrival at the ford, Brave Wolf revealed how "the fighting [at the ford] had been going on for some time [when] [t]he soldiers (Custer's) were right down close to the stream. . . ."[205] Some historians have long condemned Custer's so-called "fatal delay" (up to three-quarters of an hour) in having allegedly spent too much time either on the high ground above the ford or in Medicine Tail Coulee before launching his attack on the ford: an entirely erroneous view resulting from the mistake of following too closely the prejudicial and distorted testimonies of Reno, Benteen, and other self-serving officers who sought to demonstrate that no time existed to go to Custer's rescue to excuse themselves of responsibility in the defeat.

Such dishonest testimony at the 1879 Reno Court of Inquiry in Chicago ensured that the 7th Cavalry's officer corps and personal reputations were not stained forever, preserving the regiment's honor. As the Indian accounts, like that of Brave Wolf, have clearly demonstrated, the far greatest amount of time was consumed by Custer not on the bluffs or in the coulee in the most un-Custer-like of all possibilities in a crucial situation (wasting precious time deliberately as if time was unimportant, when he knew that time was of the essence), but in attacking and attempting to force a crossing at the ford.[206]

After the repulse at the ford and another indication that Custer had been hit, Curley described how Captain Keogh ordered his men to dismount, form skirmish lines, and fight on foot, because Custer had lost the initiative: "Here a portion of the command were dismounted and thrown forward to the river, and returned fire with the Indians."[207] To Civil War-experienced officers like Keogh, this standard tactical theory of utilizing skirmish lines—a tactical legacy from the Civil War years—was considered the best way to fight Indians. This tactic was based upon the premise that troopers on foot were more effective in firing from cover and stationary defensive positions.

However, on the barren slopes of the high ground above the ford, the open terrain, patches of prairie grass, and sagebrush offered little cover for a lengthy line of dismounted cavalrymen, who were now sitting ducks. In overall tactical terms, what had been long taught at West Point and learned during the Civil War backfired for the men of the 7th Cavalry, paving the way to the annihilation of five companies at the Little Bighorn. Indian testimony has revealed their opinion that if the charge had been continued to cross the river, then a "great victory" would have been won.[208]

Was Custer Killed or Wounded at the Ford?

With regard to the repulse at the ford, only one possibility can explain the decisive setback at the ford, and then the tactical mistake of fighting as dismounted cavalry: Custer's fall. Clearly, while advancing at the column's head in the flank attack across the ford while leading his last charge from the front as usual, Custer had presented an ideal and most conspicuous target for warriors in concealed positions. Catching

Custer by surprise in a day of many surprises, the hot fire that erupted from this ambush position under natural cover along the slight rise had proved most effective and lethal.

Again, these were no ordinary fighting men in ideal defensive positions. They had hunted game and enemies (mostly Indian enemies) for most of their lives. Mostly importantly, as experienced warriors, these fighting men had been able to easily recognize the obvious leader at the attack's head. With his penchant for personally leading the charge, Custer was also most conspicuous because of his distinctive dress. Indian accounts described the leader of the charge on the ford in considerable detail, giving credence to Custer's fall. Realizing Custer's conspicuousness, especially in leading an attack, Lieutenant Godfrey, Company K, 7th Cavalry, described how Custer "wore a whitish gray hat, with broad brim and rather low crown, very similar to the Cowboy hat."[209]

Combining extensive Indian testimony of what actually happened in the attack on Medicine Tail Coulee Ford—especially that of White Cow Bull who emphasized the distinctive "big hat" of the charge's leader—to his own analysis, historian David Humphreys Miller concluded that Custer was shot through "his left breast [but] [n]o Indian, Crow, Sioux, or Cheyenne, could say whether he died at once or later. . . ."[210] Miller's analysis matched that of historian Nathaniel Phibrick, who recently emphasized the "wounding, if not death, of Custer at the early state of the battle. . . ."[211]

After interviewing Cheyenne and Sioux warriors, Lieutenant Oscar Long, 5th United States Infantry, learned that an "officer," who carried a compass and binoculars [Custer had borrowed and wore Lieutenant DeRudio's Austria–made field glasses, that were the most powerful in the regiment], had been killed at the ford. Custer carried a set of binoculars as verified by Trumpeter John Martin, and DeRudio was angry that his commander had borrowed his prized binoculars. Custer had long relied on a compass in navigating the open plains during campaigning. This reliance included the use of a compass during his snowy trek to attack the Washita village. At that time, he had guided the column to his objective like a sea captain sailing over the open seas, to which he compared to the prairie's vast openness.[212] The victors used a captured pair of binoculars—almost certainly Custer's pair that had been borrowed from DeRudio—to spy the arrival of Terry's column on the following day.[213]

The Northern Cheyenne grandmother of Sylvester Knows Gun emphasized that Custer was mortally wounded in attempting to cross the ford and that "he was dead by the time he reached Last Stand Hill."[214] As previously mentioned, Bobtail Horse and White Cow Bull both "claimed the man leading the troops [in the attack across the ford] was shot in the chest, and then fell in the river."[215]

However, given ample evidence, the most likely scenario was that Custer was not killed or shot through the chest in leading the charge. He most likely suffered only a wound in the right forearm. This injury (minor if only a flesh wound, but a significant injury if bone was shattered) was later discovered on his body atop Custer Hill, or Last Stand Hill. Almost certainly and from the best existing evidence, Custer received this arm wound in the first initial volley from the brushy rise, where the repeating rifles roared at relatively close range from an ambush position, as emphasized by Sitting Bull (oral testimony) and others.[216]

Custer's wounding decisively dictated the course of events, including the struggle at the ford, and especially the battle's ultimate outcome. As White Cow Bull emphasized, the fact that Custer was hit naturally sapped the momentum of the offensive thrust across the ford, while also effectively eroding overall combat capabilities of the five companies. In fact, Custer's wounding had been largely responsible for the failure of the attack across the ford. If only slightly wounded on in the forearm, Custer would have then continued to lead his troopers in his withdrawal back up the high ground from the ill-fated river bottoms.

After most likely having perhaps received medical attention from Assistant Surgeon Lord, if only a minor forearm wound, Custer then could have continued to lead right up to the bitter end atop Custer Hill, about three-quarters of a mile from Medicine Tail Coulee Ford. Therefore, the traditional image of Custer fighting heroically and falling atop Custer Hill was in fact very likely the actual reality.[217] Custer dying heroically, battling to the end, was verified by brass shell casings from his "Remington Sporting rifle, octagonal barrel," laying around and even under his body atop Custer Hill.[218]

However, if more seriously wounded by a shot in the lower left breast at the ford (which was less likely than a forearm wound, given available evidence), as was discovered after the battle, then he would have been carried by members of his staff, including no doubt brother Tom.[219] Therefore and despite his reliance on Indian testimonies, Miller was most likely incorrect when he concluded that Custer's wound at the ford "was mortal."[220]

Custer's wounding at the ford, which is almost certainly the case, was nevertheless a catastrophe at the highest leadership level, sending a wave of shock through the blue ranks. Such a disaster that so suddenly burst the lofty image of Custer's invincibility so soon after the attack began has provided the best explanation for the rapid deterioration, and "panic" in Benteen's words, of trooper morale and the overall resistance effort. Custer's fall would not have been known to the defenders, because it was not known that he led the attack. As mentioned, the Cheyenne and Sioux had no idea that Custer was anywhere near the Little Bighorn.

Once again, Wooden Leg, known for his truthful words, described the true situation despite all later claims of seemingly countless Indians who bragged that they had killed Custer: "It was not then known to us who was the chief of these white soldiers [and] [i]t was not known to us where they had come from. We supposed them to be the same men [under Crook] we had fought on the Rosebud, eight days before."[221] However, these warriors knew Custer sufficiently well to have bestowed multiple names for him. As Custer penned to his amused wife two summers before: "The Indians have a new name for me, but I will not commit it to paper."[222] Clearly, this nickname was not at all flattering.

The nephew of the hard-fighting Roan Bear, a ford defender, concluded that one officer who was killed "was dressed in a buckskin suit, had short hair; and the Indians knew Custer as Long Hair, [therefore] they did not think the man with the buckskin suit was the General."[223] However, raising the possibility of a more serious wound, which was actually more remote than only a relatively slight wound, Crow scout White Man Runs Him emphasized that on this afternoon Custer "wore buckskin."[224] A warrior named Respects Nothing stated that he "saw Custer's clothing which was buckskin, after Custer was killed."[225] In addition, Hollow Horn Bear learned from another warrior that "he saw a man with a red [traditional scarf of Custer's Michigan men during the Civil War] and yellow handkerchief around his neck and a buckskin jacket on [and he believed that] it must be Long Yellow Hair."[226]

However, the ample collaborating and reliable Indian accounts, especially that of White Cow Bull, of the shooting down of this dynamic officer in buckskin leading the charge at the ford have been dismissed by the overwhelming majority of white historians, largely because of the power of myth. Much of this dismissal has also resulted because of the assumption by historians that Custer did not wear his buckskin shirt or jacket because it was simply too hot: as mentioned, a view that does not conform with that of Crow scout White Man Runs Him and others. However, historians have conveniently overlooked the fact that a number of other officers also wore their buckskin shirts and coats—soft, durable, and ideal for campaigning—in the battle for protection against the clouds of rising dust from the parched ground in summertime, despite the day's heat. However, this automatic assumption of Custer having not worn buckskin because of the day's intense heat seemed verified when Custer's body was found, but the garments of almost all victims had been stripped off by the jubilant victors.

In fact, some Indians put on these light and comfortable buckskin shirts and coats—quite likely Custer's own garments among them—and were wearing them in the attack on Reno's men on the following day, June 26. Lieutenant DeRudio, a darkly handsome officer with gray hair of Company M with Reno's command, saw one Indian "with a buckskin jacket, pants, top boots and white hat and felt quite sure I recognized him as Capt. Tom Custer," which of course was not the case. Clearly, if the buckskin shirts were not too hot to wear for the Indians to wear in battle and in the scorching heat, then they would not have been too hot for Custer. The misconception about Custer not having worn his buckskin coat was first created by Trumpeter Martin, who was known for relating contradictory information. For example, the Italian immigrant, born Martini, later described that Custer wore "a blue-gray flannel shirt" instead of a buckskin jacket.[227]

Therefore, this general assumption that it was too hot for Custer to have worn his favorite buckskin shirt, which had been fashioned by Ireland-born Sergeant Jeremiah Finley, who was a former tailor now serving in Company C, makes relatively little overall sense with regard to the usual rationales and assumptions made by historians. After all, many of Custer's fellow officers, like Lieutenants Harrington and the Porter, wore their buckskin jackets on this afternoon under the same hot and dusty conditions.[228] Indicating that Lieutenant Porter, dignified-looking with a stylish mustache, was killed in the charge at the ford, Lieutenant Godfrey penned: "I found Porter's buckskin blouse in the village [with] shot holes in it. . . ."[229]

Crow scout White Man Runs Him emphasized in no uncertain terms how Custer led the charge and went straight into harm's way to get hit, while attempting to force his way across the ford: "I know for sure that Custer went right to the river bank. I saw him go that far [and] [t]he Sioux were right across the river."[230] White Cow Bull, the fastest-firing warrior who blasted away with either a Winchester or a Henry rifle, and almost certainly the most accurate marksman of the ford defenders, very likely hit Custer with a well-placed shot. As he explained, the "man in the buckskin jacket seemed to be the leader of these soldiers . . . I aimed my repeater at him and fired [and then] I saw him fall out of his saddle and hit the water" of Little Bighorn. Additional evidence of Custer's fall can be seen in White Cow Bull's words that described what happened after the leader of the charge was shot by him: "They all reigned up their horses and gathered around where he had fallen."[231]

Significantly, White Cow Bull also related that he cut down the "soldier chief," who was leading the charge across the ford. A good deal of evidence has revealed that this could only have been Custer (the physical description of both him and his horse matched), who always led the attack and never delegated such a leading offensive role in such a crucial situation to another officer during either the Civil War or the Indian Wars.[232] If it was indeed Custer who was hit, which was most likely the case, then Libbie's dark premonition she had felt when the confident 7th Cavalry rode out of Fort Abraham Lincoln had come true at the obscure buffalo ford along the Little Bighorn.[233]

Custer was very likely shot by White Cow Bull, although most defenders were Cheyenne, who reaped tribal revenge on the native Ohioan for his dawn attack on the Cheyenne village at the Washita. This would have been the most symbolic conclusion to what had become a private war long waged between Custer and the Cheyenne people, coming full circle along the Little Bighorn.[234]

Contrary to the seemingly endless number of books about the battle Little Bighorn, what Custer launched at Medicine Tail Coulee was not an insignificant feint as long assumed by historians, but in fact a full-fledged offensive effort with all five companies. This was Custer's last-ditch bid to reverse the day's fortunes, depending upon by his maximum manpower to fuel his desperate attack to cross the river at Medicine Tail Coulee Ford.[235]

Like Lieutenant DeRudio, this maximum offensive effort was also confirmed by Lieutenant Theodore W. Goldin, Company G, 7th Cavalry, who believed (like Captain Benteen) that Custer massed his manpower as much as possible for an offensive thrust across the ford, because the village's size and the overall tactical situation (needed a successful flank attack) warranted a maximum offensive effort.[236] Under the circumstances, it only made good tactical sense that Custer would have employed both Yates's and Keogh's battalions for an all-out offensive effort to reap what might have been one of the most impressive victories of his career: a powerful final flank attack to not only reverse the day's fortunes but also to win it all, when time was of the essence. Even if Custer's attack failed, then he at least would have saved the regiment's remainder.

Tall Bull, born around 1853 to Crow parents who had been captured and spared by the Cheyenne, which was customary (to augment manpower) in Great Plains warfare, was one of the first warriors to arrive at the ford after battling Reno's men to the south. In his words: "All rushed back on the west side of the camp, down to a small dry run that comes in from the east, and there, down close to the river, were the soldiers" under Custer who was going for broke.[237]

Custer's Decisive Repulse at Medicine Tail Coulee Ford

In his final charge, Custer had met with the most decisive repulse of his career. Coinciding with Cheyenne and Sioux accounts, the words of white and Indian scouts also tell the overlooked story of the decisive repulse at the ford. White Man Runs Him, one of Custer's most reliable Crow scouts, summarized the attack on the ford in only a few words: "Custer tried to cross the river at the mouth of Medicine Tail Creek, but was unable to do so."[238] Also only briefly describing the showdown at Medicine Tail Coulee Ford in the context of an ambush, Curley emphasized that, when the troopers reached the river, "the Indians, concealed in the undergrowth on the opposite side of the river, opened fire on the troops, which checked the advance."[239] These words agreed with Captain Benteen's initial analysis of the battlefield immediately after the fight. In a letter to his wife on July 25, 1876, Benteen was entirely correct with regard to the battle's forgotten turning point. He concluded how Custer received his "1st check" at the ford: a sharp setback that forever ordained not only the battle's outcome but also the fate of Custer and his men.[240]

Historians, however, have long dismissed Benteen's words because of his hatred of Custer. Agreeing with what Curley and others saw with their own eyes with regard to Custer's last attack on the ford, Lockwood had no personal agenda about saying anything negative about his own 7th Cavalry, of which he became a member in late August 1876. In his memoir, he emphasized how Custer's fall had a devastating effect on the troopers to alter the course of the battle: "The sudden attack [ambush] and the fall of General Custer and his staff checked the rest of the troops and seemed to demoralize them. The Indians kept up the firing. The troops soon dismounted and returned the fire."[241]

From what he saw, Curley echoed this view. He concluded how the 7th Cavalry troopers "fought splendidly until the Big Chief (Custer) fell, and then they became somewhat demoralized."[242] Curley's words even hinted that he witnessed Custer fall at the ford after having seen the beginning of the struggle for possession of the ford, before riding off the field to give General Terry the news of disaster. Curley was sufficiently close to the struggle at the ford that he even "saw two of Custer's men killed who fell into the stream" at the ford.[243]

In concurrence with Curley's account and others, Lockwood's words conformed to Indian accounts, both Cheyenne and Sioux. Tall Bull noticed the lack of "very good order" of the troopers at the ford, after the initial fire from the rise had taken affect.[244] These views are in agreement with Captain Benteen, a Civil War and Indian Wars veteran, who closely analyzed the battlefield immediately after the fight. He concluded during the attack on the ford how "the cavalry was probably thrown into a panic at the 1st check [at the ford] received."[245]

With regard to suppling collaborating evidence, the Indian accounts, the post-battle analysis of 7th Cavalry officers, and even Lockwood's memoir are in agreement with Richard Allen Fox, Jr.'s highly detailed analysis obtained from his archaeological survey of the Little Bighorn battlefield. This analysis revealed the decisiveness of Indian firepower from repeating rifles, including at the ford, which conformed with Indian oral accounts: "Thus, the repeater as an instrument of shock, coupled with the liability of the single-shot carbine in close-in fighting, probably contributed significantly to demoralization" among Custer's troopers: a process that began with Custer's repulse at the ford.[246] Indeed, Fox's keen 1993 analysis corresponded directly to the words of Horned Horse and White Cow Bull. As mentioned, Horned Horse emphasized how Custer's attack at the ford was entirely thwarted because the troopers were "met by such a tremendous fire from the repeating rifles. . . ."[247]

Watching the effects of the gunfire pouring from the brushy rise to thwart Custer's last charge, White Shield likewise described how when "the Gray Horse Company [E] got pretty close to the river, they dismounted, and all the soldiers back as far as I could see stopped and dismounted also."[248]

Revered Cheyenne shaman White Bull, known as Ice Bear and born around 1834, also saw Custer's repulse at the ford. A father and husband of Wood Woman, he spoke truthful words. Respected for his prophetic visions and healing powers, he revealed, "Custer rode down to the river bank and formed a line of battle. But then he stopped and fell back up the hill," after having been repulsed at the ford.[249]

In addition, Tall Bull, a Cheyenne veteran who was confident from the recent fight on the Rosebud with Crook, described how "Custer got onto the flat [river bottom] near [Medicine Tail Coulee Ford] within easy gunshot of the village. . . ."[250] After Custer's repulse at the ford and before his troops dismounted to fight on foot, Foolish Elk, the young Sioux warrior, described how the "bluecoats sat on their horses and fired across the river into the village," and at the defenders along the slight rise covered in the thick "undergrowth," in Curley's word, blasting away as if angry that they had been repulsed (a greater shock than Reno's defeat) and Custer's tactical dream had been thwarted.[251]

Wooden Leg confirmed Custer's decisive repulse at Medicine Tail Coulee Ford: "None of the Custer soldiers came any closer to the river than they were at the time they died."[252] What Custer and his men learned in their attack at the ford was a very hard lessons about not underestimating their opponent, especially when combined with the devastating effect of superior weaponry: a combination that all but ensured defeat. Perhaps Two Moons, the minor chief of the Kit Fox Society, said it best: "Every brave in this great camp was a veteran, as all the faint-hearts in both tribes had been left on the reservations, content to draw their rations and abide by the peace treaty. The allied fighters represented the determined spirits among the plains tribes-men who preferred the hardships and dangers of the warpath to a life of ease under the white man's dominion."[253]

Exhausted, Thirsty, and Unruly Horses
Since the hard-fought struggle at the ford evolved into the decisive turning point of the battle, what other forgotten factors also played a role in Custer's decisive repulse—besides the defenders' blazing repeating rifles and sheer determination to hold firm at any cost, especially when they were so few in numbers? Horned Horse revealed that the Medicine Tail Coulee Ford was so shallow that it could be easily crossed

by all five companies. Therefore, with regard to the river's water level, the river itself posed no obstacle for the crossing by Custer's troopers, who should have easily crossed as envisioned by their commander. This was an ancient buffalo crossing and watering spot that had been currently used by these migratory animals, which needed fresh water on the arid high plains during hot summer weather. Revealing how close Custer came to reaping a success because the river was not a formidable obstacle, Horned Horse emphasized that the river at this point was only "about eighteen inches deep. . . ."[254]

Clearly, contrary to the views of previous studies, this low water level was not a factor as an effective obstacle that played a role in stopping Custer's flank attack. If the water depth of the Little Bighorn at the ford was not a factor, then what other forgotten considerations played a role in the decisive repulse of Custer's last attack?

A forgotten factor that almost certainly played a role in Custer's repulse at the ford was the poor shape and thirstiness of the troopers' horses, including the fact that many mounts were "untrained" like a good many members of the 7th Cavalry: a most disadvantageous situation that helped to sabotage the final charge. As early as June 21, Captain Yates, who led the advance with his battalion down Medicine Tail Coulee just behind Custer and his headquarters staff, complained in a letter: "My company [F] horses are about played" out from the hard riding of this arduous campaign.[255] Ending on a hot June 18, after riding nearly 250 miles over rough terrain while pushing deep in Indian country, Reno's lengthy scout all the way to Rosebud Creek had taken a severe toll on men as well as horses. Unfortunately for Custer, the five companies that launched their attack on Medicine Tail Coulee Ford had been part of Reno's exhaustive scout and were in relatively poor shape.[256]

Four days after Yates's serious June 21 complaint (that went unanswered, as if it made no difference because of excessive optimism), the horses of Custer's command were even far more jaded, after having been ridden nearly 350 miles since leaving Fort Abraham Lincoln. In fact, the horses were already in relatively poor condition even before Custer's led his regiment from the fort on May 17, more than five weeks before the showdown at the Little Bighorn. Nevertheless, the energetic Custer always drove his men and horses exceptionally hard, and never more so than during this most grueling of campaigns in his relentless push to the Little Bighorn and to catch his opponents before they fled. In hoping to reach the village before the inhabitants escaped, Custer overlooked that fact that the horses needed more frequent watering, because the overexertion and hot summer weather had at least doubled normal water requirements.[257]

After learning the intimate details about the battle from his "young men," who rode forth against Custer on their well-watered, fresh horses, Sitting Bull gave a fundamental reason for the 7th Cavalry's defeat, including the setback at Medicine Tail Coulee Ford: "When they rode up their horses were tired and they were tired."[258] This was especially the case with regard to Custer's five companies that attacked at the ford, sapping the attack's momentum. Amid an arid landscape and scorching heat after the command's dusty advance down Medicine Tail Coulee, the river of cold, clear water was like an oasis in the desert to weary men and horses who badly needed water. The ascent from Reno Creek to the top of the commanding bluffs on the Little Bighorn's east side devastated the horses' stamina and strength on one of the year's hottest days. In the correct analysis of historian Larry Sklenar: "The ride uphill would certainly have fatigued already tired horses to the breaking point."[259]

Clearly, serious liabilities existed for the horses of Custer's troopers by the time of the charge at the ford, hindering the flank attack from the beginning. By comparison, Reno's men had also just encountered the problem of thirsty horses not watered since the previous evening, and consequently becoming uncontrollable when crossing the Little Bighorn at an old Indian ford. Indeed, "into it [the river] our horses plunged without any urging, their thirst was great and also their riders," wrote Trooper Taylor.[260] Horses drank deeply and Reno's dust-covered troopers filled canteens, resulting in a delay of from ten to fifteen minutes. Clearly, the Little Bighorn served as a significant obstacle (for both Reno and Custer) that had nothing to do with the water's depths or currents, but because of thirsty horses. Indeed, Reno had been forced to water his horses in the river because "his horses were so desperately thirsty that they would not cross the river until after they had a drink."[261]

Another one of Reno's troopers wrote of the difficulty (almost certainly experienced by Custer's men) resulting from the meeting of cold water and thirsty mounts under a searing Montana sun: "Our horses were scenting danger before we dismounted, and several at this point became unmanageable and headed straight for the opening among the Indians, carrying their helpless riders with them. One of the boys, a young fellow named [George E.] Smith [a former shoemaker born in Maine] of Boston, we never saw him again, dead or alive."[262] Some cavalrymen lost control of horses because they "smelled Indians." Trooper inexperience also played a role. Before Reno's tentative attack, Adjutant Cooke had been forced to admonish Reno's troopers about conserving their horses' stamina, yelling out in desperation: "For God's sake men, don't run those horses like that; you will need them in a few minutes."[263]

Likewise, Captain Benteen wrote of the effect that the smell and sight of water had on hot and worn animals, whose thirst was maddening amid the high heat and humidity. He described how the pack train's mules suddenly became "hell-bent on getting to the blue water [of the river] which was so plainly in sight."[264] Again, such factors reduced the effectiveness of Custer's last attack at the ford. However, more than water, according to the cavalrymen, the smell of Indians caused horses to become unruly when at the edge of the large Cheyenne village. In the words of Sergeant John Ryan: "It was pretty hard to get one of our American horses to go near an Indian," especially a village.[265]

A Sioux warrior named Little Knife emphasized the early confusion and panic for the 7th Cavalry, and how "horses and men appeared to be unmanageable from the outset," and this included at Medicine Tail Coulee Ford.[266] Company C, to Company E's rear, has provided a good representative example of trouble with horses during the attack on Medicine Tail Coulee Ford. As mentioned, at least two unfortunate Company C troopers (new 7th Cavalry recruits without adequate equestrian skills) lost control of their horses that then galloped with their terrified riders across the ford and into the Cheyenne village.[267]

Defending the slight rise in the river bottoms, Bobtail Horse even caught one trooper's uncontrollable horse that had raced across the ford to gain the river's west side.[268] This was most likely a horse whose rider had been shot off. A member of the Sioux tribe, Moving Robe Woman, explained why Custer's horses were also unmanageable after the initial repulse at the ford, because the "soldiers dismounted and fired [but then the] soldiers' horses got loose and ran to the river [out of thirst and] [t]heir packs got loose and floated down the river [because the] horses wanted water."[269]

What is clear was that when Custer's attackers were very close to the ford, thirsty horses, such as at least two (and most likely more animals) mounts of Company C, became unmanageable. Such factors almost certainly played a factor in disrupting the advancing formations, helping to sabotage Custer's overall offensive effort to force a passage across the river. As mentioned, the tragic fate of Private Gustave Korn, Company I (which had been led down the coulee by First Lieutenant Porter) of Keogh's battalion, has provided the best example of the loss of control of horses during the attack. Korn's "horse ran away with him" so far that he eventually reached Reno's command on the bluff. As if protected by Providence, the private's "unmanageable horse carried him to safety."[270]

Of course, trooper horses also became unmanageable when their riders were hit, especially when wounds were inflicted on cavalrymen's arms that held the reins. Sergeant Frank Finkel (George August

Finckle), over six feet tall and German-born, was aiming his Springfield carbine at a warrior near the river when hit by a bullet. He lost control of his horse, smelling and sighting water, and the animal then headed straight for the river at a frantic pace. Upon reaching the riverbank, Finkel's horse, a high-spirited sorrel named "Ginger," then turned left, or south, and galloped along the bank toward the Sioux village to the south.[271]

Clearly, upon nearing the river, a very real problem for Custer's attack across the ford was the combination of the exhausted condition of the horses and their desperate thirst. This then was the situation that caused some horses to often ignore their rider's digging spurs and best efforts to halt them when near the river. Again, the 7th Cavalry's horses were in terrible shape: during one of the most arduous of campaigns, men and horses had been driven to their physical limits by Custer's relentless pursuit to catch up to the Indians before they slipped away, or so he feared. Therefore, with victory seemingly within his grasp in a crisis situation that reduced tactical options, a single-minded Custer had given relatively little, if any, consideration about the condition of the horses (without proper rest or nourishment for an extended period) for a major engagement on one of the year's hottest days.[272]

Paying a high price for having worn out his command's horses in pursuing victory, Custer's actions were in marked contrast to Sitting Bull's wisdom with regard to what he knew would be the inevitable showdown. When breaking up the encampment on the Rosebud, he had recently sternly admonished his young warriors about the condition of their horses. Knowing that fresh horses in good shape would play a key role in the upcoming confrontation that was only a matter of time, Sitting Bull had wisely cautioned: "You are racing your horses now, but don't race them too hard and play them out, for you all are going to have a big fight soon."[273]

As could be expected under these circumstances, Custer's troopers faced the same challenges as Reno's men. Major Reno had similarly encountered difficulty with his battalion's horses because of their worn and famished condition. Just before unleashing his attack after crossing the Little Bighorn, thirsty horses caused "some congestion and confusion" among Reno's battalion during its crucial mission of striking the village's southern end.[274] A good number of Reno's troopers were unable to control horses when near the river, because of the animals' burning thirst under the searing summer sun. Verifying the words of White Cow Bull, who witnessed this "pause" of Custer's attack upon reaching the river's east bank, Second Lieutenant Charles A. Varnum, Custer's Chief of Scouts, was correct when he emphasized that for any "column of troop[er]s getting across [the Little Bighorn] is necessarily [the cause of] some delay, they can't keep closed up [in formation] in the water."[275]

The greatest obstacle and most destructive element that thwarted Custer's attack on the ford came from the hail of the bullets from the fast-firing repeaters along the slight rise in the river bottoms. These warriors (professional hunters) were better marksmen than the troopers, especially recruits from major urban areas, and their marksmanship skill rose to the fore. The defenders also employed the smart tactic of targeting horses, which provided easier (or larger) targets to hit than the troopers on horseback. Dropping horses was actually more effective in disrupting the attack, especially attack alignment, than shooting troopers out of saddles, especially in the van. Soldier Wolf, a Cheyenne who was part of the ford's defense, emphasized the carnage among the horses that revealed how this contest was as lengthy as it was intense. He described how the struggle for possession of the strategic ford went on "for quite a time." Soldier Wolf explained the fire's destructiveness for an extended period and longer than generally assumed by historians: "There they killed quite a good many horses, and the ground was covered with the horses of the Cheyennes, the Sioux and the white men, and two soldiers were killed and left there" at the ford.[276]

By striking in summer instead of winter as usual, Custer had already lost a key advantage, because the Indian horses were at their weakest and least durable in winter, which was in part why his Washita village attack had been so successful.[277] Indeed, unfortunately for the 7th Cavalry and with regard to Indian ponies, the situation was now exactly the opposite along the Little Bighorn. While Custer's horses were now exhausted from this lengthy campaign and most recently ascending the bluffs above the Little Bighorn and then during the dusty descent down Medicine Tail Coulee, the Indian horses were in excellent shape. They had grown strong (symbolically like the buffalo) on the luxurious new growth of spring grasses, before the summer heat turned them parched and brown. Earlier in the spring, Wooden Leg emphasized with delight how "our horses were growing stronger" as the prairie grasses grew higher.[278] In fact, the fresh Indian ponies had only heightened the confidence among the warriors, believing that the bluecoats "now would be afraid to come [because] [o]n the benchlands [just west of the village] our horses found plenty of grass."[279]

Most importantly, the fact that so many troopers had difficulty with their horses also gave credence to the words of Thunder Hawk, with regard to the attack having continued across the ford to gain the opposite shore. He maintained that Custer's attack crossed the river, because troopers were riding "down the west side [of the river and] firing into the tepees."[280] Like so many Indian accounts, Thunder Hawk's words have been long routinely dismissed by historians. In fact, Thunder Hawk's oral testimony agreed with Reno's first official report of the battle on July 5, 1876, after he had evaluated the battlefield: "Companies C and I, and perhaps part of Company E, crossed to the [Cheyenne] village, or attempted it at the charge. . . ."[281] Like others who closely inspected the battlefield not long after the fight, Major Reno revealed that Custer made a maximum offensive effort to cross at the ford and explained why troopers' remains, including those of officers, were found in the village, because the attack had penetrated so far west, including into the Cheyenne village.[282]

Terrain Difficulties

The leader of an Oglala band named Horned Horse, whose two sons fought this day (including one who was killed in the early stages of battling Reno's men), described how rough terrain had also played a role in Custer's repulse at the ford. He believed that "owing to the abruptness and height of the river banks, Custer could not get down to the edge of the stream," which was not the case.[283]

Indeed, the west bank, and the land immediately west of the ford, was several feet higher than the wide and level flat on the east side opposite the ford. Providing a far-less-credible explanation, Horned Horse was also convinced that quicksand played a role in thwarting Custer's crossing of the ford: "The Little Big Horn is a stream filled with dangerous quicksand [and troopers shot off their horses] were swallowed up in the quicksand [and] [t]his is considered an explanation of the disappearance of Lieutenant Harrington and several men whose bodies were not found on the field of battle."[284] However, Sergeant John Ryan, Company M, 7th Cavalry, verified the truth of Horned Horse's seemingly exaggerated words at first glance, with regard to the river's treacherous bottom. He explained how the river's waters were "as about three feet deep with quicksand" at the bottom.[285]

Horned Horse also revealed the most important reason why Custer's last charge was thwarted at the ford, providing the most decisive catalyst in the ultimate outcome of the hard-fought contest for the ford's possession: Custer "made a dash to get across, but was met by such a tremendous fire from the repeating rifles of the savages" that it was impossible to cross the Little Bighorn.[286]

The loss of so many officers, very likely including Custer himself and the son of the 7th Cavalry's commander, Lieutenant Sturgis (two severe blows to leadership during an attack, including symbolic ones, and the loss of other top officers like Lieutenant Porter of Company I), at the ford played a key role in turning the tide at this crucial juncture. Due to the blistering fire exploding from the underbrush along the slight rise in the bottoms, the troopers retired farther away from the embattled ford and higher up the slope, where they dismounted. Any thought of crossing the ford and attacking the village was now over, along with Custer's bold plan of delivering a flank attack to pull a victory out of the jaws of defeat. The fate of the five companies was now sealed.

After this repulse, no other offensive plan existed than simple survival, because the attack on the ford was the final tactical opportunity to reverse the day's fortunes: quite literally, it was Custer's last chance to save himself and his command. For all practical purposes, the battle was over and the five companies were doomed to annihilation, especially after they dismounted in skirmish lines on higher ground. However, Custer saved the rest of the 7th Cavalry, after having pulled the great mass of warriors to him. Thereafter, in the face of the hot fire and with no tactical options remaining, the 7th Cavalry was now entirely on the defensive. Gamely, the out-gunned troopers continued to fight dismounted in lengthy skirmish lines after the sharp setback at the ford: the loss of initiative and momentum never to return to Custer's men to guarantee the most tragic day for the United States Cavalry. It was now only a matter of time before all five companies were eliminated on the deathtrap that was the open, high ground above Medicine Tail Coulee Ford. This annihilation was the inevitable result of the repulse of Custer's last charge of his career at the ford.[287]

Horned Horse summarized the decisive turning point in the showdown at the ford in only a few words: "the head of the column reeled back toward the bluffs after losing several men who tumbled into the water" of the Little Bighorn.[288] Moving Robe Woman also concluded this forgotten turning point of America's most iconic battle: "Custer's men got to the river above the beaver dam where the water was very deep [but they] got down to the river (at Medicine Tail Creek), but did not cross [and] Custer did not know where to cross" the Little Bighorn beyond the Medicine Tail Coulee Ford.[289]

Brave Wolf was one of the late-arriving Cheyenne to reinforce the band of ford defenders. He described the dramatic turning of the tide of battle: "Just as I got there [at the river], the soldiers began to retreat up the narrow gulch" known as Medicine Tail Coulee.[290]

The ford's desperate defense was absolutely crucial with regard to buying precious time for not only saving the village, but also for the arrival of the warriors returning from Reno's sector. Quite unlike the widely separated 7th Cavalry, the warriors possessed the advantage of interior lines, with the string of villages stretching for nearly three miles along the river bottoms: an easy, relatively open avenue by which hundreds of warriors (mostly Sioux) raced north from Reno's sector for a timely concentration of force against a reeling opponent, after the repulse at the ford.

As mentioned, after holding the 7th Cavalry at bay for an extended period at the ford, the band of defenders rejoiced in the arrival of increasing numbers of Sioux and Cheyenne, who had hurled Reno rearward in panic during their first success of the afternoon. The arrival of the resurgent warriors at the ford completely altered the balance of the long-range standoff. Sioux warrior Red Feather described the early rallying cry that had galvanized the warriors before Reno: "The women and children shouted, 'Another detachment coming!' They were on the high [ground] place. There was another body of soldiers east of the Cheyennes. They left Reno and went as fast as possible to the other end, but the Cheyennes were already fighting. The Oglalas acted as reinforcements" to the relative handful of Cheyenne and Sioux warriors defending the ford.[291]

At first, these warriors reinforcing the ford had been only a mere trickle, and only later became a flood of Lakota warriors who streamed across the river. Revealing why the struggle for the ford was so important, the Sioux now possessed the ford for the easiest means for crossing the river and advancing up the high ground in pursuit of the reeling troopers: the elevated ground was now nothing more than a final resting place for the ill-fated troopers and their commander's ambitions. Mounted warriors splashed across the river shouting "*Hok–a–hey*," which was equivalent to one of Custer's bugler's blowing "Charge." With plenty of firearms and a seemingly endless supply of ammunition, these warriors poured up Medicine Tail Coulee and Deep Coulee, just to the north, to close in on the bluecoats on the high ground.

After having been punished at the ford, Yates's and Keogh's battalions were in a desperate situation, although they were now united on the high ground, fighting together for a combined defense. Dismounted troopers deployed along the heights continued to blast away in the futile hope of keeping the Cheyenne and Sioux at bay. However, because Medicine Tail Coulee Ford was in possession of the Indians after Custer's setback in attempting to cross, any chance of keeping so many warriors at bay was in vain, regardless of the amount of 7ᵗʰ Cavalry courage and determination.[292]

Indeed, nothing could now halt these warriors once they had gained the permanent possession of the ford and the momentum. One Lakota, Charles Corn, described this high-stakes contest in basic terms of survival of the fittest: "the soldiers wanted to kill us so we had to fight for our lives [and] tried to get our children and wives, so I was willing to die fighting for them. . . . The children and the women were crying so we tried to defend ourselves."[293]

Distress Signals

If Custer was hit at the ford as White Cow Bull and other warriors believed (and was almost certainly the case), then Captain Myles Walter

Keogh, the senior officer who originally hailed from County Carlow (*Contae Cheatharlach* in ancient Gaelic) in southeast Ireland, had his hands full in commanding all the five companies under mounting pressure. In a confused situation after the most unexpected repulse of the largest force of 7th Cavalry troopers in the regiment's history, the Irishman found himself in a bad fix. With the crisis escalating with each passing minute, a desperate Captain Keogh almost certainly ordered the firing of volleys as signals in the hope of hastening the arrival of Benteen's battalion and perhaps even what remained of Reno's command, if sufficiently rallied. After all, without the timely arrival of reinforcements to bolster the five companies, the Indians were destined to succeed in using the classic military axiom of divide and conquer by keep the 7th Cavalry divided into manageable segments and widely separated.[294]

Again as verified by collaborating accounts, Custer's fall at the ford paved the way to disaster. Believing that he had seen Custer hit with the first volley upon looking back, packer Lockwood (like so many Indians, especially White Cow Bull) was convinced that he "saw him fall at the head of his advancing troops and that he was 'the first to fall' *before* the real battle began."[295] In his memoir, Lockwood wrote how Custer and members of his staff were completely vulnerable to what was essentially an ambush, "when the Indians opened [fire] on them and that General [Brevet rank] Custer and his staff were the first to fall."[296] Significantly, these words (although that most of the staff fell was of course an exaggeration) agreed with a number of Indian oral accounts, especially White Cow Bull, who described how he shot Custer and a flag-bearer, and Horned Horse.[297] What has to be remembered about the controversial Lockwood memoir—and why it should not be so easily dismissed as in the past—was the fact that "the testimony of the 7th's survivors under Reno and Benteen together with that of their commanders is equally untrustworthy" like so many other Anglo written accounts.[298]

Contrary to traditional battle of Little Bighorn historiography, but as confirmed by numerous Sioux and Cheyenne oral accounts, the turning point of the struggle actually took place at the ford known as Minneconjou (Medicine Tail Coulee Ford), because of the tenacious defense and especially because Custer, staff members, and a number of leading officers were hit by a hail of gunfire, including from fast-firing repeating rifles, the 16-shot Winchester and Henry rifles: essentially a deadly ambush that caught the regimental commander by surprise and wreaked havoc on Custer's last charge and final hope for securing victory. In addition, some circumstantial evidence that Custer was hit at the ford was the systematic firing of what were distress signals to Reno's and Benteen's command, as both white and Indian (Curley) accounts verified.

These successive volleys were unleashed inordinately close together and in rapid fashion to inform Reno and Benteen that something entirely unforeseen and disastrous had happened during the attack on the ford: clear signals fired by Custer's command in a disciplined manner at a time (a short lull after the repulse from the ford) before the five companies were even threatened by ever-increasing numbers of warriors crossing the ford, after the repulse. These volleys were not directed at attackers. Instead, they were fired in desperate attempts to warn of the increasingly perilous situation of Custer's five companies in the hope of garnering reinforcements, especially from Benteen, whose troopers were fresh. Quite simply, these were distress signals: Custer's greatest opportunity to reap a decisive result had just slipped away forever and Custer had been hit, after all initiative and momentum had been lost in the most unexpected and entirely unprecedented manner. After all, this was the first repulse of a 7th Cavalry charge in the regiment's history—and with Custer leading the way.

After having withdrawn from the ford and then up the grassy slope to the Nye–Cartwright Ridge that divided the South Medicine Tail

Coulee (by which Custer had descended upon the ford) and the North Medicine Tail Coulee (Deep Coulee), the troopers continued to fire from skirmish line positions, after maneuvering into good firing positions. Keeping their single-shot Colt .45 revolvers in leather holsters, the cavalrymen blasted away with their .45-.55 caliber model 1873 Springfield carbines, while dismounted on the high ground above the river. Again, another indication of Custer's fall, the withdrawal from the ford vicinity had been conducted in some confusion, because of the ambush's effectiveness, the shock of a decisive repulse, and key losses, including among the staff.

As during the showdown at the ford and then in the gradually escalating level of combat on the high ground after the repulse, trooper firearms, the single-shot Springfield carbine, were simply no match for the faster-firing Winchester and Henry rifles. Like other troopers with Major Reno, who understood the strange uniformity of the successive volleys that sounded so unlike the usual pattern of infantry fighting (regular volleys that were more a feature of Napoleonic and Civil War warfare), an alarmed Lieutenant Winfield Scott Edgerly, Company D, 7th Cavalry, listened to the "heavy firing by volleys down the creek."[299] Now part of Benteen's command after he had departed Custer's column when it descended down Medicine Tail Coulee, Trumpeter Martin described how "we heard volleys, and Captain [Thomas Benton] Weir [answered the distress signal and] jumped on his horse and started down the river all alone [until] his troop [Company D] followed him right away."[300]

In order to justify their lack of action and failure to come to the aid of Custer's five hard-pressed companies, Reno and Benteen later falsely denied (which was part of the process of blaming Custer—the perfect scapegoat—for the disaster and to make themselves look blameless and still responsible officers) that they had heard the distinct succession of volleys during the 1879 Reno Court of Inquiry.[301]

In fact, Lieutenant Edgerly, a blue-eyed West Pointer, was incorrect about the number of distress volleys that had been evidently ordered by second-in-command Captain Keogh to communicate the disastrous news of Custer's wounding to Benteen's and Reno's men in order to hasten assistance before it was too late. Scout George B. Herendeen, born in Ohio and a Civil War veteran, wrote how he knew exactly what Custer's five companies had delivered because this was a crisis situation: "There were about nine volleys at intervals" in Custer's sector. The fact that these volleys were so mechanical, successive, and regularly spaced indicated that they were fired to send an urgent and desperate message to Benteen and Reno and not part of a typical combat situation.[302] Tall Bull also heard these regular volleys, after Custer's troopers had been repulsed at the ford and then "fell back from [the] river" and in poor "order." He emphasized how he "[h]eard the volleys" that were distress signals.[303]

Commanding Company K, 7th Cavalry, Lieutenant Edward S. Godfrey correctly concluded as to the true source of these regular volleys before Custer's men ever faced large numbers of warriors. Only a belated and gradual buildup of massive Indian strength developing would warrant the firing of so many massed volleys that were reminiscent of conventional combat, rather than those of facing an opponent who fought guerrilla-style in moving stealthy up the slope, covered in high, luxurious grass: "I have but little doubt now that these volleys were fired by Custer's orders as *signals of distress* and to indicate where he was."[304]

Indeed, these volleys unleashed by the 7th Cavalry troopers were fired at a time when "there was no mass of Indians at this point opposite any part of the command." Clearly, this series of rolling volleys that echoed down the Little Bighorn Valley were "distress signals" as Lieutenant Godfrey correctly deduced with the insight of a Civil War and Indian War veteran.[305]

As mentioned, this systemic firing of volleys came at a time when the immediate threat before Custer's men was still not of a magnitude (which only came later) that warranted the unleashing of such a large number of closely spaced successive volleys, because this was before the gradual buildup of warriors: the actual case even if the number total of Herendeen's nine volleys was mistaken and fewer. Indeed, at this time, the great number of Sioux and Cheyenne who rode north from the Reno fight had still not poured across the ford at this time.

After repulsing Custer's last charge and regaining the initiative (but only just in time), the Cheyenne and Sioux then advanced on foot after dismounting and fought as individuals on the river's east side, while taking advantage of the terrain and moving slowly up the slope. Like hunting deer, antelope, and buffalo on the plains, they steadily fired at Custer's men, poised on higher ground, while pushing up the slope in a stealthy manner under the cover of the high prairie grass that provided for ideal concealment.

Again, there was no massive onslaught to justify so many heavy volleys fired in such rapid succession, because the threat was only minimal at that time. In addition, archeological evidence has revealed that these volleys (fired into the air so that Reno and Benteen could plainly hear them as an obvious distress signal) were not fired in heated combat while facing a mounted horde of attackers, as envisioned by imaginative writers and historians. After all, only a very few bodies were found where the piles of cartridges were discovered by modern archeologists along the later-named Nye–Cartwright Ridge. This open ridge stood on the high ground situated between Deep Coulee to the north and Medicine Tail Coulee to the south. Here, the dismounted troopers fired from defensive positions on the high ground above the ford below, while Indian numbers only slowly increased over time.[306]

Cheyenne warrior Brave Wolf described how after the troopers retreated from the ford and up Medicine Tail Coulee: "They were all draw up in line of battle."[307] Brave Wolf's words also indicated that the five companies fought together in a defensive action on the Nye–Cartwright Ridge above the river of blue snaked through among the stands of cottonwoods.[308]

Providing additional evidence that the regular volley firing had been distress signals to alert Benteen and Reno of the crisis situation (Custer's fall) and to hurry up reinforcements before it was too late, Indian testimony has also revealed how the later fighting above the ford was not at all distinguished by regular volley firing. In the words of a Sioux warrior named Shoots Walking that corresponded with other Indian accounts: "They did not fire their guns together and they fought without system whatsoever."[309]

Clearly, after Custer's repulse at the ford, and after the lieutenant colonel had been hit, the reeling troopers lost far more than simply their comrades in attacking the ford, morale also gradually eroded, especially with their commander's fall. Most of all, these distress signals stemmed from the fact that, in the words of historian Pennington, "Custer must have been shot at the ford which stopped the attack, considering that with the number of warriors at the ford and the state of the village, Custer should and would have charged into the village."[310] Of course like most historians, Pennington overlooked the "tremendous fire," in Horned Horse's words, unleashed by the ford defenders that had turned the tide of battle and then set the stage for the annihilation of five full companies of America's most famous cavalry regiment and the former "boy general," who was expected by the American people to win a great victory in time for the Centennial celebration in Philadelphia.[311]

Chapter VI

Custer and His Men Pay the Ultimate Price

Command cohesion and morale continued to gradually break down among Custer's men along with overall combat capabilities, which best can be explained by Custer's being wounded at the ford.[1] With contempt because he and his comrades now fought a foe who was "similar to the guerrillas in our Civil War," in Sergeant John Ryan's words, White Bull summarized the fighting qualities of his opponent, who was exposed on the open ground and vulnerable targets to be systematically picked off, after the repulse at Medicine Tail Coulee Ford: "They don't know how to fight."[2]

Without realizing the success of the Cheyenne and Sioux last stand in defending the ford, one Sioux warrior, Brave Bear, who had fought Crook on June 17, could never understand "why all of them [Custer and his men] didn't cross over [the Little Bighorn] and fight in the village . . . Custer would have been better off if he had got in the villages and made his stand there among them. . . ."[3] Of course, this was exactly Custer's battle plan of delivering a flank attack, which had been thwarted to his shock at the ford by the "tremendous fire."[4]

As could be expected, the best tactical situation to have achieved decisive victory, as emphasized by Brave Bear, had called for Custer leading the charge at the ford in a maximum offensive effort. As mentioned, therefore, the lengthy contest for possession of the ford was the battle's turning point, especially because Custer was hit in leading the last attack of his illustrious career. In the insightful words of historian Nathaniel Philbrick: the early "wounding, if not death, of Custer at the early stages of the battle would explain much. Suddenly leaderless, the battalion" was now in serious trouble and doomed to destruction.[5]

Philbrick's on-target views were echoed by Tall Bull. This warrior emphasized the decisive turning point far below Custer Hill, when the "Soldiers fell back from [the] river [and] not in very good order."[6] A warrior of few words, Two Moons briefly summarized the repulse at the ford that set the stage for the annihilation of all five companies like no other single event on the afternoon of June 25: "Custer and his men rode up nearly to the river on their horses and were being fired upon by the Sioux [and Cheyenne] on the west bank. Here, Custer stopped momentarily" in what was his first tactical setback, from which he and his troopers never recovered, and what decided the day.[7]

As mentioned, time had been of the essence in the struggle at the ford and absolutely crucial, as Custer had fully realized, forcing him to go for broke. Therefore, he had realized that no time could be wasted for delivering his daring flank attack and crossing the river to hit the undefended northern end of the massive village, because only a narrow window opportunity existed to score a victory, after Reno had been repulsed: a golden tactical opportunity that entirely dissipated when repulsed at the ford.[8]

What other overlooked factors played a role in ensuring that the five companies never regained the initiative after the setback at the ford? What was most responsible for this development that doomed the five companies besides Custer's wounding and the ford's tenacious defense? Besides the initial repulse at the ford, what else contributed to the escalating loss of morale and combat capabilities of Custer's command? One of the forgotten keys to reversing the tide was the swiftness with which a handful of warriors regained the momentum by taking the offensive, despite being very few in number. After the repulse at the ford, the initiative had been forfeited by the 7th Cavalry and would never be regained, presenting an opportunity for the Indians to swiftly exploit the tactical opportunity.

Significantly, the ford defenders continued to play a distinguished role on the river's east side by almost immediately demonstrating initiative by taking the offensive when the pony soldiers first began to withdraw from the ford. After their successful defense of the ford, the first handful of warriors who crossed Medicine Tail Coulee Ford, upon the initial withdrawal of Custer's men who headed up the high ground, fully exploited the tactical advantage, like when hunting a buffalo bull suddenly giving ground. Leading the way across the ford were the following: Roan Bear, Bobtail Horse, Buffalo Calf (all Cheyenne), and the handful of Sioux warriors (young and old), who had fought beside their Great Plains cousins in defending the ford with bows and arrows and repeating rifles, immediately switched from the defensive to offensive without any directives from tribal leaders and entirely on their own.[9]

Wooden Leg described the forgotten vanguard role of the ford defenders in leading the way by attacking across the river and applying the initial pressure on Custer's troopers at the moment when they were reeling from the shock of having been repulsed at the ford: "Bobtail Horse, Roan Bear and Buffalo Calf, three Cheyennes, and four Sioux warriors [including White Cow Bull] with them, were . . . the first of our Indians to cross the river and go to meet the soldiers" on the river's east side.[10]

As if hoping that these heroics of Sioux and his own Cheyenne warriors would not go unrecognized in meeting the greatest threat to their way of life and very existence, Wooden Leg emphasized: "The first Indians to go across the river and fire upon the Custer soldiers far out on the ridge were two Sioux and three Cheyennes."[11]

Then, to deliver an offensive effort of their own, these resurgent warriors of the last stand at the slight rise in the bottoms were "joined soon afterward by other Indians from the valley camps and from the southward hills where the first soldiers [under Reno] had taken refuge."[12] A Sioux warrior named Red Feather described the permanent gaining of the initiative after the ford's successful defense, when larger numbers of Sioux and Cheyenne, under Two Moons (who carried a repeater like many of his followers), arrived from having confronted Reno. He and his warriors then rode across the ford after the troopers had been hurled back by the stubborn band of defenders: "The Indians charged twice in the battle at the lower [Cheyenne] end of the camp. The first time the [Custer] soldiers were on foot. Then they retreated to their horses."[13] Clearly, like its glory days, the 7th Cavalry's offensive capabilities were now a thing of the past.

After having vanquished Reno and, as mentioned, multitudes of Sioux then crossed at the Medicine Tail Coulee Ford and other points along the Little Bighorn. Boding ill for Custer's men on an afternoon when everything had gone wrong, these warriors were now elated by their unexpected success at the village's upper end against Reno, which combined with the recent Rosebud victory to fuel confidence and fighting spirit to new heights. Revealing the importance of the struggle for the ford's possession and the high stakes involved, Wooden Leg, who had a brother in this fight, described: "We forded the river where all of the Indians were crossing it [at Medicine Tail Coulee Ford], at the broad shallows immediately in front of the little valley or wide coulee on the east side."[14]

With plenty of fast-firing rifles, Winchester and Henry repeaters and newly captured Springfield carbines from Reno's dead, ample ammunition gained from white traders, fresh scalps just ripped off the heads of unfortunate 7th Cavalry troopers now hanging from leather belts and "the power of victory in them," the ever-growing number of Sioux and Cheyenne warriors crossing the river was now overwhelming.[15] These fighting men were so highly motivated and incensed because they believed that the pony soldiers had been "coming to head off the women and children . . . so we turned around and went towards them."[16]

In conclusion, "Jack" Lockwood correctly summarized the show-down not only at the ford but also in the overall battle of Little Bighorn with insightful words seldom emphasized by Anglos:

> The battle has been referred to as the Custer 'massacre.' This was a battle—real war—between two well-armed and organized forces each looking at the other and ready to attack. The Indians had two very definite advantages. First, a great superiority in numbers which looked to me to be as much as fifteen or twenty to one . . . and second, in superior fire power. They had the very latest and best types of long-range Springfield and Sharps rifles, while the soldiers were equipped with shorter range carbines. It was commonly believed that the Indians got their rifles and ammunition from white Indian agents who violated the government's orders against the sale of arms and ammunition to them. The agents appeared to grow prosperous in a surprisingly short time. . . . Five entire troops had been wiped out inside of twenty minutes.[17]

Again as mentioned, the torrent of bullets that poured from the repeating rifles had played a leading role in a successful defense of the ford, and in the overall battle's outcome, because the retiring troopers then became vulnerable on the high, open ground above the river: an ideal killing ground.[18] For good reason, consequently, Sergeant John Ryan, Company M, 7th Cavalry, had strongly condemned the system-atic arming of the Indians by the corrupt Indian agents and money-hungry Indian traders, who had bestowed the already formidable Great

Plains warriors with the best and most lethal weapons with the highest cutting-edge technology: "so that his men [Sitting Bull's warriors] were better armed than the troops of the United States Government. Individually, the Indians were better soldiers than our troops, for every Indian was a perfect rider and a good shot."[19]

Without an understanding of the harsh realities of the Indians' massive amount of superior firepower, newspapers across America incorrectly emphasized that the showdown along the Little Bighorn was nothing more than a horrid "massacre," as if this much-derided foe was entirely incapable of a legitimate and thorough victory over the 7th Cavalry. For generations, "the public perception was that a group of savages had inexplicably managed to wipe out the United States Army's most elite group of soldiers. That perception remained uncontested for over a hundred years, finding its way into history books, novels, documentaries, and even feature films [while] the victors of the Little Bighorn have had scant opportunity to tell their story. . . ."[20] And this great silencing of the truth was especially the case with regard to the decisive turning point at Medicine Tail Coulee Ford, to long obscure what happened at along the Little Bighorn, and exactly why.

Like Sitting Bull's Sun Dance vision along the Rosebud that had become a reality and the fulfillment of a beautiful dream, Box Elder, the aged Northern Cheyenne prophet, also had been right. He had seen the pony soldiers in blue uniforms falling into their villages in what was little more than a divine sacrifice and tribute to honor the Great Spirit. In the end, their pain-induced Sun Dance visions derived from the wisdom and blessings of the Great Spirit had come to pass with Custer's last charge. In this sense, perhaps it had been the Great Spirit who had stopped Custer's last charge, as the warriors believed.

An unprecedented victory had been won on the afternoon of June 25 in an amazing triumph that the warriors called "the Greasy Grass Fight." The Cheyenne people now realized the truth of Box Elder's

June 24 words of the expected pony soldier attack because he had understood how:

> the wolves had known of the danger. The four-legged ones had known of the danger [because] [t]hey had trailed the white-faced strangers with the loud voices all the way from the Elk River, and since the wolves understood their language, they had learned the intentions of the whites. The loud strangers were now moving towards the Goat River [Little Bighorn] to attack the prairie people camped along the banks. It was said that the wolves had raced ahead and, from the rim-rocks overlooking the valley floor, they had howled their warnings of the impending danger. But not one of the two-legged beings below paid any attention to the howling, except an elderly blind Cheyenne named Old Brave Wolf [Box Elder] who understood their language. Yet, when he told his people of the terrible danger about to confront them, they doubted the wisdom of his words and ridiculed his pleas to heed the warning.[21]

Most of all, as the Cheyenne and Sioux believed, it had been the "Spirit Who Rules the Universe" that had brought the remarkable one-sided success at the Little Bighorn with the wiping out of Custer's five companies and the defeat of Reno's troopers. In consequence, they gave thanks to their God.[22] As if the Great Spirit had directed the bullet, the fact that Custer was most likely hit, but not killed, in leading the attack at Medicine Tail Coulee ford [as elsewhere] paved the way for one of the greatest disasters in American military history.[23]

Custer's defeat shocked America, and despite the endless sensationalism printed in hundreds of newspapers across the United States, one realistic-thinking newspaperman of the *Chicago Times* finally hit upon the undeniable truth of the battle of Little Bighorn on July 22, 1876, when he emphasized: how: "The country might as well reach a just conclusion . . . however, much it may reflect unfavorably upon the dead [because] There was no 'massacre' [as] Custer fell in a fair fight which he himself invited and inaugurated, and which resulted as it did wholly from his rashness, his desire to distinguish himself, to his personal and entirely unwarranted ambition."[24]

In the end, the obscure buffalo ford opposite the Medicine Tail Coulee was the exact point where the legendary Custer's Luck finally came to a bitter and dismal end: a lengthy winning streak that was bound to end, but no one had expected it to come at the hands of so few fighting men at an obscure ford on the Little Bighorn and in the middle of nowhere. Naturally, the thoroughness of this repulse at the ford came as an absolute shock to troopers (and of course Custer) who had long seen themselves as invincible and the elite of the United States military. Here at the old buffalo ford, like some dangerous game of musical chairs that he had played almost recklessly since the Civil War's early days, it had been only a matter of time before the good fortune of America's most famous cavalry commander ended in a disastrous manner. Indeed, not long after the battle, a Kansas newspaperman got it right, attributing the most shocking military defeat of his generation to a blind overreliance on and faith in Custer's Luck to overcome any odds.[25]

Indeed, Custer's Luck was shattered forever by the tenacious defense of the relatively few Cheyenne and Sioux warriors at the Medicine Tail Coulee Ford and, more than on any other place, on the sprawling battlefield on the afternoon of June 25. The tragic end of Custer and his command was thereafter cruelly ordained by fate, tactics, a divided regiment, and balking top lieutenants who refused to come to Custer's aid. Agreeing with the tactical analysis of Benteen, Lieutenant Winfield Scott Edgerly described the inevitable fate of Custer's five companies after the repulse at the ford, where Custer "attempted to cross and was attacked and driven back to where he was found dead. Dead bodies [of 7th Cavalry troopers] were found all the way from the ford to where Custer's body was found."[26]

In fact, the greatest and most forgotten cause of Custer's swift elimination and the destruction of his five companies was the superior combat qualities of the Cheyenne and Sioux fighting men, which was demonstrated most decisively at Medicine Tail Coulee Ford, armed with their superior weaponry. In a surprise admission in the wake of the disaster, the editor of the *New York Times* on July 7, 1876, correctly placed credit (a definite minority position among white Americans) where it was due: "The Sioux [and Cheyenne] are a distinct race of men from the so-called Indians of the Southwest, among whom the army [and General Crook] found much easy work two or three years ago. . . ."[27]

Obscuring the Importance of the Story of the Last Stand at Medicine Tail Coulee Ford

Of course, the most fundamental reason why the last stand of the Cheyenne and Sioux at Medicine Tail Coulee Ford has been overlooked for so long was the obvious fact that Custer's five companies were destroyed, leaving no survivors to tell the tale. Ironically, even conflicting Indian oral accounts likewise doomed this all-important story of the ford's defense to obscurity, thanks to the misunderstandings of interpreters and the vast cultural differences between the two people. Unlike Cheyenne words, the vast majority of Sioux oral accounts about the battle were guilty of having a marked tendency to deny any action at the ford or emphasized that it was a fight of no significance, because this was largely a Cheyenne victory: the establishment of a central foundation for the failure of later generations of white historians to fully understand the importance of the decisive showdown at the ford. This confused situation and lack of understanding led to an over-reliance on Sioux oral testimony that dismissed the importance of the Cheyenne achievements at the ford, because of tribal rivalries and jealousies. The words of a Sioux warrior named He Dog helped to obscure what really happened at the ford and its supreme importance in the battle's final outcome. Failing to mention the Cheyenne, he explained the battle in the following manner: "Those Santees and other [Sioux] Indians had come out to hunt buffalo and not to fight, and the Sioux only fought when attacked."[28]

As presented by an interpreter, He Dog's most misleading—or even misunderstood—words can be found in his conclusion: "Custer never got near the river."[29] However, one of Reno's men, Massachusetts-born Private George W. Glenn, Company H, surveyed the battlefield shortly after the fight. He wrote: "We found [the] trail going down in the river, but it seems that Custer got repulsed before he got across the river [since] we never found any trail of him on the other side of the river."[30] He also penned about what happened to some troopers who fell at the ford, "Lieutenant [James "Jack" Garland] Sturgis' trousers were found but we did not find the body at the time [but in the village] [w]e found two heads of men that were captured [and] we buried the two heads. . . . "[31]

Ireland-born Sergeant John Ryan, Company M, explained the terrible fate of men who were captured in the attack on the ford and paid a high price for that sharp setback, because fallen soldiers could not be taken rearward or saved by their withdrawing men: "I think the Indians took some of our men prisoners [because] we found what appeared to be human bones and parts of blue cloth uniforms where men had been tied to stakes or trees. Some of the bodies of our officers were not found. Among them were Lieutenant Harrington, Lieutenant Porter and Lieutenant Sturgis."[32]

The ugly final fate (a traditional one against common enemies) of these unfortunate men also can be seen in the words of Wooden Leg, who fought at Little Bighorn. He described the customary and ritualistic treatment of a dead enemy. In this sense, it made no difference if this foe were red or white, negating the overemphasized racial factor as having engendered greater hatred than usual. After killing one

Shoshone warrior, the members of a Cheyenne war party went about a ritualistic procedure to ensure that they would not have to face this same whole, able-bodied warrior in the afterlife: "We cut off his hands, his feet, his head [and] [w]e ripped open his breast and his belly," and then threw the remains in a bonfire.[33]

Small wonder that the physical remains of Custer's men who fell in and around Medicine Tail Coulee Ford were never found. Sergeant Ryan described what little was discovered among the missing men who had confidently followed their commander down the coulee and attacked the ford: "We also found three of our men's heads suspended by wires through the back of the ears from a lodge pole with the hair singed off."[34] Clearly, this was a sad ending for some of the best and brightest of the 7th Cavalry officers and enlisted men, but this was nothing unusual. At the Washita, Major Elliott and his more than a dozen men likewise had been decapitated so that a burial detail was "unable to find them" (the missing heads).[35]

Such was the high price paid for valor, audacity, and their determination to follow Custer to hell and back if necessary. In the end, perhaps a Sioux fighter named Two Moons best summarized the battle of Little Bighorn, because of the unexpected repulse of Custer's flank attack at the ford: "Custer was a brave man. I give him credit for attacking a people that vastly outnumbered his—but something was the matter with his men. They did not run or seek shelter, but stayed right out in the open where it was easy to shoot them down. Any ordinary bunch of men would have dropped into a watercourse, or a draw, where they could have fought for a long time."[36] What Two Moons and other Sioux warriors failed to reveal, or acknowledge, was that this tragic scenario for more than 200 men of five companies was only an inevitable fate that had been earlier ordained by the repulse of Custer's last charge at Medicine Tail Coulee Ford.

Most of all, this decisive repulse and the subsequent disaster along the Little Bighorn was primarily due to the courage and determination of the band of warriors along the low, brushy rise in the river bottoms near the river's west bank. Against the odds for success, they had defiantly stood their ground, and unleashed a "tremendous fire from the[ir] repeating rifles," in Horned Horse's words, that could not be overcome.[37] In a description that applied to the ford's spirited defense, Sitting Bull also emphasized how the blistering fire from so many Henry and Winchester rifles of these relatively few veteran warriors was so severe that Custer and his command had no chance for either success or survival on truly a day in hell for the troopers of the 7th Cavalry: "They could not stand up under such a fire."[38]

Recent Archeology

As mentioned, one of the great myths of the battle of the Little Bighorn was that nothing of significance occurred at Medicine Tail Coulee Ford, and that Custer never launched a strong attack with all five companies, to force a crossing at this strategic point. Instead, Custer's final offensive effort has been incorrectly viewed by generations of historians as nothing more than a mere tactical feint of little relative importance, especially with regard to determining the battle's outcome.

Even modern archeology has played a role in fostering the erroneous popular belief that no heavy fighting or anything of importance occurred at the ford: ironically, the scene of Custer's last attack. In the introductory words of Sandy Barnard's 1998 book, entitled *Digging Into Custer's Last Stand*: "In the 122 years since the battle, artifacts indicating an action of some kind have been found in the vicinity of the ford, though their relative paucity seems to indicate the fighting there was brief."[39]

Therefore, based on limited evidence from a recent archaeological dig conducted more than a century after the battle, Barnard concluded: "In the Medicine Tail Coulee area, the archeological findings seem to support the present-day thinking of many who have studied the battle 'that only a light action occurred at the ford'."[40] In another study of the Little Bighorn, three established historians and scholars concluded: "In the years since the battle, artifacts indicating an action of some kind have been found in the vicinity of the ford, though their relative paucity seems to indicate that the fighting there was brief."[41] Again, this has been a premature and erroneous evaluation based entirely upon too little evidence having been found more than a century after the battle: something that should have been fully expected. The romance and lore of what happened far from the river on the commanding heights of Last Stand Hill, or Custer Hill has continued to play a role in obscuring the more important story of the dramatic showdown of what happened at Medicine Tail Coulee Ford. Consequently, the general assumption that the fight at the ford was insignificant has become one of the greatest myths about the battle of Little Bighorn, enduring to this day.

A host of good reasons have existed to fully explain why so little battle relics were discovered around the ford by modern archaeologists. White relic hunters, who even collected skulls, and Indian scavengers looking for anything of use, scoured the battlefield. Sergeant John Ryan explained the situation of how large numbers of Indians, especially women and children, had scoured the battlefield for everything of possible use, including brass cartridges that could be reloaded for future use: "Strange to say, none of the saddle or horse equipment, not even a strap that I could see, nor cartridge shells, could be found on the field except five or six shells that were found under General Custer's body [which were] afterwards sent to Mrs. Custer with a lock of the general's hair. . . ."[42] Followed by hordes of latter-day tourists, white soldiers, including Scotland-born Private Peter Thompson, Company C, 7th Cavalry, searched the battlefield for "some trophy as a memento of this affair," not long after the battle. They secured souvenirs, such as brass cartridges, from the scene of strife, including in the Cheyenne village.[43]

However, with regard to the scarcity of relics found by archaeologists, what has been most often overlooked was the fact that significant changes have altered the battlefield since June 25, 1876, to guarantee the lack of physical evidence of the struggle at Medicine Tail Coulee Ford. For more than a century after the battle, overgrazing by herds of domestic cattle and sheep denuded the native vegetation, especially its thick carpet of prairie grasses that covered the landscape when the battle raged with such fury. Without natural vegetation, especially a thick layer of native grasses, protecting the thin top soil, heavy erosion from the rains of more than a century washed many battle artifacts, especially lightweight rifle and revolver cartridges, into the river. Then, annual flooding of the Little Bighorn (especially the winter runoff and heavy spring rains) washed artifacts (including empty, lightweight metallic cartridges that have been long used as the ultimate barometer by modern archaeologists to designate tactics, troop positions, and locations of heavy combat) away from the site of the struggle at the ford and farther downstream or were covered in deeper layers of sediment.

Therefore, relatively few artifacts at the ford were found, unlike other portions of the battlefield that were on much higher ground, and less erosion prone, far from Medicine Tail Coulee Ford. What has been found by modern archeologists in the ford area has been only heavier (than a brass cartridge) objects, such as an 1874 pattern United States Amy mess knife, a bullet, a butcher knife (evidently Indian), and a cylinder retention pin from a Colt model 1873 six–shoot revolver. These artifacts were found near the mouth of Medicine Tail Coulee, where it entered the river, during archeological digs in 1994.[44]

Worst of all, since the battle's end and for more than a century, large numbers of relic hunters and souvenir seekers have heavily scoured the mouth of the coulee and ford area, stripping these places of battle artifacts and relics. Members of the nearby Crow Agency on the north border of today's Little Bighorn National Battlefield also took a toll on the physical reminders of the struggle, removing items at the ford and selling relics, especially brass cartridges, to tourists for generations. Such developments have caused recent archaeologists more than a century later to incorrectly conclude that no significant contest was waged at the ford because of the paucity of artifacts discovered during their meticulous archaeological projects. In addition, the ground around the ford has been disturbed by many years of the activities of man and beast, including even by camera crews in the filming of the battle of the Little Bighorn sequences for the popular 1971 Arthur Penn movie, *Little Big Man.*[45]

The notable lack of artifacts found in and around the ford can also be partly explained by the fact that, in the words of Sioux warrior Horned Horse, the river "is a stream filled with dangerous quicksand," which allegedly "swallowed up" fallen troopers, including equipment and weapons.[46] Some bodies of unlucky troopers and their gear at the ford almost certainly washed downstream to the north because the rushing waters from the melting snow of the Big Horn Mountains were more rapid at the ford's shallow crossing than elsewhere along the river.

Ample evidence also exists that bodies of Custer's fallen men (only several were found at the ford) were removed from the ford's vicinity by the Indian women and taken into the village, because they were never found. Lieutenants Sturgis and Porter were among those officers who fell in the attack on the ford. After the battle, Taylor explained: "Some of the officers went galloping over the field looking at different bodies in the hope of recognizing the three missing Lieutenants; Harrington, Porter, and young 'Jimmy' Sturgis. . . . But their search was fruitless [however] Some of the clothing of young Sturgis, bearing his name was found in the deserted Indian camp. But his body was never found, to be recognized. . . . "[47]

Civil War veteran Lieutenant Godfrey, who commanded Company K and hailed from Ohio, wrote how the "bodies of Dr. Lord and Lieutenants Porter, Harrington, and Sturgis were not found, at least not recognized."[48]

Clearly, as Lieutenants Sturgis, Harrington, and Porter and so many others had discovered on bloody June 25, the 7th Cavalry troopers learned, in the sardonic words of Trooper Taylor, that in "seeking to deprive a strange and brave people of their birthright and all they held dear, was not altogether a picnic," especially along the Little Bighorn. For such reasons, the head of a Company G corporal, with red hair, was found under an overturned kettle in the Cheyenne village.[49]

However, some meager recognition for the importance of what had happened at the ford has come belatedly, but this has remained entirely insufficient. Offering a more positive analysis than other digs in the past, a 1989 archeological study by Douglas D. Scott, Richard A. Fox, Jr., Melissa A. Connor, and Dick Harmon emphasized that "artifactual evidence (e.g., government cartridge cases, etc.) found over the years at the ford may suggest that Custer's battalion, or parts of it, progressed to the river intent on crossing into the heart of the encampment."[50]

The displacement and removal of troopers' bodies in the alleged exact positions where they were supposedly killed, and hence buried, has also contributed to the misconception that nothing occurred of importance at the ford. For example, a total of fifty-two headstones stand today on Custer Hill. This is a misrepresentation that has helped to fuel the romantic imagery and fictions of the famous Last Stand" In truth, only forty-two bodies were first buried on Custer Hill. Even more, "about seventy markers now stand where no body was found" on the battlefield, representing "surplus" marble headstones that had been originally meant for proper placement on the Reno battlefield.[51]

The burial marker of reporter Mark Kellogg has provided a good representative example of the obscuring of proper positions of where bodies were actually found. The ill-fated newspaperman was killed near the river, but his white marble marker is located a good distance from where he was killed. In the words of Sandy Barnard, only "a few hundred yards from Custer Hill, [the Kellogg marker stands] but today we believe it represents Kellogg's actual death or burial site. Instead, his death almost certainly occurred three quarters of a mile to the west on the flats close to the river, as traditional accounts, such a [Colonel John] Gibbon's, suggest."[52]

The case of Lieutenant James "Jack" Garland Sturgis, who was killed in the attack on the ford (as evidenced by his clothing and head that were found in the Cheyenne village), has provided an even better example of misplaced burials than Kellogg. However, no indication today can be found that Sturgis, who was leading Company E, Yates's battalion, was cut down at the ford, additionally obscuring what happened at this strategic crossing point and its importance.[53]

Likewise, the marble marker of handsome Lieutenant Sturgis is nowhere near the ford where it rightfully belongs today. He was the promising son of the commander of the 7th Cavalry, Colonel Samuel Davis Sturgis, age fifty-four. As mentioned, the regimental commander had been conveniently ordered by headquarters to detached service at the Cavalry Depot in St. Louis to allow Custer to take charge of the regiment during his final campaign. For the colonel's sensibilities, and those of his wife, the truth of the young lieutenant's grisly demise in the Cheyenne village near the ford was deliberately obscured and falsified. When the lieutenant's mother visited the battlefield in June 1878, she was shown an entirely "fictitious" grave of her son southwest of Custer Hill and far from Medicine Tail Coulee Ford, where he had been hit.[54] Likewise and in the case of other 7th Cavalry troopers, Lieutenant Henry Moore Harrington's headstone has no connection to where he was actually killed near the ford.[55]

Again, like service records, the tragic fate of Lieutenant Sturgis and other officers has provided evidence of a much larger fight at the ford than has been recognized by historians, but in accordance with an abundant number of Indian accounts, especially Cheyenne. Lieutenant Godfrey described: "The clothing of Porter and Sturgis I found in the [Cheyenne] village, and they showed that they had been killed."[56] As mentioned, Scout George B. Herendeen was less delicate than the diplomatic lieutenant of Company M, explaining how the "heads of four white soldiers were found in the Cheyenne village."[57] These unfortunate soldiers were almost certainly officers and men who fell in Custer's attack on the ford. The distinct possibility existed that at least Lieutenants Porter and Sturgis and Dr. Lord, whose surgical box was found in the Cheyenne village, were unhorsed or even wounded to become captives, where they were later killed by their captors in the village—as seen by Reno and other officers.[58]

Ironically, one supposed eyewitness of the battle has been widely discredited, for good reason, as part of the fabricated post-battle stories from so many allegedly battle survivors and witnesses. In the September 8, 1876, issue, *The Pioneer Press and Tribune* of Minneapolis, Minnesota, presented an "interview with an old trapper" named Ridgely. Again, this account is false, but has corresponded with some existing evidence. D. H. Ridgely stated that he had been trapping in the Yellowstone country, when he was captured in March 1876.[59] Barely two months after the battle, Ridgely presented a scenario that was actually surprisingly close to what actually happened, because toward "this ford Custer followed the trail down to the river's edge. There were only twenty-five teepes [sic] visible behind the bluffs not visible [when] Custer attacked the small village [Cheyenne], and was immediately met" with resistance.[60]

He also emphasized how "Custer began the fight in the ravine [Medicine Tail Coulee] near the ford, and full half of his command seemed to be unhorsed at the first fire [and] [t]hen the soldiers retreated" up to the hills above the river.[61] Of course, these losses were an exaggeration. Interestingly, however, Ridgely also stated how after the battle "the Indians returned to camp with six soldiers as prisoners [who were then] tied to stakes at a wood-pile in the village and were burned to death."[62]

A comparable observation was made by Major Reno (Ridgely had almost certainly read the major's accounts) from the top of the bluff where he found an ideal defensive position, after his command had been routed from the river valley. As mentioned, he actually saw that missing men were "burned at the stake, for while the great battle was going on I, and some other officers, looking through field glasses, saw the Indians miles away engaged in a war dance about three captives. They were tied to the stake and my impression was that [Lieutenant] Harrington was one of them."[63]

Again, the Ridgely account is entirely false, but it has revealed that there was widespread knowledge and a common consensus about the importance of the struggle at the Medicine Tail Coulee Ford not long after the battle, and that some of Custer's officers had been captured in the combat for the ford's possession: ironically, realizations and conclusions of early observers of the field, including Benteen and Reno, immediately after the battle, which have been obscured by the fiction and romance of "Custer's Last Stand."[64]

Symbolically, after the battle, reports circulated that several open graves of 7th Cavalry troopers were found near the ford, where the fighting had raged in the battle's forgotten turning point. Indeed, to coincide with warrior oral testimony, the bodies of at least several troopers were found at the ford and others in the village.[65] Nevertheless, one of the greatest myths of the battle of Little Bighorn has doggedly persisted even among leading historians to this day: that nothing of any importance occurred at Medicine Tail Coulee Ford, when it was actually the scene of Custer's last—and most desperate—charge and the turning point of the battle.

Conclusion

A photographer named Stanley J. Morrow took a series of photographs of the Custer battlefield in the early spring of 1879. Not surprisingly, in realizing the importance of this remote place about three-quarters of a mile from the famous "Custer Hill," he made sure that he took a photograph of Medicine Tail Coulee Ford. Most significantly, Morrow correctly labeled the photograph, "Ford on the Little [Big] Horn where Custer met his first reverse. . . . The ford, where Custer attempted to cross to attack the Indian village."[1]

Morrow was entirely correct, after having learned first–hand from reliable sources about what had happened at the ford on June 25. This was indeed a significant and historic site as Morrow fully realized: the location of Custer's last attack, and one of the few times, from the Civil War to the Indian Wars, when one of his trademark hard-hitting charges had failed to garner victory. This same tactical evaluation was early voiced by Curley, who was one of the very few who saw Custer's last attack when he went for broke: "Several times Curley described an

276 • DEATH AT THE LITTLE BIGHORN

attempt by Custer's forces to charge across the ford at the mouth of
Medicine Tail Coulee. . . . "[2]

Coinciding with Morrow's views, Crow scout Little Man Runs
Him also emphasized how "Custer had come down Medicine Tail
Creek [with all five companies] and was moving toward the river [and
then] Custer tried to cross the river at the mouth of Medicine Tail
Creek, but was unable to do so."[3] However, because of the enduring
romance and popular mythology of what happened on Custer Hill,
generations of historians have casually overlooked or dismissed what
Morrow first got right less than three years after the battle: the supreme
importance of this dramatic showdown at the ford, where the battle
of the Little Bighorn was ultimately decided, and not on the much-
celebrated "Custer Hill."

Equally significant (although he was not referring specifically to
the ford's defense, which nevertheless applied in this case), archae-
ologist and historian Richard Allen Fox, Jr., summarized: "Cartridge
cases, primarily from repeating rifles, suggest that warriors at least took
advantage of the shock effects of rapid fire massed against enemy positions."[4] Unfortunately for Custer, this was indeed the exact situation
with regard to the ford's defense that led to the most disastrous repulse
of his lengthy professional career. Fox's analysis coincided with Sitting
Bull's words. The revered Hunkpapa holy man told the secret of the
remarkable success of only a handful of warriors successfully defending
Medicine Tail Coulee Ford to make a dramatic contribution to the battle's outcome far out of proportion of their numbers: "Our young men
rained lead across the river and drove the white braves back."[5]

In this regard, Fox's insightful analysis was right on target, which
was verified by not only Sitting Bull, but also the words of Horned
Horse with regard to the tenacious defense of the ford, where Custer
was "met by such a tremendous fire from the repeating rifles" that the
five companies were repulsed and forced to withdrawal to seal the
command's fate.[6] An Indian woman who saw the struggle at the ford

also emphasized "the withering fire which greeted [Custer's] approach" to the ford.[7] From the heights of Bouyer's Bluff that overlooked the ford, towering 170 feet above the river just to the south, Crow scout White Man Runs Him personally viewed the hard-fought contest. He later described the battle's decisive turning point in only a few concise, but accurate words: "Custer tried to cross the river at the mouth of Medicine Tail Creek, but was unable to do so [and] This was the last we saw of Custer."[8]

Despite the ample amount of available and reliable Indian (Cheyenne, Crow, and Sioux) testimony and even leading 7th Cavalry officers who analyzed the battlefield not long after the battle, white historians have continued to ignore the importance of what occurred at Medicine Tail Coulee Ford. This was a most ironic development with regard to the last charge of the boldest cavalry commander of his generation, and whose distinguished career was founded upon successful charges across America. It's one of the great, if not inexplicable, paradoxes of Little Bighorn historiography. As mentioned, most historians have concluded that Custer's final offensive effort was nothing more than a mere feint because it was inconceivable that his last attack could have been stopped by so few warriors: a complete dismissal of the importance of Custer's final attack and the ample amount of existing reliable and collaborating Indian (especially Cheyenne) testimony that exists. All in all, this has been a most implausible conclusion with regard to the last attack of America's most aggressive and dynamic cavalry officer. After all, Custer had almost always attacked with everything and anything that he had available during the Civil War and Indian Wars. The time-proven tactical concept of "the charge" meant victory in the mind of the native Michigander, whose reputation had been built on the aggressive offensive, even in impossible tactical situations and against the odds. In fact, the fallacy of Custer's most fundamental axiom of a brilliant cavalry career had been revealed only once: the dramatic showdown at Medicine Tail Coulee Ford.

Indeed, this longtime common and traditional view that nothing of importance happened at Medicine Tail Coulee Ford has been a rather bizarre general consensus by generations of historians. After all, even an early article in *The Sun* (New York, New York) reported on February 26, 1876: "Custer struck the Indians at a ford . . . with the full belief that Reno was fighting in the bottom, and Benteen 'coming on' to join in the fight."[9] Even more importantly, General Terry's first report, sent by telegraph to headquarters in Chicago, Illinois, on June 27 about the fight revealed a good deal of accurate information: Custer's "trail . . . comes down to the bank of the river, but at once diverges from it as if he had unsuccessfully attempted to cross."[10] There was even a forgotten 7th Cavalry survivor of the struggle at the ford: Captain Keogh's horse Comanche, a fourteen-year-old bay gelding. Scout Girard and Benteen found 7th Cavalry "horse, wounded, lying on its side in a pool of mud and water on the bank of a stream where it was supposed Custer and his men had attempted to cross in his attack on the Indian [Cheyenne] village" in the words of historian Ernst L. Reedstrom.[11]

Significantly, the contemporary accounts of those individuals who were actually at the battle revealed the truth in contrast to the outright speculation of latter-day armchair historians. After surveying the battlefield, veteran Sergeant John Ryan, 7th Cavalry, wrote how at "the end of this bluff there was a ford [Medicine Tail Coulee] and I think Custer attempted to cross at that point to the Indian [Cheyenne] camp, as we found some of the bodies of his men lying there. Those were the first bodies we found belonging to Custer's command."[12] He also penned that at "the top of this bluff, we halted and at the foot was a ford, and it was where Custer first encountered the Indians, as we found some of the dead soldiers there two days afterward."[13]

Clearly, the cavalrymen's dead bodies later found, combined with those remains of prisoners taken by their captors into the Cheyenne village and whose bodies were never found after the battle—these numerous casualties revealed that a much larger engagement, in accordance with an ample number of reliable Indian accounts, took place at the ford than has been acknowledged by historians. This long-time denial has developed because it did not fit in the traditional tactical and romantic formula of the standard narrative of the famous last stand of Custer atop Custer Hill. The mystique and romantic legacy of Custer's Last Stand atop the hill (abut three-quarters of a mile above the river) ensured that what occurred at the ford remained in the dark historical shadows to this day.[14]

Perhaps John Stands in Timber, whose grandfather Lame White Man was killed in the battle, best described what happened at the ford with regard to the battle's true turning point: "The Custer men tried to cross the river [at Medicine Tail Coulee Ford but] Cheyennes [and Sioux] hidden in the brush on the south side of the ford drove the solders back and killed a couple of them in the brush by the river [and] [t]hen the Custer men retreated" to the high ground above the river where they were wiped out to a man.[15]

Contrary to the traditional narrative steeped in romance and lore, one of those attackers who was hit, but not killed, was Custer himself. Along with members of his headquarters staff (literally the regiment's command and control center in the saddle) who were killed and wounded in the attack on the ford, Custer's wounding not only played a key part in the repulse at the ford but also in the overall collapse of command cohesion and combat capabilities, which led to the ultimate destruction of the five companies on the high ground far from the ford. Custer's early loss had provided the best explanation of the fatal catalyst that led to the ultimate disaster. Therefore, everything that happened after the repulse of Custer's last attack on the ford was anti-climactic in overall tactical terms, because the true turning point of the battle had already been reached during the struggle for possession of the ford.[16]

Nevertheless, despite the ample existing, reliable evidence and primary documentation, the ford fight has been ignored almost out-of-hand by traditional historians as little more than a feint or an "ineffective bluff." However, in striking contrast to these conventional views, the existing tactical situation that confronted Custer had called for an all-out offensive effort with all five companies, because this flank attack was his last chance to achieve success.

In many ways, the story of the ford's defense and how so few Indian defenders (including boys and older men beyond prime fighting age) saved the day by thwarting Custer's last offensive effort of his famed career, seems almost incomprehensible at first glance, especially for the general public and historians who have been unduly influenced by traditional historiography since childhood days. After all, from the Civil War to the Washita, no opponent had been able to withstand an all-out Custer cavalry charge until the afternoon showdown at Medicine Tail Coulee Ford: not a very memorable or glorious chapter for Custer enthusiasts, especially because America's hero was cut down in the attack, guaranteeing that it was best to leave this most overlooked story to its undeserved obscurity.

Of course, because none of Custer's men of five companies survived the battle, the only way to understand how the ford's defense could have reversed the day's fortunes against the odds can only be seen through warrior's words. One veteran leader of the Cheyenne Kit Fox Society, Two Moons, perhaps said it best with regard to explaining how only a mere handful of determined warriors defended the Medicine Tail Coulee Ford with a stubbornness seldom seen among Great Plains warriors: "We wanted our revenge, and it came with Custer."[17]

Nevertheless, the dramatic showdown for possession of this vital ford across the Little Bighorn—so suddenly made strategic, and the key to the success of the overall battle plan—has been the most overlooked and ignored chapter of the battle of Little Bighorn. In fact, this all–important fight at the Medicine Tail Coulee Ford has been often regulated to little more than a footnote by traditional historians, who have not deviated from the popular romanticized portrayal of the final clash. For them, the climactic showdown of the day was on Custer Hill and never at this obscure ford far below the hill's crest.

To be entirely fair, this has been only a natural, if not inevitable, development because of the power of the modern media: popular films, dramatic paintings, and hundreds of books that have faithfully fueled the traditional romance and myth for generations. Popular culture and films have been most responsible for laying the central romantic foundations and creating the enduring myths of Custer's Last Stand that have gone unquestioned for so long. These views have become so deeply ingrained in the popular memory and consciousness that no avenue has been left open for new interpretations and fresh views of one of the most iconic battles in American history, thus guaranteeing the silencing of the truth about the climactic showdown at the ford.

Even the most recent books about Custer's Last Stand, like James Donovan's popular book of 2008, *A Terrible Glory* (which presented the traditional view that predictably minimized the importance of the struggle at the Medicine Tail Coulee Ford)—and despite the publisher's glowing claims of groundbreaking contributions—have basically offered very little truly new with regard to scholarship. Such popular works have only continued the same old, well-worn story that we have been long taught to us since childhood.

In a rather sad but only too true commentary, battle of the Little Bighorn historian Walt Cross, a distinguished combat veteran of the Vietnam War, correctly emphasized why the crucial confrontation (certainly one of the most forgotten—if not *the* most important—chapters of the battle of the Little Bighorn) at Medicine Tail Coulee Ford, has continued to be grossly minimized in terms of overall importance by today's even most revered historians: "People tend to just go along with the prevailing attitude and that is what has happened to Medicine Tail Coulee. But if you listen to the Indian voices, they will understand that it was a very important reason why Custer was defeated."[18]

Even a perplexed veteran cavalryman and former Confederate general, Thomas "Tom" Lawrence Rosser, who reflected the common white perspective with regard to not understanding how Custer could have been repulsed by mere "savages," never seriously considered that such so-called barbarians could possibly have stopped the last charge of America's greatest cavalryman: "Were the nature of the river banks such . . . where he approached the river, that he could have crossed without great difficulty? Did he approach at the point where these 'cut banks' . . . are met?"[19]

In a great paradox, Custer saw the last charge of his illustrious military career stopped by only a mere handful of warriors, who seldom fought together but now united as one, in a true emergency situation: a surprising development not previously experienced by the "boy general" in attacking the Confederacy's finest troops, cavalry, and infantry, during the Civil War. However, perhaps in the end this most unexpected of possible setbacks for Custer's last attack was entirely appropriate, because before June 25, 1876, Custer's fame as an Indian fighter and postwar status as a "national hero" rested solely on "the sordid, hardly heroic reality of the Indian wars of the West, where torching a village of noncombatants [Black Kettle's camp along the Washita] was considered a great victory. . . ."[20]

An even more surreal irony of Custer's Last Stand was that the cutting-edge technological weapon, the latest Winchester (model 1876) that had killed so many of Custer's men on this bloody afternoon, was featured at the Centennial Exposition while the battle was being fought. Ironically, Custer had visited the Centennial Exposition in Philadelphia in April 1876, just before riding off to a rendezvous with disaster. Here at the Exposition, the 1876 campaign's brain trust and architects, Generals Sherman and Sheridan, first heard the shocking news of the Custer fiasco. Like the 16-shot Henry rifle, the highly effective Winchester rifle was proudly displayed at the Exposition as part of the overall theme of "A Century of Progress," to thousands of gawking visitors from around the world. Little could these visitors have realized that they were looking at the day's most advanced small arms weaponry that had just sent so many of Custer's men (perhaps Custer himself) to early graves on a remote Montana hill in the middle of nowhere.[21]

Sergeant John Ryan, Company M, 7th Cavalry and the son of Irish immigrants, was perplexed by the striking paradox, which made him angry at the America's Indian policy had proved such a monumental folly: "It seemed a strange fact that the government was . . . equipping these Indians to go out and kill the soldiers who were doing all they could to protect the frontier."[22] A sickened Major Reno described how the "harrowing sight of the dead bodies [reminded him of the Indians had been] armed, clothed, and equipped" by government agencies. Reno's and Ryan's nagging concerns were proven entirely correct by the archaeological evidence (shell cartridges): large numbers of Winchester and Henry rifles were used to wipe out Custer's five companies with a relative swiftness seldom seen on any battlefield, and certainly not during the Civil War years.[23]

Custer had never faced such a heavy volume of superior weaponry when he fought against Rebels, who were armed with single-shot rifled muskets. The first example of the devastating effect of heavy firepower in dramatically altering the battle's course was demonstrated in the ford's defense. Here, the 7th Cavalry troopers were "met by such a tremendous fire from repeating rifles," in Horned Horse's words, that revealed the most forgotten factor that had paved the way to Custer's defeat.[24]

This book's special focus on the decisiveness of the showdown at Medicine Tail Coulee Ford has revealed the fact that fresh views and interpretations can still be found even in one of the most written about fields in the annals of American military history. As revealed in this work, this new focus on the importance of the struggle at Medicine Tail Coulee has revealed the value of rethinking and reanalyzing some of the most fundamental assumptions and long-accepted axioms that have been so long embraced as gospel.

Imbedded deeply into the American consciousness, Custer's defeat at the height of America's Centennial celebration was one of the most traumatic experiences in American national life: a psychologically devastating defeat for the republic not unlike the Japanese surprise attack on Pearl Harbor, Hawaii, on December 7, 1941. The romantic visual representations of Custer going down courageously fighting atop Custer Hill as a prime example of doomed heroism—from the first contemporary newspaper sketches to epic oil paintings that continue to be created well into the twentieth first century as opposed to uncomfortable truths found in the historical record, especially from Indian oral testimony—has become one of the most iconic images in American history.

However, this enduring image of Custer's Last Stand is inaccurate and romanticized. The most popular and glorified presentation is the 1941 film starring Errol Flynn (who played Custer with the appropriate dash), *They Died With Their Boots On.* This influential film left its deep imprint on the American consciousness and memory to this day. Creating the story of a heroic martyrdom, talented scriptwriters of the Hollywood film-producing machine allowed their creative imaginations to soar to new heights. In timely fashion, Errol Flynn's 1941 film was released to raise patriotism across the United States in preparation for America's massive military effort in the Second World War.

Equally guilty in distorting the truth and creating the romantic myth, wildly distorted popular paintings were immensely popular across America. One of the most popular depictions of "the battle was "Custer's Last Fight," painted by Cassilly Adams in 1884, prepared as a lithograph by F. Otto Becker in 1889, and widely distributed by Anheuser-Busch to millions of Americans, which helped to permanently mold modern and popular memory using the power of advertising. The lithograph first appeared in 1896 just before the Spanish–American War and immediately caught the imagination of the American nation.

Transforming one of the greatest disasters in American military history into a great moral victory and a shining example of noble sacrifice on the expansionist nation's altar of Manifest Destiny, the fabled last stand was a manufactured creation now used as propaganda. Most significantly, all of the divergent promoters of romantic myth simply ignored the truth about what happened at Medicine Tail Coulee Ford, because the truth was a much less glorious, dramatic, and important story that failed to fit the popular romanticized narrative that was part of popular memory.

In the traditional scenario of Custer and the 7th Cavarly troopers standing firm in courageous defiance before waves of a great tide of charging mounted warriors, until ultimately overwhelmed, the heroic image of fighting to the bitter end bestowed a comforting national view of victory through defeat. This traditional nationalist and racist portrayal of western expansion influenced generations of Americans, including highly respected historians, regardless of their lofty academic status and number of prestigious degrees.[25]

In consequence, what has been most of all long ignored were some of the most reliable Indian accounts that have deviated so sharply from the traditional last stand portrayal of romance and myth, especially with regard to the defense of Medicine Tail Coulee Ford. As could be expected, even the most accurate and corroborating Indian accounts were not sufficient to even slightly counterbalance these glowing romantic images. The traditional requirements of a glorified history, based upon deep-seated racial and national priorities rooted in cultural perspectives, only made the situation worse with regard to the ignoring Indian accounts, which were too often deemed entirely unworthy because of their non-white source. To fuel the belief in the nobility of heroic sacrifice against the odds with the Second World War looming near, Hollywood steadily churned out a good many historical and war films. These films emphasized martial glory and moral redemption through defeat that disguised ugly realities and hard truths about

America, thus masking the folly, errors, and betrayals that made the annihilation of Custer's five companies inevitable.[26]

Consequently, the combined effect of the dominance of the influential modern media, popular images and paintings, and romantic-minded historians, the disproportionate power of the enduring image of Custer's heroic death left no place for even the most reliable Cheyenne and Sioux oral accounts of the Medicine Tail Coulee Ford showdown. Some of the most revealing and dependable eyewitness Indian accounts of what really happened at the ford have continued to be routinely ignored and dismissed by historians primarily because of the power of myth. The Cheyenne oral accounts (more thoroughly ignored in general compared to Sioux oral accounts) are vitally important for any true understanding of the confrontation. However, Cheyenne oral accounts (the most important ones about the ford fight) have been always superseded by the far more numerous Sioux oral accounts by the relatively few historians who had relied upon them, because Cheyenne accounts have presented the most contrarian views that have questioned the deeply entrenched romance about Custer's Last Stand. Ironically, in the end, even a degree of cultural prejudice, both white and Indian, existed with regard to the routine dismissal of Cheyenne testimonies.

Obvious and inevitable errors (similar to those in the Sioux accounts) of some oral accounts due to interpreters and wide differences in language and culture have meant that Cheyenne testimonies have been too often routinely dismissed by white historians far more the Sioux oral accounts. Unfortunately, and most importantly, these revealing Cheyenne accounts have been overwhelmingly ignored primarily because they presented views that have overturned some of the most romanticized interpretations of the glorified Last Stand.

This widespread dismissal of these invaluable accounts by white historians was especially the case because of the mere suggestion in Cheyenne accounts that Custer might have been one of the first to fall at the ford, so far from where the romantic legend had him dying atop Custer Hill. Therefore, almost universally, the crucial confrontation at the ford (primarily a Cheyenne defensive effort) has been viewed by traditional historians as simply not only of no importance, but also hardly even worthy of mention: dismissed as just another case of untrustworthy and lying Indians. Such an unorthodox view—that the contest at the ford was more tactically important than the much-embellished fight on Custer's Hill—has been long viewed as little more than heresy in traditional battle of Little Bighorn historiography, and especially by respected historians with a vested interest in orthodoxy.

Therefore, for the first time, this present work has incorporated the most accurate and corroborating testimony of Cheyenne and Sioux oral accounts to reveal the unvarnished story of the ford's defense in full. These Indian accounts have been interwoven into the overall mosaic of this book's narrative to bring to life the forgotten story of the contest at Medicine Tail Coulee Ford, and present the fullest and most complete narrative today of that all-important struggle. Clearly, this is the most effective means of filling in the gaps with regard to the greatest omission, and most glaringly forgotten chapter, in the annals of battle of Little Bighorn historiography.[27]

Unfortunately, however, the sheer power of the mythical aspects of Custer's Last Stand has left relatively little opportunity for the ready acceptance for the breaking of any new ground in a largely sterile field devoid of fresh, new ideas, regardless of the amount of evidence. No single aspect of the story of the Little Bighorn has suffered more extensively from this systematic neglect than the crucial struggle at Medicine Tail Coulee Ford, especially with regard to its overall importance.

Due to the dense shroud of romanticism and myth-making about Custer's Last Stand, the distortion of the facts about the battle of Little Bighorn has been far more pervasive than Custer's surprise attack on the peaceful Washita village, since the ugly realities "would not square with the portrait of heroic sacrifice required. . . ."[28]

Indeed, to the Cheyenne people, Custer's attack on the sleeping Washita village left a deep scar that was destined to last for generations, fueling a powerful motivation among the mostly Cheyenne defenders to stand firm at the old buffalo ford against the odds.[29] To this day, therefore, some Indian people of the Great Plains still are "not inclined to look with favor on anyone whose name and appearance bear any resemblance to 'Custer.'" [30]

Indicative of its power to motivate, this feeling still exists among some Lakota people to this day. After all, the devastating attack at the Washita only made the Indians realize the truth of the prophetic vision of the benevolent spirit of Sweet Medicine, who warned that a light-skinned people would one day invade this pristine land, and that they would be bent on the Cheyenne's destruction.[31]

Contrary to some of the most popular works about this iconic engagement, the truth of the actual, but forgotten, turning point of the battle of the Little Bighorn at the old buffalo ford was voiced by Cheyenne and Sioux warriors, including Sitting Bull, who learned as much from warriors, himself. With regard to a forgotten, but golden, opportunity for the 7th Cavalry to still win the day,

> they agree[d] further that if Custer had continued his charge and gone to and through the villages, the Indians would have fled, and he would have killed many of them [and] 'If the soldiers [at the ford] had not stopped, they would have killed lots of Indians,' said one of their most famous chiefs. Anyone familiar with Indian ways, mode of thought, and war customs knows very well that as a rule the Indian avoids coming to close quarters with his enemy. If the enemy charges, the Indian runs away, but as soon as the vigor of the charge lessens or the enemy stops, the Indian becomes discouraged, turns about, and himself charges. This was characteristic of the old intertribal wars, which consisted largely of charges backward and forward by the two opposing forces.[32]

After succeeding in deciphering and then understanding the nuances of Custer's tactics, an insightful George Bird Grinnell, who knew the Cheyenne people like no other white historian, concluded that

> a part of Custer's command did come nearly down to the ford, and if [the troopers of only two companies] had kept on and crossed the river, they would no doubt have been followed by the rest of the command [the other three companies], and a great victory might have followed. . . . If Custer had kept moving [and] crossed the river at the ford at the mouth of the dry gulch [Medicine Tail Coulee then], I have no doubt that the Indians would have run.[33]

If so, then Custer would have won his long-envisioned victory with his bold flank attack. Custer actually came closer to achieving an impressive tactical success than has been generally recognized by white historians: he was within only a relatively short distance of his target when he was stopped at Medicine Tail Coulee Ford. If Reno and Benteen had only played their parts in supporting their regimental commander as he fully anticipated, then Custer very likely would have emerged victorious.

Private William O. Taylor understood what really happened at the ford, which was in general agreement with the Indian accounts (both Cheyenne and Sioux) and Curley. In overall tactical terms, Taylor correctly emphasized the possibility that Custer could have done anything other than unleash his main offensive effort at the ford, which was exactly in keeping with Custer's aggressive style, the secret of all his past successes: "My [main] reason is the statements made by the two messengers that Custer dispatched from near the crests of the bluffs, and my inability to believe that he would, after seeing the village close at hand, move his command nearly a mile away [on the ridges above the ford] from the foe he had so eagerly sought."[34]

After carefully studying the field not long after the fight, Lieutenant Winfield Scott Edgerly, Company D, 7ᵗʰ Cavalry, summarized the battle's course in basic, but realistic, terms. He concluded that Custer "found a ford, and the general belief was that he attempted to cross and was attacked and driven back to where he was found dead [because] [d]ead bodies were found all the way from the ford to where Custer's body was found."³⁵

Revealing the supreme importance of the ford fight, and from what they had seen in analyzing the field not long after the guns ceased to roar at the Little Bighorn, surviving 7ᵗʰ Cavalry officers, including Benteen, "believed that the Custer fight had been nothing more than a panicked rout from Medicine Tail Coulee [because of the decisive repulse] to Custer Hill [because] [t]hat was the only explanation they could come up with for the disorganized appearance of the five companies. . . ."³⁶

Benteen was more accurate with regard to explaining why this tactical situation that led directly to the destruction of five companies developed. In a letter to his beloved wife, "My Trabbie Darling," on July 25, 1876, Benteen wrote with tactical astuteness, based upon his many years of combat experience in the Civil War and the Indian Wars, to reveal the battle's turning point: "Just one month ago—today—at just about this time of day, Genl. Custer and his command [of five companies] commenced the attack on the indian village [and were] probably thrown into a panic at the 1ˢᵗ check received" at Medicine Tail Coulee Ford.³⁷

After closely surveying the field, Major Benteen described with insight what he saw in surveying the battlefield: Custer's trail "shows that he moved rapidly down the river for three miles to the ford, at which he attempted to cross into their village, and with the conviction that he would strike a retreating enemy. . . . The [fleeing] Indians made him overconfident by appearing to be stampeded, and, undoubtedly, when he arrived at the ford, expecting to go with ease through their village, he rode into an ambuscade" of waiting warriors.³⁸

Of course, not Benteen nor anyone else could have imagined how few warriors had defended the ford. Reno and Benteen, both veteran officers with Civil War experience, were correct in their early tactical analysis that emphasized the vital importance of the showdown at the ford: Custer's final offensive effort of his career at Medicine Tail Coulee was in truth the battle's decisive turning point.[39] More importantly, Benteen's and Reno's on-target tactical analysis was confirmed by Indian accounts, both friendly and hostile. Once Custer was repulsed at the ford, the battle for all practical purposes was over, except for the grim process of killing every trooper of five companies. Tall Bull, a Cheyenne, described how the stage was set for systematic annihilation, after the repulse at the ford: "Soldiers fell back from [the] river, some mounted and some on foot and not in very good order."[40] Curley, the young Crow scout, indicated as much to reveal that friendly Indian and hostile Indian accounts were in general agreement with regard to the importance of the struggle at the ford.[41]

Like Benteen, Reno came very close to correctly analyzing what exactly happened at the ford: "The Indians made [Custer] overconfident by appearing to be stampeded, and, undoubtedly, when he arrived at the ford, expecting to go with ease through their village, he rode into an ambuscade" at Medicine Tail Coulee Ford that sealed his fate.[42] Even more from what he deduced from looking over and studying the field immediately after the battle, Reno wrote that "his trail shows that [Custer] moved rapidly down the river for three miles to the ford, at which he attempted to cross into the village, and with the conviction that he would strike a retreating enemy."[43] The tenacious defense at the ford was the antithesis of this fatal assumption on Custer's part, setting the tragic stage for Custer's Last Stand.

Major Reno's best description of what happened at the ford was revealed in his official report, July 5, 1876, to Terry's adjutant general, years before the official court of inquiry when such views were amended. In his tactical analysis, which clearly shows he was more of a thinker than fighter (like his June 25 performance), Reno summarized the fight at the ford with keen tactical insight that revealed an extended battle:

> After following over his trail it was evident to me that Custer intended to support me by moving farther down the stream and attacking the village in flank; that he found the distance greater to the ford than he anticipated; that he did charge, but his march had taken so long, although his trail shows he moved rapidly, that they were ready for him; that Companies C and I, and perhaps part of Company E, crossed to the village, or attempted it at the charge, and were met by a staggering fire, and that they fell back to secure a position from which to defend themselves. . . .[44]

Clearly, Reno explained the turning point of the battle of the Little Bighorn.

To maintain the honor of the officer corps and the 7th Cavalry's overall image at the Reno Court of Inquiry, and to save themselves, a self-serving Reno and Benteen conveniently reversed course after the battle to de-emphasize the importance of the ford fight. After all, an emphasis of the ford struggle would have given validity to Custer's battle plan of delivering a flank attack (the correct winning tactical formula) in conjunction with the expected offensive efforts of his two lieutenants from the opposite direction, if they had obeyed their commander's wishes and orders with regard to reinforcing him. Consequently, the showdown at Medicine Tail Coulee Ford had to be minimized to obscure Custer's plan of the flank attack calculated to reverse the day's fortunes: the most necessary requirement to shift all blame off the survivors, especially Reno and Benteen, for not assisting Custer's flank attack, and so that it would all then fall upon one person, Custer. They failed Custer—with regard to Reno's abortive attack at the village's opposite end, and Benteen's expected reinforcements never coming to exploit Custer's success if he had crossed the river in force—and therefore had to deny any knowledge that Custer possessed a winning tactical plan to launch a flank attack. After all, to admit that Custer possessed a very good tactical plan, which might well have worked, would have implicated Reno and Benteen for their lack of assistance. Most of all, they provided the collaborating excuses for failing to come to Custer's aid and leaving him on his own, and to his doom. Ironically, the truth spoken by Benteen and Reno immediately after the battle was not heard from them at the 1879 Court of Inquiry.[45]

The truth of what actually happened at the ford was found in the words of 7th Cavalry privates, as opposed to the official testimony of the self-serving officers, who together at the 1879 Court of Inquiry conveniently transformed Custer into the perfect scapegoat. Private William O. Taylor explained:

> Custer, after seeing what he did from his position on the bluffs, must have realize at once that there was but one course of pursue, and that was to get into the fight at some effective point and as soon as possible. . . . A short distance to his right was a dry creek which ran into the river opposite the Indian camps, and [this was] a fording place [so] he followed the dry creek down trying to find a crossing place and when near the river was met with such an overwhelming fire that he had to fall back to the ridge which seemed to offer the best chance for a successful defence.[46]

The New York-born Taylor was correct. With regard to the strength of resistance at the ford, Taylor's words corresponded with those of Horned Horse (and others) that in attempting to charge across the ford, Custer was repulsed because he "met by such a tremendous fire from the repeating rifles. . . ."[47]

In agreement with Indian testimony, Custer expert Sandy Barnard likewise correctly emphasized: "Some students of the battle concluded Custer was killed during the cavalry approach to the river crossing at Medicine Tail Coulee; if he remained alive, the disaster never would have occurred."[48] Indeed, this seldom stated view of white historians about the true cause of the disaster at the Little Bighorn was right on target, agreeing with Indian accounts. No other logical or rational tactical possibility can more adequately explain the relatively quick and systematic collapse of resistance among the five 7th Cavalry companies than the fact that Custer was hit (but most likely wounded and carried to the top of Custer Hill) in leading the attack across the ford. After all, Custer had been long viewed as invincible to the troopers, a talisman of sorts, especially in a crisis situation. As penned in a 1902 poem by John Hay, the most crucial "scorpion sting" that doomed five entire companies was when Custer was hit by gunfire and then repulsed at the ford: the fatal one-two punch that delivered the true knockout blow to nearly half of the 7th Cavalry during its last offensive effort. After analyzing the battlefield and in agreement with Indian accounts, one anonymous 6th Infantry sergeant correctly concluded that Custer "gave the order to charge [the ford], which was gallantly done, but no resistance was met. . . until they arrived at the other side of the village location, when they received a terrific volley which put an end to many a noble fellow's existence. . . ."[49]

By then crossing the ford and charging into the Cheyenne village, Custer would have snatched victory from the jaws of defeat to win the greatest and most improbable victory of his career, especially if adequately supported as ordered. For Custer and his troopers, the flank attack on the ford presented the day's greatest tactical opportunity, although that fact has been generally unrecognized by dismissive historians, who had overlooked the Cheyenne testimony.

To this day, no memorial markers dedicated to any fallen 7th Cavalry trooper can be found around the Medicine Tail Coulee Ford, despite the fact that troopers were known to have fallen and the remains of soldier graves had been discovered in this area: the result partly from partisan politics and the power of Custer Hill romanticism. A diverse range of factors (from the whitewashing of the actual events at the Court of Inquiry that obscured Custer's flank attack at the ford for political and personal reasons, to the disproportionate focus on Custer Hill) has led to the misconception that nothing of importance occurred at Medicine Tail Coulee Ford, not even the losses among Custer's ford attackers. All in all, this was part of a political whitewashing: Custer was an outspoken Democrat highly critical of the Republican Administration (one of the most corrupt in American history) and appeasing 7th Cavalry officers wanted to garner the president's favor, particularly for future promotion.

Ironically, in the end, the mass outpouring of books, popular films, and paintings (which have never focused on what happened at Medicine Tail Coulee Ford) devoted to the enduring romance of Custer's Last Stand would have been actually closer to the truth had they depicted "Custer's Last Charge" on the strategic ford at the mouth of Medicine Tail Coulee in his final bid to win it all. To this day, no dramatic paintings of the struggle at the ford have depicted this hard-fought contest, despite its decisiveness, playing a role in its general obscurity. Almost everything about the battle of the Little Bighorn has continued to be centered on the traditional story and fanciful imaginary of the Last Stand Hill.

Indeed, long unrecognized and forgotten in terms of its overall importance, the repulse of Custer's last attack at Medicine Tail Coulee Ford doomed all five companies to set the stage for last stand on the high ground. In this sense, generations of historians and the historiography of battle studies have been focused entirely in the wrong direction and at the wrong place: nearly three-quarters of a mile farther north on the less tactically significant killing ground on Custer Hill, after Custer's fate had been already sealed at the ford.

As he would have almost certainly preferred in his last hour of life on this Earth, and symbolically in keeping with the popular former "boy general" image of the Civil War years, a mounted Custer had once again charged at the head of his troopers as during his glory days at Gettysburg and the Appomattox Campaign.

Like no other single event on June 25, the failure of Custer's attack at the ford set the stage for the tragic finale on Last Stand Hill, paving the way to the unprecedented disaster. Instead of the insignificant tactical feint long incorrectly assumed by historians, Custer's desperate attack at the ford was in fact the battle's forgotten decisive turning point and the key to its final outcome. More than the traditional culprits of Benteen and Reno in explaining Custer's destruction and that of his command, the true reason why Custer was defeated stemmed primarily from one single source: the repulse of his last attack by a relative handful of Cheyenne and Sioux warriors at Medicine Tail Coulee Ford. Unlike any previous work to date, this book has finally explored in depth the forgotten story of the repulse of Custer's final, but most forgotten, attack on his illustrious career. In a final paradox, Custer's Luck was finally broken forever on the unluckiest day of his life, because of the combat prowess of the band of Cheyenne and Sioux defenders of the Medicine Tail Coulee Ford accomplished what even Lee's best officers and fighting men had failed to achieve year after year. Ironically, Custer had been repulsed in his last attack because, in his own words, "love of country is almost a religion with them," especially those warriors who defended the ford.[50]

Custer's Last and Most Forgotten Victory

What has been most forgotten about Custer's Last Stand was the victory that Custer actually achieved in the midst of the most miserable of all defeats. With his flank attack at the ford, Custer unleashed a desperate bid to gain the initiative—and the success that Reno and Benteen had so quickly forfeited: a bold decision that saved the majority of his regiment by drawing off the greatest mass of warriors away from Reno, while leading to a most noble sacrifice of his five companies that was not in vain in the end.

Without Custer's audacious flank attack, the distinct possibility existed that the 7th Cavalry might have been entirely wiped out. Private Taylor understood as much after carefully studying the terrain and overall situation:

> I am disposed to account for [Custer] on the ridge by my belief, that after being checked in his attempt to cross the river, and seeing the strength at his front, he believed that by drawing his foes away from the river and village he would render Reno's purpose more successful. And at the same time give Benteen, whom he was expecting every moment, a chance to strike the Indians on their flank or cut in between them and their village.[51]

Quite simply and paradoxically, Custer's last charge rescued the remainder of the 7th Cavalry, who survived to fight another day: a most ironic development, considering that Benteen and Reno failed to come to Custer's assistance during his supreme hour of need. Reno was saved, and almost certainly Benteen as well, because Custer's attack at the ford drew thousands of warriors in the opposite direction in a timely manner to relieve the pressure that might have well destroyed the two remaining battalions.[52]

In the end, perhaps one of Custer's Michigan men from the Civil War years said it best with regard to the iconic battle's forgotten truths, writing with disgust that the "Administration was led, through a pack of worthless, jealous officers [especially Reno and Benteen in the Reno

298 • DEATH AT THE LITTLE BIGHORN

Court of Inquiry cover-up], to heap insult after insult upon the brave Custer, and I now say, his blood is upon their heads. They murdered him, with Indian Bullets."[53]

Captain Benteen's failure to assist his commander in his greatest hour of need was partly seen in his words that revealed a sadistic delight upon first viewing Custer's dead body on the nightmarish hilltop of death: "There he is, God damn him! He'll never fight any more."[54] However, others would never fight again for entirely different reasons. In a July 6, 1876, letter to his daughters, interpreter Frederic Francis Girard was more thankful than the smug Benteen or Reno: "I escaped through the grace of God [and] I shall never go out again with an expedition."[55]

Another architect of the unprecedented disaster, the smug lawyer General Terry, lamented how the "flower of the American Army is dead," but he failed to fully understand that this was primarily the result of Custer's "1st check"—the repulse at the obscure buffalo ford along the Little Bighorn.[56] Indeed, the decisive turning point of one of America's most famous and iconic battles came when Custer's last charge failed at Medicine Tail Coulee Ford, sealing the fate of himself and his command, after having achieved his great goal of having surprised his normally vigilant opponent not once but twice (an unprecedented tactical feat in the annals of Indian warfare) in broad daylight: perhaps the greatest paradox of the battle of Little Bighorn.

In the end, there was nothing fatalistic or foolish about Custer's bold leadership and battle plan that was tactically innovative and hard-hitting: the most admirable qualities that were required for any chance of winning victory. Catching his opponent with a surprise flank attack, he had brought his five companies of the verge of winning the most dramatic of victories. In the end, Custer was tactically correct, because his tactical plan of delivering a flank attack worked to perfection, until he was hit (wounded) in leading the charge and was unexpectedly stopped at the ford. Ironically, Custer would have won his victory had the smallest and weakest village (northernmost) along the Little Bighorn had been struck first instead of the strongest at the encampment's southern end by Reno: the necessary tactical formula for his pincer movement to have succeeded. No one more than the Sioux and Cheyenne realized this undeniable tactical reality. Of course, Custer had no idea that Reno's attack was directed at the strongest part of the village, while his own attack was aimed at the weakest part: the inverse of what was needed for success.

After talking to his warriors who destroyed Custer and his five companies in systematic fashion, Sitting Bull certainly knew the most hidden truths about the battle. When an early white interviewer, who had placed a map of the battlefield before him, asked Sitting Bull: "Was there any heavy fighting after [Reno's] retreat of the soldiers to the bluffs?," he did not hesitate. Knowing exactly where the battle had been decided better than any white historian, Sitting Bull immediately responded, "Not then; not there." This careful interviewer from a major eastern newspaper then asked, "Where, then." Pointing on the map to reveal the undeniable truth about what actually happened on the afternoon of June 25, Sitting Bull then said: "'Why, down there;' and Sitting Bull indicated with his finger the piece [place] where Custer approached and touched the river. 'That,' said he, 'was where the big fight was fought. . . .'"[57]

Most significantly, what Sitting Bull meant by "big fight" was in fact the scene far below Custer Hill,: the dramatic showdown at Medicine Tail Coulee Ford, where America's most iconic battle was decided. Custer first fell not atop Custer Hill, but in fact where few believed possible or even imaginable, at an obscure buffalo ford in the middle of nowhere.

Even more than Custer's tactical mistakes, it was the folly of the nation's leaders at the White House and the highest-ranking military men at army headquarters that paved the way for the Little Bighorn defeat that shocked the American nation to the core. However, most of all, it was only a relatively few Cheyenne and Sioux warriors who were most responsible for stopping Custer's last charge: the true, but forgotten, apotheosis, and the most important and decisive last stand on June 25, 1876.

Appendix A

The Last Link to the Little Bighorn

This article by Mark Boardman first appeared within the pages of *True West* magazine on October 12, 2009.

From sharing the stories of the Custer battle to fighting in WWII, Joe Medicine Crow is a national treasure.
He is the one living connection to the Battle of the Little Bighorn, or Custer's Last Stand if you prefer.

He's an old man now, ninety-six on October 27. His hearing is bad, his eyes are weak and he's been sick a fair amount in the past year.

But Joe Medicine Crow's mind is clear and his voice is strong as he tells the stories of that hot and dry day—June 25, 1876—when a large force of Indians destroyed the U.S. 7th Cavalry in southeastern Montana. Medicine Crow heard the stories from the men who were there, both Custer foes and allies.

Voices of the Elders
Medicine Crow's mind retreats to 1920, when he was six or seven and living near Lodge Grass, Montana, about five miles from the battlefield.

In the fall and spring, the old men gathered in the sweat lodges to purify their bodies and minds, to reminisce about the past and mourn for its loss.

Usually, they recounted their bravery in battle. As you might expect, the Little Bighorn was a favorite subject.

One of those men was his grandmother's stepbrother (stay with us here), who by Crow tradition is also considered his grandfather. White Man Runs Him, born around 1858, was one of Custer's scouts on the ill-fated mission. He took the boy Joe to the lodges to hear the tales.

The elders said the problems began before the fighting started. "White Man Runs Him insisted that Custer's soldiers had been drinking that day," Medicine Crow remembers. The men of the 7th weren't ready for a tough fight.

Then the scouts went to a high point of rocks to spy on the Indian encampment—and realized that they faced several thousand warriors (just how many is still unclear). Custer didn't really believe them, and he certainly wasn't fazed; his only concern was that the Indian force might escape before he could get to them.

"Custer did not take the advice of his Crow scouts, who told him to wait for reinforcements before attacking the Sioux and Cheyenne camp," Medicine Crow says. "Instead, he divided his force of seven hundred soldiers into three parts and attacked right away." The scouts knew what awaited; they began changing from army uniforms into their native clothing and singing their death songs. Custer asked an interpreter to explain the Indians' actions. When he was told, Custer accused them of being cowards and sent them away. That saved their lives.

The last White Man Runs Him saw of Custer and his detail, they were charging toward the Little Bighorn River, heading for the huge Indian village—estimates range from several hundred lodges to a couple thousand—and the stuff of legend.

At that point, White Man Runs Him said, "we went back along the ridge and found [Maj. Marcus] Reno's men entrenched there. We stayed there all afternoon," fighting off the Indians. When darkness fell, the scout made his way through enemy lines and found troops coming to support Custer.

It was a story that Joe Medicine Crow would hear many times.

They Didn't Want to Hear

Frequently, the young man served as interpreter for his grandfather, especially when white newspapermen and writers came for interviews about the Custer fight.

Medicine Crow says that most refused to believe the stories, which flew in the face of the white image of Custer as a brave fighter who was ambushed by savages. Finally, White Man Runs Him had his fill: facing a skeptical interviewer, he told the boy in Crow, "Send him home. He does not want to know the truth." The mid-sixties man rarely spoke of the battle to whites after that.

Medicine Crow faced similar disbelief throughout the years yet he didn't stop telling the Crow stories.

Feet in Two Worlds

Medicine Crow's relatives were not afraid to face the truth—the younger people would have to live in the white man's world. So while they brought them up with the old customs—speaking the Crow language and learning the way of the warrior—the elders sent the children to white schools. It was tough, Medicine Crow says. The Indian kids faced physical and emotional bullying from their mainly white peers, and either indifference or discrimination from the teachers.

Most dropped out. Medicine Crow stayed, but he didn't get his high school diploma until he was twenty-one years old. Then he became the second member of the tribe to attend college, and the first to obtain a graduate degree, earning a master's in anthropology from the University of Southern California. He was well on his way to a PhD when WWII interrupted. Combat action in Europe provided an opportunity to bring his two worlds together—and to prove his own worth as a warrior.

In early 1945, Medicine Crow and the 103rd Army Division were driving through Germany, trying to finish up the war in Europe. He put war paint on his arms and a sacred eagle feather under his helmet, believing the strong medicine would protect him. It apparently did more than that. In an era of advanced warfare, Medicine Crow accomplished four tasks required of a Crow war chief—steal an enemy's horse, touch an enemy in battle, take away an enemy's weapon, and lead a successful war party. Nobody since has achieved that honor. It probably won't be done again.

To this day, he proudly tells stories of his accomplishments in battle—just like White Man Runs Him and his other ancestors did.

A Twenty-First-Century Crow

More honors have come Medicine Crow's way over the years, including his receipt of this year's Presidential Medal of Freedom, the nation's highest civilian honor. He's written numerous books and articles, and given more interviews than one can count.

In the oral tradition of his Crow tribe, he passes the stories on to younger generations—Indian as well as white—who need to understand their history and culture if they are to be successful in the modern world. Joe Medicine Crow has already blazed that path, a nearly one-hundred-year journey filled with great achievements.

A Song of Healing

I served on the Little Bighorn Monument advisory commission, which was to establish an Indian memorial at the Little Bighorn. And we had very studiously avoided using the word "Custer" anywhere.

Custer's name was to be eradicated in all of our deliberations. There would be nothing in this to memorialize him.

[In November 1999] we were doing the groundbreaking. And Leonard Bruguier, who was head of American Indian Studies at the University of South Dakota and the chair of the commission, was giving a speech.

Up from the crowd comes Joe Medicine Crow, dressed in his WWII uniform. He walked up to Bruguier and said, "I've come to sing an honor song for Custer." A hush came over the crowd. Leonard graciously stepped aside, and Joe sang this wonderful honor song for Custer in both Crow and English.

> —*Historian Paul Andrew Hutton, on Joe Medicine Crow's work to bridge the divide between Indians and whites; shown here is the 1926 gathering, with White Man Runs Him shaking hands with Gen. E.S. Godfrey.*

These Boots Were Made for Walkin'

In 1941, Joe Medicine Crow was undergoing his graduate study at the University of Southern California when he saw an ad in the *Los Angeles Times*. Warner Brothers was casting extras for the Custer film *They Died with Their Boots On*.

Medicine Crow thought it might be fun (and provide some pocket change), so he attended the audition. The producers were delighted to have an Indian show up, and even happier that he had actual connections to the Little Bighorn battle. They asked him to help with the script.

Medicine Crow's efforts did not work out. The powers that be threw out historical accuracy in favor of a pro-military, patriotic approach, believing (correctly) that the U.S. entry into WWII was coming fast. Their Custer (played by Errol Flynn) would be a heroic figure, sacrificing himself for his country.

When Medicine Crow told the producers that their depiction was way off, they fired him.

"I said, 'Someday I'm going to write my own Custer production and tell it like it is.'" Medicine Crow grabbed his chance in 1964, when he authored the script for the Little Bighorn reenactment that still runs each June in Hardin, Montana.

Epilogue

For nearly seventy years, Joe Medicine Crow (whose Crow name is Bako Dagak, or High Bird) served as the official tribal historian on the Crow Reservation in Montana where he was born on October 27, 1913. He died on April 3, 2016.

Appendix B:

Battle Participants

7th Cavalry Officers at the Battle of the Little Bighorn
- Commanding Officer: Lt. Col. George Armstrong Custer (killed)
- Maj. Marcus Reno
- Adjutant: 1st Lt. William W. Cooke (killed)
- Assistant Surgeon George Edwin Lord (killed)
- Acting Assistant Surgeon James Madison DeWolf (killed)
- Acting Assistant Surgeon Henry Rinaldo Porter
- Chief of Scouts: 2nd Lt. Charles Varnum (detached from A Company, wounded)
- 2nd in Command of Scouts: 2nd Lt. Luther Hare (detached from K Company)
- Pack Train Commander: 1st Lt. Edward Gustave Mathey (detached from M Company)
- A Company: Capt. Myles Moylan, 1st Lt. Charles DeRudio
- B Company: Capt. Thomas McDougall, 2nd Lt. Benjamin Hodgson (killed)

- C Company: Capt. Thomas Custer (killed), 2nd Lt. Henry Moore Harrington (killed)
- D Company: Capt. Thomas Weir, 2nd Lt. Winfield Edgerly
- E Company: 1st Lt. Algernon Smith (killed), 2nd Lt. James G. Sturgis (killed)
- F Company: Capt. George Yates (killed), 2nd Lt. William Reily (killed)
- G Company: 1st Lt. Donald McIntosh (killed), 2nd Lt. George Wallace
- H Company: Capt. Frederick Benteen, 1st Lt. Francis Gibson
- I Company: Capt. Myles Keogh (killed), 1st Lt. James Porter (killed)
- K Company: 1st Lt. Edward Settle Godfrey
- L Company: 1st Lt. James Calhoun (killed), 2nd Lt. John J. Crittenden (killed)
- M Company: Capt. Thomas French

Indian Leaders and Warriros in the Battle

- **Hunkpapa (Lakota):** Sitting Bull, Four Horns, Crow King, Chief Gall, Black Moon, Rain-in-the-Face, Moving Robe Women, Spotted Horn Bull, Iron Hawk, One Bull, Bull Head, Chasing Eagle
- **Sihasapa (Blackfoot Lakota):** Crawler, Kill Eagle
- **Minneconjou (Lakota):** Chief Hump, Black Moon, Red Horse, Makes Room, Looks Up, Lame Deer, Dog-with-Horn, Dog Back Bone, White Bull, Feather Earring, Flying By
- **Sans Arc (Lakota):** Spotted Eagle, Red Bear, Long Road, Cloud Man
- **Oglala (Lakota):** Crazy Horse, He Dog, Kicking Bear, Flying Hawk, Chief Long Wolf, Black Elk, White Cow Bull, Running Eagle, Black Fox II

- **Brule (Lakota):** Two Eagles, Hollow Horn Bear, Brave Bird
- **Two Kettles (Lakota):** Runs-the-Enemy
- **Lower Yanktonai (Dakota):** Thunder Bear, Medicine Cloud, Iron Bear, Long Tree
- **Wahpekute (Dakota):** Inkpaduta, Sounds-the-Ground-as-He-Walks, White Eagle, White Tracking Earth
- **Northern Cheyenne:** Two Moons, Wooden Leg, Old Bear, Lame White Man, American Horse, Brave Wolf, Antelope Women, ThunderBull Big Nose, Yellow Horse, Little Shield, Horse Road, Bob Tail Horse, Yellow Hair, Bear-Walks-on-a-Ridge, Black Hawk, Buffalo Calf Road Woman, Crooked Nose, Noisy Walking
- **Arapahoes:** Waterman, Sage, Left Hand, Yellow Eagle, Little Bird

Notable Scouts/Interpreters in the Battle
- The 7th Cavalry was accompanied by a number of scouts and interpreters:
- Bloody Knife: Arikara/Lakota scout (killed)
- Bob Tailed Bull: Arikara scout (killed)
- Boy Chief: Arikara scout
- Charley Reynolds: scout (killed)
- Curley: Crow scout
- Curling Head: Arikara scout
- Fred Gerard: interpreter
- Goes Ahead: Crow scout
- Goose: Arikara scout (wounded in the hand by a 7th Cavalry trooper)
- Hairy Moccasin: Crow scout
- Half Yellow Face, leader of Crow Scouts, also known as Paints Half His Face Yellow

- Isaiah Dorman: interpreter (killed)
- Little Brave: Arikara scout (killed)
- Little Sioux: Arikara scout
- Mitch Bouyer: scout/interpreter (killed)
- One Feather: Arikara scout
- Owl: Arikara scout
- Peter Jackson: half-Pikuni and half-Blackfoot brother of William, scout
- Red Bear: Arikara scout
- Red Star: Arikara scout
- Running Wolf: Arikara scout
- Sitting Bear: Arikara scout
- Soldier: Arikara scout
- Strikes The Lodge: Arikara scout
- Strikes Two: Arikara scout
- Two Moons: Arikara/Cheyenne scout
- White Man Runs Him: Crow scout
- White Swan, Crow Scout (severely wounded)
- William Jackson: half-Pikuni and half-Blackfoot scout
- Young Hawk: Arikara scout

About the Author

Phillip Thomas Tucker received his PhD in American history from St. Louis University (St. Louis, Missouri) in 1990. He has written about some of the most iconic moments in American history, including *George Washington's Surprise Attack, A New Look at the Battle that Decided the Fate of America* (Skyhorse Publishing, 2014), *Pickett's Charge: A New Look at Gettysburg's Final Attack* (Skyhorse Publishing, 2016), and *Alexander Hamilton's Revolution: His Vital Role as Washington's Chief of Staff* (Skyhorse Publishing, 2017). He lives outside of Washington, DC.

Notes

Chapter I

1.   Roy Morris, Jr., *Sheridan, The Life and Wars of General Phil Sheridan* (New York: Crown Publishers, 1992), p. 184; Perry D. Jamieson, *Crossing the Deadly Ground, United States Military Tactics, 1865–1899*, (Tuscaloosa: University of Alabama Press, 1994), pp. 22–38, 48–53.

2.   Thom Hatch, *Glorious War, The Civil War Adventures of George Armstrong Custer* (New York: St. Martin's Press, 2013), pp. 105–294; Duane Schultz, *Coming Through Fire, George Armstrong Custer and Chief Black Kettle* (Yardley, Penna. Westholme Publishing, 2012), pp. ix, 45–68, 142–180.

3.   Schultz, *Coming Through Fire*, pp. ix–2, 65–66.

4.   Ibid., pp. 182–184, 202–214.

5.   Ibid., pp. 222–235.

6.   Jamieson, *Crossing the Deadly Ground*, pp. 49–50; Schultz, *Coming Through Fire*, pp. x, 249.

7.   Michael A. Elliott, *Custerology, The Enduring Legacy of the Indian Wars and George Armonstrong Custer* (Chicago, Ill. University of Chicago Press, 2008), p. 119.

8.   Ibid. p. 107.

9.   Dee Brown, *Bury My Heart at Wounded Knee, An Indian History of the American West* (Chicago, Ill. Holt, Reinhart and Winston, 1971), pp. 68–91.

10. Ibid., p. 83.

11. Larry Sklenar, *To Hell with Honor, Custer and the Little Bighorn*, (Norman: University of Oklahoma Press, 2000), p. 132.

12. Jamieson, *Crossing the Deadly Ground*, p. 25.

13. Michael Johnson, *Sioux, Warriors of the Plains* (Edison, N.J.: Chartwell Books, Inc., 2008), pp. 6, 34.

14. Jeffry D. Wert, *Custer, The Controversial Life of George Armstrong Custer* (New York: Touchstone Books, 1997), p. 313; William O. Taylor, *With Custer on the Little Bighorn* (New York: Penguin Books 1996), pp. ix–x, 9; Morris, *Sheridan*, pp. 184, 347–348; Colin C. Calloway, *One Vast Winter Count, The Native American West before Lewis and Clark* (Lincoln: University of Nebraska Press, 2003), p. 305.

15. Thomas B. Marquis, interpreter, *Wooden Leg, A Warrior who Fought Custer* (Lincoln: University of Nebraska Press, 2003), p. 1.

16. Morris, *Sheridan*, p. 348; Wert, *Custer*, p. 313.

17. James E. Mueller, *Shooting Arrows and Slinging Mud, Custer, the Press, and the Little Bighorn* (Norman: University of Oklahoma Press, 2013), p. 18; Wert, *Custer*, pp. 313, 325; Mike Sajna, *Crazy Horse, The Life behind the Legend* (Edison, N.J.: Castle Books, 2005), p. 259; Peter Panzeri, *Little Big Horn 1876, Custer's Last Stand*, (Oxford: Osprey Publishing, 1995), pp. 8–10.

18. Wert, *Custer*, p. 325.

19. Ibid., p. 317; Sajna, *Crazy Horse*, pp. 25, 259.

20. Thomas B. Marquis, *Custer on the Little Bighorn* (Algonac, Mich.: Reference Publications, Inc., 1987), p. 82.

21. Johnson, *Sioux*, p. 39; Taylor, *With Custer on the Little Bighorn*, pp. 9–10; Richard G. Hardorff, *Indian Views of the Custer Fight, A Source Book* (Norman: University of Oklahoma Press, 2005), p. 132.

22. Brown, *Bury My Heart at Wounded Knee*, p. 70.

23. Jay Monaghan, *Custer, The Life of General George Armstrong Custer* (Lincoln: University of Nebraska Press, 1959), p. 373.

24. Wert, *Custer*, p. 317.

25. Ibid.

26. Brown, *Bury My Heart at Wounded Knee*, p. 67.

27. Sandy Barnard, editor, *Ten Years with Custer, A 7th Cavalry-man's Memoirs* (Terre Haute, Ind.: AST Press, 2001), p. 250.

28. Sajna, *Crazy Horse*, pp. 269–270; Taylor, *With Custer on the Little Bighorn*, pp. 9–10; Panzeri, *Little Big Horn 1876*, p. 13; Tim Lehman, *Bloodshed at Little Bighorn* (Baltimore, Md.: John Hopkins University Press, 2010), p. 22.

29. Barnard, ed., *Ten Years With Custer*, p. 44; Panzeri, *Little Big Horn 1876*, p. 8.

30. Taylor, *With Custer on the Little Bighorn*, p. 9.

31. Morris, *Sheridan*, pp. 359–360; Wert, *Custer*, p. 325; Lehman, *Bloodshed at Little Bighorn*, p. 77; *New York Times*, New York, May 1, 1873; Ernest R. Reedstrom, *Bugles, Banners and War Bonnets* (New York: Bonanza Books, 1986), pp. 84, 92, 102; Marguerite Merington, editor, *The Custer Story, The Life and Intimate Letters of General Custer and His Wife Elizabeth* (New York: Devin-Adair Company, 1950), p. 268.

32. Sklenar, *To Hell with Honor*, p. 49.

33. Taylor, *With Custer on the Little Bighorn*, p. 11; Reedstrom, *Bugles, Banner and War Bonnets*, pp. 103–109.

34. Barnard, ed., *Ten Years with Custer*, pp. 6, 285, 287.

35. *Bismark Tribune*, Bismark, Dakota Territory, May 24, 1876; Mary Thomas, *Canadians with Custer* (Toronto , Ont.: Dundurn, 2012), p. 165.

36. Ronald H. Nichols, editor, *Men with Custer, Biographies of the 7th Cavalry* (Hardin, Mont.: Custer Battlefield Historical & Museum Association, 2000), p. 93.

37. Ibid.

38. Ibid., p. 225.

39. Sajna, *Crazy Horse*, p. 274; Jamieson, *Crossing the Deadly Ground*, pp., N.J.37–38; Frank B. Linderman, *Plenty-Coups, Chief of the Crows* (Lincoln: University of Nebraska Press, 1962), p. 153.

40. Wert, *Custer*, pp. 329, 331.

41. Sklenar, *To Hell with Honor*, p. 93.

42. Wert, *Custer*, p. 332.
43. Ibid., p. 335; Nichols, ed., *Men with Custer*, p. 95.
44. *Bismark Tribune*, May 17, 1876; Taylor, *With Custer on the Little Bighorn*, p. 14.
45. *New York Times*, May 1, 1873.
46. Richard G. Hardorff, compiled and edited, *Lakota Recollections of the Custer Fight, New Sources of Indian Military History*, (Lincoln: University of Nebraska Press, 1997), pp. 131–132.
47. W. A. Graham, *The Custer Myth, The Source Book of Custeriana*, (Mechanicsburg, Penna.: Stackpole Books, 2000), p. 289.
48. Graham, *The Custer Myth*, p. 289.
49. *Bismark Tribune*, June 14, 1876.
50. Hardorff, *Indian Views of the Custer Fight*, p. 177.
51. Merington, ed., *The Custer Story*, p. 168.
52. Ibid., p. 217.
53. Sklenar, *To Hell with Honor*, p. 336.
54. Graham, *The Custer Myth*, p. 148.
55. Merington, ed., *The Custer Story*, p. 179.

Chapter II

1. Richard Drinnon, Facing West, *The Metaphysics of Indian–Hating and Empire–Building*, (Minneapolis: University of Minnesota Press, 1980), p. xii.
2. Ibid., p. 450.
3. Marquis, *Custer on the Little Bighorn*, p. 81.
4. Merington, ed., *The Custer Story*, p. 76.
5. Wert, *Custer*, p. 333.
6. Schultz, *Coming Through Fire*, p. 221.
7. Hardorff, *Lakota Recollections of the Custer Fight*, p. 92.
8. Jamieson, *Crossing the Deadly Ground*, p. 50; Merington, *The Custer Story*, pp. 3, 57–161.
9. Johnson, *Sioux*, p. 34; Panzeri, *Little Big Horn 1876*, pp. 9–10; Thomas E. Mails, *Dog Soldiers, Bear Men and Buffalo Women, A Study of the Societies and Cults of the Plains Indians* (Englewood, N.J.: Prentice-Hall, Inc., 1973), pp. 34–35.

10. Grinnell, George Bird, *The Fighting Cheyennes* (Norman: University of Oklahoma Press, 1985), p. 346; Nathaniel Philbrick, *The Last Stand, Custer, Sitting Bull, and the Battle of Little Bighorn* (New York: Viking, 2010), pp. 27–28, 67, 69–70; Sklenar, *To Hell with Honor*, p. 98; Lehman, *Bloodshed at Little Bighorn*, p. 8; Marquis, *Wooden Leg*, p. 19; Reedstrom, *Bugles, Banners and War Bonnets*, pp. 342–344.

11. Lehman, *Bloodshed at Little Bighorn*, p. 100.

12. Philbrick, *The Last Stand*, pp. 32, 34–35.

13. Ibid., pp. 69–70.

14. Marquis, *Custer on the Little Bighorn*, pp. 102, 104.

15. Hardorff, comp. and ed., *Cheyenne Memories of the Custer Fight*, (Lincoln: University of Nebraska Press, 1998), pp. 152, 153, note 3.

16. Ibid., p. 152.

17. Ibid., p. 64; Linderman, *Plenty-Coups*, p. 127.

18. Hardorff, *Cheyenne Memories of the Custer Fight*, pp. 81.

19. Grinnell, *The Fighting Cheyennes*, pp. 4–8.

20. Mails, *Dog Soldiers, Bear Men and Buffalo Women*, pp. 20, 42–46, 49–50, 318–335; Walt Cross, *Custer's Lost Officer, The Search for Lieutenant Henry Moore Harrington, 7th U. S. Cavalry* (Stillwater, Oklahoma: Cross Publications, 2006), p. 203.

21. Richard G. Hardorff, *Hokahey!, A Good Day to Die!, The Indian Casualties of the Custer Fight* (Lincoln: University of Nebraska Press, 1999), pp. 12–13.

22. Wert, *Custer*, p. 317.

23. Ward Churchill, *A Little Matter of Genocide, Holocaust and Denial in the Americas, 1492 to the Present* (San Francisco, Calif.: City Lights Books, 1997), pp. 229–233; Brown, *Bury My Heart at Wounded Knee*, pp. 86–87.

24. Brown, *Bury My Heart at Wounded Knee*, p. 87; Thomas, *Canadians with Custer*, pp. 71–72, 81–82.

25. Mails, *Dog Soldiers, Bear Men and Buffalo Women*, pp. 17, 27–28, 32; Joseph M. Marshall, III, *The Day the World Ended at Little Bighorn, A Lakota History* (New York: Penguin Books, 2007), p. 68; Philbrick, *The Last Stand*, p. 31.

26. Hatch, *Glorious War*, p. 302; Stephen E. Ambrose, *Crazy Horse and Custer, The Parallel Lives of Two American Warriors* (New York: Anchor Books, 1996), p. xiii.
27. *Bismarck Tribune*, June 14, 1876.
28. Marquis, *Wooden Leg*, pp. 39–40, 155–156.
29. Ibid., p. 56.
30. Milo Milton Quaife, editor, *My Life on the Plains by General George A. Custer* (New York: Promontory Press, 1995), p. 23.
31. Merington, *The Custer Story*, p. 217; Ambrose, *Crazy Horse and Custer* p. 87.
32. Philbrick, *The Last Stand*, p. xx.
33. Graham, *The Custer Myth*, pp. 181–182.
34. Philbrick, *The Last Stand*, pp. 13–16, 117, 120, 135–137; Schultz, *Coming Through Fire*, pp. 248–249; Graham, *The Custer Myth*, pp. 157, 189, 197, 202–203; Pohanka, *A Summer on the Plains with Custer's 7th Cavalry*, p. 150; Jack L. Pennington, *Custer Vindicated* (New York: iUniverse, Inc., 2007), p. xiii; Merington, *The Custer Story*, p. 222.
35. Graham, *The Custer Myth*, pp. 189–190, 197–198.
36. Gary Paul Johnston, James A. Fischer, and Harold A. Geer, *Custer's Horses* (Prescott, Az.: Wolfe Publishing Company, 2001), pp. 2, 27–33; Philbrick, *The Last Stand*, pp. 10, 44; Nichols, *Men with Custer*, p. 322; Skenlar, *To Hell with Honor*, p. 63.
37. Merrington, *The Custer Story*, p. 300.
38. Philbrick, *The Last Stand*, p. 44.
39. *Bismarck Tribune*, June 21, 1876.
40. Ibid.
41. Reedstrom, *Bugles, Banners and War Bonnets*, p. 117.
42. Philbrick, *The Last Stand*, p. 82; Cross, *Custer's Lost Officer*, p. 69; Reedstrom, *Bugles, Banners and War Bonnets*, p. 118.
43. Reedstrom, *Bugles, Banners and War Bonnets*, p. 118.
44. Graham, *The Custer Myth*, p. 129.
45. Merington, *The Custer Story*, p. 301; Ambrose, *Crazy Horse and Custer*, pp. 418–419.
46. Merington, *The Custer Story*, p. 303; Ambrose, *Crazy Horse and Custer*, pp. 418–419, 421–424.

47. Merington, *The Custer Story*, p. 79.

48. Reedstrom, *Bugles, Banners and War Bonnets*, pp. 119–120, 124; Philbrick, *The Last Stand*, pp. 101–103; Taylor, *With Custer on the Little Bighorn*, pp. 26, 30; Skenlar, *To Hell with Honor*, pp. 77, 92–93; Edgar I. Stewart, *Custer's Luck* (Norman: University of Oklahoma Press, 1987), p. 281.

49. *New York Herald*, July 11, 1876.

50. Merington, *The Custer Story*, p. 228.

51. Ibid., p. 305.

52. Taylor, *With Custer on the Little Bighorn*, pp. 26–27; Reedstrom, *Bugles, Banners and War Bonnets*, p. 122; Sklenar, *To Hell with Honor*, pp. 79, 97–98.

53. Sklenar, *To Hell with Honor*, p. 97.

54. Merrington, *The Custer Story*, p. 306.

55. Cross, *Custer's Lost Officer*, pp. 83, 86.

56. Ibid., pp. 67, 95; Philbrick, *The Last Stand*, p. 10.

57. Taylor, *With Custer on the Little Bighorn*, pp. 27–30; Philbrick, *The Last Stand*, pp. 69–70, 89; Ambrose, *Crazy Horse and Custer*, pp. 396, 412–413, 416–417.

Chapter III

1. Gerald Jasmer, Little Bighorn National Battlefield, email to author, April 4, 2013; Jules C. Ladenheim, *The Life of Frederick W. Benteen* (Bowie, Md.: Heritage Books, 2007), p. 177.

2. Marquis, *Wooden Leg*, pp. 61–62, 206; Ladenheim, *Custer's Thorn*, p. 173; Graham, *The Custer Myth*, p. 180; Donovan, *A Terrible Glory*, p. 146; Ambrose, *Crazy Horse and Custer*, pp. 416–416; Stewart, *Custer's Luck*, pp. 308–309.

3. Marquis, *Wooden Leg*, p. 206; Gerald Jasmer, Little Bighorn Battlefield National Monument, to author, April 23, 2013 email.

4. Marquis, *Wooden Leg*, pp. 11, 18–20, 28, 33–34, 95, 206, 208–209; Ambrose, *Crazy Horse and Custer*, pp. 308–309.

5. Hardorff, *Cheyenne Memories of the Custer Fight*, pp. 25, 27; *New York Herald*, August 8, 1876.

6.   Marquis, *Wooden Leg*, p. 214; Donovan, *A Terrible Glory*, pp. 149–155; Ambrose, *Crazy Horse and Custer*, pp. 414–418, 421–424.

7.   Hardorff, *Cheyenne Memories of the Custer Fight*, pp. 95, 100.

8.   Marquis, *Wooden Leg*, p. 33; Ladenheim, *Custer's Thorn*, p. 173.

9.   Marquis, *Wooden Leg*, pp. 15, 17.

10.   Ibid., p. 156.

11.   Ibid., p. 215; John Koster, *Custer Survivor, The End of a Myth, the Beginning of a Legend* (Palisades, N.Y.: Chronology Books, 2010), p. 8.

12.   Hardorff, *Indian Views of the Custer Fight*, p. 162.

13.   Koster, *Custer Survivor*, pp. 18–19.

14.   Marquis, *Wooden Leg*, p. 216.

15.   Hardorff, *Cheyenne Memories of the Custer Fight*, p. 50; Marquis, *Wooden* Leg, p. 89; Stewart, *Custer's Luck*, p. 307.

16.   Sklenar, *To Hell with Honor*, pp. 41–42.

17.   Hardorff, *Cheyenne Memories of the Custer Fight*, pp. 11, 46, and note 1, 75; Marquis, *Custer on the Little Bighorn*, p. 84; Wert, *Custer*, p. 340; Hardorff, *Indian Views of the Custer Fight*, p. 205; Taylor, *With Custer on the Little Bighorn*, p. 35.

18.   Marquis, *Wooden Leg*, p. 208.

19.   Ibid., p. 209.

20.   Ibid., pp. 106, 209–210.

21.   Ibid., p. 205.

22.   Ibid., p. 160; Sklenar, *To Hell with Honor*, p. 3.

23.   Marquis, *Wooden Leg*, p. 178.

24.   Marquis, *Custer on the Little Bighorn*, p. 84; Hardorff, *Lakota Recollections of the Custer Fight*, p. 35; Cross, *Custer's Lost Officer*, pp. 93–94.

25.   Hardorff, *Indian Views of the Custer Fight*, p. 101.

26.   Hardorff, *Cheyenne Memories of the Custer Fight*, p. 50.

27.   Hardorff, *Indian Views of the Custer Fight*, p. 188.

28.   Hardorff, *Cheyenne Memories of the Custer Fight*, pp. 152, 153, note 3.

29.   Ibid., p. 11.

30.   Hardorff, *Indian Views of the Custer Fight*, pp. 57, 59.

31. Ibid., p. 82 and note 1.
32. *New York Herald*, June 27, 1867.
33. Taylor, *With Custer on the Little Bighorn*, p. 33; Ladenheim, *Custer's Thorn*, pp. 163, 166; Sklenar, *To Hell with Honor*, pp. 110–111.
34. Taylor, *With Custer on the Little Bighorn*, p. 31; Nichols, *Men with Custer*, p. 327.
35. Nichols, *Men with Custer*, p. 206; Graham, *The Custer Myth*, p. 289; Sklenar, *To Hell with Honor*, p. 94.
36. Graham, *The Custer Myth*, p. 289; Ladenheim, *Custer's Thorn*, pp. 163, 165.
37. Graham, *The Custer Myth*, p. 289; Stewart, *Custer's Luck*, p. 314.
38. Sklenar, *To Hell with Honor*, p. 110; Barnard, *Ten Years with Custer*, p. 289.
39. Taylor, *With Custer on the Little Bighorn*, p. 34.
40. Ibid., p. 3; Sklenar, *To Hell with Honor*, pp. 110, 114; Barnard, *Ten Years with Custer*, p. 289; Linderman, *Plenty-Coups,* p. 127.
41. Monaghan, *Custer*, p. 387; Nichols, *Men with Custer*, p. 175; Barnard, *Ten Years with Custer*, pp. 289–290.
42. Nichols, *Men with Custer*, pp. 20, 177, 215, 276, 365; Barnard *Ten Years with Custer*, p. 290; Military Service Records, Record Group 94, National Archives, Washington, D.C.; Sklenar, *To Hell With Glory*, pp. 39, 88, 111–117, 143, 337; Wert, *Custer*, p. 342; Taylor, *With Custer on the Little Bighorn*, p. 65; James S. Brust, Brian C. Pohanka, and Sandy Barnard, *Where Custer Fell*: Photographs of the Little Bighorn Battlefield Then and Now, (Norman: University of Oklahoma Press, 2005), p. 31; Graham, *The Custer Myth*, pp. 157–158; Reedstrom, *Bugles, Banners and War Bonnets*, p. 111.
43. Sklenar, *To Hell with Honor*, pp. 49–50, 75, 80–84, 116–117, 119, 124; Myles Dungan, *Distant Drums, Irish Soldiers in Foreign Armies* (Belfast, Ireland: Appletree Press, 1993), p. 42; Reedstrom, *Bugles, Banners and War Bonnets*, p. 117; Drinnon, *Facing West*, p. xvii; Nichols, *Men with Custer*, pp. 82, 100, 109, 147, 340; Donovan, *A Terrible Glory*, p. 220.

44. Taylor, *With Custer on the Little Bighorn*, p. 108; Wert, *Custer*, pp. 342–343; Reedstrom, *Bugles, Banners and War Bonnets*, pp. 60, 67; Stewart, *Custer's Luck*, pp. 319–320.
45. Graham, *The Custer Myth*, p. 289; Sklenar, *To Hell with Honor*, pp. 114, 122–125.
46. Reedstrom, *Bugles, Banners and War Bonnets*, p. 113; Merington *The Custer Story*, p. 239; Wert, *Custer*, p. 321; Nichols *Men with Custer*, p. 76; Roy Bird, *The Better Brother, Tom and George Custer and the Battle for the American West* (New York: Turner Publishing Company, 2011), pp. xii–xiii, 18–230.
47. Merington, *The Custer Story*, pp. 179–180, 217; Graham, *The Custer Story*, pp. 5, 52, 71–72, 85.
48. Wert, *Custer*, p. 337; Nichols, *Men with Custer*, p. 95; Graham, *The Custer Myth*, pp. 5, 52, 71–72, 85.
49. Taylor, *With Custer on the Little Bighorn*, pp. 30–31; Joan Nabseth Stevenson, *Deliverance from the Little Big Horn, Doctor Henry Porter and Custer's Seventh Cavalry* (Norman: University of Oklahoma Press, 2012), p. 71.
50. Nichols, *Men with Custer*, p. 96.
51. Taylor, *With Custer on the Little Bighorn*, p. 24.
52. Philbrick, *The Last Stand*, p. 84.
53. Ibid.
54. Graham, *The Custer Myth*, pp. 190, 289; Sklenar, *To Hell with Honor*, pp. 218–221; Pennington, *Custer Vindicated*, pp. 32–36; Stewart, *Custer's Luck*, pp. 317–320; Ladenheim, *Custer's Thorn*, p. 169; Stevenson, *Deliverance from the Little Big Horn*, p. 73.
55. Graham, *The Custer Myth*, p. 289; Sklenar, *To Hell with Honor*, p. 128.
56. Sklenar, *To Hell with Honor*, pp. 111–114, 218–221; Taylor, *With Custer on the Little Bighorn*, p. 35.
57. Graham, *The Custer Myth*, p. 289; Sklenar, *To Hell with Honor*, pp. 113–114, 131.
58. Sklenar, *To Hell with Honor*, pp. 132–134.
59. Ibid., p. 135; Graham, *The Custer Myth*, p. 289; Wert, *Custer*, pp. 343–344.

60. Wert, *Custer*, pp. 343–344; Stewart, *Custer's Luck*, pp. 319–320; Pennington, *Custer Vindicated*, pp. 32–33.

61. Grinnell, *The Fighting Cheyenne*, p. 348.

62. Brust, Pohanka, and Barnard, *Where Custer Fell*, pp. 30–31; Nichols, *Men with Custer*, pp. 119–120; Graham, *The Custer Myth*, p. 289.

63. Nichols, *Men with Custer*, p. 120.

64. Brust, Pohanka, and Barnard, *Where Custer Fell*, p. 31; Pennington, *Custer Vindicated*, pp. 33–34; Graham, *The Custer Myth*, p. 149.

65. Graham, *The Custer Myth*, p. 289.

66. Merington, *The Custer Story*, p. 249.

67. Barnard, *Ten Years with Custer*, p. 291; Sklenar, *To Hell with Honor*, p. 124.

68. Barnard, *Ten Years with Custer*, p. 291.

69. Ibid; Nichols, *Men with Custer*, p. 288.

70. Sklenar, *To Hell with Honor*, pp. 41, 185; Graham, *The Custer Myth*, pp. 149, 289; Nichols, *Men with Custer*, p. 305; Pennington, *Custer Vindicated*, pp. 18, 63–64.

71. Barnard, *Ten Years with Custer*, pp. 195, 211; Nichols, *Men with Custer*, p. 288.

72. Pennington, *Custer Vindicated*, pp. 33–34; Graham, *The Custer Myth*, p. 289; Nichols, *Men with Custer*, pp. 87–88; Reedstrom, *Bugles, Banners and War Bonnets*, p. 5.

73. Graham, *The Custer Myth*, p. 289.

74. Nichols, *Men with Custer*, p. 177; Wert, *Custer*, p. 348; Brust, Pohanka, and Barnard, *Where Custer Fell*, p. 73; Graham, *The Custer Myth*, pp. 149, 289, 328; Pennington, *Custer Vindicated*, p. 36; Donovan, *A Terrible Glory*, pp. 152–155.

75. Wert, *Custer*, p. 354; Brust, Pohanka, and Barnard, *Where Custer Fell*, p. 73; Donovan, *A Terrible Glory*, pp. 152–155.

76. Sklenar, *To Hell with Honor*, p. 94; Mari Sandoz, *The Battle of the Little Bighorn* (Lincoln: University of Nebraska Press, 1966), p. 115.

77. Brust, Pohanka, and Barnard, *Where Custer Fell*, pp. 8, 31, 73; Wert, *Custer*, pp. 348–349; Graham, *The Custer Myth*, pp. 149,

289; Pennington, *Custer Vindicated*, p. 51; Sklenar, *To Hell with Honor*, pp. 194–195.

78. Wert, *Custer*, pp. 348–349; Graham, *The Custer Myth*, p. 289; Brust, Pohanka, and Barnard, *Where Custer Fell*, p. 74; Sklenar, *To Hell with Honor*, p. 197; Graham, *The Custer Myth*, pp. 289–290.

79. Hardorff, *Indian Views of the Custer Fight*, p. 46.

80. Graham, *The Custer Myth*, p. 290; Sklenar, *To Hell with Honor*, p. 197.

81. Hardorff, *Indian Views of the Custer Fight*, pp. 64, 82–83, 95; Gregory F. Michno, *Lakota Noon, The Indian Narrative of Custer's Defeat* (Missoula, Mo.: Mountain Press Publishing Company, 2004), p. 98.

82. Graham, *The Custer Myth*, pp. 289–290; Michno, *Lakota Noon*, p. 101.

83. Graham, *The Custer Myth*, pp. 289–290.

84. Merington, *The Custer Story*, p. 262.

85. Burst, Pohanka, and Barnard, *Where Custer Fell*, p. 73; Cross, *Custer's Lost Officer*, pp. 98–99; Wert, *Custer*, p. 349; Stewart, *Custer's Luck*, p. 414; Frederic C. Wagner, III, *The Strategy of Defeat at the Little Bighorn, A Military and Timing Analysis of the Battle* (Jefferson, NC: McFarland Publishing Company, 2014), p. 113. Ladenheim, *Custer's Thorn*, p. 174.

86. Hardorff, *Indian Views of the Custer Fight*, pp. 151, 153, and note 20; Philbrick, *The Last Stand*, p. 67; Graham, *The Custer Myth*, pp. 289–290; Geoffrey Regan, *Great Military Disasters* (New York: M. Evans and Company, Inc., 1987), pp. 22–23; Ambrose, *Crazy Horse and Custer*, p. 436.

87. Marquis, *Wooden Leg*, p. 179.

88. Merington, *The Custer Story*, p. 262; Stewart, *Custer's Luck*, p. 316.

89. Brust, Pohanka, and Barnard, *Where Custer Fell*, p. 9; Cross, *Custer's Lost Officer*, p. 99; Nichols, *Men with Custer*, p. xiii; Walt Cross, *Thompson and White's Little Big Horn Narratives of 1876* (Stillwater, Okla.: Dire Wolf Books, 2011), p. 246; Ladenheim, *Custer's Thorn*, pp. 172–173.

90. Graham, *The Custer Myth*, pp. 289–290; Nichols, *Men with Custer*, pp. 206–207; Brust, Pohanka, and Barnard, *Where Custer Fell*, p. 9; Graham, *The Custer Myth*, pp. 289–290; Regan, *Great Military Disasters*, pp. 22–23; Stewart, *Custer's Luck*, p. 338; Donovan, *A Terrible Glory*, pp. 152–153.

91. Graham, *The Custer Myth*, p. 290.

92. Ibid.; Nichols, *Men with Custer*, pp. 62, 206–207; Barnard, *Ten Years with Custer*, p. 69; MSR, RG 94, NA.

93. Graham, *The Custer Myth*, p. 290.

94. Merington, *The Custer Story*, p. 222; Reedstrom, *Bugles, Banners and War Bonnets*, p. 261; Ladenheim, *Custer's Thorn*, p. 166.

95. Skenlar, *To Hell with Honor*, p. 161; Barnard, *Ten Years with Custer*, p. 290.

96. Donovan, *A Terrible Glory*, pp. 152–153.

97. Graham, *The Custer Myth*, p. 25; Stewart, *Custer's Luck*, p. 338; Nichols, *Men with Custer*, p. 133.

98. Graham, *The Custer Myth*, p. 290; Brust, Pohanka, and Barnard, *Where Custer Fell*, p. 9.

99. Graham, *The Custer Myth*, p. 11.

100. Hatch, *Glorious War*, p. 24.

101. *New York Herald*, June 28, 1876.

102. Ibid.

103. Hatch, *Glorious War*, p. 24; Merington, *The Custer Story*, pp. 178, 262; Daria Olivier, *The Burning of Moscow 1812* (London: George Allen & Unwin, Ltd., 1966), p. 157.

104. Mueller, *Shooting Arrows and Slinging Mud*, pp. 3–4, 13; Sklenar, *To Hell with Honor*, pp. 34–36, 41, 86, 142–144, 146; Stewart, *Custer's Luck*, p. 414; Monaghan, *Custer*, pp. 385–386; Graham, *The Custer Myth*, pp. 202, 289–290.

105. Grinnell, *The Fighting Cheyennes*, p. 357; Graham, *The Custer Myth*, pp. 289–290; Merington, *The Custer Story*, p. 98.

106. Cross, *Custer's Lost Officer*, pp. 133, 138; Bird, *The Better Brother*, p. 109.

107. Ambrose, *Crazy Horse and Custer*, pp. 352, 412; Wert, *Custer*, p. 342; Sklenar, *To Hell with Honor*, p. 33; Graham, *The Custer Myth*, p. 290.

108. Wert, *Custer*, p. 342.
109. Sklenar, *To Hell with Honor*, p. 100; Johnston, Fischer, and Geer, *Custer's Horses*, p. 13; Graham, *The Custer Myth*, p. 345; Ladenheim, *Custer's Thorn*, pp. 166, 168.
110. Merrington, *The Custer Story*, pp. 250, 307.
111. Philbrick, *The Last Stand*, pp. 155–156; Merington, *The Custer Story*, p. 303; Reedstrom, *Bugles, Banners and War Bonnets*, p. 110.
112. Sklenar, *To Hell with Honor*, pp. 73–74; Ambrose, *Crazy Horse and Custer*, p. 360; Donovan, *A Terrible Glory*, pp. 317–319.
113. Merington, *The Custer Story*, p. 198.
114. Hardorff, *Hokahey!*, p. 62; Hardorff, *Lakota Recollections of the Custer Fight*, p. 25, note 2.
115. Michno, *Lakota Noon*, p. 100; Stewart, *Custer's Luck*, p. 435; Pennington, *Custer Vindicated*, pp. 90, 92; Gerald "Jerry" Jasmer, Park Ranger, Little Bighorn Battlefield National Monument, Montana, two emails to author, August 29, 2015; Ladenheim, *Custer's Thorn*, pp. 172–173; Nichols, *Men with Custer*, p. viii.
116. Taylor, *With Custer on the Little Bighorn*, p. 35; Stewart, *Custer's Luck*, p. 308.
117. Graham, *The Custer Myth*, p. 137; Nichols, *Men with Custer*, p. 121.
118. Hardorff, *Indian Views of the Custer Fight*, p. 46.
119. Sklenar, *To Hell with Honor*, p. 33; Schultz, *Coming Through Fire*, pp. 241–243.
120. Marshall, *The Day the World Ended at Little Bighorn*, p. 72; Hardorff, *Indian Views of the Custer Fight*, p. 107; Marquis, *Wooden Leg*, pp. 212, 213; Graham, *The Custer Myth*, pp. 289–290.
121. Marquis, *Wooden Leg*, pp. 121, 167, 209, 212, 215, 381.
122. Hardorff, *Cheyenne Memories of the Custer Fight*, p. 43; Graham, *The Custer Myth*, pp. 289–290; Stewart, *Custer's Luck*, p. 469.
123. Hardorff, *Cheyenne Memories of the Custer Fight*, p. 50; Michno, *Lakota Noon*, p. 104.

124. Hardorff, *Cheyenne Memories of the Custer Fight*, pp. 50 and 51, note 2.
125. Sandoz, *The Battle of the Little Bighorn*, p. 116; Marshall, *The Day the World Ended at Little Bighorn*, p. 72; Hardorff, *Indian Views of the Custer Fight*, p. 109.
126. Schultz, *Coming Through Fire*, pp. 222–224; Barnard, *Ten Years with Custer*, pp. 74–75.
127. Marshall, *The Day the World Ended at Little Bighorn*, p. 72.
128. Hardorff, *Cheyenne Memories of the Custer Fight*, p. 43; Michno, *Lakota Noon*, p. 98; Marquis, *Wooden Leg*, p. 214.
129. Hardorff, *Cheyenne Memories of the Custer Fight*, p. 43.
130. Graham, *The Custer Myth*, p. 11; Hardorff, *Lakota Recollections of the Custer Fight*, p. 28.
131. Graham, *The Custer Myth*, p. 11; Schultz, *Coming Through Fire*, pp. 222–224; Merrington, *The Custer Story*, p. 303.
132. Barnard, *Ten Years with Custer*, p. 185.
133. Merington, *The Custer Story*, p. 119.

Chapter IV

1. Merington, *The Custer Story*, p. 179.
2. Graham, *The Custer Myth*, p. 262; Wert, *Custer*, p. 333; Grinnell, *The Fighting Cheyennes*, p. 357; Barnard, *Ten Years with Custer*, p. 28; Reedstrom, *Bugles, Banners and War Bonnets*, pp. 258–259; Nichols, *Men with Custer*, p. 29.
3. Schultz, *Coming Through Fire*, p. 212; Donovan, *A Terrible Glory*, p. 218; Reedstrom, *Bugles, Banners and War Bonnets*, p. 55.
4. Pohanka, *A Summer on the Plains with Custer's 7th Cavalry*, p. 157.
5. Morris, *Sheridan*, p. 362; Sklenar, *To Hell with Honor*, pp. 76–79; Merington, *The Custer Story*, p. 239; Reedstrom, *Bugles, Banners and War Bonnets*, p. 108.
6. Graham, *The Custer Myth*, p. 147; Sklenar, *To Hell with Honor*, p. 56.
7. Sklenar, *To Hell with Honor*, pp. 61–62; Bird, *The Better Brother*, pp. 216–217.

8. Stewart, *Custer's Luck*, pp. 414, 494; Sklenar, *To Hell with Honor*, pp. 26–43, 203–204, 218–239, 260, 263, 267; Gerald Jasmer, Little Bighorn National Battlefield, email to author, April 24, 2013; Donovan, *A Terrible Glory*, p. 274; Ladenheim, *Custer's Thorn*, pp. 168–170.

9. Bird, *The Better Brother*, pp. 169, 217–218; Kenneth Hammer, editor, *Custer in '76, Walter Camp's Notes on the Custer Fight* (Norman: University of Oklahoma Press, 1976), p. 86; Sklenar, *To Hell with Honor*, pp. 26–43, 203–204, 218–239, 269, 263, 267–268, 274, 340–341; Graham, *The Custer Myth*, pp. 272, 275–276; Brust, Pohanka, and Barnard, *Where Custer Fell*, pp. 9, 75; Nichols *Men with Custer*, p. 124; Custer, *Tenting on the Plains*, p. 234; Pennington, *Custer Vindicated*, pp. 108, 110; Reedstrom, *Bugles, Banners and War Bonnets*, p. 43.

10. Brian W. Dippie, *Custer's Last Stand, The Anatomy of an American Myth* (Lincoln: University of Nebraska Press, 1994), p. 127; Hammer, *Custer in '76*, p. 86.

11. John C. Lockwood Memoir, John C. Lockwood Papers, 1860–1926, OCLC No. 12254–5861, 3 Volumes of Memoirs, Huntington Library, San Marino, California; Four Miscellaneous Letters from Elizabeth Bacon-Custer to John C. Lockwood, HM 65754, HM 65763, HM 65764, and HM 65765, John C. Lockwood Papers, Huntington Library, Marino, California; Stewart, *Custer's Luck*, pp. 181, 248; Hammer, *Custer in '76*, p. 86; Barnard, *Ten Years with Custer*, p. 242; Graham, *The Custer Myth*, p. 188; MSR, RG 94, NA; Ryan, *Custer Fell First*, pp. 20–48, 56; Nichols, *Men with Custer*, pp. 277, 389, 394–395; Pennington, *Custer Vindicated*, pp. 108, 110; Sklenar, *To Hell with Honor*, p. 274.

12. Lockwood Memoir, LP, HL; Ryan, *Custer Fell First*, pp. 14–49; Cross, *Custer's Lost Officer*, p. 132; Graham, *The Custer Myth*, p. 188.

13. Sklenar, *To Hell with Honor*, p. 210; Hammer, *Custer in '76*, p. 86.

14. Hammer, *Custer in '76*, p. 86; Sklenar, *To Hell with Honor*, p. 274.

15. Lockwood Memoir, LP, HL; Four Miscellaneous Letters from Elizabeth Bacon-Custer to John C. Lockwood-Custer to Lockwood, HL; Ryan, *Custer Fell First*, pp. xxv, 13–58; Hammer, ed., *Custer in '76*, p. 86; Nichols, *Men with Custer*, pp. 100, 277, 394–395; Barnard, *I Go with Custer*, pp. 77–87; Cross, *Custer's Lost Officer*, p. 132; Brust, Pohanka, and Barnard, *Where Custer Fell*, p. 75; Graham, *The Custer Myth*, pp. 11, 188, 205, 227; MSR, RG 94, NA; Pennington, *Custer Vindicated*, pp. 108, 110; Koster, *Custer Survivor*, pp. 11–197; Sklenar, *To Hell with Honor*, pp. 233, 274.

16. Lockwood Memoir, LP, HL; Koster, *Custer Survivor*, pp. 11–197; MSR, RG 94, NA; Ryan, *Custer Fell First*, pp. v, xxi,14–70; Hammer, *Custer in '76*, pp. 92–93; Nichols, *Men with Custer*, pp. 170, 206–207, 215, 277.

17. Lockwood Memoir, LP, HL; Ryan, *Custer Fell First*, pp. 47–49; Graham, *The Custer Myth*, pp. 11, 72, 272; Pennington, *Custer Vindicated*, pp. 108, 110; Hardorff, *Indian Views of the Custer Fight*, p. 40; Sklenar, *To Hell with Honor*, pp. 213, 274; Hammer, *Custer in '76*, p. 86.

18. Brust Pohanka, and Barnard, *Where Custer Fell*, p. 75; Graham, *The Custer Myth*, pp. 11, 188, 227.

19. Philbrick, *The Last Stand*, pp. 184–165; Graham, *The Custer Myth*, pp. 11, 290; Pennington, *Custer Vindicated*, pp. 108, 110; Sklenar, *To Hell with Honor*, p. 274; Brust, Pohanka, and Barnard, *Where Custer Fell*, p. 75; Hammer, *Custer in '76*, p. 86.

20. Graham, *The Custer Myth*, pp. 11, 272; Ryan, *Custer Fell First*, pp. 47–49; Graham, *The Custer Myth*, p. 290; Pennington *Custer Vindicated*, pp. 108, 110; Sklenar, *To Hell with Honor*, pp. 274, 340–341; Hammer, *Custer in '76*, p. 86; Brust, Pohanka, and Barnard, *Where Custer Fell*, p. 75.

21. Mueller, *Shooting Arrows and Slinging Mud*, pp. 15, 19; Monaghan, *Custer*, pp. 385–386; Jamieson, *Crossing the Deadly Ground*, pp. 44–45; Wert, *Custer*, p. 335; Ryan, *Custer Fell First*, pp. 47–49; Sklenar, *To Hell with Honor*, pp. 93, 100, 274, 340–341; Pennington, *Custer Vindicated*, pp. 108, 110;

Graham, *The Custer Myth*, pp. 11, 272; Bird, *The Better Brother*, pp. 48, 52–53, 64, 194; Charles E. Rankin, ed., *Legacy, New Perspectives on the Battle of the Little Bighorn* (Helena: Montana Historical Society Press,1996), p. 153.

22. Merrington, *The Custer Story*, p. 266.
23. Pohanka, *A Summer on the Plains with Custer's 7th Cavalry*, pp. 46–54, 92, 95, note 90, page 51; Monaghan, *Custer*, pp. 385–386; Graham, *The Custer Myth*, pp. 11, 272, 289–290; Pennington, *Custer Vindicated*, pp. 108, 110; Brust, Pohanka, and Barnard, *Where Custer Fell*, p. 75; Bernard, *Ten Years with Custer*, p. 68; Ryan, *Custer Fell First*, pp. 47–49; Sklenar, *To Hell with Honor*, pp. 199–202, 211–212, 269, 274; Cross, *Custer's Lost Officer*, p. 67; Rankin, *Legacy*, p. 153; Nichols, *Men with Custer*, pp. 275, 365.
24. Barnard, *Ten Years with Custer*, p. 128; Bird, *The Better Brother*, pp. 48, 52–53, 64, 194.
25. Merington, *The Custer Story*, p. 179.
26. Nichols, *Men with Custer*, pp. 233, 307–308; Cross, *Custer's Lost Officer*, pp. 100, 125; Pohanka, *A Summer on the Plains with Custer's 7th Cavalry*, p. 51; Taylor, *With Custer on the Little Bighorn*, pp. 195–196; Philbrick, *The Last Stand*, pp. 24–25; Douglas O. Scott, Robert A. Fox, Jr., Melissa A. Connor, and Dick Harmon, *Archaeological Perspectives on the Battle of Little Bighorn* (Norman: University of Oklahoma Press, 2000), p. 248; MSR, RG 94, NA; Koster, *Custer Survivor*, p. 33; Barnard, *Ten Years with Custer*, p. 68; Bird, *The Better Brother*, pp. 194, 217; Sklenar, *To Hell with Honor*, pp. 52, 269.
27. Hardorff, *Indian Views of the Custer Fight*, p. 40.
28. Skenlar, *To Hell with Honor*, pp. 73–74, 269; Hammer, *Custer in '74*, p. 172; Barnard, *Ten Years with Custer*, p. 75.
29. Graham, *The Custer Myth*, p. 11.
30. Ibid., pp. 84–85.
31. Hardorff, *Indian Views of the Custer Fight*, p. 46.
32. Ibid., p. 74, note 4.
33. Pohanka, *A Summer on the Plains with Custer's 7th Cavalry*, pp. 46–47; Taylor, *With Custer on the Little Bighorn*, p. 17; Graham, *The Custer Myth*, pp. 289–290.

34. Mueller, *Shooting Arrows and Slinging Mud*, pp. 4, 6, 31,
     34; MSR, RG 94, NA; Stewart, *Custer's Luck*, p. 231; Eric
     J. Wittenberg, editor, and Karla Jean Husby, compiler,
     *Under Custer's Command, The Civil War Journal of James
     Henry Avery* (Washington, DC: Potomac Books, 2000), p.
     xiii; Monaghan, *Custer*, pp. 370–371, 373–376, 385–386;
     Philbrick, *Custer's Last Stand*, p. 218; Marshall, *The Day the
     World Ended at Little Bighorn*, p. 72; Graham, *The Custer
     Myth*, pp. 272, 289–290; Nichols, *Men with Custer*, pp.
     1–367; Ryan, *Custer Fell First*, pp. 47–48; Jamieson, *Cross-
     ing the Deadly Ground*, pp. 44–45, 51; Merington, *The
     Custer Story*, pp. 253, 296; Pohanka, *A Summer on the Plains
     with Custer's 7th Cavalry*, p. 155; Schultz, *Coming Through
     Fire*, pp. 222–228, 245–246; Lockwood Memoir, LP, HL;
     Wert, *Custer*, pp. 340, 342; Lehman, *Bloodshed at Little
     Bighorn*, p. 44; Sklenar, *To Hell with Honor*, pp. 32–33, 49,
     77–78, 90, 97–98, 274; Hardoff, *Indian Views of the Custer
     Fight*, p. 82; Rankin, *Legacy*, p. 153; Marquis, *Wooden Leg*,
     pp. 178, 215–216.
35. Schultz, *Coming Through Fire*, pp. 222–223.
36. Ibid; Bird, *The Better Brother*, p. 103.
37. Donovan, *A Terrible Glory*, pp. 191, 210; Monaghan, *Custer*,
     pp. 370, 386; Sklenar, *To Hell with Honor*, p. 90; Ladenheim,
     Custer's Thorn, p. 166.
38. Graham, *The Custer Myth*, p. 294.
39. Pohanka, *A Summer on the Plains with Custer's 7th Cavalry*,
     pp. 8–14, 20; Philbrick, *The Last Stand*, p. 18.
40. Pohanka, *A Summer on the Plains with Custer's 7th Cavalry*,
     pp. 87, 89–90.
41. Philbrick, *The Last Stand*, p. 71.
42. MSR, RG 94, NA; Sklenar, *To Hell with Honor*, pp. 52–53,
     72–74, 95, 125, 199–202, 274; Nichols, *Men with Custer*, pp.
     62, 74, 76, 89, 100–101, 130, 160, 216, 272, 300, 341; Brust,
     Pohanka, and Barnard, *Where Custer Fell*, pp. 9, 205, note 5;
     Donovan, *A Terrible Glory*, pp. 218–219; Ryan, *Custer Fell
     First*, pp. 47–48; Barnard, *Ten Years with Custer*, p. 298; Reed-
     strom, *Bugles, Banners and War Bonnets*, pp. 55, 83, 123, 125,

127; Lockwood Memoir, LP, HL, Pohanka, *A Summer on the Plains with Custer's 7th Cavalry*, pp. 151, 153, 163; Graham, *The Custer Myth*, pp. 11, 135–136, 272; Barnard *Ten Years with Custer*, p. 68; Shultz, *Coming Through Fire*, pp. 222–223; Johnston, Fischer, and Geer, *Custer's Horses*, p. 51;.Meringtion, *The Custer Story*, pp. 61, 66, 232, 253; Pennington, *Custer Vindicated*, p. 3; Cross, *Custer's Lost Officer*, pp. 65, 67–68, 85, 150–153, 190, 204; Hardorff, *Indian Views of the Custer Fight*, p. 49, note 17, and p. 55, note 2, and page 104, note 14; Taylor, *with Custer on the Little Bighorn*, p. 65; Hammer, *Custer in '76*, p. 172; Edward B. Cummings, "Steamboat at the Little Big Horn," *On Post*, vol. 13, no. 3 (2007–2008), p. 10; Thomas, *Canadians With Custer*, pp. 17, 51–57, 91–99, 105, 192; Bird, *The Better Brother*, pp. 2–230; Kostser, *Custer Survivor*, pp. 35–36.

43. Sklenar, *To Hell with Honor*, p. 125; Nichols, *Men with Custer*, pp. 197–198.

44. Sandy Barnard, *I Go with Custer, The Life and Death of Reporter Mark Kellogg* (Bismacrk, N.D.: *The Bismarck Tribune*, 1996), pp. 5–117, 123, 130–141; Sandy Bernard, *Digging into Custer's Last Stand*, (Terre Haute, Ind.: AST Press, 1988), p. 107; Nichols, *Men with Custer*, pp. 173–174; Taylor, *With Custer on the Little Bighorn*, p. 65; Barnard, *Ten Years with Custer*, p. 130; Stevenson, *Deliverance from the Little Big Horn*, p. 12.

45. Barnard, *I Go with Custer*, p. 79.

46. Ibid., p. 98.

47. Merrington, *The Custer Story*, pp. 305–306.

48. Donovan, *A Terrible Glory*, p. 85; Stewart, *Custer's Luck*, pp. 138–139.

49. *Bismarck Tribune*, June 14, 1876.

50. Ryan, *Custer Fell First*, pp. 47–49; Lockwood Memoir, LP, HL; MSR, RG 94, NA.

51. Cross, *Custer's Lost Officer*, p. 89.

52. Nichols, *Men with Custer*, p. 261; Koster, *Custer Survivor*, p. 33; Graham, *The Custer Myth*, pp. 289–290.

53. Donovan, *A Terrible Glory*, pp. 218–219.

54. Merington, *The Custer Story*, p. 133.

55. Ibid., p. 178; Bird, *The Better Brother*, pp. 23–234.

56. Hardorff, *Cheyenne Memories of the Custer Fight*, p. 50; Graham, *The Custer Myth*, pp. 289–290.

57. Hardorff, *Cheyenne Memories of the Custer Fight*, pp. 50 and 51, note 2.

58. Michno, *Lakota Noon,* pp. 31, 102, 104; Graham, *The Custer Myth*, pp. 11, 289–290; Sklenar, *To Hell with Honor*, pp. 73–74; White Cow Bull's Story of the Battle of the Little Bighorn #1, astonisher@com. library, internet.

59. Michno, *Lakota Noon*, p. 102.

60. Hardorff, *Cheyenne Memories of the Custer Fight*, p. 50; White Cow Bull's Story of the Battle of the Little Bighorn #1, astonisher@com.library, internet.

61. Barnard, *Ten Years with Custer*, pp. 45–46; Nichols, *Men with Custer*, p. 288.

62. Hardorff, *Cheyenne Memories of the Custer Fight*, p. 50; Grinnell, *The Fighting Cheyennes*, p. 350; Marshall, *The Day the World Ended at Little Bighorn*, p. 72; Michno, *Lakota Noon*, p. 102.

63. Hardorff, *Cheyenne Memories of the Custer Fight*, pp. 50 and 51, note 4.

64. Ibid.; Grinnell, *The Fighting Cheyennes,* p. 350; Bob Snelson, *Death of a Myth: Seventh Cavalry at the Little Bighorn, June 25–26, 1876* (private printing, 2002), p. 93; Graham, *The Custer Myth*, pp. 11, 289–290.

65. Merington, *The Custer Story*, p. 296; MSR, RG 94, NA; Koster, *Custer Survivor*, p. 37; Nichols, *Men with Custer*, pp. 1–364; Sklenar, *To Hell with Honor*, p. 274; Stevenson, *Deliverance from the Little Big Horn*, pp. 110–111.

66. Ryan, *Custer Fell First*, pp. xxv, 47, 55–56; Lockwood Memoir, LP, HL.

67. Grinnell, *The Fighting Cheyennes*, p. 350; Ryan, *Custer Fell First*, p. 47; Sklenar, *To Hell with Honor*, pp. 32–34; Hatch, *Glorious War*, pp. 105–299; Lockwood Memoir, LP, HL; Graham, *The Custer Myth*, p. 272.

68. Taylor, *With Custer on the Little Bighorn*, p. 11.
69. Barnard, *Ten Years with Custer*, p. 68; Cross, *Custer's Lost Officer*, p. 126.
70. Nichols, *Men with Custer*, pp. 301, 321.
71. Ibid., pp. 20, 317.
72. Hardorff, *Cheyenne Memories of the Custer Fight*, p. 50; Cross, *Custer's Lost Officer*, p. 135; Koster, *Custer Survivor*, pp. 33, 37; Barnard *Ten Years with Custer*, p. 68.
73. Nichols, *Men with Custer*, p. 275; Reedstrom, *Bugles, Banners and War Bonnets*, p. 122
74. Sklenar, *To ell with Honor*, p. 58.
75. Pennington, *Custer Vindicated*, p. 91; MSR, RG 94, NA; Graham, *The Custer Myth*, p. 231; Nichols, *Men with Custer*, pp. 89, 216, 341.
76. Merrington, *The Custer Story*, p. 307; Sklenar, *To Hell with Honor*, p. 17; Graham, *The Custer Myth*, pp. 11, 188; Hammer, *Custer in '76*, p. 86.
77. Graham, *The Custer Myth*, p. 16; Nichols, *Men with Custer*, p. 356.
78. Elizabeth B. Custer, *Tenting on the Plains, General Custer in Kansas and Texas* (New York: Barnes and Noble, 2006), p. 1.
79. Donovan, *A Terrible Glory*, pp. 261–263; Miles Doleac, *In the Footsteps of Alexander, The King Who Conquered the Ancient World* (New York: Metro Books, 2014), p. 60.

Chapter V

1. Nichols, *Men with Custer,* p. 9
2. Johnston, Fischer, and Geer, *Custer's Horses*, p. 53; Nichols, *Men with Custer,* pp. 9, 25; Sklenar, *To Hell with Honor*, p. 145; Graham, *The Custer Myth*, p. 11; Schultz, *Coming Through Fire*, pp. vii–269.
3. Nichols, *Men with Custer*, p. 9.
4. Mails, *Dog Soldiers, Bear Men and Buffalo Women*, p. 20; Fox, *Archeology, History, and Custer's Last Stand*, p. 280; Grinnell, *The Fighting Cheyennes*, pp. 350, 357; Marshall, *The Day the World*

Ended at Little Bighorn, p. 72; Hardorff, *Indian Views of the Custer Fight*, pp. 40, 114, note 13, and p. 115, note 18; Michno, *Lakota Noon*, pp. 101–102; Sklenar, *To Hell with Honor*, p. 274; Hardorff, *Cheyenne Memories of the Custer Fight*, p. 50; Lehman, *Bloodshed at Little Bighorn*, p. 105; Rankin *Legacy*, p. 153; Marquis, *Wooden Leg*, pp. 11, 39, 56–57, 211–212; Bird, *The Better Brother*, pp. 194, 217–230; White Cow Bull's Story of the Battle of Little Bighorn #1, astonisher@com. library, internet; Cross, *Custer's Lost Officer*, p. 103; Reedstrom, *Bugles, Banners and War Bonnets*, p. 43.
5. Michno, *Lakota Noon*, pp. 103–104.
6. Hardorff, *Cheyenne Memories of the Custer Fight*, p. 50; White Cow Bull's Story of the Battle of the Little Bighorn #1, astonisher@com.library, internet; Grinnell, *The Fighting Cheyennes*, p. 350; Marshall, *The Day the World Ended at Little Bighorn*, p. 72; Hardorff, *Indian Views of the Custer Fight*, p. 115, note 18, and p. 179; Michno, *Lakota Noon*, p. 102.
7. Hardorff, *Indian Views of the Custer Fight*, p. 115, note 18; Miller, *Custer's Fall*, pp. 123–124; White Cow Bull's Story of the Battle of the Little Bighorn #1, astonisher@com.library, internet; Bird, *The Better Brother*, p. 215; Marshall, *The Day the World Ended at Little Bighorn*, p. 72; Michno, *Lakota Noon*, pp. 102, 104, 118.
8. Grinnell, *The Fighting Cheyennes*, p. 350; Rankin, ed., *Legacy*, p. 152; Lehman, *Bloodshed at Little Bighorn*, p. 105.
9. Hardorff, *Cheyenne Memories of the Custer Fight*, p. 50.
10. Ibid.; Marquis, *Wooden Leg*, pp. 229–230; Miller, *Custer's Fall*, pp. 123–125; Grinnell, *The Fighting Cheyennes*, p. 350; Hardorff, *Cheyenne Memories of the Custer Fight*, pp. 50, p. 51, note 3, and p. 51, note 5; Michno, *Lakota Noon*, pp. 102, 104, 118; Graham, *The Custer Myth*, pp. 27–28, 139; David A. Dary, *The Buffalo Book, The Saga of an American Symbol* (New York: Avon Books, 1974), p. 63; Bird, *The Better Brother*, p. 122.
11. Hardorff, *Cheyenne Memories of the Custer Fight*, pp. 50, 51, note 2, and p. 52, note 6; Michno, *Lakota Noon*, p. 102; Miller, *Custer's Fall*, p. 125; Jamieson, *Crossing the Deadly Ground*, p.

30; White Cow Bull's Story of the Battle of the Little Bighorn #1, astonisher@com.library, internet; Richard Hook, *Warriors at the Little Bighorn 1876* (Oxford: Osprey Publishing, Inc., 2004), p. 11; Rankin *Legacy*, p. 122.

12. Michno, *Lakota Noon*, p. 102; Cross, *Thompson and White's Little Big Horn Narratives 1876*, p. 246; White Cow Bull's Story of the Battle of the Little Bighorn #1, astonisher@com.library, internet.
13. Michno, *Lakota Noon*, p. 102.
14. Hardorff, *Indian Views of the Custer Fight*, p. 114, note 13; Michno, *Lakota Noon*, p. 101; Miller, *Custer's Fall*, pp. 124–125; Marquis, *Wooden Leg*, p. 187.
15. Hardorff, *Cheyenne Memories of the Custer Fight*, pp. 48–50; White Cow Bull's Story of the Battle of the Little Bighorn #1, astonisher@com.library, internet.
16. Hardorff, *Cheyenne Memories of the Custer Fight*, p. 50; Pennington, *Custer Vindicated*, pp. 108, 110.
17. Hardorff, *Cheyenne Memories of the Custer Fight*, p. 50; Sandoz, *The Battle of the Little Bighorn*, p. 115; Merington *The Custer Story*, p. 303.
18. Marshall, *The Day the World Ended at Little Bighorn*, p. 11.
19. Schultz, *Coming Through Fire*, pp. 2–3.
20. Ibid., pp. 127, 142, 157.
21. Marquis, *Wooden Leg*, p. 225.
22. White Cow Bull's Story of the Battle of the Little Bighorn #1, astonisher@com.library, internet; Marquis, *Wooden Leg*, pp. 83–84; Hook, *Warriors of the Little Bighorn 1876*, pp. 10–13.
23. Marquis, *Wooden Leg*, pp. 83–84.
24. Merington, *The Custer Story*, p. 303.
25. Marshall, *The Day the World Ended at Little Bighorn*, p. 72; White Cow Bull's Story of the Battle of the Little Bighorn #1, astonisher@com.library, internet; Brown, *Bury My Heart at Wounded Knee*, p. 89; Hook, *Warriors of the Little Bighorn 1876*, pp. 10–13.
26. Hardorff, *Indian Views of the Custer Fight*, pp. 113, 115; Michno, *Lakota Noon*, pp. 101, 117–118; Cross, *Custer's Lost Officer*,

pp. 103, 134; Johnston, Fischer, and Geer, *Custer's Horses*, pp. 13–14; Reedstrom, *Bugles, Banners and War Bonnets*, p. 53; Graham, *The Custer Myth*, p. 16.

27.   Michno, *Lakota Noon*, p. 118; White Cow Bull's Story of the Battle of the Little Bighorn #1, astonisher@com.library, internet; Marshall, *The Day the World Ended at Little Bighorn*, p. 72.

28.   Marshall, *The Day the World Ended at Little Bighorn*, p. 72; Hook, *Warriors at the Little Bighorn 1876*, pp. 7, 9; Rankin, *Legacy*, p. 122; Hardorff, *Indian Views of the Custer Fight*, pp. 40, 113, 115; White Cow Bull's Story of the Battle of the Little Bighorn #1, astonisher@com.library, internet.

29.   Philbrick, *The Last Stand*, pp. 69–70.

30.   Graham, *The Custer Myth*, p. 65.

31.   Philbrick, *The Last Stand*, pp. 69–70; Hardorff, *Ceyenne Memories of the Custer Fight*, p. 50.

32.   Michno, *Lakota Noon*, p. 115.

33.   Graham, *The Custer Myth*, p. 230.

34.   Michno, *Lakota Noon*, p. 114.

35.   Hardorff, *Cheyenne Memories of the Custer Fight*, pp. 29, 50; Michno, *Lakota Noon*, p. 106.

36.   Hardorff, *Indian Views of the Custer Fight*, p. 115, note 19; Hardorff, *Cheyenne Memories of the Custer Fight*, p. 11; Graham, *The Custer Myth*, pp. 147, 231, 289–290.

37.   Michno, *Lakota Noon*, p. 118; Stewart, *Custer's Luck*, p. 307; Marshall, *The Day the World Ended at Little Bighorn*, p. 72; Michno, *Lakota Noon*, p. 102; White Cow Bull's Story of the Battle of the Little Bighorn #1, astonisher@com.library, internet; Cross, *Custer's Lost Officer*, p. 103; Pennington, *Custer Vindicated*, p. 117; Miller, *Custer's Fall*, p. 125; Lehman, *Bloodshed at Little Bighorn*, p. 106; Schultz, *Coming Through Fire*, pp. 222–224; Graham, *The Custer Myth*, pp. 11, 85, 289–290; Fox, *Archaeology, History, and Custer's Last Battle*, p. 280.

38.   Graham, *The Custer Myth*, p. 85.

39.   Pennington, *Custer Vindicated*, p. 117; Stewart, *Custer's Luck*, p. 444.

40. Hardorff, *Cheyenne Memories of the Custer Fight*, p. 142.
41. White Cow Bull's Story of the Battle of the Little Bighorn #1, astonisher@com.library, internet; Michno, *Lakota Noon*, p. 118.
42. Michno, *Lakota Noon*, p. 102.
43. Barnard, *Ten Years with Custer*, p. 64.
44. Miller, *Custer's Fall*, p. 125; Graham, *The Custer Myth*, pp. 11, 85; Hardorff, *Indian Views of the Custer Fight*, p. 40; Cross, *Custer's Lost Officer*, p. 103; Sklenar, *To Hell with Honor*, pp. 33, 62, 73–74.
45. Hardorff, *Indian Views of the Custer Fight*, pp. 64–65; Schultz, *Coming Through Fire*, pp. 222–224; White Cow Bull's Story of the Battle of the Little Bighorn #1, astonisher@com.library, internet; Philbrick, *The Last Stand*, pp. 33–34.
46. Hardorff, *Cheyenne Memories of the Custer Fight*, p. 52; Hook, *Warriors of the Little Bighorn*, p. 11.
47. Graham, *The Custer Myth*, p. 15; Nichols, *Men with Custer*, p. 356.
48. Sklenar, *To Hell with Honor*, p. 272; White Cow Bull's Story of the Battle of the Little Bighorn #1, astonisher@com.library, internet.
49. Michno, Lakota Noon, p. 118; Graham, *The Custer Myth*, p. 11.
50. Michno, *Lakota Noon*, p. 118.
51. Ibid., pp. 104, note 195, 118–119; Marshall, *The Day the World Ended at Little Bighorn*, p. 72; Michno, *Lakota Noon*, p. 119; Graham, *The Custer Myth*, pp. 11, 85, 289–290; Fox, *Archaeology, History, and Custer's Last Battle*, p. 280; White Cow Bull's Story of the Battle of the Little Bighorn #1, astonisher@com.library, internet; Rankin, *Legacy*, p. 152; Hook, *Warriors of the Little Bighorn 1876*, p. 12.
52. Michno, *Lakota Noon*, p. 119; Marquis, *Wooden Leg*, pp. 35–37; Sklenar, *To Hell with Honor*, p. 88.
53. Stewart, *Custer's Luck*, p. 444; Lockwood Memoir, LP, HL; Ryan, *Custer Fell First*, p. 48; Miller, *Custer's Fall*, p. 127; Cross, *Custer's Lost Officer*, pp. 103; Song of Solomon, 6:10, Bible-Gateway, internet; Hook, *Warriors of the Little Bighorn 1876*, p. 9; Graham, *The Custer Myth*, p. 11.

54. Pennington, *Custer Vindicated*, p. 121; Lockwood Memoir, LP, HL; Cross, *Custer's Lost Officer*, p. 103; Stewart, *Custer's Luck*, p. 444; Rankin, *Legacy*, pp. 73–74.

55. Graham, *The Custer Myth*, p. 15; Stewart, *Custer's Luck*, p. 444; Lockwood Memoir, LP, HL; Rankin, *Legacy*, pp. 73–74; White Cow Bull's Story of the Battle of the Little Bighorn #1, astonisher@com.library, internet; Ryan, *Custer Fell First*, p. 48.

56. Ibid., p. 16; Ryan, *Custer Fell First*, pp. 47–48; SR, Lockwood Memoir, LP, HL; MRG 94, NA; Hammer, *Custer in '76*, p. 87; White Cow Bull's Story of the Battle of the Little Bighorn #1, astonisher@com.library, internet.

57. Hardorff, *Indian Views of the Custer Fight*, p. 40; Stewart, *Custer's Luck*, p. 444; Lockwood Memoir, LP, HL; White Cow Bull's Story of the Battle of the Little Bighorn #1, astonisher@com.library, internet.

58. Hardorff, *Indian Views of the Custer Fight*, p. 40; Lockwood Memoir, LP, HL.

59. Graham, *The Custer Myth*, p. 11.

60. Ibid., p. 85.

61. *The Billings Gazette* (Billings, Montana), May 27, 1961.

62. Pennington, *Custer Vindicated*, p. 121; Cross, *Custer's Lost Officer*, p. 103.

63. Pennington, *Custer Vindicated*, pp. 120–121; Stewart, *Custer's Luck*, p. 444.

64. White Cow Bull's Story of the Battle of the Little Bighorn #1, astonisher@com.library, internet; Pennington, *Custer Vindicated*, pp. 120–121; Michno, *Lakota Noon*, p. 119; Cross, *Custer's Lost Officer*, p. 103.

65. Graham, *The Custer Myth*, p. 16.

66. Ibid., p. 11.

67. Ibid., p. 72.

68. Taylor, *With Custer on the Little Bighorn*, p. 108.

69. Hardorff, *Indian Views of the Custer Fight*, p. 40; MSR, RG 94, NA; Michno, *Lakota Noon*, p. 119; Graham, *The Custer Myth*, pp. 11, 85; Lockwood Memoir, LP, HL.

70. Michno, *Lakota Noon*, p. 102; White Cow Bull's Story of the Battle of the Little Bighorn #1, astonisher@com.library, internet; Graham, *The Custer Myth*, p. 72.

71. Michno, *Lakota Noon*, p. 119; Graham, *The Custer Myth*, p. 72; Hardorff, *Indian Views of the Custer Fight*, p. 40.

72. Hardorff, *Indian Views of the Custer Fight*, p. 40; Graham, *The Custer Myth*, p. 72.

73. Hardorff, *Indian Views of the Custer Fight*, p. 40; Pohanka, *A Summer on the Plains with Custer's 7th Cavalry*, p. 109.

74. Dean K. Boorman, *The History of Winchester Firearms* (Guilford, Conn.: The Lyons Press, 2001), pp. 6–10, 30–46.

75. Ibid., pp. 12–29; Wiley Sword, *The Historic Henry Rifle, Oliver's Winchester's Famous Civil War Repeater* (Lincoln, Neb.: Andrew Mowbray Publishers, 2002), pp. 8–66; Hardorff, *Indian Views of the Custer Fight*, p. 40.

76. Marquis, *Wooden Leg*, p. 72; Michno, *Lakota Noon*, p. 119; Scott, Fox, Conner, and Harmon, *Archaeological Perspectives on the Battle of the Little Bighorn*, pp. 188–189, 191; Graham, *The Custer Myth*, pp. 11, 85; White Cow Bull's Story of the Battle of the Little Bighorn #1, astonisher@com.library, internet; Hook, *Warriors of the Little Bighorn 1876*, p. 11.

77. Jamieson, *Crossing the Deadly Ground*, p. 30.

78. Michno, *Lakota Noon*, p. 119; Hardorff, *Indian Views of the Custer Fight*, p. 40; Graham, *The Custer Myth*, pp. 11, 72.

79. Custer, *Tenting on the Plains*, pp. 242, 247; Reedstrom, *Bugles, Banners and War Bonnets*, p. 87; Sklenar, *To Hell With Honor*, p. 52.

80. Brust, Pohanka, and Barnard, *Where Custer Fell*, p. 11; Graham, *The Custer Myth*, p. 203; Nichols, *Men with Custer*, pp. 307–308.

81. Mails, *Dog Soldiers, Bear Men and Buffalo Women*, pp. 20, 42, 46, 49–50; Grinnell, *The Fighting Cheyennes*, p. 12; Hardorff, *Indian Views of the Custer Fight*, pp. 40, 140, 184; Scott, Fox, Connor, and Harmon, *Archaeological Perspectives on the Battle of the Little Bighorn*, p. 86; Michno, *Lakota Noon*, p. 102; White Cow Bull's Story of the Battle of the Little Bighorn #1, astonisher@com.library, internet; Hardorff, *Cheyenne Memories of the Custer Fight*, pp. 29, 35–36, 43, 52, 76.

82. Michno, *Lakota Noon*, pp. 118–119; Hardorff, *Indian Views of the Custer Fight*, p. 40; Graham, *The Custer Myth*, pp. 11, 72.

83. Graham, *The Custer Myth*, p. 221.
84. Mails, *Dog Soldiers, Bear Men and Buffalo Women*, pp. 26–28; Graham, *The Custer Myth*, pp. 11, 72; Hardorff, *Indian Views of the Custer Fight*, p. 40.
85. Mails, *Dog Soldiers, Bear Men and Buffalo Women*, p. 35; Miller, *Custer's Fall*, pp. 123–124; Donovan, *A Terrible Glory*, p. 147; Hammer, *Custer in '76*, p. 87; Hook, *Warriors at the Little Bighorn 1876*, pp. 10, 41.
86. Grinnel, *The Fighting Cheyennes*, p. 338; Charles M. Robinson, III, *The Plains Wars, 1757–1900* (New York: Osprey Limited Publishing, 2003), p. 9; Hardorff, *Cheyenne Memories of the Custer Fight*, p. 49.
87. Jamieson, *Crossing the Deadly Ground*, p. 33; Cross, *Custer's Lost Officer*, p. 88.
88. Michno, *Lakota Noon*, pp. 118–119.
89. Jamieson, *Crossing the Deadly Ground*, p. 30; Hardorff, *Lakota Recollections of the Custer Fight*, p. 77.
90. Hardorff, *Lakota Recollections of the Custer Fight*, p. 179.
91. Hatch, *Glorious War*, p. 123; Bird, *The Better Brother*, p. 221.
92. Nichols, *Men with Custer*, p. 76; Hardorff, *Indian Views of the Custer Fight*, pp. 72 and 73, note 2; Philbrick, *The Last Stand*, pp. 116, 129; Bird, *The Better Brother*, pp. 176, 214, 239; Skenlar, *To Hell with Honor*, p. 90; Hammer, *Custer in '76*, p. 72; Reedstrom, *Bugles, Banners and War Bonnets*, p. 299.
93. Hardorff, *Indian Views of the Custer Fight*, pp. 73, note 2, 115, 119; Graham, *The Custer Myth*, pp. 57, 289, 346; Cross, *Custer's Lost Officer*, pp. 150–153, 157, note 25; Skenlar, *To Hell with Honor*, p. 90.
94. Lockwood Memoir, LP, HL; Ryan, *Custer Fell First*, pp. 47–49; Cross, *Custer's Lost Officer*, p. 103; Rankin, *Legacy*, pp. 73–74.
95. Lockwood Memoir, LP, HL; Ryan, *Custer Fell First*, p. xiii.
96. Pennington, *Custer Vindicated*, p. 119.
97. Miller, *Custer's Fall*, p. 128.
98. Philbrick, *The Last Stand*, p. 257; Rankin, *Legacy*, pp. 73–74.
99. Philbrick, *The Last Stand*, p. 257.

100. White Cow Bull's Story of the Battle of the Little Bighorn #1, astonisher@com.library, internet; Graham, *The Custer Myth*, p. 11; Lockwood Memoir, LP, HL; Cross, *Custer's Lost Officer*, p. 103.
101. Hardorff, *Indian Views of the Custer Fight*, p. 40; White Cow Bull's Story of the Battle of the Little Bighorn #1, astonisher@com.library, internet.
102. Graham, *The Custer Myth*, p. 72; White Cow Bull's Story of the Battle of the Little Bighorn #1, astonisher@com.library, internet; Cross, *Custer's Lost Officer*, p. 103.
103. Hardorff, *Indian Views of the Custer Fight*, p. 40.
104. Hardorff, *Cheyenne Memories of the Custer Fight*, p. 154.
105. Merington, *The Custer Story*, p. 287.
106. Taylor, *With Custer on the Little Bighorn*, p. 88.
107. Barnard, *Ten Years with Custer*, p. 273.
108. Sklenar, *To Hell with Honor*, p. 9.
109. Scott, Fox, Connor, and Harmon, *Archaeological Perspectives on the Battle of the Little Bighorn*, pp. 104–113, 117–121, 124–130, 162–166; Fox, *Archaeology, History, and Custer's Last Battle*, pp. 55–56, 78–80, 87, 96, 103–111, 250, 253.
110. Nichols, *Men with Custer*, p. 109; Graham, *The Custer Myth*, p. 341; Sklenar, *To Hell with Honor*, p. 55; Bird, *The Better Brother*, p. 176.
111. Barnard, *Ten Years with Custer*, p. 273; Hardorff, *Indian Views of the Custer Fight*, p. 40; Reedstrom, *Bugles, Banners and War Bonnets*, p. 100.
112. Graham, *The Custer Myth*, p. 112.
113. Ibid., pp. 71–72.
114. Miller, *Custer's Fall*, p. 129; Lockwood Memoir, LP, HL; Cross, *Custer's Lost Officer*, p. 103; 47–49; Michno, *Lakota Noon*, p. 119; Rankin, *Legacy*, pp. 73–74; Koster, *Custer Survivor*, pp. 33, 37; White Cow Bull's Story of the Battle of the Little Bighorn #1, astonisher@com.library, internet.
115. Koster, *Custer Survivor*, p. 37; Nichols, *Men with Custer*, p. 130.

116. Hardorff, *Indian Views of the Custer Fight*, p. 40; Reedstrom, *Bugles, Banners and War Bonnets*, pp. 247–249, 250, 254; Hook, *Warriors of the Little Bighorn 1876*, p. 11.

117. Sklenar, *To Hell with Honor*, pp. 80–86; Cross, *Custer's Lost Officer*, pp. 136–137.

118. Reedstrom, *Bugles, Banners and War Bonnets*, pp. 123, 299; Nichols, *Men with Custer*, pp. 47, 74, 177; Skenlar, *To Hell with Honor*, p. 52; MSR, RG 94, NA; Merington, *The Custer Story*, p. 236; Custer, *Tenting on the Plains*, p. 245; Bird, *The Better Brother*, pp. 176–177.

119. Nichols, *Men with Custer*, pp.140, 184; *Coldwater Republican* (Coldwater, Michigan), July 11, 1876; Cross, *Custer's Lost Officer*, pp. 7, 14, 24–25, 29, 125, 141,149, 163, 204, 215, 225–226; Walt Cross, *Out West with Custer and Crook, Verling K. Hart, 7th U. S. Cavalry* (Stillwater, Okla.: Dire Wolf Books, 2011), pp. 93–94.

120. Cross, *Custer's Lost Officer*, pp. 146, 163; Walt Cross, editor, *Thompson's Narrative of the Little Big Horn* (Stillwater, Okla.: Cross Publications, 2007), p. 90.

121. Cross, *Custer's Lost Officer*, pp. 103, 146; Hardorff, *Indian Views of the Custer Fight*, p. 40; Koster, *Custer Survivor*, p. 37; Graham, *The Custer Myth*, pp. 11, 72.

122. Hardorff, *Cheyenne Memories of the Custer Fight*, p. 126; Cross, *Custer's Lost Officer*, p. 146; Hammer, ed., *Custer in '76*, p. 97; Cross *Thompson's Narrative of the Little Big Horn*, p. 90.

123. Cross, *Thompson's Narrative of the Little Big Horn*, p. 90.

124. Ibid.

125. Hardorff, *Indian Views of the Custer Fight*, pp. 40–41, 54.

126. Ibid.; Cross, *Thompson's Narrative of the Little Big Horn*, p. 90.

127. Hardorff, *Cheyenne Memories of the Custer Fight*, pp. 95, 126.

128. Pohanka, *A Summer on the Plains with Custer's 7th Cavalry*, p. 145; Graham, *The Custer Myth*, p. 72; Hardorff, *Indian Views of the Custer Fight*, p. 40.

129. Michno, *Lakota Noon*, p. 120; Hammer, *Custer in '76*, p. 97.

130. Koster, *Custer Survivor*, p. 37; Hammer, *Custer in '76*, pp. 157, 162, 207 and note 5; Nichols *Men with Custer*, p. 44; Scott, Fox, Connor, and Harmon, *Archaeological Perspectives on the Battle of the Little Bighorn*, p. 7.

131. Reedstrom, *Bugles, Banner and War Bonnets*, p. 138; Stewart, *Custer's Luck*, p. 444.

132. Michno, *Lakota Noon*, p. 119.

133. Hardorff, *Indian Views of the Custer Fight*, p. 40; Stewart, *Custer's Luck*, p. 444; Cross, *Thompson's Narrative of the Little Big Horn*, p. 90; Cross, *Custer's Lost Officer*, pp. 146, 204; Miller, *Custer's Fall*, p. 128; Graham, *The Custer Myth*, pp. 11, 72, 346; Hammer *Custer in '76*, p. 87; Reedstrom, *Bugles, Banners and War Bonnets*, p. 138.

134. MSR, RG 94, NA; Ryan, *Custer Fell First*, pp. 47–49; Cross, *Custer's Lost Officer*, p. 103; Hardorff, *Indian Views of the Custer Fight*, p. 40.

135. MSR, RG 94, NA; Nichols, *Men with Custer*, p. 341; Cross, *Custer's Lost Officer*, p. 103; Barnard, *I Go with Custer*, p. 144.

136. Barnard, *I Go with Custer*, p. 144; White Cow Bull's Story of the Battle of the Little Bighorn #1, astonisher@com.library, internet.

137. Nichols, *Men with Custer*, p. 89; Hardorff, *Indian Views of the Custer Fight*, p. 49, note 17; MSR, RG 94, NA.

138. Lockwood Memoir, LP, HL; Ryan, *Custer fell First*, pp. 47–49; Hardorff, *Indian Views of the Custer Fight*, p. 40; Graham, *The Custer Myth*, pp. 11, 72; MSR, RG 94, NA; Cross, *Custer's Lost Officer*, p. 103; White Cow Bull's Story of the Battle of the Little Bighorn #1, astonisher@com.library, internet.

139. Nichols, *Men with Custer*, p. 160; Barnard, *I Go with Custer*, p. 144; MSR, RG 94, NA; Graham, *The Custer Myth*, pp. 11, 270; Stewart, *Custer's Luck*, p. 444.

140. Stewart, *Custer's Luck*, p. 444; White Cow Bull's Story of the Battle of the Little Bighorn #1, astonisher@com.library, internet; Cross, *Custer's Lost Officer*, p. 103.

141. Miller, *Custer's Fall*, p. 128; Stewart, *Custer's Luck*, p. 444; White Cow Bull's Story of the Battle of the Little Bighorn #1, astonisher@com.library, internet.

142. Brust, Pohanka, and Barnard, *Where Custer Fell*, p. 205, note 5; MSR, RG 94, NA; Nichols, *Men with Custer*, p. 160.

143. Michno, *Lakota Noon*, p. 119.

144. Bernard, *Digging into Custer's Last Stand*, p. 107.

145. Ibid.

146. MSR, RG 94, NA; Lockwood Memoir, LP, HL; Ryan, *Custer Fell First*, pp. 47–49; Graham, *The Custer Myth*, pp. 11, 42; Cross, *Custer's Lost Officer*, p. 103; Hardorff, *Indian Views of the Custer Fight*, p. 40; Rankin, *Legacy*, pp. 73–74.

147. Nichols *Men with Custer*, p. 173; Barnard, *I Go with Custer*, p. 128.

148. Barnard, *I Go with Custer*, p. 144.

149. Ibid., p. 141.

150. MSR, RG 94, NA; Lockwood Memoir, LP, HL; Graham, *The Custer Myth*, pp. 11, 72; Ryan, *Custer Fell First*, pp. 47–49; Cross, *Custer's Lost Officer*, p. 103; Hardorff, *Indian Views of the Custer Fight*, p. 40; Rankin, *Legacy*, pp. 73–74.

151. MSR, RG 94, NA; Cross, *Custer's Lost Officer*, pp. 103, 104, 163, 204; Hardorff, *Indian Views of the Custer Fight*, p. 40; Lockwood Memoir, LP, HL; Rankin *Legacy*, pp. 73–74; Ryan, *Custer Fell First*, pp. 47–49; Graham, *The Custer Myth*, pp. 11, 72, 260, 346.

152. *Daily Record*, (Greensboro, North Carolina), April 27, 1924; Nichols *Men with Custer*, p. 170.

153. Nichols, *Men with Custer*, pp. 321–322; Cross, *Custer's Lost Officer*, pp. 28, 125–126, 163; Sklenar, *To Hell with Honor*, p. 17; MSR, RG 94, NA; Donovan, *A Terrible Glory*, p. 124.

154. Graham, *The Custer Myth*, pp. 260, 346; Cross, *Custer's Lost Officer*, pp. 104, 126, 163, 204; Cross, *Thompson's Narrative of Little Big Horn*, p. 90.

155. Brust, Pohanka, and Barnard, *Where Custer Fell*, pp. 112, 204, note 9; Graham, *The Custer Myth*, pp. 260, 346.

156. Sklenar, *To Hell with Honor*, pp. 16–17.

157. Cross, *Custer's Lost Officer*, p. 146; Cross, *Thompson's Narrative of the Little Big Horn*, p. 90.

158. Cross, *Thompson's Narrative of the Little Big Horn*, p. 90; Cross, *Custer's Lost Officer*, pp. 146, 163.

159. Reedstrom, *Bugles, Banners and War Bonnets*, p. 39.
160. Barnard, *Ten Years With Custer*, p. 80; Cross *Thompson's Narrative of the Little Big Horn*, p. 90.
161. Barnard *Ten Years with Custer*, p. 302.
162. Reedstrom, *Bugles, Banners and War Bonnets*, p. 138; Cross, *Custer's Lost Officer*, pp. 146, 163, 179; Graham, *The Custer Myth*, p. 260, 346.
163. Graham, *The Custer Myth*, p. 260.
164. Hammer, *Custer in '76*, pp. 147, 177; Cross, *Custer's Lost Officer*, p. 163.
165. Miller, *Custer's Fall*, pp. 128–130; Hardorff, *Indian Views of the Custer Fight*, pp. 20, 40; Cross, *Custer's Lost Officer*, p. 103; MSR, RG 94, NA; Graham, *The Custer Myth*, p. 72.
166. Miller, *Custer's Fall*, p. 128–130; Rankin *Legacy*, pp. 73–74; Cross, *Custer's Lost Officer*, p. 130; Hardorff, *Indian Views of the Custer Fight*, p. 40; Graham, *The Custer Myth*, pp. 11, 72.
167. Reedstrom, *Bugles, Banners and War Bonnets*, p. 138; Graham, *The Custer Myth*, p. 260.
168. Grinnell, *The Fighting Cheyennes*, p. 350; Miller, *Custer's Fall*, pp. 128–130; Graham, *The Custer Myth*, pp. 11, 72; Hardorff, *Indian Views of the Custer Fight*, p. 40; MSR, RG 94, NA; Stewart, *Custer's Luck*, p. 441; Brust, Pohanka, and Barnard, *Where Custer Fell*, p. 9.
169. Miller, *Custer's Fall*, pp. 128–130; Graham, *The Custer Myth*, pp. 11, 72; Hammer *Custer in '76*, p. 86; Sklenar, *To Hell with Honor*, p. 274; Hardorff, *Indian Views of the Custer Fight*, p. 40.
170. Hardorff, *Cheyenne Memories of the Custer Fight*, p. 29.
171. Ibid., pp. 33, 35–36; Reedstrom, *Bugles, Banners and War Bonnets*, p. 138.
172. Bernard, *Digging into Custer's Last Stand*, pp. 105, 114; Graham, *The Custer Myth*, p. 72; Miller, *Custer's Fall*, pp. 128–130; Hardorff, *Views of the Custer Fight*, p. 40.
173. Grinnell, *The Fighting Cheyennes*, p. 350; Ryan, *Custer Fell First*, pp. 47–49.
174. Grinnell, *The Fighting Cheyennes*, p. 350.
175. Hardorff, *Indian Views of the Custer Fight*, p. 181; Graham, *The Custer Myth*, p. 11.

176. Hardorff, *Indian Views of the Custer Fight*, pp. 40, 48, note 15; Cross, *Custer's Lost Officer*, p. 103; Graham, *The Custer Myth*, p. 11, 72.

177. Hardorff, *Indian Views of the Custer Fight*, p. 48; Barnard *Ten Years with Custer*, p. 68.

178. Hardorff, *Cheyenne Views of the Custer Fight*, pp. 42–43.

179. Ibid., p. 52.

180. Barnard, *Ten Years with Custer* p. 306; Hammer, *Custer in '76*, p. 86.

181. Hardorff, *Cheyenne Views of the Custer Fight*, p. 43.

182. Pennington, *Custer Vindicated*, p. 118.

183. Reedstrom, *Bugles, Banners and War Bonnets*, p. 138.

184. Hardorff, *Cheyenne Views of the Custer Fight*, p. 43; Barnard, *Ten Years with Custer*, p. 306; Graham, *The Custer Myth*, pp. 11, 188; Hardorff, *Indian Views of the Custer Fight*, p. 40; Hammer, *Custer in '76*, p. 86.

185. John Martin Folder, Walter Mason Camp Manuscript, 1873–1918, Collection No. LMC 1167, Field Notes, vol. 3, The Lilly Library, Indiana University, Bloomington, Indiana.

186. Marquis, *Wooden Leg*, p. 226; Graham, *The Custer Myth*, p. 72.

187. Koster, *Custer Survivor*, p. 37; Graham, *The Custer Myth*, p. 11, 72; Hardorff, *Indian Views of the Custer Fight*, p. 40; Miller, *Custer's Fall*, pp. 128–130; Graham, *The Custer Myth*, p. 72.

188. Koster, *Custer Survivor*, p. 37; Hardorff, *Indian Views of the Custer Fight*, p. 40.

189. MSR, RG 94, NA; Koster, *Custer Survivor*, p. 37; Hardorff, *Indian Views of the Custer Fight*, pp. 40, 48, and note 15; Reedstorm, *Bugles, Banners and War Bonnets*, p. 138; Ryan, *Custer Fell First*, pp. 47–49; Dungan, *Distant Drums*, pp. 45–47; Brust, Pohanka, and Barnard, *Where Custer Fell*, pp. 75, 197, note 32; Lockwood Papers, LP, HL; Graham, *The Custer Myth*, pp. 11, 72, 188, 345; Miller, *Custer's Fall*, pp. 128–130; Schultz, *Coming Through Fire*, pp. 222–224; Barnard, *Ten Years with Custer*, p. 68; Pennington, *Custer Vindicated*, pp. 108, 110; Nichols *Men with Custer*, pp. 12, 177, 196; Hook, *Warriors of the Little Big Horn 1876*, p. 41; Hammer *Custer in '73*, pp. 86–87, 102; Rankin

Legacy, pp. 73–74; Sklenar, *To Hell with Honor*, pp. 54–55, 83, 213, 274.

190. Nichols, *Men with Custer*, p. 44; Reedstrom, *Bugles, Banners, and War Bonnets*, p. 138; Ryan, *Custer Fell First*, pp. 47–49; Hammer, *Custer in '76*, p. 86.

191. Donovan, *A Terrible Glory*, p. 218; Cross, *Custer's Lost Officer*, pp. 7, 126, 163, 204; Nichols, *Men with Custer*, pp. 177, 264–265; Graham, *The Custer Myth*, p. 346; Philbrick, *The Last Stand*, p. 255; Brust, Pohanka, and Barnard, *Where Custer Fell*, p. 103.

192. Graham, *The Custer Myth*, p. 346.

193. Reedstrom, *Bugles, Banners and War Bonnets*, p. 138; Cross, *Thompson's Narrative of the Little Big Horn*, p. 90; Nichols, *Men with Custer*, p. 39.

194. MSR, RG 94, NA; Edward Godfrey, "Custer Last Battle," *Century Magazine*, (1892), p. 381; Nichols *Men with Custer*, pp. 44–45, 121–122.

195. Reedstrom, *Bugles, Banners and War Bonnets*, p. 138; Nichols, *Men with Custer*, pp. 183–184.

196. Nichols *Men with Custer*, pp. 153–154.

197. Lockwood Memoir, LP, HL; Ryan, *Custer Fell First*, p. 47; Hammer *Custer in '76*, p. 86.

198. Snelson, *Death of a Myth*, p. 93; Miller, *Custer's Fall*, pp. 128–130; Graham, *The Custer Myth*, p. 72; Hammer *Custer in '76*, p. 86.

199. Lockwood Memoir, LP, HL; Ryan, *Custer Fell First*, pp. 47–49; Cross, *Custer's Lost Officer*, pp. 7, 150–154, 157, note 25; Bird, *The Best Brother*, p. 214; Reedstorm, *Bugles, Banners, and War Bonnets*, p. 299.

200. Hardorff, *Indian Views of the Custer Fight*, p. 41.

201. Ibid., p. 40; Rankin, *Legacy*, pp. 73–74; White Cow Bull's Story of the Battle of the Little Bighorn #1, astonisher@com. library, internet.

202. Fox, *Archaeology, History, and Custer's Last Battle*, p. 285.

203. Pennington, *Custer Vindicated*, pp. 172–173; Hammer, *Custer in '76*, p. 97.

204. Reedstrom, *Bugles, Banners and War Bonnets*, p. 138.

205. Hardorff, *Cheyenne Memories of the Custer Fight*, pp. 35–36.
206. Ibid.; Michno, *Lakota Noon*, pp. 108–110; Pennington, *Custer Vindicated*, pp.13–56; Miller, *Custer's Fall*, pp. 128–130.
207. Graham, *The Custer Myth*, p. 11.
208. Jamieson, *Crossing the Deadly Ground*, pp. 43–44; Stewart, *Custer's Luck*, p. 441; Nichols, *Men with Custer*, p. 177.
209. Graham, *The Custer Myth*, pp. 11, 72, 345; Pennington, *Custer Vindicated*, p. 121; Cross, *Custer's Lost Officer*, p. 103; Miller, *Custer's Fall*, pp. 128–130; Hardorff, *Indian Views of the Custer Fight*, p. 40; Rankin, *Legacy*, pp. 73–74; Stewart, *Custer's Luck*, p. 441.
210. Miller, *Custer's Fall*, p. 128; White Cow Bull's Story of the Battle of the Little Bighorn #1, astonisher@com.library, internet.
211. Philbrick, *The Last Stand*, p. 258.
212. Skenlar, *To Hell with Honor*, p. 272; Hammer, *Custer in '76*, p. 84; Graham, *The Custer Myth*, p. 290; Reedstrom, *Bugles, Banners and War Bonnets*, p. 51; Quaife *My Life on the Plains*, p. 5.
213. Hardorff, *Lakota Recollections of the Custer Fight*, p. 28; Hammer, *Custer in '76*, 84.
214. Philbrick, *The Last Stand*, p. 257.
215. Pennington, *Custer Vindicated*, p. 121.
216. Sklenar, *To Hell with Honor*, p. 330; Lockwood Memoir, LP, HL; Ryan, *Custer Fell First*, pp. 47–49; Graham, *The Custer Myth*, p. 11, 72; Philbrick, *The Last Stand*, p. 275; Miller, *Custer's Fall*, pp. 128–130; Rankin, *Legacy*, pp. 73–74; Pennington, *Custer Vindicated*, pp. 119–121; Hardorff, *Indian Views of the Custer Fight*, p. 40.
217. Sklenar, *To Hell with Honor*, p. 330; Nichols, *Men with Custer*, p. 197; Philbrick, *The Last Stand*, pp. 257–258; Graham, *The Custer Myth*, p. 188; Pennington, *Custer Vindicated*, pp. 119–121, 187, 195, 197; Rankin, *Legacy*, pp. 73–74; Stewart, *Custer's Luck*, p. 441.
218. Graham, *The Custer Myth*, pp. 345; Philbrick, *The Last Stand*, p. 258; White Cow Bull's Story of the Battle of the Little Bighorn #1, astonisher@com.library, internet.

219. Sklenar, *To Hell with Honor*, p. 330; Nichols, *Men with Custer*, p. 76.
220. Miller, *Custer's Fall*, p. 128.
221. Marquis, *Wooden Leg*, p. 377; Graham, *The Custer Myth*, pp. 72,188; Pennington, *Custer Vindicated*, pp. 119–121; Stewart, *Custer's Luck*, p. 448; Philbrick, *The Last Stand*, pp. 257–258; Rankin, *Legacy*, pp. 73–74.
222. Merington, *The Custer Story*, p. 274.
223. Hardorff, *Indian Views of the Custer Fight*, p. 115.
224. Graham, *The Custer Myth*, pp. 16, 72; Philbrick, *The Last Stand*, p. 258.
225. Hardorff, *Lakota Recollections of the Custer Fight*, p. 28.
226. Ibid., p. 185.
227. Graham, *The Custer Myth*, pp. 16, 72, 254, 289; Rankin *Legacy*, pp. 73–74; White Cow Bull's Story of the Battle of the Little Bighorn #1, astonisher@com.library, internet; Philbrick, *The Last Stand*, pp. 255–258; Donovan, *A Terrible Glory*, p. 308.
228. Nichols, *Men with Custer*, p. 100; Donovan, *A Terrible Glory*, pp. 200, 305; Reedstrom, *Bugles, Banners and War Bonnets*, pp. 296– 299.
229. Graham, *The Custer Myth*, p. 346.
230. Rankin, *Legacy*, pp. 73–74; Graham, *The Custer Myth*, p. 15.
231. Philbrick, *The Last Stand*, pp. 257–258; White Cow Bull's Story of the Battle of the Little Bighorn #1, astonisher@com.library, internet; Cross, *Custer's Lost Officer*, p. 103.
232. Brust, Pohanka, and Barnard, *Where Custer Fell*, p. 197, note 32; White Cow Bull's Story of the Battle of the Little Bighorn #1, astonisher@com.library, internet; Philbrick, *The Last Stand*, pp. 257–258; Michno, *Lakota Noon*, pp. 190; Rankin, *Legacy*, pp. 73–74; Grinnell, *The Fighting Cheyennes*, pp. 349–352.
233. Reedstrom, *Bugles, Banners and War Bonnets*, p. 110; Rankin, *Legacy*, pp. 73–74.
234. Schultz, *Coming Through* Fire, pp. vii–269; Michno, *Lakota Noon*, pp. 190; White Cow Bull's Story of the Battle of the Little Bighorn #1, astonisher@com.library, internet; Philbrick,

The Last Stand, pp. 257–258; Grinnell, *The Fighting Cheyennes*, pp. 349–352.

235. Brust, Pohanka, and Barnard, *Where Custer Fell*, pp. 9, 75; Graham, *The Custer Myth*, pp. 11, 72; Sklenar, *To Hell with Honor*, p. 274; Hammer, *Custer in '76*, p. 86; MSR, RG 94, NA.

236. Graham, *The Custer Myth*, pp. 272–273; Hammer *Custer in '76*, p. 86.

237. Hardorff, *Cheyenne Memories of the Custer Fight*, pp. 45, 47.

238. Graham, *The Custer Myth*, p. 23.

239. Ibid., p. 11.

240. Ibid., p. 188.

241. Lockwood Memoir, LP, HL; Ryan, *Custer Fell First*, pp. 48, 56; Graham, *The Custer Myth*, pp. 11, 188, 227.

242. Graham, *The Custer Myth*, p. 260.

243. Ibid., p. 11.

244. Lockwood Memoir, LP, HL; Ryan, *Custer Fell First*, pp. 47–49; Hardorff, *Cheyenne Memories of the Custer Fight*, p. 76; Rankin, *Legacy*, pp. 73–74; Graham, *The Custer Myth*, pp. 11, 188, 227.

245. Graham, *The Custer Myth*, p. 188.

246. Fox, *Archaeology, History, and Custer's Last Battle*, p. 253; Hardorff, *Indian Views of the Custer Fight*, p. 40; Cross, *Custer's Lost Officer*, p. 103; Lockwood Memoir, LP, HL; Graham, *The Custer Myth*, pp. 11, 72, 188, 227; MSR, RG 94, NA; White Cow Bull's Story of the Battle of the Little Bighorn #1, astonisher@com.library, internet.

247. Hardorff, *Indian Views of the Custer Fight*, p. 40; MSR, RG 94, NA; White Cow Bull's Story of the Battle of the Little Bighorn #1, astonisher@com.library, internet.

248. Hardorff, *Cheyenne Memories of the Custer Fight*, p. 52.

249. Ibid., pp. 37, 39–40.

250. Ibid., p. 75.

251. Michno, *Lakota Noon*, p. 120; Graham, *The Custer Myth*, p. 11.

252. Marquis, *Wooden Leg*, p. 380.

253. Hardorff, *Cheyenne Memories of the Custer Fight*, p. 119; Hardorff, *Indian Views of the Custer Fight*, p. 40; Graham, *The Custer Myth*, pp. 11, 72.

254. Hardorff, *Indian Views of the Custer Fight*, p. 40; Graham, *The Custer Myth*, pp. 11, 72.

255. Pohanka, *A Summer on the Plains with Custer's 7th Cavalry*, p. 126; Skenlar, *To Hell with Honor*, p. 75; Cross, *Thompson and White's Little Big Horn Narratives of 1876*, p. 248; Taylor, *With Custer on the Little Bighorn*, pp. 98, 108.

256. Skenlar, *To Hell with Honor*, pp. 72, 75.

257. Ibid., p. 75; Johnston, Fischer, and Geer, *Custer's Horses*, pp. 2, 25–40, 48–58, 62–65; Donald W. Engels, *Alexander the Great and the Logistics of the Macedonian Army* (Berkeley: University of California Press, 1978), pp. 126–127; Taylor, *With Custer on the Little Bighorn*, p. 179.

258. Graham, *The Custer Myth*, p. 71.

259. Skenlar, *To Hell with Honor*, p. 207.

260. Taylor, *With Custer on the Little Bighorn*, p. 35; Stewart, *Custer's Luck*, p. 331.

261. Ladenheim, *Custer's Thorn*, p. 169; Stewart, *Custer's Luck*, p. 331.

262. Nichols, *Men with Custer*, pp. 308–309; MSR, RG 94, NA.

263. Pennington, *Custer Vindicated*, p. 50; Hammer, *Custer in '76*, pp. 118–119.

264. Graham, *The Custer Myth*, p. 193.

265. Barnard, *Ten Years with Custer*, p. 60.

266. Hardorff, *Indian Views of the Custer Fight*, p. 54.

267. Koster, *Custer Survivor*, p. 37.

268. Michno, *Lakota Noon*, p. 119.

269. Hardorff, *Indian Views of the Custer Fight*, p. 186.

270. Nichols, *Custer Fell First*, pp. 183–184; Koster, *Custer Survivor*, p. 37.

271. Nichols, *Men with Custer*, p. 100; Koster, *Custer Survivor*, pp. 38, 47.

272. Johnston, Fischer, and Geer, *Custer's Horses*, pp. 2, 25–40, 48–58, 62–65; Koster, *Custer Survivor*, p. 37.

273. Hardorff, *Indian Views of the Custer Fight*, p. 178.

274. Sklenar, *To Hell with Honor*, p. 151.

275. Ibid.; Nichols, *Men with Custer*, pp. 183–184; John M. Carroll, Custer's Chief of Scouts, *The Reminiscences of Charles A. Varnum*

(Lincoln: University of Nebraska Press, 1987), p. 119; White Cow Bull's Story of the Battle of the Little Bighorn #1, astonisher@com.library, internet.

276. Hardorff, *Cheyenne Memories of the Custer Fight*, p. 43; Graham, *The Custer Myth*, p. 72; Cross, *Custer's Lost Officer*, p. 103; MSR, RG 94, NA; Rankin, *Legacy*, pp. 98–99; Hardorff, *Indian Views of the Custer Fight*, p. 40; White Cow Bull's Story of the Battle of the Little Bighorn #1, astonisher@com.library, internet.

277. Cross, *Out West with Custer and Crook*, p. 83.

278. Marquis, *Wooden Leg*, p. 183; Johnston, Fischer, and Geer, *Custer's Horses*, pp. 25–77; Dary, *The Buffalo Book*, p. 31.

279. Marquis, *Wooden Leg*, p. 204.

280. Pennington, *Custer Vindicated*, pp. 172–173.

281. Reedstrom, *Bugles, Banners and War Bonnets*, p. 138.

282. Graham, *The Custer Myth*, pp. 260, 346; Hammer, *Custer in '76*, p. 97.

283. Hardorff, *Indian Views of the Custer Fight*, p. 40.

284. Ibid., pp. 40–41; Stewart, *Custer's Luck*, p. 307.

285. Barnard, *Ten Years with Custer*, p. 291.

286. Hardorff, *Indians Views of the Custer Fight*, p. 40.

287. Ibid.; Phibrick, *The Last Stand*, pp. 257–258; Cross, *Custer's Lost Officer*, pp. 103–104; Graham, *The Custer Myth*, pp. 11, 72, 346; MSR, RG 94, NA; White Cow Bull's Story of the Battle of the Little Bighorn #1, astonisher@com.library, internet; Stewart, *Custer's Luck*, p. 441; MSR, RG 94, NA.

288. Hardorff, *Indian Views of the Custer Fight*, p. 40; Graham, *The Custer Myth*, p. 72.

289. Hardorff, *Indian Views of the Custer Fight*, p. 186.

290. Hardorff, *Cheyenne Memories of the Custer Fight*, p. 36.

291. Hardorff, *Lakota Recollections of the Custer Fight*, pp. 84–85; Ryan, *Custer Fell First*, pp. 74–75.

292. Cross, *Custer's Lost Officer*, pp. 103–105; Hardorff, *Indian Views of the Custer Fight*, p. 179.

293. Hardorff, *Indian Views of the Custer Fight*, p. 94.

294. Brust, Pohanka, and Barnard, *Where Custer Fell*, p. 197, note 32; Philbrick, *The Last Stand*, pp. 257–258; Rankin, *Legacy*,

pp. 73–74; White Cow Bull's Story of the Battle of the Little
Bighorn #1, astonisher@com.library, internet.

295. Ryan, *Custer Fell First*, p. xiii; Rankin, *Legacy*, pp. 73–74;
Lockwood Memoir, LP, HL; White Cow Bull's Story of
the Battle of the Little Bighorn #1, astonisher@com.library,
internet.

296. Lockwood Memoir, LP, HL; Ryan, *Custer Fell First*, p. 49.

297. Hardorff, *Indian Views of the Custer Fight*, p. 40; White Cow
Bull's Story of the Battle of the Little Bighorn #1, astonish-
er@com.library, internet; Cross, *Custer's Lost Officer*, p. 103;
Rankin, *Legacy*, pp. 73–74.

298. Reedstrom, *Bugles, Banners and War Bonnets*, p. 139; Lockwood
Memoir, LP, HL.

299. Wert, *Custer*, p. 348; Lockwood Memoir, LP, HL; Nichols, *Men
with Custer*, p. viii; Cross, *Custer's Lost Officer*, pp. 130–132;
White Cow Bull's Story of the Battle of the Little Bighorn #1,
astonisher@com.library, internet; Rankin, *Legacy*, pp. 73–74;
Stewart, *Custer's Luck*, p. 441; Ryan, *Custer Fell First*, pp.
47–49; Hardorff, *Cheyenne Memories of the Custer Fight*, pp.
29, 35–36, 43, 52, 76; Philbrick, *The Last Stand*, pp. 257–258;
Hardorff, *Indian Views of the Custer Fight*, p. 40; MSR, RG 94,
NA; Sklenar, *To Hell with Honor*, p. 281; Graham, *The Custer
Myth*, pp. 11, 72,142, 264.

300. Graham, *The Custer Myth*, p. 291; Nichols, *Men with Custer*,
p. 350.

301. Sklenar, *To Hell with Honor*, pp. 18–25; Pennington, *Custer
Vindicated*, pp. vii–202; Wert, *Custer*, p. 348.

302. Graham, *The Custer Myth*, p. 264; Nichols, *Men with Custer*,
p. 95; p. 146; MSR, RG 94, NA; Ryan, *Custer Fell First*, pp.
74–75.

303. Hardorff, *Cheyenne Memories of the Custer Fight*, p. 76.

304. Graham, *The Custer Myth*, p. 142; MSR, RG 94, NA; Fox,
Archaeology, History, and Custer's Last Battle, p. 280.

305. MSR, RG 94, NA; Sklenar, *To Hell with Honor*, p. 281; Graham, *The Custer Myth*, p. 142; Nichols, *Men with Custer*, p.
121; Philbrick, *The Last Stand*, pp. 257–258.

306. Bernard, *Digging into Custer's Last Stand*, p. 6; Fox, *Archaeology,
History, and Custer's Last Battle*, p. 280.

307. Hardorff, *Cheyenne Memories of the Custer Fight*, p. 36.
308. Ibid.
309. Hardorff, *Indian Views of the Custer Fight*, p. 169; White Cow Bull's Story of the Battle of the Little Bighorn #1, astonisher@com.library, internet.
310. Pennington, *Custer Vindicated*, p. 119; Graham, *The Custer Myth*, p. 188, Philbrick, *The Last Stand*, p. 258; Rankin, *Legacy*, pp. 73–74; Stewart, *Custer's Luck*, p. 441; White Cow Bull's Story of the Battle of the Little Bighorn #1, astonisher@com.library, internet.
311. Hardorff, *Indian Views of the Custer Fight*, p. 40.

Chapter VI

1. Pennington, *Custer Vindicated*, pp. 119–121; Philbrick, *The Last Stand*, pp. 257–258; Graham, *The Custer Myth*, p. 188; Rankin, *Legacy*, pp. 73–74; Stewart, *Custer's Luck*, p. 441; White Cow Bull's Story of the Battle of the Little Bighorn #1, astonisher@com.library, internet.
2. Hardorff, *Indian Views of the Custer Fight*, p. 163; Barnard *Ten Years with Custer*, p. 89.
3. Hardorff, *Indian Views of the Custer Fight*, pp. 85–86.
4. Ibid., p. 40.
5. Philbrick, *The Last Stand*, p. 258; Hardorff, *Indian Views of the Custer Fight*, pp. 85–86; White Cow Bull's Story of the Battle of the Little Bighorn #1, astonisher@com.library, internet.
6. Hardorff, *Cheyenne Memories of the Custer Fight*, p. 76.
7. Ibid., p. 126.
8. Ibid., p. 98; Graham, *The Custer Myth*, pp. 289–290.
9. Marquis, *Wooden Leg*, p. 229; Hardorff, *Indian Views of the Custer Fight*, p. 40; Graham, *The Custer Myth*, p. 188; Philbrick, *The Last Stand*, pp. 257–258; Marshall, *The Day that World Ended at Little Bighorn*, p. 72.
10. Marquis, *Wooden Leg*, p. 229; Philbrick, *The Last Stand*, pp. 257–258.
11. Marquis, *Wooden Leg*, p. 381.
12. Ibid., p. 230.

13. Hardorff, *Lakota Recollections of the Custer Fight*, p. 85; Marquis, *Wooden Leg*, p. 213; Sandoz, *The Battle of Little Bighorn*, p. 120; Hardorff, *Indian Views of the Custer Fight*, p. 110.

14. Marquis, *Wooden Leg*, p. 228.

15. Sandoz, *The Battle of Little Bighorn*, pp. 119–120; Fox, *Archaeology, History, and Custer's Last Battle*, pp. 55–56, 78–80, 87, 96, 103–114, 250, 253.

16. Hardorff, *Indian Views of the Custer Fight*, p. 62.

17. Lockwood Memoir, LP, HL; Ryan, *Custer Fell First*, pp. 47–49, 52–53.

18. Hardorff, *Indian Views of the Custer Fight*, p. 40; Fox, *Archaeology, History, and Custer's Last Battle*, pp. 55–56, 78–80, 87, 96, 103–114, 250, 253–255; Graham, *The Custer Myth*, p. 72.

19. Barnard, *Ten Years with Custer*, p. 273.

20. Marshall, *The Day the World Ended at Little Bighorn*, pp. 16–17.

21. Hardorff, *Cheyenne Memories of the Custer Fight*, p. 11; Marshall, *The Day the World Ended at Little Bighorn*, pp. 11, 16.

22. Mails, *Dog Soldiers, Bear Men and Buffalo Women*, pp. 17, 26–29, 31–33.

23. Philbrick, *The Last Stand*, p. 258; White Cow Bull's Story of the Battle of the Little Bighorn #1, astonisher@com.library, internet.

24. *Chicago Times* (Chicago, Illinois), July 22, 1876.

25. *Chanute Times* (Chanute, Kansas), July 13, 1876; Nichols, *Men with Custer*, pp. 9, 261; Philbrick, *The Last Stand*, pp. 257–258; MSR, RG 94, NA; Graham, *The Custer Myth*, p. 188.

26. Graham, *The Custer Myth*, pp. 188, 221; Hardorff, *Indian Views of the Custer Fight*, p. 40.

27. *New York Times* (New York, New York), July 7, 1876; Hardorff, *Indian Views of the Custer Fight*, p. 40; Graham, *The Custer Myth*, p. 72.

28. Hardorff, *Lakota Recollections of the Custer Fight*, p. 78.

29. Ibid., p. 75.

30. George W. Glenn Paper, Walter Camp Collection, Little Bighorn Battlefield National Monument, Crow Agency, Montana; Nichols, *Men with Custer*, p. 121.

31. Glenn Paper, LBBNM.
32. Barnard, *Ten Years with Custer*, p. 301.
33. Marquis, *Wooden Leg*, p. 12.
34. Barnard, *Ten Years with Custer*, p. 306.
35. Ibid., p. 85.
36. Hardorff, *Lakota Recollections of the Custer Fight*, p. 138.
37. Hardorff, *Indian Views of the Custer Fight*, p. 40.
38. Graham, *The Custer Myth*, p. 72.
39. Bernard, *Digging into Custer's Last Stand*, p. 6; Brust, Pohanka, and Barnard, *Where Custer Fell*, p. 9.
40. Bernard, *Digging into Custer's Last Stand*, p. 105.
41. Brust, Pohanka, and Barnard, *Where Custer Fell*, p. 10.
42. Barnard, *Ten Years with Custer*, p. 303; Rankin, *Legacy*, pp. 197–198.
43. Cross, *Thompson's Narrative of the Little Big Horn*, p. 87; Nichols *Men with Custer*, p. 329.
44. Barnard, *Digging into Custer's Last Stand*, pp. 111, 114; Koster, *Custer Survivor*, p. 166.
45. Rankin, ed., *Legacy*, pp. 197–198; Barnard, *Digging into Custer's Last Stand*, pp. 105, 114; Scott, Fox, Connor, and Harmon, *Archaeological Perspectives on the Battle of Little Bighorn*, p. 246; Cross, *Thompson's Narrative of the Little Big Horn*, p. 87.
46. Hardorff, *Indian Views of the Custer Fight*, pp. 40–41.
47. Taylor, *With Custer on the Little Bighorn*, p. 76; MSR, RG 94, NA; Graham, *The Custer Myth*, pp. 260, 346; Stewart, *Custer's Luck*, pp. 443–444.
48. Graham, *The Custer Myth*, p. 377; Nichols, *Men with Custer*, p. 121.
49. Taylor, *With Custer on the Little Bighorn*, p. 118; Hammer, *Custer in '76*, p. 147.
50. Scott, Fox, Connor, and Harmon, *Archaeological Perspectives on the Battle of Little Bighorn*, pp. 17, 19.
51. Brust, Pohanka, and Barnard, *Where Custer Fell*, pp. 13, 127.
52. Barnard, *I Go with Custer*, p. xv.
53. Graham, *The Custer Myth*, pp. 260, 377; MSR, RG 94, NA; Brust, Pohanka, and Barnard, *Where Custer Fell*, p. 115; Nichols, *Men with Custer*, p. 321.

54. Brust, Pohanka, and Barnard, *Where Custer Fell*, pp. 115–116; MSR, RG 94, NA; Nichols, *Men with Custer*, pp. 321–322.

55. Brust, Pohanka, and Barnard, *Where Custer Fell*, p. 127; Cross, *Custer's Lost Officer*, pp. 7, 103, 179; MSR, RG 94, NA.

56. MSR, RG 94, NA; Graham, *The Custer Myth*, p. 377; Rankin, *Legacy*, pp. 73–74.

57. Graham, *The Custer Myth*, p. 260.

58. Cross, *Custer's Lost Officer*, p. 146; Cross, *Thompson's Narrative of the Little Big Horn*, p. 90; Hammer, *Custer in '76*, p. 87.

59. *The Pioneer Press and Tribune*, September 8, 1876; Dippie, *Custer's Last Stand*, p. 82.

60. *The Pioneer Press and Tribune*, September, 8, 1876.

61. Ibid.

62. Ibid.

63. Cross, *Custer's Missing Officer*, p. 146; Cross, *Thompson's Narrative of the Little Big Horn*, p. 90.

64. Dippie, *Custer's Last Stand*, p. 82; Graham, *The Custer Myth*, pp. 188, 227.

65. Fox, *Archaeology, History, and Custer's Last Battle*, p. 285; Hammer, *Custer in '76*, pp. 87, 162, 207, 248, note 5; White Cow Bull's Story of the Battle of the Little Bighorn #1, astonisher@com.library, internet; Stewart, *Custer's Luck*, p. 443.

Conclusion

1. Brust, Pohanka, and Barnard, *Where Custer Fell*, pp. 178, 185.

2. Ibid., p. 75; Graham, *The Custer Myth*, pp. 188, 227.

3. Graham, *The Custer Myth*, p. 23.

4. Fox, *Archaeology, History, and Custer's Last Battle*, p. 21.

5. Graham, *The Custer Myth*, p. 72; Hardorff, *Indian Views of the Custer Fight*, p. 40.

6. Hardorff, *Indian Views of the Custer Fight*, p. 40.

7. Graham, *The Custer Myth*, p. 85.

8. Ibid., p. 23.

9. Ibid., pp. 23, 188, 227; *The Sun* (New York, New York), February 26, 1879; Brust, Pohanka and Barnard, *Custer Fell Here*, p. 9; Rankin, *Legacy*, pp. 73–74.

10. Reedstrom, *Bugles, Banners, and War Bonnets*, p. 133.

11. Ibid., p. 230; Philbrick, *A Terrible Glory*, p. 281.

12. Barnard, *Ten Years with Custer*, p. 302; Graham, *The Custer Myth*, pp. 188, 227.

13. Barnard, *Ten Years with Custer*, p. 297.

14. Hardorff, *Cheyenne Memories of the Custer Fight*, pp. 29, 35–36, 43, 52, 76, 169; Cross, *Custer's Lost Officer*, p. 103; Graham, *The Custer Myth*, pp. 11, 72, 260, 346; Hardorff, *Indian Views of the Custer Fight*, p. 40; Stewart, *Custer's Luck*, pp. 443–444; Cross, *Thompson's Narrative of the Little Big Horn*, p. 90.

15. Hardorff, *Cheyenne Memories of the Custer Fight*, p. 169.

16. Pennington, *Custer Vindicated*, pp. 119–121, 144–146; Hardorff, *Indian Views of the Custer Fight*, p. 40; MSR, RG 94, NA; Rankin, *Legacy*, pp. 73–74; Philbrick, *The Last Stand*, pp. 257–258; Stewart, *Custer's Luck*, p. 441; White Bull's Story of the Battle of the Little Bighorn #1, astonisher@com.library, internet.

17. Hardorff, *Lakota Recollections of the Custer Fight*, p. 133; Hardorff, *Indian Views of the Custer Fight*, p. 40; Sklenar, *To Hell with Honor*, p. 273; Brust, Pohanka, and Barnard, *Where Custer Fell*, pp. 9, 72; Philbrick, *The Last Stand*, pp. 257–258; Graham, *The Custer Myth*, pp. 11, 72, 188, 227; White Bull's Story of the Battle of the Little Bighorn #1, astonisher@com.library, internet; Rankin, *Legacy*, pp. 73–74, 122; Hardorff, *Cheyenne Memories of the Custer Fight*, pp. 29, 35–36, 43, 52, 76.

18. Walt Cross, Stillwater, Oklahoma, to author, July 7, 2015; Donovan, *A Terrible Glory*, pp. 261–263; Dippie, *Custer's Last Stand*, pp. 1–144.

19. Graham, *The Custer Myth*, p. 231.

20. Philbrick, *The Last Stand*, pp. xix, 12; Rankin, *Legacy*, pp. 73–74, 122; Schultz, *Coming Through Fire*, pp. ix–x, 245.

21. Boorman, *The History of Winchester Firearms*, pp. 8, 46; Barnard, *Ten Years with Custer*, pp. 243–244, 271, 273–274, 279;

Lehman, *Bloodshed at Little Bighorn*, p. 3; Hardorff, *Indian Views of the Custer Fight*, p. 40; Merington, *The Custer Story*, p. 292; Rankin, *Legacy*, pp. 73–74; Cross, *Custer's Lost Officer*, p. 103; Hardorff, *Cheyenne Memories of the Custer Fight*, pp. 29, 35–36, 43, 52, 76; Fox, *Archaeology, History, and Custer's Last Stand*, pp. 55–56, 78–114, 250–255; Graham, *The Custer Myth*, pp. 5, 11, 52, 71–72, 85.

22. Barnard, *Ten Years with Custer*, p. 243; Nichols, *Men with Custer*, p. 288.

23. Scott, Fox, Connor, and Harmon, *Archaeological Perspectives on the Battle of Little Bighorn*, pp.104–113, 117–121, 124–130, 162–166; Rankin, *Legacy*, p. 98.

24. Hardorff, *Indian Views of the Custer Fight*, p. 40.

25. Dipple, *Custer's Last Stand*, pp. 1–61, 89–107; Rankin, *Legacy*, pp. 73–74.

26. Ibid.; Peter C. Rollins and John E. O'Connor, editors, *Why We Fought, America's Wars in Film and History* (Lexington: University of Kentucky Press, 2008), p. 287; Hardorff, *Cheyenne Memories of the Custer Fight*, pp. 29, 35–36, 43, 52, 76.

27. Dipple, *Custer's Last Stand*, pp. 1–61, 89–107; Ryan, Lockwood Memoir, LP, HL; *Custer Fell First*, pp. 47–49; Hardorff, *Indian Views of the Custer Fight*, p. 40; Cross, *Custer's Lost Officer*, p. 103; Graham, *The Custer Myth*, p. 11; Fox, Archaeology, History and Custer's Last Battle, p. 278.

28. Elliott, *Custerology*, pp. 124, 139.

29. Ibid., p. 139.

30. Koster, *Custer Survivor*, p. 5.

31. Ibid.; Shultz, *Coming Through Fire*, pp. 2–4, 245.

32. Graham, *The Custer Myth*, p. 72; Grinnell, *The Fighting Cheyennes*, pp. 356–357; Hardorff, *Indian Views of the Custer Fight*, p. 40; Cross, *Custer's Lost Officer*, p. 103.

33. Grinnell, *The Fighting Cheyennes*, pp. 357–358.

34. Taylor, *With Custer on the Little Bighorn*, p. 71; Hardorff, *Indian Views of the Custer Fight*, p. 40; Graham, *The Custer Myth*, p. 11; Cross, *Custer's Lost Officer*, p. 103; Ryan, *Custer Fell First*, pp. 47–49; Schultz, *Coming Through Fire*, pp. ix–245.

35. Graham, *The Custer Myth*, p. 221.
36. Snelson, *Death of a Myth*, p. 160; Graham, *The Custer Myth*, pp. 188, 227.
37. Graham, *The Custer Myth*, p. 188.
38. Ibid., p. 227.
39. Ibid., 188, 227; Snelson, *Death of a Myth*, p. 160; Ryan, *Custer Fell First*, pp. 47–49.
40. Hardorff, *Cheyenne Memories of the Custer Fight*, p. 76; Graham, *The Custer Myth*, pp. 11, 118, 227; Stewart, *Custer's Luck*, p. 444; Rankin, *Legacy*, pp. 73–74; Hardorff, *Indian Views of the Custer Fight*, p. 40.
41. Graham, *The Custer Myth*, p. 11; White Cow Bull's Story of the Battle of the Little Bighorn, #1, astonisher@com.library, internet; Hardorff, *Indian Views of the Custer Fight*, p. 40.
42. Graham, *The Custer Myth*, p. 227.
43. Ibid.
44. Reedstrom, *Bugles, Banners and War Bonnets*, p. 138.
45. Pennington, *Custer Vindicated*, pp. vii–202.
46. Ibid.; Taylor, *With Custer on the Little Bighorn*, p. 70.
47. Hardorff, *Indian of the Custer Fight*, p. 40; Nichols, *Men with Custer*, p. 327.
48. Barnard, *I Go with Custer*, p. 142.
49. *New York Herald*, August 1, 1876; Drinnon, *Facing West*, p. 261; Cross, *Custer's Lost Officer*, p. 129; Rankin, *Legacy*, pp. 73–74; Stewart, *Custer's Luck*, p. 444; Graham, *The Custer Myth*, pp. 188; Philbrick, *The Last Stand*, pp. 257–258.
50. Hardorff, *Indian Views of the Custer Fight*, p. 40; Graham, *The Custer Myth*, pp. 11, 72; Dippie, *Custer's Last Stand*, pp. 1–118; MSR, RG, NA; Rankin, *Legacy*, p. 94.
51. Taylor, *With Custer on the Little Bighorn*, p. 71; Sklenar, *To Hell with Honor*, pp. 262, 340–341; Fox, *Archeology, History, and the Custer Battle*, p. 285; Pennington, *Custer Vindicated*, pp. vii–202.
52. Sklenar, *To Hell with Honor*, p. 262.
53. Wittenberg and Husby, *Under Custer's Command*, p. 147.
54. Sklenar, *To Hell with Honor*, p. 328.

55. Nichols, *Men with Custer*, p. 121; Stewart, *Custer's Luck*, p. 414.
56. Sklenar, *To Hell With Honor*, p. 328; Hardorff, *Indian Views of the Custer Fight*, p. 40; Graham, *The Custer Myth*, p. 188.
57. Reedstrom, *Bugles, Banners and War Bonnets*, p. 345; Graham, *The Custer Myth*, pp. 11, 72; Philbrick, *The Last Stand*, pp. 258, 319; White Cow Bull and the Battle of the Little Bighorn #1, astonisher@com.library, internet; Rankin, *Legacy*, pp. 73–74; Stewart, *Custer's Luck*, p. 444.

Index

Frankel, Frank /Finckle, George August
(Sergeant), 113–114, 116
French, Thomas Henry (Captain), 64,
200

G
Galaxy Magazine, 127–128
Garry Owen/Garryowen, 18, 25, 94,
123, 130–131
Gibbon, John (Colonel), 36–38, 41,
271
Girard, Frederic Francis, 298
Glenn, George W. (Private), 263–264
Goat River/ Little Sheep Creek. *see*
Little Bighorn River
Godfrey, Edward Seattle (Lieutenant),
109, 223, 227, 251, 269, 271–272
Goes Ahead, 196–197
gold and sacred lands, 9–14
Goldin, Theodore W. (Lieutenant), 233
Grant, Ulysses S. (President), xviii, xix,
1–2, 10–11, 87
Gray Horse Company. *see* Company E,
7th Cavalry, Grey Horse Company
Greasy Grass River battle, xiv, 14–15,
260–261
Great Medicine Dance Creek/Green
Grass Creek, 66
Great Medicine or Great Spirit Dance
(Sun Dance), 26–27, 46
Great Reservation, 15
Griffin, Patrick (Private), 201
Grinnell, George Bird, 215–216, 289
Gun That Won the West, 188–190

H
Hairy Moccasin (Crow scout), 77, 90,
196–197
Hamilton, Alexander, 129
Hamilton, Louis McLane (Captain),
129

Hard Robe (Cheyenne), 167
Harmon, Dick, 270
Harper's Weekly, May 19, 1864, 126
Harrington, Henry Moore (Second
Lieutenant), 134, 196, 202–204,
209–211, 213, 269–272
Hay, John, 294
He Dog (Sioux), 179, 263–264
headquarters staff, Custer's, 131–143
headstones, on Custer Hill, 270
"helper birds," 193–194
Henry rifle, xxii, 188–190, 197, 209,
232, 249–250, 282–283
Herendeen, George B. (Crow Scout),
70–72, 213, 251, 271–272
Hetesimer, Adam (Private), 65
Hi-es-tzie (Long Hair), 24
"Hills that are Black," 9–14
Hollow Horn Bear (Sioux warrior),
195, 230
Horn, Marion E., 224
Horned Horse
and artifacts at battle site, 269
on defense of Ford, 188
describes rough terrain at Ford,
244–245
describes wounded falling into
water, Custer's wounding, 185,
198, 224
effects of rapid rifle fire by Indians,
235–237, 265–266, 276, 283,
293
ignored testimony of, xxviii
quicksand swallows troopers (supposedly), 244–245, 269
on success of rapid fire, 276–277,
293–294
surprising sight of Custer's column,
123
horses, at Medicine Tail Coulee Ford,
236–244